Misinformation and Mass Audiences

Information, a series edited by Andrew Dillon

EDITED BY
BRIAN G.
SOUTHWELL,
EMILY A.
THORSON,
AND LAURA
SHEBLE

Misinformation
and Mass Audiences

University of Texas Press
Austin

Requests for permission to reproduce material from this work should be
sent to:
    Permissions
    University of Texas Press
    P.O. Box 7819
    Austin, TX 78713-7819
    utpress.utexas.edu/rp-form

♾ The paper used in this book meets the minimum requirements of
ANSI/NISO Z39.48-1992 (R1997) (Permanence of Paper).

Library of Congress Cataloging-in-Publication Data

Names: Southwell, Brian G. (Brian Glen), 1974–, editor. |
    Thorson, Emily A., editor. | Sheble, Laura, editor.
Title: Misinformation and mass audiences / edited by Brian G. Southwell,
    Emily A. Thorson, and Laura Sheble.
Description: First edition. | Austin : University of Texas Press, 2018. |
    Series: Information | Includes bibliographical references and index.
Identifiers: LCCN 2017025953
    ISBN 978-1-4773-1455-5 (cloth : alk. paper)
    ISBN 978-1-4773-1456-2 (pbk. : alk. paper)
    ISBN 978-1-4773-1457-9 (library e-book)
    ISBN 978-1-4773-1458-6 (non-library e-book)
Subjects: LCSH: Mass media—Audiences. | Communication. | Common
    fallacies—Social aspects. | Deceptive advertising—Social aspects.
Classification: LCC P91.27 .M57 2018 | DDC 302.23—dc23
LC record available at https://lccn.loc.gov/2017025953
doi:10.7560/314555

Contents

Acknowledgments

This project reflects the work of many authors, both those listed formally and others who helped behind the scenes. Collectively, we would like to thank the external reviewers as well as the University of Texas Press for their enthusiastic help in constructing this volume, especially Robert Devens, Sarah McGavick, and Lynne Chapman, and series editor Andrew Dillon at the University of Texas, who with a light hand nurtured this project as it grew. Many thanks also to freelance copyeditor Tana Silva, indexer Lisa Rivero, and proofreader Melissa McGee Tullos for their outstanding work.

In addition, Brian is grateful for the ongoing patience and support of his family, including Jessica, Gavin, and Ellerie. Emily would like to thank her family and coeditors. Laura thanks her family and friends for their encouragement and uncanny ability to know perfectly just when to share a joke, a walk, a sandwich—and especially their time. We would also like to thank all who have contributed to our understanding of misinformation. Finally, we thank those who are reading these pages for your interest in joining this conversation.

Misinformation and Mass Audiences

Misinformation among Mass Audiences as a Focus for Inquiry

BRIAN G. SOUTHWELL, EMILY A. THORSON,
AND LAURA SHEBLE

Misinformation—both deliberately promoted and accidentally shared—is a noteworthy and perhaps inevitable part of the world in which we live. People likely have lied to one another for roughly as long as verbal communication has existed. Deceiving others can offer an apparent opportunity to gain strategic advantage, to motivate others to action, or even to protect interpersonal bonds. Moreover, people inadvertently have been sharing inaccurate information with one another for thousands of years. We currently live in an era of mass audiences, however, which means that the potential for immediate and widespread misinformation effects now looms larger than in the past. Yet in those same patterns of mass communication and facilitated peer-to-peer information spread might also be the seeds of misinformation correction over time. Investigating the spread and effects of misinformation is as compelling now as it has ever been in human history.

As a focus for research and debate, the phenomenon of misinformation crosses disciplinary bounds; misinformation exists in and across topical domains, from science to politics to consumer advertising, and can quickly spread through a range of media, including television, radio, and pixels shared via social media on the Internet. Understanding misinformation requires working at many levels of analysis, from the policy infrastructure for mass media content to individual information processing ability. Thor-

1

oughly understanding and addressing the proliferation, effects, and correction of misinformation calls for a multidisciplinary approach.

In assembling this collection of essays, we have brought together evidence and ideas from communication research, public health, psychology, political science, environmental studies, information science, and other literatures to explore what constitutes misinformation, how it spreads, and how best to counter it. We consider various angles, such as the extent to which audiences consciously notice misinformation, possibilities for audience deception, the ethics of satire in journalism and public affairs programming, the diffusion of rumors, the role of Internet search behavior, and the development of efforts such as fact-checking programs.

Curation of a broad sweep of ideas related to misinformation admittedly risks creation of a smorgasbord that lacks useful argument and thematic coherence. In light of that risk, we have organized contributions into three types of essays—conceptualization and measurement of individual engagement with misinformation, discussion of potential effects, and exploration of remedies—and also have accepted some framing assumptions and boundaries as to what we can discuss in this book and what is best left for future exploration. The consequence of that is a book that simultaneously reminds us that misinformation will continue to pose a dilemma for mass media systems for the foreseeable future and that there are ways we can address concerns. Below, we argue that misinformation exists, that it is problematic in the context of mass audiences and societies for particular reasons, and that the essays we have selected contribute in different ways to thought in this arena, an arena we claim is a worthy one for future inquiry, policy making, and public discussion.

What Is Misinformation?

Misinformation is concerning because of its potential to unduly influence attitudes and behavior, leading people to think and act differently than they would if they were correctly informed. In other words, we worry that misinformation (or false information) might lead people to hold misperceptions (or false beliefs) and that these misperceptions, especially when they occur among mass audiences, may have downstream consequences for health, social harmony, and political life.

Here we are assuming the common existence of mass audiences as Price (1992) and Webster and Phalen (1996) have defined them: more than a dyad or family unit and large enough that members do not necessarily communicate with one another directly but rather are connected primarily through exposure to a common message or piece of information. The possibility that *mass audiences* would consider false information to be true and would act on that false information implies a serious social problem, in that a mass communication system employs technology to simultaneously and immediately reach and connect large, heterogeneous groups of geographically dispersed people but cannot be fully protected against repeated and widespread claims that are not true. Given this potential problem, we are interested in the diffusion, use, persistence, and refutation of false information on a mass scale.

As Stahl (2006) has noted, critical theorists have raised important concerns about the possibility of information having objective truth value, concerns that complicate any distinction of misinformation and information on the basis of the former being false and the latter being true. On this point, nonetheless, thinking by Habermas (1984, 1987) is useful, as he focuses on a speaker's intent to deceive and distinguishes between *mis*information and *dis*information. Habermas views truth as only possible collectively among people as a product of consensus; one's collegial participation in collective understanding also matters. Misinformation from such a perspective, then, is contentious information reflecting disagreement between people, whereas disinformation is more problematic, as it involves the deliberate alienation or disempowerment of other people. Lewandowsky, Stritzke, Freund, Oberauer, and Krueger (2013) have carried forward this sense of disinformation as intentionally incorrect information.

We respectfully reject a worldview in which no degree of consensus between people is possible. Moreover, misinformation can occur and mislead those exposed, at least relative to what they would have believed if exposed to more complete and accurate information. Habermas's triad of concepts—information, misinformation, and disinformation—offers a path forward and useful category distinctions for our discussion. If we allow a claim acknowledged by consensus to hold truth value, we then can position misinformation as a category of claim for which there is at least substantial disagreement (or even consensus rejection) when judged as to truth value among the widest feasible range of observers. That approach would include disinformation as a special type of misinformation distinguished by the intent of the promoter. From an ethical perspective, many people will worry most about active promotion of disinformation. Nonetheless, we will use the word *misinformation* throughout this book to acknowledge that false information can mislead people even if unintention-ally promoted or mistakenly endorsed as being true. We acknowledge that such an approach opens the door for certain claims to evolve from being information to becoming misinformation and vice versa over time as a function of a society's changing consensus. For our purposes, though, we will focus on misinformation as being claims to which mass audiences are exposed that do not actually enjoy universal or near-universal consensus as being true at a particular moment in time.

Mass Audience Exposure to Misinformation as a Cause for Concern

As argued elsewhere (Southwell & Thorson, 2015), at least three obser-vations related to misinformation in the contemporary mass media en-vironment warrant the attention of researchers, policy makers, and lay-people. First, people who encounter misinformation tend to believe it, at least at first. Second, many types of misinformation can appear in con-tent available to mass audiences without being blocked or censored in many media systems. Third, countering misinformation once it has en-joyed wide exposure can be a resource-intensive effort.

What happens when people initially encounter misinformation holds tremendous importance for estimating the potential for subsequent problems. Although individuals generally have considerable routine ex-perience encountering information now considered to be false, the ques-tion of exactly how—and when—we should label information as true or false has garnered philosophical debate. As outlined later in this volume, the dilemma is neatly summarized by a contrast between how the phi-losophers Descartes and Spinoza described human information engage-ment centuries ago with conflicting predictions that only recently have been empirically tested in robust ways. Descartes argued that a person ac-cepts or rejects information only after considering its truth or falsehood; Spinoza argued that people accept all encountered information (or mis-information) by default and then subsequently verify or reject it through a separate process. Empirical evidence in recent decades has supported Spinoza's account (Asp & Tranel, 2012; Gilbert, Krull, & Malone, 1990; Gilbert, Tafarodi, & Malone, 1993): people appear to encode all new in-formation as if it were true, even if only momentarily, and later tag the information as being either true or false, a pattern that seems consis-tent with the observation that skepticism physically resides in a different part of the brain than the resources used in perceiving and encoding. We also know people judge source credibility as a heuristic cue in determining message acceptability and will turn to others for confirmation of the truth value of a claim (Lewandowsky, Ecker, Seifert, Schwarz, & Cook, 2012; Southwell, 2013). If the people surrounding someone tend to initially believe misinformation, then it raises the specter of network reinforcement of misinformation, meaning that misinformation could become even more difficult to debunk over time as the false claim becomes held by more and more people.

What about our claim that misinformation often can appear in electronic or print media without being preemptively blocked? One might consider the nature of regulatory structures in countries such as the United States: regulatory agencies tend to focus on post hoc detection of broadcast information. Organizations such as the U.S. Federal Trade Commission, Federal Election Commission, and Food and Drug Administration offer considerable monitoring and notification functions, but these typically do not involve preemptive censoring. The Food and Drug Administration (FDA) oversees direct-to-consumer prescription drug advertising, for example, and has developed mechanisms such as the "Bad Ad" program through which people can report advertising in apparent violation of FDA guidelines on the presentation of drug risks and benefits (O'Donoghue et al., 2015). Such programs, though laudable and useful, do not guarantee that false advertising never appears on the airwaves and, moreover, do not prevent false news stories from appearing. In addition, even misinformation that is successfully corrected can continue to affect attitudes (Thorson 2015).

Lastly, countering misinformation with new information requires effort not only to develop new content that is understandable but also to ensure adequate message exposure. As Hornik (2002) has argued, a communication campaign can succeed or fail, at least in part, as a function of exposure or lack thereof. A campaign to correct misinformation, even if rhetorically compelling, requires resources and planning to accomplish the necessary reach and frequency. For corrective information to be persuasive it needs to be comprehended by audiences, which requires either effort to frame messages in ways that are understandable or effort to educate and sensitize audiences to the possibility of misinformation. That audiences might not be aware of the potential for misinformation also suggests the potential utility of media-literacy efforts as early as elementary school. Even with journalists, pundits, and scholars pointing to the phenomenon of "fake news" (Amarasingam, 2011), when scanning and processing information people often do not distinguish between demonstrably false stories and those based in fact.

As we consider mass audience vulnerability to misinformation, we should note how changes in electronic media have suggested to various scholars new possibilities for an individual actor to seed the world with falsehood. Social media offer the potential for a single person in a small town in South Dakota, for example, to reach people directly around the world with a video full of false information. Jenkins (2008) has noted the increased possibilities for user-produced content to be uploaded and shared with other individual information consumers. Such an emphasis on the potential for individual audience members' agency relative to well-funded and centralized media institutions itself is not new, as media studies scholars have sought for decades to understand how people use media content for their own purposes in their daily lives (Brooker & Jermyn, 2003; Katz, Blumler, & Gurevitch, 1973–1974). Although these technology changes offer paths for problematic diffusion and dissemination of misinformation, evidence suggests that conventional media institutions still play a crucial role regarding message reach and immediacy in cases when information that first appears on a single page somewhere on the Internet subsequently diffuses widely (Weeks & Southwell, 2010). Although any one person can tell another a lie standing on a street corner, the dilemma of widespread misinformation among mass audiences should be understood as a problem of scope and scale not entirely appreciated from the vantage point of a single conversation.

An Overview of the Book

We have organized the chapters to address three important dimensions of misinformation that current and future scholars working in this arena will need to consider as we move forward to understand the phenomenon. First, we have asked a group of researchers to articulate what we know about conceptualizing and measuring audience awareness of misinformation. Second, we have gathered theoretical essays on the ways in which misinformation could have consequences for outcomes that matter to societal governance, individual decision making, and the everyday lives of audience members. Last, we approach the question of potential solutions and remedies for misinformation. Our particular focus on cognition, communication, and policy reflects concern for human engagement with misinformation and consequent potential for dysfunction in human societies. The human brain, interactions of people, and regulations and laws all shape problems and solutions in this arena and will continue to be relevant even as developing information technologies may automate some aspects of future detection, prevention, and correction of misinformation.

Our distinguished contributors for the first section of the book, on dimensions of audience awareness, cover a wide range of topical areas; as they do, some common themes surface about the importance of carefully defining variables and ensuring that measures are valid and reliable. Marsh and Yang approach this concern from a cognitive science perspective, highlighting human biases that favor misinformation acceptance to facilitate information-processing efforts. In this they set the stage for discussion of information encoding, forgetting, and retrieval in a manner that offers useful considerations for the rest of the chapters in the book. Boudewyns and colleagues consider consumer awareness in the specific context of health-related advertising. They find that although some researchers have investigated the prevalence and consequences of problematic claims in advertising, relatively little work to date sheds direct light on audience ability to detect deception. Cappella, Ophir, and Sutton argue for an approach to knowledge measurement that is relevant not only to the tobacco advertising research they have conducted but also to various situations in which knowing whether people hold specific factual claims in mind matters. They argue that many knowledge-based approaches to measuring audience exposure to misinformation are too narrow in scope and fail to take into account alternatives for measuring knowledge that would demonstrate manifestations of misinformation in relevant ways. Ahler and Sood also offer a measurement perspective, theirs grounded in thinking about political issues rather than health. Hemsley and Snyder extend our thinking to consider the possibility of visual misinformation, meaning the possibility for graphics and figures to lead people to misperceptions over and above verbal information. They argue that our current media environment offers numerous opportunities for visual deception.

As we turn to the theoretical consequences of misinformation, a group of experienced researchers reminds us that the ways in which we define and consider misinformation exposure and acceptance, as we do in the first part of the book, affect the range of possibilities for effects. Green and Donahue assess the potential effects of false information in news stories. They look at both immediate misinformation acceptance and persistence of such acceptance over time, and they usefully consider how what we know about audience transportation in the face of narratives helps account for such acceptance. Part of what is intriguing about Green and Donahue's account is their consideration of news stories, a type of content in which misinformation sometimes can occur unintentionally. What about situations in which an author contorts or ignores some facts in an effort to shed light on truth? One can encounter such a situation with the use of satire and ironic humor. Young considers the possible effects of satire and irony and offers some answers to the question of whether satire and irony even should be categorized as misinformation. With the rise of political satire programs on channels such as Comedy Central and outlets such as the *Onion* in the United States and elsewhere, Young's essay should be useful and timely for many years. Weeks focuses on the political realm in his essay on political misperceptions; he outlines factors such as the prevalence of ideologically oriented media content and the proliferation of social media tools as key considerations. Similarly, Maki, Carrico, and Vandenbergh look at misperceptions in the environmental arena. They specifically examine behavior with consequences for the environment, such as hand-washing and energy-saving practices, and they conclude that various fallacies sometimes have led to behavior at odds with recommended practice. Sheble helpfully reminds us that sometimes misperceptions about science stem not from explicit scientific fraud but by the diffusion of scientific information through social networks, a process that can result in the spread of misinterpretations over time.

The last section of the book addresses the difficult question of what, if anything, can be done to solve the problems caused by misinformation. Eliminating the existence of misinformation itself may be an impossible task in the media systems of relatively free and democratic societies, but nonetheless remedies may well exist to counter the *effects* of misinformation. Understanding whether such corrective efforts can work requires theory on the mechanisms of misinformation acceptance and rejection, for which we can draw on parts of section 1 as well as an artful review of mechanisms for corrective effect by Swire and Ecker. They note that many corrections are ineffective but also point out some reason for optimism. On a similar note, Thorson offers comparative evidence regarding the efficacy of various political campaign fact-checking approaches. She reports compelling reason for third-party fact-checking entities and journalists to get involved with the process, as she finds that adjudication by a fact-checking organization is more likely to offer corrective traction than simply allowing each side of a campaign to fact-check the other. Not all corrective efforts perform equally.

Corrective action is not limited to the political sphere. Researchers, professionals, and volunteers have attempted to develop remedies for misinformation for decades; we have even seen formal use of corrective remedies commissioned by agencies such as the FDA (Aikin et al., 2015). Our discussion would be incomplete without a look at the evolution of political campaign fact checking, and Poulsen and Young offer such an assessment with their discussion of the history of fact-checking initiatives related to political contests in the United States. At the same time, we can learn from the emerging literature on consumer product marketing as well. In this vein, Bullock reviews the consumer product label arena and concludes that regulations need to move beyond current practice to ideally combat fraudulent labeling claims. Strong remedies, however, also will face challenges from those who worry about censorship, as Kaplan notes in her review of efforts to provide balanced information about vaccine safety. The corrective-policy story is still being written, but our discussion nonetheless reveals some of the practical struggles that have been faced in balancing free speech concerns with worry about lying in stump speeches, political ads, or product promotion.

In the third section of the book, we again acknowledge the role that diffusion through networks can play in accounting for misinformation proliferation. A sociological approach not only highlights how information and misinformation move through communities but also might suggest yet another site for mitigation. In this regard, Hemsley's chapter on what he calls "middle-layer gatekeepers," people who serve as network hubs as information spreads from elite outlets to audience members with few followers, suggests a twist on the prospect of unmitigated diffusion as he notes the power of such information hubs to filter or stop the flow of misinformation. Such an approach harks back to the opinion-leader concept articulated by Katz and Lazarsfeld (1955), offering not just a description of the flow of information but potential remedy for the spread of misperceptions.

Concluding Thoughts

The importance of misinformation as a concern has appeared to grow in recent years as technology affords quicker and more widespread dissemination of information and misinformation while various individual and societal constraints make the presentation and acceptance of misinformation common. At the same time, there is a growing interest in this dilemma from academics and policy makers, as evidenced by the contributions throughout this book. Moreover, technological change and human innovation have evolved in recent years to suggest some possibilities for immediate counterefforts that hold promise. One is real-time fact checking like the U.S. cable news channel CNN did for some presidential speeches in 2016; by immediately posting graphics noting claims that were not factually accurate, the organization leveraged technology to offer a potentially useful frame for viewers interested in the truth, a strategy recommended by Graves (2016). We live in a moment in which widespread misinformation is common. Yet, this is also a time in which many people are passionately developing potential solutions and remedies. The journey forward undoubtedly will be a long one. The way in which media systems have developed in many democratic societies inherently calls for both vulnerability to occasional misinformation and robust systems to detect and address it. Airtight preemptory systems, in fact, ultimately would be suffocating and unappealing. With this collection of essays, then, we hope to inform future efforts in what will be an ongoing struggle that stems from the nature of mass audience systems.

References

Aikin, K. J., Betts, K. R., O'Donoghue, A. C., Rupert, D. J., Lee, P. K., Amoozegar, J. B., & Southwell, B. G. (2015). Correction of overstatement and omission in direct-to-consumer prescription drug advertising. *Journal of Communication, 65*(4), 596–618.

Amarasingam, A. (2011). *The Stewart/Colbert effect: Essays on the real impacts of fake news.* Jefferson, NC: McFarland.

Asp, E. W., & Tranel, D. (2012). False tagging theory: Toward a unitary account of prefrontal cortex function. In D. T. Stuss & R. T. Knight (Eds.), *Principles of frontal lobe function* (pp. 383–416). New York, NY: Oxford University Press.

Brooker, W., & Jermyn, D. (Eds.). (2003). *The audience studies reader.* London, UK: Routledge.

Gilbert, D. T., Krull, D. S., & Malone, P. S. (1990). Unbelieving the unbelievable: Some problems in the rejection of false information. *Journal of Personality and Social Psychology, 59,* 601–613.

Gilbert, D., Tafarodi, R., & Malone, P. (1993). You can't not believe everything you read. *Journal of Personality and Social Psychology, 65*(2), 221–233.

Graves, L. (2016). *Deciding what's true: The rise of political fact-checking in American journalism.* New York, NY: Columbia University Press.

Habermas, J. (1984). *The theory of communicative action: Vol. 1. Reason and the rationalization of society* (T. McCarthy, Trans.). Boston, MA: Beacon Press.

Habermas, J. (1987). *The theory of communicative action: Vol. 2. Lifeworld and system: A critique of functionalist reason* (T. McCarthy, Trans.). Boston, MA: Beacon Press.

Hornik, R. C. (Ed.). (2002). *Public health communication: Evidence for behavior change.* Mahwah, NJ: Lawrence Erlbaum.

Jenkins, H. (2008). *Convergence culture: Where old and new media collide.* New York, NY: New York University Press.

Katz, E., Blumler, J. G., & Gurevitch, M. (1973–1974). Uses and gratifications research. *Public Opinion Quarterly, 37*(4), 509–523.

Katz, E., & Lazarsfeld, P. F. (1955). *Personal influence: The part played by people in the flow of mass communications.* Glencoe, IL: Free Press.

Lewandowsky, S., Ecker, U. K. H., Seifert, C. M., Schwarz, N., & Cook, J. (2012). Misinformation and its correction: Continued influence and successful debiasing. *Psychological Science in the Public Interest, 13*(3), 106–131.

Lewandowsky, S., Stritzke, W. G. K., Freund, A. M., Oberauer, K., & Krueger, J. I. (2013). Misinformation, disinformation, and violent conflict: From Iraq and the "War on Terror" to future threats to peace. *American Psychologist, 68*(7), 487–501.

O'Donoghue, A. C., Boudewyns, V., Aikin, K. J., Geisen, E., Betts, K. R., & Southwell, B. G. (2015). Awareness of FDA's Bad Ad program and education regarding pharmaceutical advertising: A national survey of prescribers in ambulatory care settings. *Journal of Health Communication, 20*(11), 1330–1336.

Price, V. (1992). *Public opinion.* Thousand Oaks, CA: Sage.

Southwell, B. G. (2013). *Social networks and popular understanding of science and health: Sharing disparities.* Baltimore, MD: Johns Hopkins University Press.

Southwell, B. G., & Thorson, E. A. (2015). The prevalence, consequence, and remedy of misinformation in mass media systems. *Journal of Communication, 65*(4), 589–595.

Stahl, B. C. (2006). On the difference or equality of information, misinformation, and disinformation: A critical research perspective. *Informing Science Journal, 9*, 83–96.

Thorson, E. (2015). Belief echoes: The persistent effects of corrected misinformation. *Political Communication,* 1–21.

Webster, J., & Phalen, P. F. (1996). *The mass audience: Rediscovering the dominant model.* New York, NY: Routledge.

Weeks, B., & Southwell, B. (2010). The symbiosis of news coverage and aggregate online search behavior: Obama, rumors, and presidential politics. *Mass Communication and Society, 13*(4), 341–360.

PART I Dimensions of Audience Awareness of Misinformation

Believing Things That Are Not True

ONE A Cognitive Science Perspective on Misinformation

ELIZABETH J. MARSH AND BRENDA W. YANG

One of these rather silly anecdotes is an actual news story: some newer Canadian hundred-dollar bills smell like maple syrup; England is considering issuing a coin featuring the pop band One Direction; the U.S. Treasury recently introduced Perry the Pyramid, a terrifying one-eyed mascot for the dollar. Choosing the real story was the task of a college student who called in to the "Bluff the Listener" game on the National Public Radio program *Wait Wait . . . Don't Tell Me!* (Danforth, 2013). He won the game by correctly selecting the true but rather obscure story about scented Canadian currency. How did the listener make this choice, given it was unlikely he had the relevant information in mind to make that decision?

In this chapter, we review the cognitive strategies and heuristics people use when deciding whether something is true. Our approach to understanding this issue is an experimental one, with the goal of isolating particular mechanisms that contribute to illusions of truth and the propagation of falsehoods. Many of the misconceptions covered in this volume are powerful precisely because they result from combinations of mental processes; there is not one simple trick to convincing people that Barack Obama was not born in the United States, that climate change is a hoax, or that other claims percolating through mass media are unsupported. Here, we consider how statements can be manipulated to seem more truthful than they are, why people unwittingly trust information from sources they initially knew to be unreliable, and how certain features of claims and arguments increase their persuasiveness; our objective in revealing these processes is to inform our overall understanding of misinformation in and out of the laboratory.

An Assumption of Truth

We begin with a very basic issue, namely, that even the most skeptical people have a bias toward accepting what they hear as true. This partly comes out of a need to have successful conversations; to do so, a person shapes what she says to be understood by those around her and assumes others are doing the same. Thus people expect what others say to be truthful, relevant, informative but not overly so, and clear (Grice, 1975). While these guidelines can be stretched or even broken—for instance, through deception, comedy, tall tales, and long academic lectures—they describe what people expect from others in everyday discourse; violations can be noticed in children as young as three years old (Eskritt, Whalen, & Lee, 2008). Our focus here is on the expectation that speakers are truthful. While this assumption is cognitively efficient compared to a strategy of evaluating each and every claim that comes one's way, it can become problematic.

At issue is that people are often willing to be flexible in how they define "truth." We found evidence for this in a study in which Stanford undergraduates tracked instances when they shared their memories with others (Tversky & Marsh, 2000). Over the course of four weeks, students submitted more than a thousand reports of such conversations. Consistent with conversational norms not to tell more than the listener needs to know, more than a third of retellings were reported to be selective in some way. For example, a student sharing a story about an annoying dinner guest focused on the guest's criticisms of the cooking, omitting how the guest also "commented on how another one of my appetizers was tasty. . . . I mentioned everything except the positive comment [when sharing this story]. . . . I was already too annoyed to let it change my reaction." Intriguingly, this speaker also labeled this retelling "complete and accurate," presumably because the story was consistent with the overall theme of the event. In this study, a third of retellings containing distortions like omissions and elaborations were considered accurate by the teller. As Neisser (1981) has noted, truth and accuracy are not simple notions: something can be true on one level and inaccurate on another. This discussion of different levels of truth is meaningful beyond psychological theory. The legal testimony of John Dean, former counsel to President Nixon, was crucial to prosecuting the cover-up at Watergate although large parts of what he said were factually inaccurate (Neisser, 1981). While Dean was inaccurate about many of the details, he was in another sense fundamentally right about the gist of the case and the key parties involved.

However, the problem runs deeper than people taking liberties with the truth. For example, people self-report lying in conversation at surprising rates (DePaulo, Kashy, Kirkendol, Wyer, & Epstein, 1996). This problem is pervasive; politicians stretch the truth or lie outright, advertisements exaggerate claims, textbooks contain errors (Steuer & Ham, 2008), and people's own naïve beliefs about the world can be wrong (Markman & Guenther, 2007). People often have little knowledge to use when assessing incoming information (as in picking out the actual news story in "Bluff the Listener"), but even when they do, such monitoring may be superficial, and they miss errors that are "close enough," as described in partial-match theory (Reder & Kusbit, 1991). People may fail to notice a problem with the question "How many animals of each kind did Moses take on the ark?" This is true even when those people otherwise demonstrate that they know that the biblical ark was built by Noah, not Moses (Erickson & Mattson, 1981). Accepting close matches makes sense, as everyday speech is surprisingly error-filled (Fox Tree, 1995). Not surprisingly, however, people's tolerance for errors drops as errors become more blatant and further from the truth (Hinze, Slaten, Horton, Jenkins, & Rapp, 2014).

Even knowing someone is violating conversational norms and speaking untruthfully, people seem to believe what they are processing automatically. Not believing a falsehood requires an active second step that occurs after initial belief, which can be disrupted (Gilbert, 1991). Evidence for this claim comes from a study in which participants read crime reports about robberies and were instructed to play the role of judge for these cases (Gilbert, Tafarodi, & Malone, 1993). The reports contained a mix of true and false statements—similar to what a judge might actually hear—and subjects were told that true statements were printed in black, while false statements were printed in red. In one report, the false statements exacerbated the crime, such as "The robber had a gun"; in the other report, the false statements made the crime less severe. Critically, half the participants were asked to complete a secondary task while reading these reports; this subjected them to the interruption condition. The results showed that participants who were interrupted were more likely to behave as if the false statements were true; interrupted would-be judges recommended longer prison sentences after reading exacerbating, untrue statements like "The robber had a gun." This is worrisome, as it demonstrates that even explicitly false information can be used when making the kind of judgments regularly made in the real world by distracted individuals. Gilbert's work is supplemented by more recent neuropsychological evidence that the second step in unbelieving a claim can be localized to a region of the prefrontal cortex (ventromedial prefrontal cortex); patients with damage to this brain area show global increases in credulity (Asp et al., 2012).

Reliance on Credible Sources

One way to estimate truth is simply to assess the credibility of the source. It makes sense that people are more likely to believe or act on information when its source is perceived as credible (Pornpitakpan, 2004); if a source is trustworthy, one's own lack of knowledge is unimportant. Advertisers and businesses take advantage of this strategy, spending time and money to acquire celebrity endorsements or develop refer-a-friend models. To investigate this experimentally, Unkelbach and Stahl (2009) exposed participants to a mix of true and false trivia statements, such as "Europe's biggest glacier is the Vatnajökull on Iceland," read by two different voices. They told participants that statements read by the female voice were true and those read by the male voice were false, or vice versa. In these studies, participants were able to use their recollection of the source—whether the voice was male or female—to evaluate the claim by simply applying the credibility of the source to the claim. One would hope that people discount information from sources that are not credible or may have an agenda to deceive.

However, the story regarding belief and source is more complicated than it first appears. Source information is often forgotten, with the result that people frequently do not know where they learned information. While a person is likely to know that Washington, DC, is the capital of the United States and that Mark Twain is the author of *Huckleberry Finn*, he likely does not remember how, when, and where he learned these facts (Tulving, 1985). Some source information is never attended to in the first place; other source information is lost as time passes or as information is encountered in multiple settings (Conway, Gardiner, Perfect, Anderson, & Cohen, 1997).

Even when people do have source information stored in memory, they often fail to apply that knowledge. This problem explains at least some instances of cryptomnesia, unconscious plagiarism as documented in work by Marsh, Landau, and Hicks (1997). In that work, students were asked to generate 15 ways the university might be improved. Critically, subjects returned one week later and were divided into two groups. Subjects in one group took a test containing a list of old and new ideas and selected one of three options for each: "I generated it"; "Someone else generated it"; or "The solution is new." Subjects in the other group were simply asked to generate new ideas they had not given in the first session. Plagiarism was rare in the first testing condition, in which students were explicitly asked to consider the source of ideas, but much higher in the group asked to generate ideas without thinking about the ideas' sources. Similar effects have been found using other paradigms; for instance, eyewitness suggestibility is lessened when people must explicitly attribute information to a set of sources (Lindsay & Johnson, 1989). To the extent that a situation does not prompt people to specifically attribute source, they will act as if the source is forgotten.

For these reasons, discounting less credible sources is not a very powerful strategy; as people forget the source or do not think about where the information came from, they will be influenced by information from that source. This basic idea has a long history, dating to Hovland's classic work on the *sleeper effect* during World War II. A propaganda video affected the opinions and morale of U.S. soldiers more when their attitudes were measured nine weeks after watching the movie than five days after seeing it (Hovland, Lumsdaine, & Sheffield, 1949; for a review, see Kumkale & Albarracín, 2004). This is surprising, given that memory typically declines over time. The key insight is that source information is usually lost at a faster rate than the content of the communication; the persuasiveness of the message increases over time as the source and message become disassociated. This same effect can occur in very different situations. Eyewitnesses generally reject misinformation from a low-credibility source, such as a child, if tested immediately afterward but demonstrate more suggestibility as time passes (Underwood & Pezdek, 1998).

Rather than the quality of a source, another possibility is to look at the number of sources providing the same information, the assumption being that something is more likely to be true if multiple people are saying it. Such a heuristic would be a valuable one, as there is evidence to support "the wisdom of crowds" (Surowiecki, 2005); averaging over a group of responses is more likely to approach the actual truth than is relying on any one individual's response. However, the problem here, again, is that people's relative insensitivity to source information extends to the number of sources making a claim. People treat a repeated claim from the same source as similar to a claim repeated by different sources: "a repetitive voice can sound like a chorus" (Weaver, Garcia, Schwarz, & Miller, 2007). Results of a large-scale study with high school and college students indicate that students' ability to discern reliable from unreliable sources is "bleak" even when explicitly probed, as measured by tasks such as discerning ads from news stories on website homepages and evaluating claims on Twitter (Stanford History Education Group, 2016). This work suggests that even initial evaluations of sources may be lacking; future work might examine general population performance beyond the classroom on similar tasks.

Ease of Processing as a Heuristic for Truth

On average, easy processing, or *fluency*, is interpreted as evidence of truth (Alter & Oppenheimer, 2009). One is less likely to believe another who is hard to understand, such as a speaker with a foreign accent (Lev-Ari & Keysar, 2010), or speech containing disfluencies like "uh" and "um" (Brennan & Williams, 1995). We rate a high-contrast, bolded statement (e.g., **Osorno is in Chile**) as truer than a hard-to-read, low-contrast version (*Osorno is in Chile*) (Reber & Schwarz, 1999). Rhyming aphorisms ("What sobriety conceals, alcohol reveals") are judged to be more accurate than similar but nonrhyming versions ("What sobriety conceals, alcohol unmasks") (McGlone & Tofighbakhsh, 2000).

Fluency is a feeling that is interpreted. Depending on the circumstances, it can be taken as evidence of liking (Bornstein & D'Agostino, 1992; Zajonc, 1968), fame (Jacoby, Kelley, Brown, & Jasechko, 1989), intelligence (Alter & Oppenheimer, 2008), confidence (Alter, Oppenheimer, Epley, & Eyre, 2007; Simmons & Nelson, 2006), and other domain-specific judgments. Our focus here is on the interpretation of fluency as evidence for truth. Unkelbach (2007) argues that this heuristic reflects our knowledge of a natural correlation in the world between fluency and truth. That is, on average, any one true statement is more likely to have been encountered before than any of the infinite possible falsifications of that statement. Something repeated is easier to process than something novel (Jacoby & Whitehouse, 1989). For example, it is easy to process "Washington, DC, is the capital of the United States" for someone who has heard and read this statement many times, and it is not arbitrary that it is heard more often than any of the following false statements: "Lompoc is the capital of the United States"; "Nashville is the capital of the United States"; "El Paso is the capital of the United States." It is important to note that while repetition often drives fluency—it gets easier and easier to read the same statement—it is not a requirement; fluent processing can also result from easy-to-read fonts, from rhymes, and from other variables.

Fluency is not limited to what is easy to process but also can refer to ease of understanding (*conceptual fluency*). Whittlesea (1993) compares the processing of the word "BOAT" in the sentence "The stormy seas tossed the BOAT" as compared to the sentence "He saved up his money and bought a BOAT." Both sentences make sense, but the former is more fluent because the earlier part of the sentence is related to the concept of a BOAT. This eased processing through *priming* (for example) can be interpreted as evidence for prior presentation (Whittlesea, 1993). Parks and Toth (2006) used a similar manipulation and found that people rated claims as more true after being primed by a related paragraph.

Similar explanations involving conceptual fluency have been offered to explain why people are more likely to rate a claim as true if it is accompanied by a photograph that provides no additional support for that claim (Newman, Garry, Bernstein, Kantner, & Lindsay, 2012). The statement "Macadamia nuts are in the same evolutionary family as peaches" is rated more true when it appears with a picture of macadamia nuts than without. Critically, the photo of macadamia nuts provides no new evidence with which to assess the claim about peaches, but it may nevertheless help process the claim. The effect does not occur when a random picture is paired with a statement (Newman et al., 2015), presumably because an unrelated photo causes conceptual disfluency. Newman and colleagues (2015) dubbed this effect of nonprobative photos a "truthiness" effect (p. 1337), borrowing a term from the comedian Stephen Colbert to describe "truth that comes from the gut, not books" (p. 1338) . Colbert (2005) was lampooning the tendency for people to rely on whether claims felt true rather than evaluating them based on evidence—which is, in fact, just what people do when they rely on fluency heuristics, although it is an adaptive strategy in most cases.

Scientific Window Dressing as Evidence of Truth

We have already discussed how people sometimes interpret credible sources as evidence of truth and how claims that are easier to process perceptually and conceptually seem truer. Now we turn to the influence of symbols that are commonly associated with truth to examine whether such trappings of science as formulas, graphs, brain images, irrelevant neuroscience references, and pictures of scientists can affect belief even if they do not add information.

The short answer to this question is yes—certain types of scientific references appear to affect belief in the science. Adding meaningless mathematics such as an irrelevant equation to a scientific abstract tends to encourage higher quality ratings (Eriksson, 2012). References to brain areas (e.g., "the frontal lobe brain circuitry") increased people's satisfaction with scientific explanations even though the references added nothing to the logic of the explanations (Weisberg, Keil, Goodstein, Rawson, & Gray, 2008; see also Fernandez-Duque, Evans, Christian, & Hodges, 2015). Estimates of a drug's longevity increased when the chemical formula ($C_{21}H_{29}FO_5$) was included in addition to the information that the compound is "carbon-oxygen-helium-and-fluorine based" (Tal & Wansink, 2016).

One open question involves whether ostensibly scientific pictures like graphs and brain images are powerful above and beyond images described as having a truthiness effect. Some data suggest that a graph increases belief even when the same results are presented in the text (Tal & Wansink, 2016). Without a control condition with an image that is not a graph, however, we cannot be sure whether the effect is driven by the graph or the inclusion of an image, that is, its truthiness. At a minimum, the Tal and Wansink effect seems to be related to scientific images, in that the effect was stronger in participants who agreed with the statement "I believe in science." More controversial are the effects of brain images. Initial results of another study indicate that undergraduates who read scientific texts paired with brain images were more likely to rate the articles as making more sense than articles without images (McCabe & Castel, 2008), but more recent work has failed to replicate this finding (Michael, Newman, Vuorre, Cumming, & Garry, 2013).

Features of Stories as Promoting Belief

Often one must evaluate information structured as narratives rather than as one-off claims about, for example, macadamia nuts or Icelandic glaciers. As with other types of claims, however, people are not very good at discerning honest narratives from misleading ones (Ekman & O'Sullivan,

1991). The question we consider here is whether there is anything differ- ent about evaluating a story compared to a claim. The fact-checking web- site Snopes presents variations on an urban legend that goes like this: "Drugged travelers awaken in ice-filled bathtubs only to discover one of their kidneys has been harvested by organ thieves" (Mikkelson, 2008). A 1997 version of the tale posted to Snopes begins, "I wish to warn you about a new crime ring that is targeting business travelers." It proceeds through grim details of a lone traveler being slipped a drug and awakening in an ice-filled bathtub to discover that, preposterously, not one but both kid- neys have been removed. A note instructs the victim to call 911, whose dis- patchers "have become quite familiar with this crime." The tale concludes with the assurance "This is not a scam or out of a science fiction novel, it is real" and the warning "If you travel or someone close to you travels, please be careful" (in Mikkelson 2008).

There are many differences between the statement and story. For one, the story is longer and contains additional information, two features that are likely to affect how truthfulness is perceived. Presenting infor- mation as a story is known to afford the extraction of gist (McDaniel, Einstein, Dunay, & Cobb, 1986). Moreover, this gruesome tale and other urban legends tend to be of high interest, and interesting information may take less attention to process, thus freeing up cognitive resources to allow "more flexible, increased processing" (McDaniel, Waddill, Fin- stad, & Bourg, 2000). And the very form of a story may have properties that render information "sticky" (Heath & Heath, 2007); it can guide re- membering by providing a "story schema" for people to follow (Mandler & Johnson, 1977). Furthermore, predictable patterns constrain the infor- mation and make stories more stable as they pass from one person to another (Wallace & Rubin, 1991).

A key feature particular to stories is that they have the ability to trans- port the reader. While experiencing stories, one can feel emotionally in- volved and as if being swept away as a participant (Green & Brock, 2000). There is some evidence that being transported into a story requires a sus- pension of disbelief; enjoying *Jurassic Park* or a Harry Potter tale may in- volve putting aside what one knows about the world that contradicts the story (Gerrig, 1989). A story that suggests an unexpected outcome ("George Washington declined the nomination to become the first president of the United States") results in readers being slower to verify well-known facts ("George Washington was elected first president of the United States"). This suspension of disbelief may make one less likely to spot problems in a narrative, as illustrated by a study in which participants read a story and circled any "false notes" or parts that did not make sense (Green & Brock, 2000). Green and Brock refer to this method as "Pinocchio circling": just as the puppet's nose signaled when he told a falsehood, authors also leave clues when they are being untruthful. But readers who were more transported by the story spotted fewer "Pinocchios," consistent with the idea that people are less likely to doubt highly transporting stories.

The Roles of Motivation and Emotions

While our approach draws heavily on cognitive psychology, the present discussion would be incomplete without at least briefly considering the role of affective processes in shaping belief, particularly the role of existing worldviews and political positions. Misconceptions such as "Tax cuts increase government revenue" and "President Bush banned stem cell research" are evaluated differently by Republicans and Democrats, and such biases are likely to limit some of the effects discussed thus far—a fluency manipulation is highly unlikely to swing someone to the opposite position.

The Truth We Want to Exist

Prior beliefs affect how people process and evaluate incoming information. "Motivated reasoning" describes a set of findings showing that people's goals and predispositions influence how they interpret information (Kunda, 1990); or, in Colbert's words, we sometimes find "the truth we want to exist" (as cited in Sternbergh, 2006, p. 2). People tend to look for and remember information that is consistent with what they already believe; this is *confirmation bias* (Nickerson, 1998). People also subject information inconsistent with what they already believe to more scrutiny and rate it less favorably; this tendency is called *disconfirmation bias* (Edwards & Smith, 1996). In one study, participants were chosen so that half supported capital punishment and the other half opposed it (Lord, Ross, & Lepper, 1979). Before the experiment began, both groups believed most of the relevant research supported their respective positions; proponents of capital punishment believed it had a deterrent effect on crime, while opponents believed the opposite. Each person read about two research studies on capital punishment, one supporting the efficacy of the death penalty in bringing down crime and the other discrediting the death penalty's deterrent effect. Not only did participants rate the facts that confirmed their existing beliefs to be more convincing and accurate than ones that contradicted their existing beliefs, but exposure to this mixed evidence actually polarized people's beliefs more. This *motivated skepticism* has also been found in studies wherein people evaluate other controversial issues, such as affirmative action and gun control (Taber, Cann, & Kucsova, 2009; Taber & Lodge, 2006). Taber and colleagues (2009) argue that people are powerfully motivated to confirm their own beliefs while rejecting arguments that challenge prior positions, and that these processes happen automatically.

Another line of research examines how political affiliation affects the ways retractions of information are handled. Media coverage of the beginning of the U.S.-Iraq war in 2003 provided Lewandowsky and colleagues (2005) fertile ground for testing these ideas, as corrections and retractions of earlier information occurred frequently. They found that American participants were more likely than German participants to rely on information that had been later retracted, such as the existence of weapons of mass destruction in Iraq, even when they had heard and confidently knew about the retraction (Lewandowsky, Stritzke, Oberauer, & Morales, 2005). The authors argue that these differences occurred because American and German participants held different beliefs about reasons for the war; while Americans listed "destroying weapons of mass destruction" as the most important reason for the war (on average), Germans did not consider this very important. Another study shows that Republicans were less likely than Democrats to correct the misconception that weapons of mass destruction were found in Iraq when the United States invaded (Nyhan & Reifler, 2010). In fact, such retractions may actually further cement the mistaken belief.

The Effect of Emotions

Emotions play a critical role in shaping how information is processed and evaluated. Anecdotally, examples include children saying nice things to their parents before asking favors and advertising strategies and political campaigns eliciting fear or hope. While we cannot cover all of the effects of emotion here, we simply note that the effects are powerful and have consequences that can extend to real-world contexts, such as courtrooms. Images that provoke emotion—gruesome photos of a victim's injuries or from a crime scene—can lead jurors to award more damages to accident victims (Edelman, 2009; Thompson & Dennison, 2004) or make it more likely for jurors to find a defendant guilty (Bright & Goodman-Delahunty, 2006; Douglas, Lyon, & Ogloff, 1997).

Our focus here is on the effects of emotion on the transmission of misinformation. Many studies have shown how misinformation can spread when one person reproduces false information in conversation with another (*social contagion*) (Roediger, Meade, & Bergman, 2001). Emotion may play a key role, in that people are more likely to share emotional stories. In a diary study with Stanford undergraduates, retellings were more likely to involve emotional memories than neutral ones (Tversky & Marsh, 2000); another study shows that people who are more physiologically aroused (disgusted, amused, anxious, angered) are more likely to share information (Berger, 2011). This can be seen anecdotally, as urban legends often elicit high arousal, like the story about the ring of organ thieves or other false rumors, such as those about KFC serving a fried rat or people hiding razor blades in children's Halloween candy. Heath and colleagues argue that *emotional selection* helps determine which ideas get passed on and survive (Heath, Bell, & Sternberg, 2001). Their participants rated the emotional content of a sample of stories and urban legends, as well as their own willingness to pass them along. People reported being more willing to pass on stories that were more disgusting. A follow-up study by Heath and Heath (2007) shows that urban legends containing disgust-inducing motifs are distributed more widely online.

Stored Knowledge Is Insufficient

Are people susceptible to misinformation even when they know better? Conversations with our own stubborn family members, along with the overall difficulty we have encountered counteracting sticky falsehoods in mass media, suggest that the answer is yes. While we have alluded to the role of knowledge, it is worth stating explicitly that heuristics are not limited to cases of ignorance. People rely on heuristics for truth even when they have the option of retrieving the relevant information in memory that would enable them to avoid endorsing errors; knowledge affords limited protection from misinformation. There are many cases of people failing to use their knowledge logically. One is the common belief that the Great Wall of China is one of the only man-made objects that is visible from space. While the Great Wall is indeed quite long, it is not particularly wide. If it is visible from space, so would be other large structures, including wide multilane freeways. And while most people could identify H_2O as the chemical notation for water, some are nevertheless susceptible to hoaxes and pranks involving the dangers of a colorless and odorless chemical compound; two radio DJs were suspended for eliciting a minor panic on April Fool's Day when they joked that "dihydrogen monoxide" was coming out of county residents' taps (Braun, 2013).

The problem is not limited to logical extensions of knowledge. People can have the exact information necessary stored in their memory and still fail to bring it to bear. In the Moses illusion, people fail to notice an incorrect reference to Moses even though they demonstrate that they know the biblical reference should be to Noah. In our experiments investigating knowledge and illusions of truth, we find that repetition affects the rated truth of statements even when the statements contradict well-known facts. Prior exposure to falsehoods like "A sari is a short pleated skirt worn by Scots" increases ratings of truth later on, just as is observed for statements for which people have little knowledge, such as "The Arno is the river that runs through Rome" (Fazio, Brashier, Payne, & Marsh, 2015).

Moreover, such effects are not simply a matter of failing to notice the error and reading over it. We know the errors are processed because people later repeat them despite having the correct information stored in memory as well. In one study, we asked people general questions such as "What is the largest ocean?" two weeks before exposing them to misinformation such as "The Atlantic is the largest ocean" (Fazio, Barber, Rajaram, Ornstein, & Marsh, 2013). Some of the people who gave the correct answer, "Pacific," switched to "Atlantic" two weeks later. And this same effect occurs even if people demonstrate their knowledge just 10 minutes before reading the stories (Mullet, Umanath, & Marsh, 2014). Similar effects occur with films. Reading a veridical passage about how Mozart was respectful and polite as a child does not prevent the viewer from later relying on an incorrect movie clip from *Amadeus* that shows the young Mozart as childish and eccentric (Butler, Zaromb, Lyle, & Roediger, 2009; Umanath, Butler, & Marsh, 2012). In our studies we reliably find that people are susceptible to influence from misinformation even if it blatantly contradicts what they already know. These effects do not depend on forgetting the source of the information. In our experiments, people claimed they knew that the Atlantic was the largest ocean before coming into the laboratory, demonstrating evidence of prior knowledge (Marsh, Meade, & Roediger, 2003). We also find that repeating the misinformation makes it more likely to persist (Barber, Rajaram, & Marsh, 2008). In other words, sharing the error will not only propagate it to others but also make it more likely to be remembered by the teller.

For an example of these ideas in the real world, we can revisit the study on media retractions on coverage of the Iraq War (Lewandowsky et al., 2005). Critically, after measuring whether people's beliefs were in line with the retractions, the researchers asked people whether they remembered reading retractions of the errors. Remembering a retraction did not guarantee an effect on belief; people could have knowledge of the retraction stored in memory and yet act as if they did not know it. Our experimental work shows that people use heuristics to evaluate truth even when knowledge is available in memory. However, such relatively neutral trivia stimuli are unlikely to provoke motivated reasoning by which people more actively interpret information to be consistent with their worldviews. The limitations of knowledge in preventing errors may be even starker for more partisan contexts, as in the case of the Iraq War (see Nyhan, 2016, for related open questions).

Conclusion

Chris Yamas was the caller who successfully chose the correct news story about Canadian currency out of two similarly silly distractors on the NPR game "Bluff the Listener" (Danforth, 2013). He explains his reasoning on air as follows: "You know, I dated a lovely Canadian girl, and I have many Canadian friends, and I know they're a bunch of maple-loving loonies. So I'm going to go with A [the Canadian $100 bill smelling like maple syrup]." While it is impossible to know exactly how Chris came to his decision—it could easily have been a lucky guess—we have discussed several strategies he may have relied on in making his correct decision. Chris could have recollected a conversation with his ex or a friend from Canada as reliable sources in discussing their currency's curious scent. And even if he could no longer remember when or how he heard the story previously, prior exposure would have generated a feeling of fluency that Chris could take as a heuristic for truth. In either case, Chris would have used a proxy for truth instead of directly retrieving knowledge from memory, a strategy people commonly use when evaluating claims. This reliance on heuristics normally works, as it did for Chris, but it can also lead people astray. A casual listener tuning in to the radio program could have been distracted, making the listener less likely to take the active second step necessary to unbelieving the falsehoods after understanding them. And perhaps a reader, forgetting that she originally read the stories about One Direction on British coins and Perry the Pyramid from this text, will one day misconstrue these made-up stories for truth and circulate them in conversation.

In our experimental work, we find that creating situations in which people repeat misinformation or fail to notice it is relatively easy, even when they should know better. Such errors matter, as they form the bases for confusions that are propagated through people and the media while being shaped by emotions and preexisting motives. Correcting such beliefs can prove challenging. In an ideal world, we would advocate for such errors to be unbelieved immediately upon encountering them rather than needing correction after they have been believed and shared with others. However, this kind of online detection is a real challenge, given that people's goals in life often are at odds with a monitoring focus; they consume media to be entertained, to have beliefs confirmed, and to be distracted from other things. We know that people can sometimes be encouraged to bring their knowledge to bear, through explicit instructions to mark errors (Green & Brock, 2000; Marsh & Fazio, 2006), or to take the perspective of a proofreader (Rapp, Hinze, Kohlhepp, & Ryskin, 2014), but these laboratory studies not do suggest realistic interventions. Future research should focus on this early stage of belief, before people develop large misconceptions that require massive interventions to correct.

References

Alter, A. L., & Oppenheimer, D. M. (2008). Effects of fluency on psychological distance and mental construal (or why New York is a large city, but New York is a civilized jungle). *Psychological Science*, 19(2), 161–167.

Alter, A. L., & Oppenheimer, D. M. (2009). Uniting the tribes of fluency to form a metacognitive nation. *Personality and Social Psychology Review*, 13(3), 219–235.

Alter, A. L., Oppenheimer, D. M., Epley, N., & Eyre, R. N. (2007). Overcoming intuition: Metacognitive difficulty activates analytic reasoning. *Journal of Experimental Psychology: General*, 136(4), 569–576.

Asp, E., Manzel, K., Koestner, B., Cole, C., Denburg, N. L., & Tranel, D. (2012). A neuropsychological test of belief and doubt: Damage to ventromedial prefrontal cortex increases credulity for misleading advertising. *Decision Neuroscience*, 6, 100.

Barber, S. J., Rajaram, S., & Marsh, E. J. (2008). Fact learning: How information accuracy, delay, and repeated testing change retention and retrieval experience. *Memory*, 16(8), 934–946.

Berger, J. (2011). Arousal increases social transmission of information. *Psychological Science*, 22(7), 891–893.

Bornstein, R. F., & D'Agostino, P. R. (1992). Stimulus recognition and the mere exposure effect. *Journal of Personality and Social Psychology*, 63(4), 545.

Braun, M. (2013, April 2). DJs' April Fools' prank leads to small-scale panic. *USA Today*. Bonita Springs, FL. Retrieved from http://www.usatoday.com/story/news/nation/2013/04/02/florida-water-prank/2046639

Brennan, S. E., & Williams, M. (1995). The feeling of another's knowing: Prosody and filled pauses as cues to listeners about the metacognitive states of speakers. *Journal of Memory and Language*, 34, 383–398.

Bright, D. A., & Goodman-Delahunty, J. (2006). Gruesome evidence and emotion: Anger, blame, and jury decision-making. *Law and Human Behavior*, 30(2), 183–202.

Butler, A. C., Zaromb, F. M., Lyle, K. B., & Roediger, H. L. (2009). Using popular films to enhance classroom learning: The good, the bad, and the interesting. *Psychological Science*, 20(9), 1161–1168.

Colbert, S. (Producer). (2005, October 17). "The Word—Truthiness." [Television series clip]. *Colbert Report*. New York, NY: Comedy Central.

Conway, M. A., Gardiner, J. M., Perfect, T. J., Anderson, S. J., & Cohen, G. M. (1997). Changes in memory awareness during learning: The acquisition of knowledge by psychology undergraduates. *Journal of Experimental Psychology: General*, 126(4), 393.

Danforth, M. (Producer). (2013, June 1). *Wait wait . . . don't tell me!* [Radio broadcast]. Chicago, IL: National Public Radio. Retrieved from http://www.npr.org/templates/story/story.php?storyId=187762247

DePaulo, B. M., Kashy, D. A., Kirkendol, S. E., Wyer, M. M., & Epstein, J. A. (1996). Lying in everyday life. *Journal of Personality and Social Psychology*, 70(5), 979.

Douglas, K. S., Lyon, D. R., & Ogloff, J. R. P. (1997). The impact of graphic photographic evidence on mock jurors' decisions in a murder trial: Probative or prejudicial? *Law and Human Behavior*, 21(5), 485–501.

Edelman, B. (2009). The impact of graphic injury photographs on liability verdicts and non-economic damage awards. *The Jury Expert: The Art and Science of Litigation Advocacy*, 21(5), 1–4.

Edwards, K., & Smith, E. E. (1996). A disconfirmation bias in the evaluation of arguments. *Journal of Personality and Social Psychology*, 71(1), 5.

Ekman, P., & O'Sullivan, M. (1991). Who can catch a liar? *American Psychologist*, 46(9), 913.

Erickson, T. D., & Mattson, M. E. (1981). From words to meaning: A semantic illusion. *Journal of Verbal Learning and Verbal Behavior*, 20, 540–551.

Eriksson, K. (2012). The nonsense math effect. *Judgment and Decision Making*, 7(6), 746.

Eskritt, M., Whalen, J., & Lee, K. (2008). Preschoolers can recognize violations of the Gricean maxims. *British Journal of Developmental Psychology*, 26(3), 435–443.

Fazio, L. K., Barber, S. J., Rajaram, S., Ornstein, P. A., & Marsh, E. J. (2013). Creating illusions of knowledge: Learning errors that contradict prior knowledge. *Journal of Experimental Psychology: General*, 142(1), 1–5.

Fazio, L. K., Brashier, N. M., Payne, B. K., & Marsh, E. J. (2015). Knowledge does not protect against illusory truth. *Journal of Experimental Psychology: General, 144*(5), 993–1002.

Fernandez-Duque, D., Evans, J., Christian, C., & Hodges, S. D. (2015). Superfluous neuroscience information makes explanations of psychological phenomena more appealing. *Journal of Cognitive Neuroscience, 27*(5), 926–944.

Fox Tree, J. E. (1995). The effects of false starts and repetitions on the processing of subsequent words in spontaneous speech. *Journal of Memory and Language, 34,* 709–738.

Gerrig, R. J. (1989). Suspense in the absence of uncertainty. *Journal of Memory and Language, 28*(6), 633–648.

Gilbert, D. T. (1991). How mental systems believe. *American Psychologist, 46*(2), 107–119.

Gilbert, D. T., Tafarodi, R. W., & Malone, P. S. (1993). You can't not believe everything you read. *Journal of Personality and Social Psychology, 65*(2), 221.

Green, M. C., & Brock, T. C. (2000). The role of transportation in the persuasiveness of public narratives. *Journal of Personality and Social Psychology, 79*(5), 701–721.

Grice, H. P. (1975). Logic and conversation. In P. Cole & J. L. Morgan, *Syntax and semantics: Vol. 3. Speech acts* (pp. 41–58). New York, NY: Academic Press.

Heath, C., Bell, C., & Sternberg, E. (2001). Emotional selection in memes: the case of urban legends. *Journal of Personality and Social Psychology, 81*(6), 1028.

Heath, C., & Heath, D. (2007). *Made to stick: Why some ideas survive and others die.* New York, NY: Random House.

Hinze, S. R., Slaten, D. G., Horton, W. S., Jenkins, R., & Rapp, D. N. (2014). Pilgrims sailing the Titanic: Plausibility effects on memory for misinformation. *Memory & Cognition, 42*(2), 305–324.

Hovland, C. I., Lumsdaine, A. A., & Sheffield, F. D. (1949). *Studies in social psychology in World War II: Vol. 3. Experiments on mass communication.* Princeton, NJ: Princeton University Press.

Jacoby, L. L., Kelley, C., Brown, J., & Jasechko, J. (1989). Becoming famous overnight: Limits on the ability to avoid unconscious influences of the past. *Journal of Personality and Social Psychology, 56*(3), 326.

Jacoby, L. L., & Whitehouse, K. (1989). An illusion of memory: False recognition influenced by unconscious perception. *Journal of Experimental Psychology: General, 118*(2), 126.

Kumkale, G. T., & Albarracín, D. (2004). The sleeper effect in persuasion: A meta-analytic review. *Psychological Bulletin, 130*(1), 143–172.

Kunda, Z. (1990). The case for motivated reasoning. *Psychological Bulletin, 108*(3), 480–498.

Lev-Ari, S., & Keysar, B. (2010). Why don't we believe non-native speakers? The influence of accent on credibility. *Journal of Experimental Social Psychology, 46*(6), 1093–1096.

Lewandowsky, S., Stritzke, W. G. K., Oberauer, K., & Morales, M. (2005). Memory for fact, fiction, and misinformation: The Iraq War 2003. *Psychological Science, 16*(3), 190–195.

Lindsay, D. S., & Johnson, M. K. (1989). The eyewitness suggestibility effect and memory for source. *Memory & Cognition, 17*(3), 349–358.

Lord, C. G., Ross, L., & Lepper, M. R. (1979). Biased assimilation and attitude polarization: The effects of prior theories on subsequently considered evidence. *Journal of
Personality and Social Psychology, 37*(11), 2098.

Mandler, J. M., & Johnson, N. S. (1977). Remembrance of things parsed: Story structure and recall. *Cognitive Psychology, 9*(1), 111–151.

Markman, K. D., & Guenther, C. L. (2007). Psychological momentum: Intuitive physics
and naive beliefs. *Personality and Social Psychology Bulletin, 33*(6), 800–812.

Marsh, E. J., & Fazio, L. K. (2006). Learning errors from fiction: Difficulties in reducing
reliance on fictional stories. *Memory & Cognition, 34*(5), 1140–1149.

Marsh, E. J., Meade, M. L., & Roediger, H. L. R. (2003). Learning facts from fiction.
Journal of Memory and Language, 49(4), 519–536.

Marsh, R. L., Landau, J. D., & Hicks, J. L. (1997). Contributions of inadequate source
monitoring to unconscious plagiarism during idea generation. *Journal of Experimental Psychology: Learning, Memory, and Cognition, 23*(4), 886.

McCabe, D. P., & Castel, A. D. (2008). Seeing is believing: The effect of brain images on
judgments of scientific reasoning. *Cognition, 107*(1), 343–352.

McDaniel, M. A., Einstein, G. O., Dunay, P. K., & Cobb, R. E. (1986). Encoding difficulty
and memory: Toward a unifying theory. *Journal of Memory and Language, 25*(6),
645–656.

McDaniel, M. A., Waddill, P. J., Finstad, K., & Bourg, T. (2000). The effects of text-based
interest on attention and recall. *Journal of Educational Psychology, 92*(3), 492–502.

McGlone, M. S., & Tofighbakhsh, J. (2000). Birds of a feather flock conjointly (?):
Rhyme as reason in aphorisms. *Psychological Science, 11*(5), 424–428.

Michael, R. B., Newman, E. J., Vuorre, M., Cumming, G., & Garry, M. (2013). On the
(non)persuasive power of a brain image. *Psychonomic Bulletin & Review, 20*(4),
720–725.

Mikkelson, D. (Fact checker). (2008, March 12). Kidney theft. Snopes.com. Retrieved
from http://www.snopes.com/horrors/robbery/kidney.asp

Mullet, H. G., Umanath, S., & Marsh, E. J. (2014). Recent study, but not retrieval, of
knowledge protects against learning errors. *Memory & Cognition, 42*(8), 1239–1249.

Neisser, U. (1981). John Dean's memory: A case study. *Cognition, 9*, 1–22.

Newman, E. J., Garry, M., Bernstein, D. M., Kantner, J., & Lindsay, D. S. (2012). Nonprobative photographs (or words) inflate truthiness. *Psychonomic Bulletin & Review,
19*(5), 969–974.

Newman, E. J., Garry, M., Unkelbach, C., Bernstein, D. M., Lindsay, D. S., & Nash,
R. A. (2015). Truthiness and falsiness of trivia claims depend on judgmental contexts. *Journal of Experimental Psychology: Learning, Memory, and Cognition, 41*(5),
1337–1348.

Nickerson, R. S. (1998). Confirmation bias: A ubiquitous phenomenon in many guises.
Review of General Psychology, 2(2), 175–220.

Nyhan, B. (2016, June). The challenge of false beliefs. Presented at *How We Can Improve
Health Science Communication*, University of Michigan, Ann Arbor. Retrieved from
https://www.isr.umich.edu/cps/events/Nyhan_20160613.pdf

Nyhan, B., & Reifler, J. (2010). When corrections fail: The persistence of political misperceptions. *Political Behavior, 32*(2), 303–330.

Parks, C. M., & Toth, J. P. (2006). Fluency, familiarity, aging, and the illusion of truth. *Aging, Neuropsychology, and Cognition, 13*(2), 225–253.

Pornpitakpan, C. (2004). The persuasiveness of source credibility: A critical review of five decades' evidence. *Journal of Applied Social Psychology, 34*(2), 243–281.

Rapp, D. N., Hinze, S. R., Kohlhepp, K., & Ryskin, R. A. (2014). Reducing reliance on inaccurate information. *Memory & Cognition, 42*(1), 11–26.

Reber, R., & Schwarz, N. (1999). Effects of perceptual fluency on judgments of truth. *Consciousness and Cognition, 8*, 338–342.

Reder, L. M., & Kusbit, G. W. (1991). Locus of the Moses illusion: Imperfect encoding, retrieval, or match? *Journal of Memory and Language, 30*, 385–406.

Roediger, H. L., Meade, M. L., & Bergman, E. T. (2001). Social contagion of memory. *Psychonomic Bulletin & Review, 8*(2), 365–371.

Simmons, J. P., & Nelson, L. D. (2006). Intuitive confidence: Choosing between intuitive and nonintuitive alternatives. *Journal of Experimental Psychology: General, 135*(3), 409–428.

Stanford History Education Group. (2016). *Evaluating information: The cornerstone of civic online reasoning.* Stanford Graduate School of Education. Retrieved from https://sheg.stanford.edu/upload/V3LessonPlans/Executive%20Summary%20 11.21.16.pdf

Sternbergh, A. (2006, October 16). Stephen Colbert has America by the ballots. *New York Magazine.* New York, NY. Retrieved from http://nymag.com/news/politics/22322

Steuer, F. B., & Ham, K. W. (2008). Psychology textbooks: Examining their accuracy. *Teaching of Psychology, 35*(3), 160–168.

Surowiecki, J. (2005). *The wisdom of crowds.* New York, NY: Anchor.

Taber, C. S., Cann, D., & Kucsova, S. (2009). The motivated processing of political arguments. *Political Behavior, 31*(2), 137–155.

Taber, C. S., & Lodge, M. (2006). Motivated skepticism in the evaluation of political beliefs. *American Journal of Political Science, 50*(3), 755–769.

Tal, A., & Wansink, B. (2016). Blinded with science: Trivial graphs and formulas increase ad persuasiveness and belief in product efficacy. *Public Understanding of Science, 25*(1), 117–125.

Thompson, C. M., & Dennison, S. (2004). Graphic evidence of violence: The impact on juror decision-making, the influence of judicial instructions and the effect of juror biases. *Psychiatry, Psychology and Law, 11*(2), 323+.

Tulving, E. (1985). Memory and consciousness. *Canadian Psychology, 26*(1), 1–12.

Tversky, B., & Marsh, E. J. (2000). Biased retellings of events yield biased memories. *Cognitive Psychology, 40*(1), 1–38.

Umanath, S., Butler, A. C., & Marsh, E. J. (2012). Positive and negative effects of monitoring popular films for historical inaccuracies: Learning history from popular films. *Applied Cognitive Psychology, 26*(4), 556–567.

Underwood, J., & Pezdek, K. (1998). Memory suggestibility as an example of the sleeper effect. *Psychonomic Bulletin & Review, 5*(3), 449–453.

Unkelbach, C. (2007). Reversing the truth effect: Learning the interpretation of processing fluency in judgments of truth. *Journal of Experimental Psychology: Learning, Memory, and Cognition, 33*(1), 219–230.

Unkelbach, C., & Stahl, C. (2009). A multinomial modeling approach to dissociate different components of the truth effect. *Consciousness and Cognition, 18*(1), 22–38.

Wallace, W. T., & Rubin, D. C. (1991). Characteristics and constraints in ballads and their effects on memory. *Discourse Processes, 14*(2), 181–202.

Weaver, K., Garcia, S. M., Schwarz, N., & Miller, D. T. (2007). Inferring the popularity of an opinion from its familiarity: A repetitive voice can sound like a chorus. *Journal of Personality and Social Psychology, 92*(5), 821–833.

Weisberg, D. S., Keil, F. C., Goodstein, J., Rawson, E., & Gray, J. R. (2008). The seductive allure of neuroscience explanations. *Journal of Cognitive Neuroscience, 20*(3), 470–477.

Whittlesea, B. W. A. (1993). Illusions of familiarity. *Journal of Experimental Psychology: Learning, Memory, and Cognition, 19,* 1235–1253.

Zajonc, R. B. (1968). Attitudinal effects of mere exposure. *Journal of Personality and Social Psychology Monograph Supplement, 9*(2). Retrieved from http://isites.harvard.edu/fs/docs/icb.topic472736.files/Zajonc.pdf

Awareness of Misinformation in Health-Related Advertising

A Narrative Review of the Literature

VANESSA BOUDEWYNS, BRIAN G. SOUTHWELL,
KEVIN R. BETTS, CATHERINE SLOTA GUPTA,
RYAN S. PAQUIN, AMIE C. O'DONOGHUE,
AND NATASHA VAZQUEZ

TWO

Health-related advertisements, such as direct-to-consumer (DTC) and direct-to-physician (DTP) advertisements for prescription drugs, are a consequential source of information for consumers and physicians alike. Ideally, information provided in advertisements should be of high quality to support consumers and health care providers (HCPs) in making informed, evidence-based decisions. This information should contain no false or misleading claims in text, graphics, or any other format. Critically, this is not always the case. In regard to prescription drug advertising, the U.S. Food and Drug Administration (FDA) frequently issues compliance letters addressing false and misleading claims and presentations (FDA, 2004, 2009). False claims are expressly untrue and contain factually incorrect information. Misleading claims can be factually truthful but result in erroneous beliefs about what is true. Misleading claims come in many forms, but in the context of existing research, the term "misleading" is usually applied to claims that exaggerate effectiveness beyond the evidence or that de-emphasize important details (Hastak & Mazis, 2011; Hyman, 1990).

Interest in the problem of false and misleading claims in health-related advertising has a long history in the behavioral sciences. Numerous studies have examined the prevalence of false or misleading claims in DTC advertising, in regard to both prescription drugs (Faerber & Kreling, 2013; Symonds, Hackford, & Abraham, 2014) and other medical products (Hastak & Mazis, 2011; Mitra, Raymond, & Hopkins, 2008). Although some researchers have begun to investigate the prevalence of problematic claims in health-related advertising and some studies provide evidence regarding the behavioral consequence of such claims on consumer and HCP understanding, relatively little work sheds direct light on consumer and HCP awareness of false or misleading claims per se. Therefore, we conducted a literature review of published scholarship appearing through August 2015 to summarize available research related to the ability of either consumers or HCPs to independently identify false or misleading claims in advertising and, by extension, the impact these claims have on attitudes and behavioral intentions. After synthesizing the available literature, we identified gaps in the available research and have provided recommendations for future research.

Methods

To understand past research on consumer and HCP response to misinformation in advertising, we collected broadly related published scholarship appearing through August 2015. We limited our search to English-language journals in a series of prominent databases (including PubMed, PsycINFO, Science Direct, and Business Source Corporate) and supplemented this search with a hand search of relevant articles. Our search terms included "deception," "misinformation," "deceptive advertis*," "deceptive claim*," "misleading advertis*," "misleading claim*," "false advertis*," and "false claim*" combined with "effect OR perceive OR detect OR notice OR recogni* OR comprehen* OR understand." As is evident from this list, we did not limit our search terms to health-related advertising. Rather, we sought literature on advertising in general in order to facilitate a highly inclusive approach though still ultimately limiting the search to literature with clear implications for health-related advertising. With that in mind, we use the terms "deception" and "deceptive claims" colloquially in the remainder of the chapter and do not intend to evoke any specific legal standard or definition. Our database search produced 212 unique citations. To be included, articles had to focus on empirical research studies of adult populations, have full texts available, and be relevant to the research topic. We did not search gray literature (including project reports and white papers) or unpublished studies. Two project team members reviewed the abstracts, and the full text was retrieved for all abstracts that met the relevance and selection criteria. After screening the full text once again for eligibility and adding articles from citation searches, we retained 47 articles.

Results

Our search of the available literature, in combination with other relevant studies, suggests that researchers are concerned about deception in health-related advertising, and our results suggest numerous opportunities for future research. As we outline in this chapter, we know a fair amount about the human tendency to be misled and why that happens. We know less about when people are able to consciously detect deceptive claims and to reject them as deception attempts.

Ability to Detect Deceptive Claims

To investigate the extent to which people can detect deception, we need to first ask what happens when people encounter and comprehend an advertisement. Humans process information by attending to new stimuli and, crucially, by comparing that information to existing knowledge structures. As work on schemata has demonstrated, readers engage with new information by using old information. When new information sufficiently fits together with the old, the reader is able to comprehend and move forward with relatively little effort; that is, the new information clicks with the old (Anderson, 1984). Advertising researchers have embraced this perspective on comprehension and posited that incongruity between preexisting schema and advertisement messages can motivate the viewer to resolve the incongruity.

Drawing inferences—generating information to fill gaps between what is explicitly stated and what a viewer knows—is a natural and important part of comprehending written and conversational language. A person's ability to extrapolate from the information explicitly given in a text is developed at a young age and is essential to fully understand the meaning of most messages (Johnson & Smith, 1981). In turn, inferences derived from a text have an impact on its perceived meaning after the initial point of encounter. For example, people tend to incorrectly remember texts as having explicitly stated propositions that in fact were merely implied (Alba, 1984; Gaeth & Heath, 1987; Graesser, Singer, & Trabasso, 1994; Harris, Dubitsky, & Bruno, 1983; Harris, Pounds, Maiorelle, & Mermis, 1993; McKoon & Ratcliff, 1992; Snyder, 1989; Wyckham, 1987). Pragmatic inferences, which are derived from associations among propositions that suggest or imply an unstated piece of information, may not fully align with the text's explicit and logical interpretation (Harris & Monaco, 1978; Morgan, 1977). In some instances the implicit meaning of a text goes well beyond the literal meaning of the explicit statements from which it is derived. Consider the following hypothetical advertising script provided by Harris (1977): "Get through a whole winter without colds. Take Eradicold pills as directed." Neither of the imperative sentences makes any explicit claims about Eradicold pills; however, when placed in close proximity to one another, the statements strongly imply that Eradicold pills prevent winter colds.

Importantly, human brains also harbor a distinct resource for questioning the validity of information. One might think about this resource as a capacity for skepticism. Asp and colleagues (2012) present evidence suggesting that such capacity might physically reside in the prefrontal cortex; people with damage to the prefrontal cortex tended to accept information from a deceptive advertisement as credible and were more likely to intend to purchase the advertised products than those without prefrontal cortex damage. As a locatable mental resource, skepticism may well vary among people and as a function of circumstances that might hinder or aid activation of associated brain function.

Part of what is noteworthy about the idea that people harbor distinct resources for skepticism is what that means for the initial moment of engagement with new stimuli. Philosophers Descartes and Spinoza were proponents of different theories of human information engagement, Descartes arguing that one accepts or rejects information only after considering its truth or falsehood and Spinoza arguing that people accept information by default but verify or reject it in a subsequent process. Numerous researchers have shown support for Spinoza's account (Asp et al., 2012; Gilbert, Krull, & Malone, 1990; Gilbert, Tafarodi, & Malone, 1993; Skurnik, Yoon, Park, & Schwarz, 2005), suggesting that people encode all new information as if it were true, even if only momentarily, and later tag the information as being either true or false. Such a default stance makes the presentation of misinformation about health-related products a potentially challenging act to overturn, requiring relatively timely and explicit corrective efforts to relabel that information as false in order to overturn misperceptions from misleading claims (Aikin et al., 2015; Southwell & Thorson, 2015).

For decades, researchers have measured deception as an outcome among advertisement audiences (e.g., Andrews, Burton, & Netemeyer, 2000; Armstrong, Gurol, & Russ, 1979; Lammers, 2000; Olson & Dover, 1978; Romani, 2006). In many of these studies, researchers have randomly assigned people to view claims known to be false or that imply inaccurate information and then assessed the effects on product perceptions or intentions. In a review of experimental research on deceptive advertising over the past 30 years, Xie and Boush (2011) assert that consumers can be highly susceptible to such deceptive advertising claims, especially when the literal claims in question may be true but implications of those claims evoke erroneous inferences. Since the 1980s, research on comparative claims in DTC and over-the-counter drug advertisements has suggested that even factually true comparative claims can mislead consumers about the relative effectiveness of competing brands by implying (either intentionally or not) that attribute-based comparisons reflect how well the drugs work (Burke, DeSarbo, Oliver, & Robertson, 1988; O'Donoghue, Williams, et al., 2014). People routinely make inferences when comprehending text and derive information from advertisements beyond what is directly stated in the text (Harris, 1977). In fact, previous research suggests that consumers not only routinely make inferences from advertisements but also then tend to believe that such inferences were stated directly in the advertisement (Harris et al., 1983). Shimp (1978) finds that the majority of participants (64%) thought that an implied claim was stated directly when it was not, and another 30% thought that even though the implied claim was not stated directly in the advertisement, the advertiser intended the advertisement to be interpreted in that fashion.

What the studies highlighted by our literature search tend not to do, however, is directly measure detection of deception in advertising among consumers or HCPs. Some studies, like Denburg et al. (2007) and Arai (2013), operationalize deception or even skepticism through claim-acceptance measures but not through indicators of awareness of deceit; in such studies a person is counted as being deceived if he or she accepts or believes a false claim as though it were true. Conceptually, this outcome aligns with a simplified definition of deception derived from Chisholm and Feehan (1977), wherein deception occurs when a message source contributes causally to the recipient's belief in a false claim. On this operationalization, it is tempting to treat the inverse of claim acceptance as evidence of skepticism or awareness of attempted deception, reasoning that a person who does not accept a false claim has not been deceived. However, the inverse of claim acceptance as an outcome is not quite the same as explicit awareness of an advertiser's intent to deceive or even awareness of the deceptive potential in an advertisement. In terms of measuring an audience's ability to detect deception in advertising, disbelief in a false claim is an insufficient criterion because there may be other explanations for this disbelief. In order to rule out other explanations, such as that the claim was misunderstood or not read or heard in the first place, it is also important to establish that the recipient is at least minimally aware that the advertiser attempted to represent the false claim as if it were true. Awareness of deception should be negatively related to claim acceptance, but the two constructs are nevertheless not entirely equivalent.

Potential Moderators of Deception Awareness

To date, we do not have a robust model of general advertising skepticism, particularly in the context of health-related advertising. Moreover, in the case of prescription drug advertising, much regulatory focus resides at the level of specific claims in advertisements. That suggests we need to better understand whether people differ in their skepticism of individual statements and propositions in advertisements.

Personal characteristics. Media dependency theory generally suggests that the extent to which people have access to alternative sources of information has implications for whether they tend to rely on the information presented from any one source (Ball-Rokeach, 1985). Similarly, when judging advertised products, consumers who rely solely on advertisements for information appear to be more likely to be deceived or to accept problematic claims compared with consumers who are presented with comprehensive and truthful informational materials in which questionable claims are removed or disclosed (e.g., Xie & Boush, 2011). Results from a number of studies suggest that experience with the product in question also seems to matter as an additional source of information beyond advertising (Andrews et al., 2000; Arai, 2013; Barone & Miniard, 1999; Bone, Shimp, & Sharma, 1990; Cowley & Janus, 2004; Olson & Dover, 1978; Snyder, 1989). Work on this topic shows that participants who were familiar with the product were less likely to misperceive misleading advertising than were their counterparts, who were less familiar with it (Cowley & Janus, 2004); that consumers who had used a product had a greater tendency toward advertising-claim skepticism compared to their less experienced counterparts (Bone, Shimp, & Sharma, 1990); and that participants generally perceived deception only for attributes they could verify through their own experiences, such as a product's color or taste (Held & Germelmann, 2014). Combined, these studies suggest that product novelty or lack of direct consumer experience could play an important role in heightening vulnerability to deception and decreasing awareness of deception. As an example, people who are newly diagnosed with a health condition would have reason to suddenly view a set of prescription drugs as being relevant to them but would not have extensive experience with using such drugs.

The difference in the ability of novices such as newly diagnosed patients versus experts like HCPs to identify deception has not been extensively investigated in the advertising literature. Although relatively little work has been done to date to investigate HCP awareness of advertising deception, O'Donoghue and colleagues (2015) have found that the majority of HCPs were confident they could recognize false or misleading advertising, and roughly half of respondents indicated some intention to report such advertising to the FDA. However, it is unclear whether confidence in detecting deception in advertising translates to actual ability to detect deception. Outside of the advertising context, work on deception awareness in general has tended to find that experts are no better than novices at detecting deception (Laczniak & Grossbart, 1990; Nysse-Carris, Bottoms, & Salerno, 2011; Strömwall & Granhag, 2003).

Persuasion knowledge. Other researchers have drawn from Friestad and Wright's (1994) persuasion knowledge model (PKM) to examine consumer reactions to misleading claims in advertisements (e.g., Xie & Quintero Johnson, 2015). The PKM asserts that individuals develop an ability to identify persuasion tactics through "tactic recognition" heuristics—an extension of previous work on peripheral cues in the elaboration likelihood model (ELM) (Petty & Cacioppo, 1986). People with high persuasion knowledge would be more likely to recognize deceptive persuasion tactics and exercise greater diligence. Johnson, Grazioli, and Jamal (1993) describe cognitive subprocesses by which individuals, based on their domain knowledge and the available information cues, determine whether information provided by a sender is deceptive. They argue that to be successful in detecting deception in a drug advertisement, consumers must be able to notice the anomalies as a result of the deceptive information practices and attribute the noticed anomalies to deception by the advertiser. Consumers with high persuasion knowledge may have a better chance of noticing and being suspicious of questionable claims and judging that the advertisement is deceptive.

Age. Aging also appears to play a role in predicting skepticism regarding advertising claims, at least in terms of exacerbating the effects of brain damage. Earlier we mentioned the important role of the prefrontal cortex in governing decision making. In a study of individuals with and without prefrontal cortex lesions, older individuals with prefrontal cortex lesions were less skeptical of misleading advertisements (Denburg et al., 2007). However, this difference appears open to mitigation; the explicit inclusion of a disclaimer clarifying the potentially deceptive portion of the advertisement erased the differences in skepticism; young and old people, with and without brain lesions, accepted the claims to the same extent when shown the disclaimer. Asp et al. (2012) also found higher credulity and increased purchase intention associated with misleading advertisements among those with prefrontal cortex damage, but the use of a disclaimer did not seem to substantially mitigate effects. Asp and colleagues (2012) offer the explanation that people always initially believe their first perceptions, then engage in a falsification process in which they compare the claims to other information. However, the researchers explain that this falsification process is disrupted in people with prefrontal cortex disruption, who are therefore less likely to later tag this information as false. Ventromedial prefrontal dysfunction—whether the result of brain injury or aging—appears to be an important factor in an individual's ability to discern deceptive advertising.

Another related phenomenon associated with aging is source confusion, whereby people forget the original context of a piece of information over time (Mares, 1996; Marsh & Yang, this volume). Given that older people have more difficulty retrieving details from different media (see, for example, Southwell et al., 2010), this phenomenon is a potentially pressing concern for older audiences and the influence of deceptive advertising. Skurnik and colleagues (2005) studied older and younger adults and found that over time, older adults tended to forget key contextual information regarding the falseness of claims. Both younger and older adults appeared to be able to process and retain a warning about the falseness of information in the short term; however, after several days, older participants tended to misremember original claims as being true, having forgotten subsequent contextual statements warning that the original information was false. Such work, although relevant to our discussion, nonetheless does not signal distinct age-based differences in deception awareness as much as underscore age-based differences in retention of false information warnings over time. Finally, new research suggests that older adults focus on and recall positive information more than negative information, unlike their younger counterparts (Reed & Carstensen, 2012). This may have implications for their susceptibility to deception.

Emotion. Independent of age, we know that a person's emotional state or mood over time can affect information processing and deception detection by inviting deeper, more elaborative message processing (e.g., Ashby, Isen, & Turken, 1999; Wegener, Smith, & Petty, 1995). Across several studies, LaTour and LaTour (2009) find that participants in a relatively positive mood were more likely to scrutinize and identify pieces of false information in an ad. However, the researchers found that people did not tend to integrate their awareness that the information was false when evaluating the brand; those in a positive mood had a more favorable response toward the brand in a subsequent implicit association task. Based on these results, although positive mood seems to enhance the extent to which people elaborate on various elements of advertisements and to notice information that is discordant with their personal experiences, the net impact of such processing on subsequent product perceptions is not necessarily negative. Although we found no articles focused on the impact of negative emotions, drawing from the broader emotion research there is evidence to suggest that negative affect narrows focus and that negative moods, especially sadness, may trigger a more vigilant form of processing (Cohen, Pham, & Andrade, 2008). More research is needed to explore the impact of positive and negative emotions and mood (i.e., incidental affect) on awareness of misinformation.

Advertisement characteristics. We might consider at least three dimensions of advertising content in predicting differences in people's ability to detect deception: claim contextualization, claim refutation or qualification (inclusion and prominence), and visual deception.

Claim contextualization is the degree to which a claim is made without a clear structure to ease audience interpretation—such as claiming that "Brand X is the best" rather than providing more context about what "the best" means—and appears to complicate audience detection of deception (Harris et al., 1993; Johar, 1995; Shimp, 1978). Claims presented without explicit comparison references may invite unwarranted inferences by audiences, and such interpretation mistakes may make it more challenging for people to notice missteps in accepting explicitly false claims.

Claim refutation or qualification entails the inclusion and prominence of information intended to refute or qualify potentially deceptive claims, such as disclosures or disclaimers, and seems to matter when it comes to consumer detection of misleading information (e.g., Andrews, Netemeyer, & Burton, 1998; Burke et al., 1988; Denburg et al., 2007). Importantly, though, the evidence in this arena is mixed. Andrews and colleagues (1998) find that the positive impact of a disclosure related to nutrition claims was mainly apparent among high-knowledge consumers who had been exposed to relatively ambiguous claims. At the same time, clarifying information is not necessarily automatically engaged. The visual prominence of material clarifying or disclaiming problematic claims also appears to affect people's ability to detect deception. Foxman, Muehling, and Moore (1988) observe that respondents performed less well in remembering footnoted material intended to qualify claims than in remembering similar material that appeared in the regular body copy of a print advertisement. Moreover, the success of intentionally clear and direct corrective advertising—such as in advertisements that explicitly use the word "correct" (Aikin et al., 2015)—suggests that direct mitigation of misleading claim acceptance in the case of prescription drugs is more likely when correction of potentially misleading information is unambiguous and easily noticed by audience members. Ambiguity or subtlety appears to undermine potential corrective or clarification effects.

Visual deception can be considered when visually depicted content—presented through graphics, charts, or photographs—holds distinct potential for deception. Data-visualization scholars have long warned about the possibilities for visual deception (Tufte, 1983). Awareness of visual deception in advertisements is a new arena for research, so we do not have much evidence to date. However, researchers have noted that a sizable proportion of drug advertisements includes graphical elements that could potentially mislead people (e.g., Sansgiry, Sharp, & Sansgiry, 1999), and some have found evidence that visual depictions in food marketing can lead to misperceptions about product attributes, such as size or color (Held & Germelmann, 2014).

Regulation of visual deception is challenging theoretically. Messaris (1997) notes that judging consequential deception caused by the visual dimension of advertising is difficult because, unlike written language, visual communication lacks explicit propositional syntax to guide interpretation of elements. Nonetheless, researchers have attempted to demonstrate the deceptive effects of visuals. Pandey and colleagues studied the effect of distorted graphic elements in charts and figures that exaggerated quantity differences relative to the actual numbers being reported (Pandey, Rall, Satterthwaite, Nov, & Bertini, 2015). They found that a wide range of people are susceptible to deception; they assessed a series of individual difference variables, such as education, familiarity with charts, visual ability, and need for cognition, and found no consistent evidence of individual differences in vulnerability to visual deception.

Research Gaps

A key limitation of past research in this topic area has been the absence of explicit deception awareness measures. Furthermore, no papers explicitly examine whether (or when) laypeople or experts are comparatively more likely to detect certain types of deception. Our review of the available literature underscores the need for research designed to directly assess consumer and HCP awareness of deception in health-related advertising.

The following questions also remain relatively unaddressed, based on our literature review:

> What is the threshold at which deception tends to trigger awareness of misinformation among consumers and HCPs?
>
> When people recognize that there is an attempt to deceive, how does that affect their subsequent perceptions and actions regarding the advertised products? Do people resist or reject subsequent or related messages if they are aware of an intent to deceive?
>
> Are some populations more vulnerable to misleading advertising content in the sense of being less likely to detect deception?
>
> What role does visual content play in deception, and how does it interact with false or misleading claims?

Although papers in our literature search examine a variety of deceptive tactics, relatively few studies compare various deceptive tactics within a single study, and no study explicitly compares various combinations of deceptive techniques.

Finally, most studies were conducted before 1990, whereas the growth in DTC advertising has occurred after 1999; it is possible that consumers have grown savvier or more suspicious of advertising over time, so meta-analyses across time might be worthwhile. Even aside from historical comparisons, new research on consumer and professional ability to detect deception continues to be warranted.

Conclusion

Our review suggests that humans are vulnerable to deception in advertising, particularly for new products or in instances in which they do not have ready access to counterevidence, in part because of common information-processing tendencies. Although the literature suggests that consumers and HCPs sometimes are misled or deceived by advertising claims, relatively little empirical evidence sheds light on exactly who is able to detect and label deception as deception, when that detection is relatively more likely to happen, and what the exact influence of detecting deception is on outcomes such as perceived drug efficacy and safety. People do appear to vary to some extent in their skepticism, but, importantly, some types of advertisements hold potential for deception across a wide range of people. Moreover, we have no empirical evidence as to whether consumers or HCPs are more likely to detect deception accurately, although we do know that even medical experts make mistakes and overlook deception at times.

Future work to investigate deception effects should embrace experimental study design and consider a variety of potential effect moderators, including variables related to advertising elements and individual-level variables. Providers and consumers who have prior experience with the advertised product, who have prior exposure to related advertisements, and who are more skeptical about advertisements in general are more likely to notice anomalies in an advertisement that will, in turn, prompt them to consider whether the advertisement is deceptive. As such, we can argue for the relevance of general advertisement skepticism, product experience or knowledge, and possibly age as candidate moderating variables.

With respect to the stimuli for each study, we might consider three dimensions of advertising content in predicting people's ability to detect deception: claim contextualization, claim refutation or qualification inclusion and prominence, and visual deception. Advertisements for new products, advertisements that lack important claim contextualization, advertisements without clear and prominent qualification of potentially deceptive claims, and advertisements that present visual distortions all pose particular challenges for audiences and may present deception that escapes detection.

References

Aikin, K. J., Betts, K. R., O'Donoghue, A. C., Rupert, D. J., Lee, P. K., Amoozegar, J. B., & Southwell, B. G. (2015). Correction of overstatement and omission in direct-to-consumer prescription drug advertising. *Journal of Communication, 65*(4), 596–618.

Alba, J. (1984). Nature of inference representation. *American Journal of Psychology, 97*, 215–233.

Anderson, R. C. (1984). Role of the reader's schema in comprehension, learning, and memory. In R. C. Anderson, J. Osborn, & R. Tierney (Eds.), *Learning to read in American schools: Basal readers and content texts* (pp. 243–257). Hillsdale, NJ: Lawrence Erlbaum.

Andrews, C. J., Burton, S., & Netemeyer, R. G. (2000). Are some comparative nutrition claims misleading? The role of nutrition knowledge, ad claim type, and disclosure conditions. *Journal of Advertising, 29*(3), 29–42.

Andrews, J. C., Netemeyer, R. G., & Burton, S. (1998). Consumer generalization of nutrient content claims in advertising. *Journal of Marketing, 62*(4), 62–75.

Arai, K. (2013). Note on the need for rules on misleading representation based on experimental evidence. *Applied Economics Letters, 20*(1), 10–17.

Armstrong, G. M., Gurol, M. N., & Russ, F. A. (1979). Detecting and correcting deceptive advertising. *Journal of Consumer Research, 6*(3), 237–246.

Ashby, F. G., Isen, A. M., & Turken, A. U. (1999). A neuropsychological theory of positive affect and its influence on cognition. *Psychological Review, 106*(3), 529–550.

Asp, E., Manzel, K., Koestner, B., Cole, C. A., Denburg, N. L., & Tranel, D. (2012). A neuropsychological test of belief and doubt: Damage to ventromedial prefrontal cortex increases credulity for misleading advertising. *Frontiers in Neuroscience, 6*, 1–9.

Ball-Rokeach, S. J. (1985). The origins of individual media-system dependency: A sociological framework. *Communication Research, 12*(4), 485–510.

Barone, M. J., & Miniard, P. W. (1999). How and when factual ad claims mislead consumers: Examining the deceptive consequences of copy x copy interactions for partial comparative advertisements. *Journal of Marketing Research, 36*(1), 58–74.

Bone, P. F., Shimp, T. A., & Sharma, S. (1990). Assimilation and contrast effects in product performance perceptions: Implications for public policy. *Journal of Public Policy & Marketing, 9*(1), 100–110.

Burke, R. R., DeSarbo, W. S., Oliver, R. L., & Robertson, T. S. (1988). Deception by implication: An experimental investigation. *Journal of Consumer Research, 14*(4), 483–494.

Chisholm, R. M., & Feehan, T. D. (1977). The intent to deceive. *Journal of Philosophy, 74*, 143–159.

Cohen, J. B., Pham, M. T., & Andrade, E. B. (2008). The nature and role of affect in consumer behavior. In C. P. Haugtvedt, P. M. Herr, & F. R. Kardes (Eds.), *Handbook of consumer psychology* (pp. 297–348). New York, NY: Psychology Press.

Cowley, E., & Janus, E. (2004). Not necessarily better, but certainly different: A limit to the advertising misinformation effect on memory. *Journal of Consumer Research, 31*(1), 229–235.

Denburg, N. L., Cole, C. A., Hernandez, M., Yamada, T. H., Tranel, D., Bechara, A., & Wallace, R. B. (2007). The orbitofrontal cortex, real-world decision making, and normal aging. *Annals of the New York Academy of Science, 1121*, 480–498.

Faerber, A. E., & Kreling, D. H. (2013). Content analysis of false and misleading claims in television advertising for prescription and nonprescription drugs. *Journal of General Internal Medicine, 29*(1), 110–118.

FDA. *See* U.S. Food and Drug Administration (FDA).

Foxman, E. R., Muehling, D. D., & Moore, P. A. (1988). Disclaimer footnotes in ads: Discrepancies between purpose and performance. *Journal of Public Policy & Marketing, 7*(1), 127–137.

Friestad, M., & Wright, P. (1994). The persuasion knowledge model: How people cope with persuasion attempts. *Journal of Consumer Research, 22*(1), 1–31.

Gaeth, G. J., & Heath, T. B. (1987). The cognitive processing of misleading advertising in young and old adults: Assessment and training. *Journal of Consumer Research, 14*(1), 43–54.

Gilbert, D. T., Krull, D. S., & Malone, P. S. (1990). Unbelieving the unbelievable: some problems in the rejection of false information. *Journal of Personality and Social Psychology, 59*, 601–613.

Gilbert, D., Tafarodi, R., & Malone, P. (1993). You can't not believe everything you read. *Journal of Personality and Social Psychology, 65*(2), 221–233.

Graesser, A. C., Singer, M., & Trabasso, T. (1994). Constructing inferences during narrative text comprehension. *Psychological Review, 101*(3), 371–395.

Harris, R. J. (1977). Comprehension of pragmatic implications in advertising. *Journal of Applied Psychology, 62*(5), 603–608.

Harris, R. J., Dubitsky, T. M., & Bruno, K. J. (1983). *Psycholinguistic studies of misleading advertising. Information processing research in advertising* (pp. 241–262). Hillsdale, NJ: L. Erlbaum Associates.

Harris, R. J., & Monaco, G. E. (1978). Psychology of pragmatic implication: Information processing between the lines. *Journal of Experimental Psychology, 62*, 603–608.

Harris, R. J., Pounds, J. C., Maiorelle, M. J., & Mermis, M. (1993). The effect of type of claim, gender, and buying history on the drawing of pragmatic inferences from advertising claims. *Journal of Consumer Psychology, 2*(1), 83–95.

Hastak, M., & Mazis, M. B. (2011). Deception by implication: A typology of truthful by misleading advertising and labeling claims. *Journal of Public Policy & Marketing, 30*, 157–167.

Held, J., & Germelmann, C. C. (2014). Deceived or not deceived: How food consumers perceive deception. *Advances in Consumer Research, 42*, 313–317.

Hyman, M. R. (1990). Deception in advertising: A proposed complex of definitions for researchers, lawyers, and regulators. *International Journal of Advertising, 9*, 259–270.

Johar, G. V. (1995). Consumer involvement and deception from implied advertising claims. *Journal of Marketing Research, 32*, 267–279.

Johnson, H., & Smith, L. B. (1981). Children's inferential abilities in the context of reading to understand. *Child Development, 52*, 1216–1223.

Johnson, P. E., Grazioli, S., & Jamal, K. (1993). Fraud detection: Intentionality and deception in cognition. *Accounting, Organizations, and Society, 18*(5), 467–488.

Laczniak, R. N., & Grossbart, S. (1990). An assessment of assumptions underlying the reasonable consumer element in deceptive advertising policy. *Journal of Public Policy & Marketing, 9*, 85–99.

Lammers, H. B. (2000). Effects of deceptive packaging and product involvement on purchase intention: An elaboration likelihood model perspective. *Psychological Reports, 86*(2), 546–550.

LaTour, K. A., & LaTour, M. S. (2009). Positive mood and susceptibility to false advertising. *Journal of Advertising, 38*(3), 127–142.

Mares, M. L. (1996). The role of source confusions in television's cultivation of social reality judgments. *Human Communication Research, 23*(2), 278–297.

McKoon, G., & Ratcliff, R. (1992). Inference during reading. *Psychological Review, 99*(3), 440–466.

Messaris, P. (1997). *Visual persuasion: The role of images in advertising.* Thousand Oaks, CA: Sage.

Mitra, A., Raymond, M. A., & Hopkins, C. D. (2008). Can consumers recognize misleading advertising content in a media rich online environment? *Psychology & Marketing, 25*(7), 655–674.

Morgan, J. L. (1977). Linguistics: The relation of pragmatics to semantics and syntax. *Annual Review of Anthropology, 6*, 57–67.

Nysse-Carris, K. L., Bottoms, B. L., & Salerno, J. M. (2011). Experts' and novices' abilities to detect children's high-stakes lies of omission. *Psychology, Public Policy, and Law, 17*(1), 76–98.

O'Donoghue, A. C., Boudewyns, V., Aikin, K. J., Geisen, E., Betts, K. R., & Southwell, B. G. (2015). Awareness of the Food and Drug Administration's bad ad program and education regarding pharmaceutical advertising: A national survey of prescribers in ambulatory care settings. *Journal of Health Communication, 20*(11), 1330–1336.

O'Donoghue, A. C., Williams, P. A., Sullivan, H. W., Boudewyns, V., Squire, C., & Willoughby, J. F. (2014). Effects of comparative claims in prescription drug direct-to-consumer advertising on consumer perceptions and recall. *Social Science and Medicine, 120*, 1–11.

Olson, J. C., & Dover, P. A. (1978). Cognitive effects of deceptive advertising. *Journal of Marketing Research, 15*(1), 29–38.

Pandey, A. V., Rall, K., Satterthwaite, M. L., Nov, O., & Bertini, E. (2015). How deceptive are deceptive visualizations? An empirical analysis of common distortion techniques. In D. Brown & J. Kim (Eds.), *CHI '15 Proceedings of the 33rd Annual ACM Conference on Human Factors in Computing Systems* (pp. 1469–1478). New York, NY: Association for Computing Machinery.

Petty, R. E., & Cacioppo, J. T. (1986). *Communication and persuasion: Central and peripheral routes to attitude change.* New York, NY: Springer-Verlag.

Reed, A. E., & Carstensen, L. L. (2012). The theory behind the age-related positivity effect. *Frontiers in Psychology, 3*, 339.

Romani, S. (2006). Price misleading advertising: Effects on trustworthiness toward the source of information and willingness to buy. *Journal of Product & Brand Management*, 15(2), 130–138.

Sansgiry, S., Sharp, W. T., & Sansgiry, S. S. (1999). Accuracy of information on printed over-the-counter drug advertisements. *Health Marketing Quarterly*, 17(2), 7–18.

Shimp, T. A. (1978). Do incomplete comparisons mislead? *Journal of Advertising Research*, 18(6), 21–27.

Skurnik, I., Yoon, C., Park, D. C., & Schwarz, N. (2005). How warnings about false claims become recommendations. *Journal of Consumer Research*, 31(4), 713–724.

Snyder, R. (1989). Misleading characteristics of implied-superiority claims. *Journal of Advertising*, 18(4), 54–61.

Southwell, B. G., Gilkerson, N. D., Depue, J. B., Shelton, A. K., Friedenberg, L. M., & Koutstaal, W. (2010). Aging and the questionable validity of recognition-based exposure measurement. *Communication Research*, 37(5), 603–619.

Southwell, B. G., & Thorson, E. A. (2015). The prevalence, consequence, and remedy of misinformation in mass media systems. *Journal of Communication*, 65, 589–595.

Strömwall, L. A., & Granhag, P. A. (2003). How to detect deception? Arresting the beliefs of police officers, prosecutors and judges. *Psychology, Crime & Law*, 9(1), 19–36.

Symonds, T., Hackford, C., & Abraham, L. (2014). A review of FDA warning letters and notices of violation issued for patient-reported outcomes promotional claims between 2006 and 2012. *Value in Health*, 17, 433–437.

Tufte, E. R. (1983). *The visual display of quantitative information*. Cheshire, CT: Graphics Press.

U.S. Food and Drug Administration (FDA). (2004). FDA Prescription Drug Advertising Rule, 21 C.F.R. § 202.1e.

U.S. Food and Drug Administration (FDA), Division of Drug Marketing Advertising and Communication. (2009). *Presenting risk information in prescription drug and medical device promotion* [Draft guidance]. Retrieved from http://www.fda.gov /downloads/Drugs/GuidanceComplianceRegulatoryInformation/Guidances /UCM155480.pdf

Wegener, D. T., Smith, S. M., & Petty, R. E. (1995). Positive mood can increase or decrease message scrutiny: The hedonic contingency view of mood and message processing. *Journal of Personality and Social Psychology*, 69(1), 5–15.

Wyckham, R. G. (1987). Implied superiority claims. *Journal of Advertising Research*, 27(1), 54–63.

Xie, G. X., & Boush, D. M. (2011). How susceptible are consumers to deceptive advertising claims? A retrospective look at the experimental research literature. *Marketing Review*, 11(3), 293–314.

Xie, G. X., & Quintero Johnson, J. M. (2015). Examining the third-person effect of baseline omission in numerical comparison: The role of consumer persuasion knowledge. *Psychology & Marketing*, 32(4), 438–449.

The Importance of Measuring Knowledge in the Age of Misinformation and Challenges in the Tobacco Domain

THREE

JOSEPH N. CAPPELLA, YOTAM OPHIR, AND JAZMYNE SUTTON

The study, evaluation, and correction of misinformation require that erroneous knowledge be unearthed so that its presence can be established unequivocally and corrections appropriately marshaled. This chapter focuses on measuring knowledge and its absence in a variety of ways. Our claim is that most widely used measures of knowledge are too narrow in scope and fail to take into account a wider range of alternatives for measurement that would give us deeper and broader access to misinformation. Two broad issues in the measurement of knowledge are addressed. The first maps the landscape of measuring knowledge from the individual to the social. The most common measure of knowledge in empirical work employs simple, closed-ended recognition items. Such measures are efficient and well known but have limitations that invite alternatives: some are known to researchers but not widely used, and others are newer techniques that have just begun to make their way into researchers' tool kits. The second is conceptual. Behavior change theorists argue that measures of simple factual beliefs (one type of knowledge) have little impact on behavior. If so, why be so concerned about careful measurement of this kind of knowledge? We suggest ways to conceptualize knowledge to enhance prediction of behavioral intention and behavior change.

Most of the illustrations provided derive from work in tobacco control and tobacco products generally. This context does not limit the applicability of our arguments; rather, the same conclusions can be applied to other substantive contexts in health, politics, and social policy. We begin with an assumption that also guides many political theorists, public health agencies, and institutions of governmental policy, such as the Food and Drug Administration (FDA): a fully and accurately informed citizenry serves the public good. Methods for correcting falsehoods and misinformation first require a range of measures for uncovering misinformation.

The Importance of Knowledge

Knowledge is considered by many to be a vital element of citizenship and a prerequisite to civic engagement (Dahlgren, 2009). Gaps in knowledge are seen as a potential risk to society (Gaziano, 1983). Despite increasing information in the age of the Internet, the differences between social groups may have widened (Southwell, 2013). The information explosion has paradoxically opened the door to misinformation (Niederdeppe, Fowler, Goldstein, & Pribble, 2010), even in specialized areas of scientific knowledge (Oreskes & Conway, 2011). The prevalence of incomplete and inaccurate knowledge about established facts poses a threat to individuals and societies by affecting policy decisions and individuals' choices in their everyday lives (Lewandowsky, Ecker, Seifert, Schwarz, & Cook, 2012).

Virtually every theory of persuasion and behavior change has found a role for knowledge as a predictor in the causal processes of persuasion and behavior change. The operational and conceptual definitions have varied from the more personal and subjective ("My smoking 20 cigarettes a day will increase my chances of lung cancer by a factor of XX") to the more objective ("People who smoke 20 cigarettes a day for 20 years will increase their chances of getting lung cancer by a factor of XX") (Eagly & Chaiken, 1993). Reinforcement theories of persuasion (Hovland, Janis, & Kelly, 1953) emphasize learning as the basis for persuasion (Insko, 1967). The elaboration likelihood model (ELM) explains the interaction between knowledge transmitted through persuasive communication and prior knowledge that provides audiences with the ability to process new information (Petty & Cacioppo, 1986). The theory of reasoned action (Fishbein & Ajzen, 2010) posits personal and subjective knowledge (i.e., behavioral beliefs) as one of the key predictors of behavioral intention and ultimately behavior. Theorists of cognition and memory have argued that human knowledge, arranged into stories, is the essence of memory and the construction of reality (Schank & Abelson, 1995). Knowledge also plays a central role in foundational theories of communication and persuasion (McGuire, 1989) and self-efficacy (Bandura, 2001).

Public health educators have hewn to the belief that enhancing the public's knowledge about health issues will "close the gaps between what is known about optimum health practice and that which is actually practiced" (Griffiths, 1972, p. 7) and thereby actually increase healthy behaviors. Approaches such as the health belief model suggest that knowledge about diseases, including their severity and our vulnerability to them, drives people's health behaviors (Rosenstock, 1974). Improving public knowledge has been a high priority for federal agencies such as the FDA, especially in light of the years of misinformation about tobacco products intentionally propagated by tobacco companies (Smith et al., 2011).

Tobacco Misinformation, Regulation, and the Need to Evaluate Knowledge

In 1964, the U.S. Surgeon General concluded that smoking has deleterious health effects and may cause cancer (Glantz, Bero, & Slade, 1996). Despite the steady decline in smoking (Centers for Disease Control and Prevention [CDC], 2011), it remains a leading cause of preventable death in the United States (CDC, n.d.) and worldwide (World Health Organization [WHO], 2016). Moreover, the historical efforts of tobacco companies to conceal the harmful effects of its products on the public's health (Cappella, Maloney, Ophir, & Brennan, 2015) still leave footprints on people's beliefs. Misconceptions about tobacco products remain prevalent among smokers in regard to the risks to health (Smith et al., 2011), the benefits of using "light" cigarettes (Cummings, Hyland, Bansal, & Giovino, 2004), and the risks of secondhand smoke (Hyland et al., 2009). Despite years of governmental agencies' and nongovernmental groups' attempts to correct tobacco misinformation (McAfee, Davis, Alexander, Pechacek, & Bunnell, 2013), many smokers still believe misinformation about tobacco products.

According to the FDA's website (2015, p. 2), the Center for Tobacco Products has the task of "launching public education and health campaigns, particularly targeted at youth, about the dangers of regulated tobacco products." A crucial part of educational efforts about tobacco products is the correction of inaccurate beliefs (FDA, 2015). Misinformation can be persistent and influential, especially when that misinformation is in service of existing behaviors and values. Various studies demonstrate that correction is not easy (Ecker, Lewandowsky, & Tang, 2010; Lewandowsky et al., 2012). Even when corrective information manages to amend inaccurate beliefs, previously accepted misinformation can have a continued effect on attitudes (Thorson, 2016). Under some conditions, corrections may even lead to an increase in acceptance of the misinformation (Nyhan & Reifler, 2010). The design and testing of effective correctives is a crucial line of research in domains as disparate as climate-change denial and vaccine confidence. A necessary prerequisite to work on corrections is efficient and effective measurement of the accuracy of audiences' beliefs.

A Critical Review of Approaches to Knowledge Assessment

Several methods have been used by researchers to assess knowledge and knowledge gain, on both the individual and population levels. Some of these approaches are more familiar and common, others novel and still in the early stages of adoption. We review the most common approaches for measuring knowledge, provide examples of each within the domains of tobacco and public health, and highlight their advantages and limitations. The purpose is to expand researchers' tools for measuring knowledge and in the process discover manifestations of misinformation by deploying more sensitive measurements than have been common.

Most measures of social and psychological phenomena are imprecise and prone to error. Measurement error can be nonsystematic (random) or systematic (the result of a bias that leads to the consistent over- or under-estimation of observed units) (King, Keohane, & Verba, 1994). The following discussion will focus on approaches to knowledge measurement and their internal and external validity as well as inherent disadvantages that may lead to bias and threats to validity (Mitchell & Jolley, 2007).

Closed-Ended Questions

Most attempts to assess knowledge and beliefs within the realm of tobacco control and other contexts as well have used closed-ended survey questions. This type of assessment requires the respondent to choose the best-fitting answer out of a predefined set of options. Possible answers can appear in the form of discrete choices ("Which of the following products include nicotine: Cigar, E-cigarette, or Hookah?"), true/false ("Low-tar cigarettes can be addictive: True/False"), or Likert-scale ("How much do you agree with the following statement from 1 [*Strongly agree*] to 7 [*Strongly disagree*]?: Tobacco cigarettes cause cancer"). In order to measure an individual's knowledge, researchers must define a priori correct and incorrect answers to the questions based on experts' opinions and then calculate a knowledge score based on the number of correct and incorrect answers each individual provides.

Closed-ended questions may be used to assess two types of knowledge. The first tests existing levels of knowledge on the individual and population levels in regard to a substantive topic. As there may be an infinite number of potential questions that could be used to assess knowledge about a domain, the researcher's goal is to generate an efficient and valid subset of questions that will serve as an indicator of the entire domain. The usefulness and efficiency of this approach have been demonstrated in the political domain, showing that a short subset of questions about the presidency and Congress correlates well with other types of political knowledge and related behaviors, such as participation (Delli Carpini & Keeter, 1993). Subsets of closed-ended questions are common in research about tobacco effects as well. The Health Information National Trends Survey (HINTS) of the National Cancer Institute (NCI, n.d.) consists of specific questions such as "In your opinion, do you think that some smokeless tobacco products, such as chewing tobacco, snus [a type of smokeless tobacco, similar to snuff in some respects], and snuff, are less harmful to a person's health than cigarettes?" with the predefined answers "Yes, No, or Don't know."

A second class of closed-ended knowledge questions is used to test the effectiveness of health messages and the consequences of exposure to them. Respondents are exposed to stimulus materials intended to communicate specific information. The knowledge items in this approach tend to be much narrower in scope, as they are developed from the specific knowledge claims communicated in the messages. Studies of smoking cessation narratives (Sanders-Jackson, 2014) and cigarette packages' warning labels (Mutti, Hammond, Reid, & Thrasher, 2013) tapped into specific knowledge of claims from the narratives and the labels, respectively.

Knowledge also can be conceptualized and operationalized as the awareness and recognition of different types of tobacco products or controversies around tobacco products. Tan and Bigman (2014) tested whether smokers who had never heard of e-cigarettes were more or less likely to quit smoking combustible cigarettes than smokers who were aware of them. Signal detection methodology provides more subtle information about knowledge and biases in its measurement but requires a wider array of questions. One study tested participants' ability to accurately recognize information presented in stimuli in the presence of distractors in the form of foil answers (Lee & Cappella, 2013). The results indicate that the presence of smoking cues (objects or behaviors) led to lower recognition of stimuli from public service announcements.

Knowledge items have been used by some researchers as indicators of attention to the details of a message while assessing issues of distraction, cognitive load, and engagement with the core and peripheral content of the message. Lang, Zhou, Schwartz, and Bolls (2000) used this technique to assess individual attention and memory as the number of visual edits and emotionality varied in videos across conditions.

Closed-ended questions have been used to test the relationship between perceived-knowledge and tobacco-related behavior. In this approach, researchers attempt to evaluate whether participants perceive themselves to be knowledgeable about tobacco products and their consequences. Questions such as "How much would you say you know about the risks of waterpipe tobacco smoking?" were found to be significantly (though weakly) correlated with objective factual knowledge (Lipkus, Eissenberg, Schwartz-Bloom, Prokhorov, & Levy, 2014). The study reports that neither factual nor perceived knowledge was associated with intentions to quit smoking. The utility of knowledge-based items such as risks of tobacco use as predictors of an individual's behavior will be addressed later.

Closed-ended questions are very common in the social sciences due to their simple, straightforward, and familiar nature. They are relatively easy to generate and calculate. Moreover, closed-ended questions can be deployed conveniently to assess the impact of campaigns and messages by showing, for example, the correlation between amount of exposure and influence (Hornik, Jacobsohn, Orwin, Piesse, & Kalton, 2008). However, consideration must be given to the difficulty level of items so that questions do not produce ceiling or floor effects, thereby sharply restricting variance. Rather, the set of items deployed should be variable in difficulty so that variance is not restricted and is broad in scope to fully span the space being evaluated, whether that space is a domain of general tobacco knowledge or a domain of a particular tobacco stimulus. Core challenges to developing a knowledge questionnaire primarily or solely based on closed-ended questions include creating a set of measures that is efficient yet accurate and representative of the larger topical space, well correlated with related measures, and predictive of relevant smoking behaviors.

Most self-report survey items are prone to response bias. Such bias can be the result of social desirability, the motivation to appear in a positive light in the eyes of the researchers (Furnham, 1986), and the limitations of participants' memory and perceptions. A respondent may not remember that she heard about a product although she did; knowledge of that product may influence her decisions even when she cannot remember it. Implicit cognitive processes, often inaccessible to conscious awareness, as well as some conscious processes cannot be found through reports on closed-ended questions (Falk, Berkman, Mann, Harrison, & Lieberman, 2010). Other challenges include limitations on the number of items that can be used, the diagnostic value of items to the topic being assessed (for example, the extent to which items are central or peripheral to a target knowledge space), and cuing effects associated with the response alternatives.

Open-Ended Recall of Knowledge

Surveys commonly make use of open-ended as well as closed-ended questions. Open-ended questions allow participants to answer questions using their own words (Geer, 1988). In a study about e-cigarettes, participants were asked to write about their experiences with products. Participants wrote about where they bought their e-cigarettes, the reasons they used them, and the desired and undesired results of using them (Etter, 2010). Other studies asked people to write about their experiences with secondhand smoke (Steil, Lorenzo, & Sydeman, 2010), diseases caused by smoking (Weinstein, Slovic, Waters, & Gibson, 2004), and awareness of antitobacco campaigns (Farrelly et al., 2002).

While open-ended questions allow respondents to describe their thoughts and opinions freely and may allow researchers to avoid certain response biases, the approach has its disadvantages. Open-ended questions are more taxing for both the researchers and respondents. Participants' responses often require more time and cognitive resources. A respondent may be knowledgeable but unmotivated. Another limiting source is literacy. Those who have lower levels of literacy and who are uncomfortable with their linguistic abilities may not seem to be knowledgeable when in fact they may simply be reluctant to express themselves in written form (Geer, 1988).

For researchers, open-ended answers require developing reliable and valid coding procedures and, when using human coding (versus machine-based procedures discussed below), the allocation of additional resources to the analysis. One common approach with open-ended recall is confirmation of the accuracy of reported information either through expert opinion or against a prevailing norm such as the actual content of a recalled ad. Confirmed recall adds information about accuracy of the recall and the kinds of distortions added.

With the rise of big data, more automated methods are available (Shah, Cappella, & Neuman, 2015) though not yet fully disseminated (Baker, 2006). Like closed-ended responses, open-ended responses depend on the amount and type of information the respondent is willing to provide the researchers. It is thus still susceptible to social-desirability, literacy, and motivational biases.

On the positive side, open-ended recall is likely to generate responses that at least in the aggregate are salient to the respondents and that have been actively retrieved from memory rather than cued by the response options. The accuracy of information recalled must be established by the researchers through expert opinion or other unassailable standards, but its salience is less in doubt.

Reaction Times

When people are said to be knowledgeable about a topic, they typically have accurate beliefs about the topic that are readily accessible. Ready accessibility is usually tapped by speed of response, otherwise known as reaction time (Luce, 1986). The previously presented measurements focus on the amount, quality, and depth of knowledge as means to understand knowledge resources potentially available for decision making. The foundational assumption underlying the use of reaction times for assessing knowledge is that information that has been previously activated is more easily and rapidly accessible. The speed with which people process incoming information can be mapped into their current mental representation of the topic (Gygax, Bosson, Gay, & Ribordy, 2010). Some scholars have focused not only on the amount of information available to a person but also on the accessibility and salience of that information and its influence on attitudes (Fishbein & Ajzen, 2010) and behaviors (Roskos-Ewoldsen & Fazio, 1997). According to the accessibility-bias argument, information that can be more easily retrieved from memory tends to dominate decisions (Iyengar, 1990). The accessibility of information can be evaluated based on how quickly it can be retrieved and/or the number of contexts in which it can be retrieved (Barnes, Dennis, & Haefele-Kalvaitis, 1996).

In an investigation of the reading processes of tobacco warnings by adolescents, researchers measured the time it took participants to evaluate whether a target sentence comprised a particular behavior or not, and they compared the reaction times to severe consequences of smoking for nonsmokers and past smokers (Gygax et al., 2010). Another study compared the response times to recognition items from public service announcements (PSAs) based on their sensation value (Langleben et al., 2009).

Compared to deliberate self-reports, response times are much harder for respondents to control and manipulate and thus can provide information that is less susceptible to social-desirability and other biases. Capturing reaction times can be more complicated technically and requires the use of relatively less familiar calculations and analyses. Reaction times may not tap into the accuracy or volume of knowledge but provide relatively less controllable information indicative of accessibility. Reaction time data alone do not measure the accuracy of held beliefs and so are uninformative about misinformation by themselves. Therefore, reaction data are almost always obtained in combination with information about the accuracy of responses.

Argument Repertoire

Argument repertoire assesses quality and depth of knowledge. In this approach, participants are asked to provide arguments and counterarguments for a given topic on which they hold a position. The measure evaluates the degree of anchoring of one's own opinion and knowledge of the bases for opinions held by others (Cappella, Price, & Nir, 2002). The measure has been used in studies to assess the contribution of public deliberation (Price, Cappella, & Nir, 2002) and the effects of framing on policy support (Brewer & Gross, 2005). We could not find any use to date of the measure in the realm of tobacco and smoking.

While the argument repertoire approach is helpful for understanding the extent to which existing opinion is anchored, it is not designed to measure opinion accuracy. The ability to understand both sides of a debate is important for citizens in the context of public deliberation, but it makes them susceptible to misinformation and deception (Lewandowsky et al.,

2012). Typically, researchers who use argument repertoire couple it with more standard measures of knowledge accuracy, such as closed-ended or open-ended recall. In studies of the effects of deliberation on knowledge, some of our research has shown that deliberation has clear and strong effects on increasing argument repertoire and effects on knowledge in the form of decreasing uncertainty and increasing accuracy but not decreasing inaccuracy (Cappella, Price & Nir, 2002).

Computational Approaches to Text Analysis

The presence of and access to social media have made available a tremendously large corpus of data online. Computational tools to scrape and analyze these data have become available to scholars, increasing the opportunity to acquire knowledge, attitudes, and opinions through automated computational procedures executed on "found data" rather than "made data" (DiMaggio, 2015; Schwartz et al., 2013).

The mining of found data offers researchers opportunities previously unavailable in the study of accurate and inaccurate opinions. One simple use of found data is to conduct a "netnography" that excerpts stated opinions from online contributions by the public at large. These expressions constitute a kind of formative research that can inform subsequent intensive interviews, focus groups, or preliminary versions of survey instruments (Japec et al., 2015). In recent work in our own laboratory on "natural tobacco cigarettes," opinions shared by readers of vendors' online websites readily yielded more than 50 unique opinion statements about organic and natural tobaccos that have since become the basis for a study of misinformation about advertising about these products. Other ways to gather such responses from made data are more expensive and unlikely to be any more representative. The approach to mining data through a netnography is more qualitative than systematic, but such an approach is consistent with the preliminary use of the elements derived.

More systematic approaches to large-scale found data are disseminating rapidly into the social and communication sciences; these approaches offer researchers an opportunity to unearth the public's valid and invalid claims about social and policy issues. Social media platforms provide an online space for people to express their opinions, including claims they accept as true about issues in the public arena (González-Bailón & Paltoglou, 2015; Y. Kim, Hsu, & de Zúñiga, 2013; Murphy et al., 2014). Studies show that people use social media to make sense of health-related topics (Vos & Buckner, 2016). The huge amount of information available online requires the use of computational tools to infer the kinds of claims the public is expressing. The use of found data and computational tools for inferring topics and claims capturing public attention provides researchers with a new set of tools for describing, following, and evaluating the public's fully informed, partially informed, and uninformed opinions about issues.

One example from our research group is Rui Shi's (2016) dissertation about public response to news stories online regarding graphic warning labels proposed by the FDA. Several thousand relevant comments were extracted and subjected to supervised machine-learning algorithms. The topics that emerged (13) included both factual claims (e.g., smokers' rights are violated; tobacco companies' rights are violated; the public knows the risks already) and subjective opinions (e.g., will protect new users from smoking; will not be effective). The computational approach that Shi followed required validation and became the basis for research on the effects of competing frames in user-generated comments and news reports on policy support and thought diversity. Importantly, the content themes studied were those widely employed by members of the public debating the FDA's proposals.

The supervised machine-learning techniques are just one class of computational procedures available for studying knowledge claims buried in found data. Two commonly used computational methods — topic modeling and semantic networks — may be useful for measuring offline and online knowledge. Probabilistic topic models are algorithms used to analyze large sets of documents using a latent Dirichlet allocation (LDA) technique, a generative process based on Bayesian posterior probability calculation that is intended to track the process through which the documents were written (Blei, Ng, & Jordan, 2003). The basic assumption in topic modeling is that of collocation: words that appear in the same documents share thematic similarities (Blei, 2012). Topic modeling has become popular in the humanities (Jockers, 2013) and social sciences (Ghosh & Guha, 2013) and can be used on naturally occurring texts (Hong & Davison, 2010) as well as text generated in research contexts, such as collections of responses from open-ended questionnaires (Roberts et al., 2014). The algorithm provides researchers with a set of topics (probability lists of words that tend to appear together in the same texts) and can provide information about their prominence and distribution across a corpus.

LDA topic modeling had been used to analyze Twitter data about tobacco products and was able to identify topics important to users (Prier, Smith, Giraud-Carrier, & Hanson, 2011). Topics reported included weight loss, marijuana, and health policy, such as the Affordable Care Act (Obamacare). The authors conclude that LDA topic modeling on social media texts can be a useful tool to better understand health-related topics. Bisgin, Liu, Fang, Xu, and Tong (2011) have found that topic modeling offers a novel and efficient way for discovering hidden relationships between concepts mined from health-related documents. The method holds promise for mining information the public expresses in a variety of domains.

Semantic networks can be useful for studying, organizing, and analyzing misinformation. Semantic networks derive from work on mental models (Johnson-Laird, 1983) that can be visually represented through a network of concepts and their relationships (Carley & Palmquist, 1992). Unlike topic models, semantic networks require information about the structure of and relationships between concepts. The semantic units (e.g., concepts, words) are the nodes, and the relationships between them (e.g., collocations) are the edges (Steyvers & Tenenbaum, 2005). Semantic networks have been used for studying knowledge about genetics (Yu, Friedman, Rhzetsky, & Kra, 1999), communication (Doerfel & Barnett, 1999), and public opinion (Yang & González-Bailón, 2016). The application of semantic networks will surely grow, given the breadth and availability of found data.

Computational approaches allow researchers to study expressions of knowledge based on large amounts of data, opening a window to knowledge assessment that goes beyond the level of individuals. Such methods can also identify linguistic relationships and patterns that are hidden from the human coder and can only be noticed through a systematic analysis of large amounts of text (Campbell & Pennebaker, 2003). Since these methods are used to analyze naturally occurring discourse, certain biases inherent in self-report measures are avoided. They can provide ongoing information about the targets of the public's concerns for evolving social and policy issues and thereby allow more immediate responses to invalid claims and rapidly developing, misleading rumors. However, these methods are often based on linguistic assumptions that may or may not be accurate (e.g., collocation, "bag of words"), unrepresentative samples from individuals using social media, more advanced and less familiar programming and analysis techniques, and heavy reliance on the interpretation of the researcher.

Knowledge That Matters

In 1999, the *Journal of the National Cancer Institute Monographs* took up the question of conceptualizing and measuring health-risk information primarily because increasing people's knowledge of the objective risk associated with various cancers has so little influence on their behavior (Rothman & Kiviniemi, 1999). The authors make the argument that it is not objective knowledge of risk but felt risk, experienced subjectively, that is crucial to making the acquisition of risk information important to behavior. We agree with Rothman and Kiviniemi, as do other theorists (Fishbein & Ajzen, 2010). If knowledge measured objectively and dispassionately does not enhance behavioral changes consistently with that risk, then why worry about acquiring objective, dispassionate knowledge? Rothman and Kiviniemi hint at an approach, and Fishbein and Ajzen aggressively pursue the use of behavioral beliefs as personalizations of knowledge that are better predictors of intentions to behave.

Beliefs about consequences to the self are expected to be more important and thus more indicative of attitudes, intentions, and behaviors (O'Keefe, 2013). Due to optimistic bias, smokers may believe that smoking is dangerous and fatal for "most people who smoke" but not for themselves (Weinstein, Marcus, & Moser, 2005). Discovering that people know smoking increases the risk for heart attacks may not lead people to believe that they are at a higher risk due to their own smoking and may not influence their attitudes, intentions, and behaviors.

When assessing people's knowledge about the consequences of smoking, researchers can ask a participant whether or how strongly she believes that "people who smoke every day are more likely to suffer a heart attack than people who do not smoke every day." An important variation on this question is "If I smoke every day, I will be more likely to suffer a heart attack than people who do not smoke every day." The two items tap into the same knowledge, that is, the relative risk of heart attacks for smokers. The first version is about the effects of smoking on people, while the second is about the effects on self. The two versions will likely be processed differently by the participant.

Measuring knowledge from a person-centric point of view is not always required by the research being done, but when the goal is to enhance knowledge in order to activate behavior change consistent with that knowledge, then that knowledge should be framed to have an impact on the person's emotional well-being and self-interest. When beliefs as determinants of specific intentions and behaviors are the targets of interventions, personalizing the knowledge claim's focus is necessary (Fishbein & Cappella, 2006).

Moreover, even if people believe that they and others are at the same risk, their beliefs about the self are expected to be more influential on their own behavior. Fishbein and Ajzen (2010) have advised researchers to use measures of beliefs, attitudes, and intentions that are self-directed. Although people may hold inaccurate beliefs about the risks of smoking for themselves and others, it is the risk for oneself that is expected to be more important to their future intentions and behaviors, and thus it should be the focus of future knowledge measurements.

Conclusion

We have argued that measurements of knowledge about tobacco products and their deleterious effects may fail to predict attitudes and behavior change due to their methodological properties and limitations, as well as much past research. Our review of more and less common approaches highlights the advantages and disadvantages of each approach. Certain and unequivocal advice for best practices in measuring knowledge depends on the questions driving the specific research enterprise. Researchers should adjust their measures to their specific populations of interest and research questions, but measurement should not be driven only by familiarity and ease of use. Approaches to measuring knowledge have differing strengths and limitations. The research community's ability to address misinformation and its correction depends to a large degree on valid, subtle, and efficient measures of knowledge to uncover misinformation and to know when corrections are effective and when they are not. Researchers should also think of ways to combine and complement the approaches through triangulation. Advances in technology and data availability open the door for new and complex measurements that have not been widely adopted in the everyday practices of social and communication science and yet may be an option that is pragmatic and particularly useful for measuring knowledge in some contexts. Such computational methods can be implemented to extract data from naturally occurring language in social media to shed light on thoughts and beliefs held by highly motivated people for whom the topic is likely of relevance.

When the measurement of knowledge needs to be linked to behavior change, the focus of knowledge may need to be on its self-relevance.

Simply assuming that education through acquisition of correct information will enhance behavior change is naïve and contrary to much available evidence. The consequences of actions and inactions for one's own health will likely be more indicative of attitudes, intentions, and future behaviors. Despite years of corrective attempts, misinformation about tobacco remains a public concern and serves as a threat to individuals' health. Careful consideration and construction of an adequate and valid measurement tool of knowledge is thus an essential and crucial first step toward understanding and correcting detrimental misinformation.

References

Baker, P. (2006). *Using corpora in discourse analysis*. New York, NY: Continuum.

Bandura, A. (2001). Social cognitive theory of mass communication. *Media Psychology*, 3(3), 265–299.

Barnes, M. A., Dennis, M., & Haefele-Kalvaitis, J. (1996). The effects of knowledge availability and knowledge accessibility on coherence and elaborative inferencing in children from six to fifteen years of age. *Journal of Experimental Child Psychology*, 61(3), 216–241.

Bisgin, H., Liu, Z., Fang, H., Xu, X., & Tong, W. (2011). Mining FDA drug labels using an unsupervised learning technique — topic modeling. *BMC Bioinformatics*, 12(10), 1–8.

Blei, D. M. (2012). Probabilistic topic models. *Communications of the ACM*, 55(4), 77–84.

Blei, D. M., Ng, A. Y., & Jordan, M. I. (2003). Latent Dirichlet allocation. *Journal of Machine Learning Research*, 3, 993–1022.

Brewer, P. R., & Gross, K. (2005). Values, framing, and citizens' thoughts about policy issues: Effects on content and quantity. *Political Psychology*, 26(6), 929–948.

Campbell, R. S., & Pennebaker, J. W. (2003). The secret life of pronouns: Flexibility in writing style and physical health. *Psychological Science*, 14(1), 60–65.

Cappella, J. N., Maloney, E., Ophir, Y., & Brennan, E. (2015). Interventions to correct misinformation about tobacco products. *Tobacco Regulatory Science*, 1(2), 186–197.

Cappella, J. N., Price, V., & Nir, L. (2002). Argument repertoire as a reliable and valid measure of opinion quality: Electronic dialogue during campaign 2000. *Political Communication*, 19(1), 73–93.

Carley, K., & Palmquist, M. (1992). Extracting, representing, and analyzing mental models. *Social Forces*, 70(3), 601–636.

CDC. *See* U.S. Centers for Disease Control and Prevention (CDC).

Cummings, K. M., Hyland, A., Bansal, M. A., & Giovino, G. A. (2004). What do Marlboro Lights smokers know about low-tar cigarettes? *Nicotine & Tobacco Research*, 6(3), S323–S332.

Cummings, K. M., Hyland, A., Giovino, G. A., Hastrup, J. L., Bauer, J. E., & Bansal, M. A. (2004). Are smokers adequately informed about the health risks of smoking and medicinal nicotine? *Nicotine & Tobacco Research*, 6(3), S333–S340.

Dahlgren, P. (2009). *Media and political engagement: Citizens, communication and democracy*. New York, NY: Cambridge University Press.

Delli Carpini, M. X., & Keeter, S. (1993). Measuring political knowledge: Putting first things first. *American Journal of Political Science, 37*(4), 1179–1206.

DiMaggio, P. (2015). Adapting computational text analysis to social science (and vice versa). *Big Data & Society, 2*(2), http://dx.doi.org/10.1177/2053951715602908.

Doerfel, M. L., & Barnett, G. A. (1999). A semantic network analysis of the International Communication Association. *Human Communication Research, 25*(4), 589–603.

Eagly, A. H., & Chaiken, S. (1993). *The psychology of attitudes*. Orlando, FL: Harcourt Brace Jovanovich College Publishers.

Ecker, U. K. H., Lewandowsky, S., & Tang, D. T. W. (2010). Explicit warnings reduce but do not eliminate the continued influence of misinformation. *Memory & Cognition, 38*(8), 1087–1100.

Etter, J.-F. (2010). Electronic cigarettes: A survey of users. *BMC Public Health, 10*, 231.

Falk, E. B., Berkman, E. T., Mann, T., Harrison, B., & Lieberman, M. D. (2010). Predicting persuasion-induced behavior change from the brain. *Journal of Neuroscience, 30*(25), 8421–8424.

Farrelly, M. C., Healton, C. G., Davis, K. C., Messeri, P., Hersey, J. C., & Haviland, M. L. (2002). Getting to the truth: Evaluating national tobacco countermarketing campaigns. *American Journal of Public Health, 92*(6), 901–907.

FDA. *See* U.S. Food and Drug Administration (FDA).

Fishbein, M., & Ajzen, I. (2010). *Predicting and changing behavior: The reasoned action approach*. New York, NY: Psychology Press.

Fishbein, M., & Cappella, J. N. (2006). The role of theory in developing effective health communications. *Journal of Communication, 56*, S1–S17.

Furnham, A. (1986). Response bias, social desirability, and dissimulation. *Personality and Individual Differences, 7*(3), 385–400.

Gaziano, C. (1983). The knowledge gap: An analytical review of media effects. *Communication Research, 10*(4), 447–486.

Geer, J. G. (1988). What do open-ended questions measure? *Public Opinion Quarterly, 52*(3), 365–371.

Ghosh, D., & Guha, R. (2013). What are we "tweeting" about obesity? Mapping tweets with topic modeling and geographic information system. *Cartography and Geographic Information Science, 40*(2), 90–102.

Glantz, S. A., Bero, L. A., & Slade, J. (1996). *The cigarette papers*. Berkley, CA: University of California Press.

González-Bailón, S., & Paltoglou, G. (2015). Signals of public opinion in online communication A comparison of methods and data sources. *Annals of the American Academy of Political and Social Science, 659*(1), 95–107.

Griffiths, W. (1972). Health education: Definitions, problems, and philosophies. *Health Education & Behavior, 1*(31), 7–11.

Gygax, P. M., Bosson, M., Gay, C., & Ribordy, F. (2010). Relevance of health warnings on cigarette packs: A psycholinguistic investigation. *Health Communication, 25*(5), 397–409.

Hong, L., & Davison, B. D. (2010). Empirical study of topic modeling in Twitter. In

SOMA '10 Proceedings of the First Workshop on Social Media Analytics (pp. 80–88). New York, NY: Association for Computing Machinery.

Hornik, R., Jacobsohn, L., Orwin, R., Piesse, A., & Kalton, G. (2008). Effects of the national youth anti-drug Media Campaign on youths. *American Journal of Public Health, 98*(12), 2229–2236.

Hovland, C. I., Janis, I. L., & Kelly, H. H. (1953). *Communication and persuasion: Psychological studies of opinion change*. New Haven, CT: Yale University Press.

Hyland, A., Higbee, C., Borland, R., Travers, M., Hastings, G., Fong, G. T., & Cummings, K. M. (2009). Attitudes and beliefs about secondhand smoke and smoke-free policies in four countries: Findings from the International Tobacco Control Four Country Survey. *Nicotine & Tobacco Research, 11*(6), 642–649.

Insko, C. A. (1967). *Theories of attitude change*. New York, NY: Appleton-Century-Crofts.

Iyengar, S. (1990). The accessibility bias in politics: Television news and public opinion. *International Journal of Public Opinion Research, 2*(1), 1–15.

Japec, L., Kreuter, F., Berg, M., Biemer, P., Decker, P., Lampe, C., . . . Usher, A. (2015). Big data in survey research AAPOR task force report. *Public Opinion Quarterly, 79*(4), 839–880.

Jockers, M. (2013). *Macroanalysis: Digital methods and literary history*. Champaign, IL: University of Illinois Press.

Johnson-Laird, P. N. (1983). *Mental models: Towards a cognitive science of language, inference, and consciousness*. Cambridge, MA: Harvard University Press.

Kim, Y., Hsu, S.-H., & de Zúñiga, H. G. (2013). Influence of social media use on discussion network heterogeneity and civic engagement: The moderating role of personality traits. *Journal of Communication, 63*(3), 498–516.

King, G., Keohane, R. O., & Verba, S. (1994). *Designing social inquiry: Scientific inference in qualitative research*. Princeton, NJ: Princeton University Press.

Lang, A., Zhou, S., Schwartz, N., & Bolls, P. D. (2000). The effects of edits on arousal, attention, and memory for television messages: When an edit is an edit can an edit be too much? *Journal of Broadcasting and Electronic Media, 44*, 94–109.

Langleben, D. D., Loughead, J. W., Ruparel, K., Hakun, J. G., Busch-Winokur, S., Holloway, M. B., . . . Lerman, C. (2009). Reduced prefrontal and temporal processing and recall of high "sensation value" ads. *NeuroImage, 46*(1), 219–225.

Lee, S., & Cappella, J. N. (2013). Distraction effects of smoking cues in antismoking messages: Examining resource allocation to message processing as a function of smoking cues and argument strength. *Media Psychology, 16*(2), 154–176.

Lewandowsky, S., Ecker, U. K. H., Seifert, C. M., Schwarz, N., & Cook, J. (2012). Misinformation and its correction: Continued influence and successful debiasing. *Psychological Science in the Public Interest, 13*(3), 106–131.

Lipkus, I. M., Eissenberg, T., Schwartz-Bloom, R. D., Prokhorov, A. V., & Levy, J. (2014). Relationships among factual and perceived knowledge of harms of waterpipe tobacco, perceived risk, and desire to quit among college users. *Journal of Health Psychology, 19*(12), 1525–1535.

Luce, R. D. (1986). *Response times: Their role in inferring elementary mental organization*. New York, NY: Oxford University Press.

McAfee, T., Davis, K. C., Alexander Jr., R. L., Pechacek, T. F., & Bunnell, R. (2013). Effect of the first federally funded US antismoking national media campaign. *Lancet,* *382*(9909), 2003–2011.

McGuire, W. J. (1989). Theoretical foundations of campaigns. In R. E. Rice & C. K. Atkin (Eds.), *Public communication campaigns* (2nd ed., pp. 43–66). Thousand Oaks, CA: Sage.

Mitchell, M. L., & Jolley, J. M. (2007). *Research design explained* (6th ed.). Belmont, CA: Thomson Wadsworth.

Murphy, J., Link, M. W., Childs, J. H., Tesfaye, C. L., Dean, E., Stern, M., . . . Harwood, P. (2014). Social media in public opinion research: Executive summary of the AAPOR Task Force on Emerging Technologies in Public Opinion Research. *Public Opinion Quarterly, 78*(4), 788–794.

Mutti, S., Hammond, D., Reid, J. L., & Thrasher, J. F. (2013). The efficacy of cigarette warning labels on health beliefs in the United States and Mexico. *Journal of Health Communication, 18*(10), 1180–1192.

National Cancer Institute (NCI). (N.d.). Survey instruments. Retrieved from http://hints.cancer.gov/instrument.aspx

Niederdeppe, J., Fowler, E. F., Goldstein, K., & Pribble, J. (2010). Does local television news coverage cultivate fatalistic beliefs about cancer prevention? *Journal of Communication, 60*(2), 230–253.

Nyhan, B., & Reifler, J. (2010). When corrections fail: The persistence of political misperceptions. *Political Behavior, 32*(2), 303–330.

O'Keefe, D. J. (2013). The relative persuasiveness of different forms of arguments-from-consequences: A review and integration. In C. T. Salmon (Ed.), *Communication yearbook, 36.* New York, NY: Routledge.

Oreskes, N., & Conway, E. M. (2011). *Merchants of doubt: How a handful of scientists obscured the truth on issues from tobacco smoke to global warming.* New York, NY: Bloomsbury Press.

Petty, R. E., & Cacioppo, J. T. (1986). *Communication and persuasion.* New York, NY: Springer.

Price, V., Cappella, J. N., & Nir, L. (2002). Does disagreement contribute to more deliberative opinion? *Political Communication, 19*(1), 95–112.

Prier, K. W., Smith, M. S., Giraud-Carrier, C., & Hanson, C. L. (2011). Identifying health-related topics on Twitter. In J. Salerno, S. J. Yang, D. Nau, & S.-K. Chai (Eds.), *Social computing, behavioral-cultural modeling, and prediction* (pp. 18–25). Berlin, Germany: Springer-Verlag.

Roberts, M. E., Stewart, B. M., Tingley, D., Lucas, C., Leder-Luis, J., Gadarian, S. K., . . . Rand, D. G. (2014). Structural topic models for open-ended survey responses. *American Journal of Political Science, 58*(4), 1064–1082.

Rosenstock, I. M. (1974). Historical origins of the Health Belief Model. *Health Education & Behavior, 2*(4), 328–335.

Roskos-Ewoldsen, D. R., & Fazio, R. H. (1997). The role of belief accessibility in attitude formation. *Southern Communication Journal, 62*(2), 107–116.

Rothman, A., & Kiviniemi, M. (1999). Treating people with information: An analysis and review of approaches to communicating health risk information. *Journal of the National Cancer Institute Monographs, 25,* 44–51.

Sanders-Jackson, A. (2014). Rated measures of narrative structure for written smoking-cessation texts. *Health Communication, 29*(10), 1009–1019.

Schank, R. C., & Abelson, R. P. (1995). Knowledge and memory: The real story. In R. S. Wyer (Ed.), *Knowledge and memory: The real story* (pp. 1–86). Hillsdale, NJ: Lawrence Erlbaum.

Schwartz, H. A., Eichstaedt, J. C., Kern, M. L., Dziurzynski, L., Ramones, S. M., Agrawal, M., . . . Ungar, L. H. (2013). Personality, gender, and age in the language of social media: The open-vocabulary approach. *PLOS ONE, 8*(9), e0073791.

Shah, D. V., Cappella, J. N., & Neuman, W. R. (2015). Big data, digital media, and computational social science: Possibilities and perils. *Annals of the American Academy of Political and Social Science, 659*(1), 6–13.

Shi, R. (2016). Viewer-generated comments to online health policy news: Content, dynamics, and influence (Doctoral dissertation). Annenberg School for Communication, University of Pennsylvania, Philadelphia, PA.

Smith, P., Bansal-Travers, M., O'Connor, R., Brown, A., Banthin, C., Guardino-Colket, S., & Cummings, K. M. (2011). Correcting over 50 years of tobacco industry misinformation. *American Journal of Preventive Medicine, 40*(6), 690–698.

Southwell, B. G. (2013). *Social networks and popular understanding of science and health: Sharing disparities.* Baltimore, MD: Johns Hopkins University Press.

Steil, A. K., Lorenzo, L., & Sydeman, S. J. (2010). Demographic variables are associated with knowledge, attitudes, and preventive behaviors related to environmental tobacco smoke. *Nicotine & Tobacco Research, 12*(6), 674–678.

Steyvers, M., & Tenenbaum, J. B. (2005). The large-scale structure of semantic networks: Statistical analyses and a model of semantic growth. *Cognitive Science, 29*(1), 41–78.

Tan, A. S. L., & Bigman, C. A. (2014). E-cigarette awareness and perceived harmfulness: Prevalence and associations with smoking-cessation outcomes. *American Journal of Preventive Medicine, 47*(2), 141–149.

Thorson, E. (2016). Belief echoes: The persistent effects of corrected misinformation. *Political Communication, 33*(3), 460–480.

U.S. Centers for Disease Control and Prevention (CDC). (2011). Quitting smoking among adults—United States, 2001–2010. *MMWR. Morbidity and Mortality Weekly Report, 60*(44), 1513–1519.

U.S. Centers for Disease Control and Prevention (CDC). (N.d.). Fast facts. Retrieved July 1, 2016, from http://www.cdc.gov/tobacco/data_statistics/fact_sheets/fast_facts

U.S. Food and Drug Administration (FDA). (2015). *Center for Tobacco Products overview.* Retrieved from http://www.fda.gov/downloads/TobaccoProducts/NewsEvents/UCM265523.pdf

Vos, S. C., & Buckner, M. M. (2016). Social media messages in an emerging health crisis: Tweeting bird flu. *Journal of Health Communication, 21*(3), 301–308.

Weinstein, N. D., Marcus, S. E., & Moser, R. P. (2005). Smokers' unrealistic optimism about their risk. *Tobacco Control, 14*(1), 55–59.

Weinstein, N. D., Slovic, P., Waters, E., & Gibson, G. (2004). Public understanding of the illnesses caused by cigarette smoking. *Nicotine & Tobacco Research, 6*(2), 349–355.

World Health Organization (WHO). (2016, June). Tobacco. [Fact sheet]. Retrieved from http://www.who.int/mediacentre/factsheets/fs339/en

Yang, S., & González-Bailón, S. (2016). Semantic networks and public opinion. In Victor, J. N., Lubell, M., & Montgomery, A. H. (Eds.). *Oxford handbook of political networks*. New York, NY: Oxford University Press. http://dx.doi.org/10.1093/oxford hb/9780190228217.013.14

Yu, H., Friedman, C., Rhzetsky, A., & Kra, P. (1999). Representing genomic knowledge in the UMLS semantic network. In *Proceedings of the AMIA Symposium* (pp. 181–185). Bethesda, MD: American Medical Informatics Association.

FOUR

Measuring Perceptions of Shares of Groups

DOUGLAS J. AHLER AND GAURAV SOOD

A *misperception* is a belief in incorrect information (Luskin, Sood, & Blank, 2013). Other chapters in this volume provide provocative and disturbing examples of misperceptions: some citizens believe that former president Barack Obama was born outside the United States, just as some consumers believe that "light" cigarettes cause neither cancer nor addiction, despite abundant evidence in the information environment that those beliefs are wholly wrong.

Stereotypes about groups are a type of misperception—perhaps one of the most common. Unlike the examples above, however, stereotypes are rooted in "kernels of truth" (Bordalo, Coman, Gennaioli, & Shleifer, 2016). People develop mental images of groups to better understand the social world and their own place in it (Lippman, 1922). But society is highly complex and cognitive capacity limited. Hence, when developing these mental images, people rely on mental shortcuts, or heuristics, developing impressionistic accounts rather than photorealistic portraits of the world outside.

Stereotypes—"overgeneralizations that are especially resistant to change" (Ruggiero, 2012)—are among the most common consequences of this heuristic processing. Stereotypes tend to emerge from actual differences between groups but often greatly exaggerate differences, which can inflame intergroup animus (e.g., Ahler & Sood, forthcoming). Thus, group stereotypes lie behind some of the most fundamental questions in social science as they relate to intergroup conflict. What explains intergroup conflict? What are its consequences? And how do we temper or inflame it?

Because stereotypes tend to reflect genuine intergroup differences, social scientists increasingly study stereotypes through the broader lens of how individuals think about group and population composition, searching for psychological mechanisms for perceptual distortion (Bordalo et al., 2016; Gennaioli & Shleifer, 2010) and leveraging such distortion experimentally to better understand the effects of stereotyping (Ahler & Sood, forthcoming). In this chapter we address the measurement of perceptions of salient, stereotypical groups' numerical strength in the population and in other stereotype-relevant groups.

But what do we mean by perceptions of composition? We conceptualize them as crude beliefs about the numerical strength of a given group within a subpopulation. It is unlikely that more than a handful of people hold any beliefs about the numerical strength of most groups—for example, how many beekeepers drive sedans. When groups are salient to policy debates, however (immigrants, for example), people likely hold crude beliefs about the numerical strength of those groups both in the population generally and within other groups (such as Democrats).

We contend that these crude beliefs implicitly map to specific numbers. When people are surveyed about their beliefs about population or group composition, they translate these beliefs into specific numbers, though likely with considerable noise. A person may hold the belief that "many" undocumented immigrants live in the United States. This belief may affect the person's attitude toward immigration without his or her ever mapping "many" to a particular number. When asked about the share of undocumented immigrants among current U.S. residents, the person may report that 15% of the people living in the country are doing so illegally. (The actual number is 3.5%, per Krogstad & Passel, 2016.) We contend that the reported 15% is a function of the underlying belief and random error.

This conceptualization raises a variety of mechanistic and conceptual concerns. Does it matter how we elicit the beliefs? In particular, does it matter how much time we give people to report their beliefs? Do people honestly report what they believe? Or do they instead offer responses that reflect how they feel about the group? Does innumeracy, rather than genuine misperception, explain survey reports exaggerating certain groups' shares? Each of these concerns highlights a threat to the *validity* of measures of perceptions about composition, suggesting that something intervenes between people's crude beliefs about the numerical strength of a given group and how they report that belief on a survey.

Even if concerns like these prove unfounded, it is not clear how to interpret elicited perceptions. Notably, if we find that people overestimate the share of a given group in a subpopulation (e.g., the percentage of Democrats who are black)—what do we make of it? Could it be that people think that the share of blacks in the population is larger than it is? Or is it that people accurately perceive the share of blacks in the population but overestimate their prevalence in the Democratic Party?

We shed light on these and other such questions around conceptualization, measurement, and interpretation of perceptions of the numerical strength of groups in populations and subpopulations. We provide methods for explaining, interpreting, and assessing the validity of reported perceptions, demonstrating the use of some of the tools with two large survey experiments.

Causes and Consequences of Misperceptions of Numerical Strength of Groups

The most apparent consequence of misperceptions about the numerical strength of groups is that such misinformation can affect people's feelings toward groups and the people who belong to them. Sometimes attitudes toward groups are rooted in the zero-sum struggle between groups for resources and power (Campbell, 1965). In such a scenario, an increase in the actual or imagined share of an out-group naturally increases one's anxiety that the out-group will seize power—especially in a democracy—and execute its agenda. Members of the threatened group respond to this heightened threat with greater in-group solidarity and out-group hostility (e.g., Nadeau, Niemi, & Levine, 1993; Sides & Citrin, 2007a), greater opposition to policies that benefit the out-group, and greater likelihood of preemptive action, such as voting to reduce the power of the threatening group (Blalock, 1967; Dancygier, 2010; Key, 1949).

Social identity theory provides another explanation for how people evaluate groups and why perceptions of group shares may matter. People seek positive distinctiveness. In-group favoritism arises because individuals' self-concepts are intricately tied to their membership in social groups (Tajfel & Turner 2004). So powerful is the need for positive group distinctiveness that membership in even arbitrarily assigned groups engenders in-group favoritism (Sherif, 2015; Tajfel, 1970). The importance of social identity means that people often evaluate novel groups based on their perceptions of how known social groups compose them. For instance, people conceptualize political parties in terms of longer-standing social groups, like those based on race and social class (Green, Palmquist, & Schickler, 2002). And partisans' perceptions about the share of these groups in the parties affect their feelings toward opposing party supporters (Ahler & Sood, forthcoming). More broadly, how large people think a group is affects not only how threatened they feel by the group but also their attitudes and behaviors toward the group as well as related policy preferences (Sides & Citrin, 2007a; Wong, 2007; Wong, Bowers, Williams, & Simmons, 2012), as realistic conflict and social identity theories would predict.

Troublingly, perceptions of group shares are often biased in ways that heighten conflict (Ahler & Sood, forthcoming; Nadeau et al., 1993; Sides & Citrin, 2007a). But how is it that people come to hold these erroneous beliefs? Common pathways include reliance on accessible information, disinformation, and the use of representativeness heuristics in evaluating group composition.

People continuously but often lazily learn from their environments. They are most likely to receive and accept information that is most readily available. But what is accessible is not always apt for drawing correct inferences. Local television news covers violent crime far more than nonviolent crime even though nonviolent crime is far more common. And watching local news likely leads some people to wrongly believe that violent crime in their local area is common (Romer, Jamieson, & Aday, 2003). Similarly, it is no surprise that Americans' beliefs about the percentage of the poor who are black hew closely to media depictions of the poor (Gilens, 1996) and that perceptions of the percentage of Democrats and Republicans belonging to party-stereotypical groups are the most biased among people who report having the greatest interest in political news (Ahler & Sood, forthcoming).

Accessibility implies that people make erroneous inferences about group shares from readily available information; elite communications *indirectly* drive misinformation. By contrast, *disinformation* implies that people are directly misled. Cynical spreading of falsehoods with the aim of persuading voters to change their preferences and behaviors is not new (Jackson & Jamieson, 2007), but the 2016 U.S. presidential elections brought this concern to the fore as never before. A number of stories circulated during the campaign that grossly overstated the total number of immigrants, especially undocumented immigrants, in the country. And some of these stories were shared and read widely on social media, sometimes cynically disseminated by others; Barthel, Mitchell, and Holcomb (2016) find that "14% [said] they shared a story they knew was fake at the time [of sharing]." As such, there is reason to think that some people hold incorrect beliefs about the share of prominent social groups entangled in policy debates because they take as fact disinformation from a trusted source.

Both external information and internal processes can drive misperceptions about group strength. Foremost among these internal processes is the representativeness heuristic (Bordalo et al., 2016; Tversky & Kahneman, 1973). In the case of perceptions about group composition, this is likely to result in people neglecting base rate information. When people are asked to evaluate the percentage of poor Americans who are black, they are apt to focus on the categorical overlap in memory between blacks and the poor and not consider that just 13% of the U.S. population is black.

Perceptions of the numerical strength of groups, therefore, are of interest to social scientists not only because they affect intergroup attitudes and relations but also because misperceptions may shed light on the nature of information flows about social groups and events. Measuring these perceptions presents unique challenges.

Conceptual, Measurement, and Interpretation Concerns

A half century of survey data suggest that the average American knows little about politics (Campbell, Converse, Miller, & Stokes, 1960; Delli Carpini & Keeter, 1996). For example, roughly half of survey respondents fail to identify their members of Congress, and similar numbers fail to correctly place the political parties on major issues (Freeder, Lenz, & Turney, 2016). Such disengagement makes it unlikely that most people will encounter—much less remember—specific data on the numerical strength of even salient or stereotypical social groups in the population or in politically relevant groups. Instead, most people are likely to have crude beliefs—stereotypes founded in representativeness or impressions based on inferences from accessible information, as we describe above. These crude beliefs likely map implicitly to numbers that people use to react to situations. It is these numbers that survey researchers want to elicit. A variety of concerns and questions accompany common survey measures gauging these numerical perceptions.

Eliciting Beliefs about Groups' Numerical Strength

The quantity of interest is the numbers that people's crude beliefs about group composition implicitly "map to." From a face-validity perspective, the closer the responses are to being automatic, the better they are at capturing the implicit mapping. To obtain such responses, researchers may want to curtail the time the respondents have between accessing the crude belief and reporting its numerical mapping. Providing more time to respond may yield estimates that reflect additional deliberation and reasoning beyond what people would normally engage in when accessing and using these beliefs outside the survey environment. Given additional time, a respondent may reason that his "gut answer" is too large or too small. Thus, these considered reports are liable to be different than beliefs that inform people's judgments in the real world.

Eliciting more considered beliefs may also change the underlying beliefs that people have. Presenting people with circumstances in which they have the opportunity to carefully consider the beliefs they report may cause some to change not only what they report but also what they actually believe. Having considered the number their belief maps to, some people may find it too large and change their original beliefs. This suggests that eliciting more considered responses may be useful in evaluating the degree to which misperceptions can be corrected through slower, more effortful processing (Kahneman, 2011; Petty & Cacioppo, 1986).

Use of Denominators Larger than 100

When reporting beliefs about shares of groups, people often implicitly use denominators larger than 100 (Wong, 2007). That is, when asked to report shares of an exhaustive set of mutually exclusive groups in a population or subpopulation, respondents' summed answers often exceed 100. This implies that innumeracy about percentages and genuine misperceptions about group shares may be observationally equivalent. Two strategies exist for addressing this concern. The first is recalibration. If shares of an exhaustive, mutually exclusive set of categories sum to 125, estimates for each of the categories can be divided by the more appropriate denominator (125). Such recalibration assumes that relative error is the same across categories, though it may not be.

Alternatively, one can address the problem during measurement, amending the survey instrument in a way that makes respondents more acutely aware of the appropriate denominator. One might force respondents to sum the shares of a comprehensive set of mutually exclusive groups to 100 (Ahler & Sood, forthcoming). This solution likely has some unwanted collateral effects. Not only is it cognitively taxing for survey respondents, but it may cause them to think more effortfully about the quantities. Alternatively, and more simply, one may rephrase the question stem as "Out of 100, how many . . ." as opposed to "What percentage . . ." (Sides & Citrin, 2007b). However, it is not clear whether this strategy ameliorates the concern.

Motivated Responding

Respondents may intentionally misreport their beliefs about the numerical strength of groups to express their feelings about the groups referenced in the survey question (Bullock, Gerber, Hill, & Huber, 2013; Khanna & Sood, 2015; Prior, Sood, & Khanna, 2015). In particular, people may intentionally overstate the share of groups they (dis)like within groups they also (dis)like. For example, a white racist may purposefully overreport the percentage of poor Americans who are black, as doing so casts aspersions on a disliked racial out-group.

Evidence for motivated responding is hard to collect. A bulk of the evidence comes from experiments that pay people for providing correct answers and for confessing to ignorance. Prior et al. (2015) give a random set of respondents accuracy incentives (monetary or textual appeals) for correct answers. They find that the partisan gap in responses to affectively charged items, such as changes in the unemployment rate under a Democratic president, falls by about half. Bullock et al. (2013) also provide accuracy incentives, for either marking "Don't Know" or marking the correct answer, and arrive at similar estimates.

Interpreting the results of experiments that provide incentives can be tricky. First, incentives may encourage cheating; like Bullock et al. (2013), researchers may want to use placebo questions to gauge the extent of the concern. Second, to earn the reward, respondents may revise their responses to comport with their perceptions of the researchers' beliefs, even if they do not believe those reports. Asking respondents to guess how the researchers would answer may be one way to gauge that concern. Lastly, providing incentives likely yields more considered responses. And as we argue above, top-of-the-head answers may be closer to the beliefs respondents generally carry about salient and stereotypical groups.

Misunderstanding Question or Scale

Respondent ambiguity about what is being asked can hamper the validity of any survey item. These concerns extend to items tapping perceptions of group shares. The question "What percentage of Democrats are black?" is somewhat ambiguous. Some respondents may reasonably wonder whether "Democrats" means just people who identify themselves as Democrats or also those who lean toward the party—or, instead, those who voted for the Democratic candidate in the last presidential election. All of this assumes that these distinctions appreciably alter the elicited number. Many times they don't. Including those who lean toward a party doesn't appreciably change the share of prominent party-stereotypical groups in the party (Ahler & Sood, forthcoming). Still, precision is preferred.

There is, however, generally a trade-off between precision, compactness, and comprehensibility. And given that only a few respondents are likely to be aware of these finer distinctions, one idea may be to keep the question stem as is and ask an additional open-ended question about the definition of the quantity being estimated. People's understanding of the quantity being asked can then be used to more clearly interpret the responses.

Others have raised concerns about comprehensibility of response scales for numerical perception items. Ansolabehere, Meredith, and Snowberg (2013, p. 481) assert that "providing respondents with benchmark quantities . . . can reduce measurement error due to respondents not understanding the scale on which more complex quantities, such as the unemployment rate, are measured." We are skeptical that this improves measurement of group shares—and even numerical perceptions more broadly. It is odd to claim that people can know the unemployment rate and yet not know its scale. Simply, if a respondent knows that the unemployment rate is 4.4%, comprehension of the scale is moot—and again very likely obvious to people who know the unemployment rate. And interpreting the effect of offering a benchmark rate—lower error—as better comprehension of the scale seems unwarranted. Offering a benchmark rate is liable to reduce error not because respondents suddenly realize that the unemployment rate is based on a 101-point (0–100) scale but because respondents can better calibrate their guesses. Another adverse effect of offering benchmark quantities is that benchmarks are likely to act as low-information anchors, shrink variance, and add bias to the elicited answers (Tversky & Kahneman, 1973).

When interpreting perceptions of subpopulation composition, researchers face a unique challenge. When people are asked to assess the percentage of a given subpopulation belonging to a particular group, such as the percentage of Republicans who earn $250,000 per year or more, someone might overestimate the probability that a given person who earns more than $250,000 is a Republican for two different reasons. The respondent may believe that a larger share of Republicans fit the Republican stereotype of being wealthy than in reality. Alternatively, the respondent may believe that a larger share of Americans earn more than $250,000 than do in reality. The latter would imply that the respondent would also overestimate the percentage of Democrats and independents who are very wealthy, and naturally, such a response would reflect little about party stereotypes.

Data suggest that people are not only ignorant of base rates but also likely to neglect them even when they do know them. The *base rate fallacy* occurs when people use the representativeness heuristic, equating the likelihood that a Republican earns more than $250,0000 with the likelihood that a person earning $250,000 is a Republican (Kahneman & Frederick, 2002). Thus, researchers interested in assessing potential mechanisms behind misperceptions about subpopulation composition may find value in providing and/or experimentally manipulating base rates.

Researchers interested in correcting misperceptions may also find value in priming nonstereotypical cases. A survey might simply ask respondents about the percentage of Republicans who earn less than $250,000 per year. More creatively, it might ask respondents to think about a handful of Republican friends or associates—who, by virtue of base rates, are unlikely to earn more than $250,000 per year—or even to write down something about those friends' jobs or socioeconomic status (Thorson, 2016).

Data and Research Design

The data primarily come from two surveys with multiple embedded experiments conducted on Amazon's Mechanical Turk market for trading small services. Compared to the population, survey respondents recruited on Mechanical Turk tend to be younger, better educated, and more likely to identify with the Democratic Party (Berinsky, Huber, & Lenz, 2012). The study design and sample composition are presented in an online appendix (Ahler and Sood, 2017). Still, Mechanical Turk respondents' perceptions of party composition are similar to those of respondents from more representative samples (Ahler & Sood, forthcoming). Our data are relevant to the evolving literature on group perceptions.

We conducted Study 1 to assess concerns about the validity of the finding that Americans overestimate the share of party-stereotypical groups in the two main political parties (Ahler & Sood, forthcoming). To assess the concern, we randomly assigned respondents to one of five conditions: standard estimation, a control condition, and three other conditions designed to assess the validity of a specific alternative explanation or interpretation of our results. We describe the different conditions in greater detail as part of discussion about each specific concern.

In Study 2 we asked about perceptions of shares of a broader variety of groups: 1) the share of Democrats who are atheist/agnostic, black, gay/lesbian/bisexual, and union members; 2) the share of Republicans who are age 65+, evangelical, southern, and earning more than $250,000 per year; 3) the share of Americans who drink diet soda (for some respondents) and the percentage of American men and women who do so (all respondents); 4) the percentage of people living in America who were born outside the United States (e.g., Alba, Rumbaut, & Marotz, 2005); and 5) the percentage of American poor who are black (e.g., Gilens, 1996). As before, we describe the specific experiments in Study 2 as part of the discussion about each specific concern.

Top-of-the-Head versus Considered Responses

"Top of the head" answers are likely closest to the numbers that stereotypes implicitly map to. If so, how biased (if at all) are more considered opinions? To evaluate that, in Study 2 we assigned roughly 300 respondents to a timing experiment. Half of the respondents were randomly assigned to the time-pressure condition in which they were only given 10 seconds to answer each item, and half were assigned to the time-requirement condition in which they had to wait 15 seconds with just the question text on the screen before they could input their responses. Respondents were alerted about the timed portion of the survey before answering the questions. Depictions of all treatments in both studies are provided in an online appendix (Ahler and Sood, 2017).

Use of Denominators Larger than 100

To gauge the impact of implicit use of denominators larger than 100, we conducted two experiments. In Study 1, respondents were assigned to a sum-to-100 condition in which they reported their beliefs about the percentage of partisans belonging to a party-stereotypical group but also their beliefs about a comprehensive set of complementary, mutually exclusive categories. Respondents estimated not only the percentage of Republicans who are evangelical Christian but also the percentage of Republicans who are mainline Protestant, Catholic, and "other/no religion." We required that the estimates sum to 100. To help respondents make sure their estimates summed to 100, an on-screen counter tracked the total. The difference between results in the sum-to-100 condition and the standard-estimation condition gives us the extent to which implicit use of denominators larger than 100 affects reports of numerical strengths of various stereotypical groups in the party.

In Study 2, another 300 respondents were assigned to a wording experiment designed for the same purpose. We randomly manipulated question stems to read either "Out of every 100 [Republicans/Democrats], how many do you think are [characteristic]?" or "What percentage of [Republicans/Democrats] do you think are [characteristic]?" Following Sides and Citrin (2007b), we expect "Out of every 100 . . ." to make the correct denominator more salient. We manipulated the stems of the party composition items, foreign-born population item, and racial composition of the poor item.

Motivated Responding

We assessed the extent to which motivated responding affects responses by offering accuracy incentives to a random subset of respondents in Study 1. Respondents in the accuracy incentives condition received an additional five cents, 20% of the compensation for finishing the survey (25 cents) for each response that fell within five percentage points of the truth. While the bonus may seem small, given that respondents answered items on eight groups' shares, they had the opportunity to nearly triple what they made for the survey. If Americans' apparent misperceptions about party composition reflect motivated responding, estimates of respondents assigned to the incentives condition should be substantially different from those elicited without incentives.

Beliefs about Related Quantities
and Interpretation of Responses

Do misperceptions about the share of a group in a party merely reflect misperceptions about the share of the group and nothing particular to partisan stereotypes? We gauged the possibility in three ways. Perhaps most dispositively, in Study 1 we removed ignorance about base rates as a plausible alternative explanation. We did so by anchoring sliders at the base rate for each party-stereotypical group. After being explicitly alerted to this design feature, respondents were then asked to use the sliders to estimate the probability of a group member also being a member of the party. Significantly lower estimates in the base rates condition would mean that inflated base rates potentially explain these reported misperceptions.

Second, in the standard estimation condition, we asked respondents to estimate the groups' base rates in addition to their prevalence in a particular party. We can use these data to assess people's beliefs about base rates. Moreover, we can compare respondents' estimated group base rates to their estimates of group shares in the party to test whether misperceptions reflect anything beyond base rate ignorance. To better understand misperceptions about subpopulation composition, we can compute a difference-in-differences, which tells us whether party stereotypes or erroneous beliefs about the group's base rate more strongly color perceptions of party composition.

Finally, in Study 2 we used the diet soda items to test a hypothesis regarding beliefs about related quantities. Although roughly equal percentages of men (23%) and women (24%) report drinking diet soda (Mendes, 2013), advertising often targets women (Lin, 1998; Yoder, Christopher, & Holmes, 2008). Therefore, we suspect that Americans overestimate the gap in diet soda consumption between men and women. Since the share of men and women in the population is roughly 50% and common knowledge, we can identify the source of error in people's perceptions of women as more likely to drink diet soda than men. We randomly assigned half of respondents to provide their beliefs about the base rate of diet soda consumption in America before answering the items specific to men and women. With between-conditions data we can assess whether asking about base rates reduces error in reported perceptions of the proportion of men and women who drink soda.

Results

For all 10 items in the timing experiment—the eight party-composition items, the percentage-of-foreign-born item, and the percentage-of-poor-who-are-black item—responses are more accurate in the time-requirement condition than in the time-pressure condition. To get a sense of the average difference across conditions and items, we regressed *perceptual bias*, the signed difference between a respondent's perception and the true estimate, on an indicator for assignment to the time-requirement treatment, and fixed effects for items, clustering the standard errors by respondent. In the results, *perceptual bias* refers to the average raw, directional error in the respondents' reported quantities across items. Ahler and Sood (2017) present two alternative specifications of inaccurate perception: *absolute error*, the average raw, absolute distance from the true quantities observed in respondents' reports across items, and *percentage bias*, which averages the percentage by which respondents err (signed error) across items. Results fail to change in any meaningful way using these specifications rather than perceptual bias. On average, perceptual bias in the time-requirement condition was 4.3 points lower than in the time-pressure condition (Figure 4.1). However, it is worth noting that this is only a 22% decline in perceptual bias. Across all items, bias in reported perceptions was 19.7 points in the time-pressure condition, which fell to 15.5 points among those assigned to the time requirement condition.

Reduced bias in the time-requirement condition, however, may be due to respondents using the additional time to consult outside sources. To assess the concern, we plotted the density curve of all responses to all the items by treatment condition. If reduced bias in the time-requirement condition was a consequence of cheating, we should observe spikes in the density plot at the correct answer. But we do not see these spikes. To formally test for cheating, we compared proportion correct (within one percentage point) across conditions; the data suggest no differences. Both analyses are available in an online appendix (Ahler and Sood, 2017).

Figure 4.1 depicts 95% confidence intervals. Results are from OLS regression of perceptual bias on treatment indicators (with baseline conditions noted here), with item fixed effects and standard errors clustered by respondent. The "standard estimation" condition serves as a baseline for the "Sum-to-100," "Incentives," and "Base Rates" conditions. The "time pressure" condition serves as a baseline for the "time require-

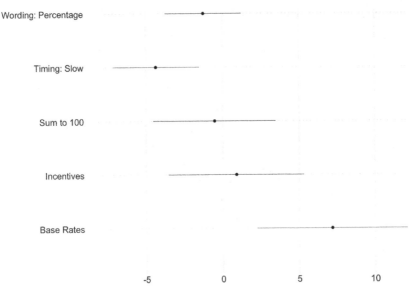

Figure 4.1. Average effects of eliciting perceptions of various groups in different ways

ment" (or "Slow") condition. The alternative stem wording ("Out of every 100") serves as a baseline for the "Percentage" (standard stem wording) condition.

Use of Denominators Larger than 100

If people implicitly use denominators larger than 100 when reporting percentages, estimates in the sum-to-100 condition should be significantly lower than in the standard-estimation condition. However, when respondents are required to ensure that shares for a comprehensive set of mutually exclusive groups sum to 100, they are generally just as biased. For just one of the eight items—the black-Democratic group-party dyad—are estimates significantly less biased (online appendix, Ahler and Sood, 2017, section 1.1). As Figure 4.1 shows, average perceptual bias across all party-group dyads fell by just 0.5 points in the sum-to-100 condition, from a baseline of 18.9 points in the standard estimation condition. (Results are from OLS regression of error on indicators for Study 1 treatments, with item fixed effects and standard errors clustered by respondent.) Thus, inflated implicit denominators appear to minimally affect perceptions of group shares.

Question stem wording fails to systematically affect responses to these items. In Study 2's wording experiment, the "Out of every 100" wording reduced bias in just three of the 10 items (for plots see Ahler and Sood, 2017, section 2.6). Pooling across items, the "Out of every 100" wording is associated with a 1.2-point increase in perceptual bias. (Again, results are from an OLS regression of perceptual bias on an indicator for the "Out of every 100" treatment, with item fixed effects and standard errors clustered by respondent.) Given that the usual "What percent" wording yields an average perceptual bias of 18.9 points, this difference is neither statistically nor substantively significant. In sum, neither priming the appropriate denominator nor constraining respondents to the right denominator significantly reduces bias in their estimates, suggesting that respondents' implicit use of denominators greater than 100 does not strongly bias reported perceptions.

Motivated Responding

In Study 1 we offered incentives to a random set of respondents to deter motivated responding. If estimations are distorted by motivated responding, they should be considerably different when incentives are given. They are not. Figure 4.1 shows that pooling across items, average perceptual bias in the incentives condition is roughly the same as in the standard condition. Furthermore, responses are distributed similarly in the two conditions.

Beliefs about Related Quantities

Even if these estimates capture genuine beliefs, they can still be difficult to interpret. Notably, without additional data, it is unclear whether the perceptions reflect beliefs about the composition of the subpopulation or perceptions of the group's share in the population. In Study 1 we measured beliefs about the share of party-stereotypical groups in the population. Respondents generally overestimate groups' base rates, especially for groups that compose a small share of the population. For example, gays, lesbians, and bisexuals are just 3.8% of the population but perceived at a mean estimate of 14.9%. Similarly, respondents on average estimate that those who earn more than $250,000 per year are 11.4% of the population (versus 2% in reality). People generally overestimate the share of these groups in the parties they "represent" more than their share in the overall population. These differences are significant for all eight party-group dyads except for the black-Democratic dyad. Like Wong (2007), we find that respondents greatly overestimate the share of African Americans in the U.S. population.

The difference between the extent to which people overestimate the share of party-stereotypical groups in their own parties and in the population can shed light on the extent to which party stereotypes are more influential than base rates in people's estimates. These difference-in-differences estimates are significantly positive, implying a larger role for party stereotypes, for five of the eight dyads; estimates are not significantly different from zero for the others.

In addition to these descriptive and observational analyses, we conducted an experiment in Study 1 to more cleanly estimate the extent to which beliefs about base rates explain beliefs about party composition. As we discuss above, we randomly assigned one group of respondents to answer the party-composition items with sliders anchored at the groups' base rates, informing respondents we had done so. As Figure 4.1 shows, reported perceptions became more biased, not less so. These results suggest that perceptions like these are driven by *representativeness*; people's focus on the idea that "like goes with like" leads them to ignore other pertinent information like base rates (Gilovich & Savitsky, 1996).

Lastly, asking people about their beliefs about base rates before asking about share of subgroups does not reduce bias. In Study 2 we randomly assigned half of respondents to report their beliefs about the percentage of Americans who drink diet soda (24% in reality) before eliciting their beliefs about the percentage of men (23%) and women (24%) who do so. Respondents in the "no base rate" condition significantly overestimated the gender gap in diet soda consumption, reporting that 46.2% of women drink diet soda compared to 30.0% of men. If anything, those who were first asked about the base rate (estimated on average as 41.0%) became less accurate; rather than altering their estimates about women (46.7%), they may have changed their beliefs about men's diet soda consumption (27.4%). This difference in the estimated gender gap fails to reach statistical significance at conventional levels (95% CI: [−1.0, 7.2]) but comports with the evidence from Study 1. Overall, priming or providing base rates has little effect on people's reported beliefs about subpopulation composition and may even make those reports more biased.

Conclusion

A variety of politically salient concerns are linked to misperceptions about the share of groups in the population or in various subpopulations. Nativist sentiment is associated with inaccurate beliefs about the share of immigrants in the population (Alba et al., 2005), antiwelfare attitudes are linked to misperceptions about the share of poor who are black (Gilens, 1996, 1999), and partisan antipathy to erroneous beliefs about the share of out-party supporters who belong to party-stereotypical groups (Ahler & Sood, forthcoming). These concerns take on additional heft given how often they are exploited in political campaigns. For instance, in 2016 both the "Brexit" referendum and Donald Trump's presidential campaign prominently highlighted claims about immigration levels.

These concerns, as well as the broader social scientific study of stereotyping (Bordalo et al., 2016), raise questions regarding valid measurement of perceptions of share of groups. This is vital not just for accurate description of people's perceptions but also for accurate estimates of the causes and consequences of misperceptions. In this chapter, our aim has been to describe and probe several of these unique concerns, suggest methods for gauging these concerns, and demonstrate the use of some of the tools.

Results from these experiments suggest that people carry cognitions about the share of some politically salient and stereotypical groups in the population and some subpopulations and that these beliefs can be reliably elicited by asking respondents to give numerical estimates of the share of these groups. In particular, the data suggest that commonly noted concerns like motivated responding, use of denominators larger than 100, and cheating—as well as less commonly noted concerns like considered responding—do not appear to significantly bias responses. Apparent effects may even be in the opposite direction than hypothesized in some cases. Providing groups' base rates made reported beliefs about those groups' shares in certain subpopulations slightly less accurate.

This conclusion, however, may not hold for items other than those discussed here. In particular, we have addressed items tapping prevalent group stereotypes, which we contend are more likely to give rise to crude but firm beliefs about the numerical strength of groups. Our claim is not that the concerns raised about these measures never apply; we cannot even confidently rule out all the concerns for all the measures presented here without collecting significant additional data. Instead, our purpose is to highlight and illustrate some of the inferential strategies researchers can use to assess the severity of the most pressing of these concerns in the data they collect.

Much of science reduces to measurement—of a phenomenon, its causes, and its consequences. And much of scientific progress has been built on improvements in measurement. We aim to highlight challenges and strategies in assessing misperceptions of group shares as well as to open a systematic conversation about how to best administer these novel and increasingly important survey measures. It is our hope that a better measurement machinery for assessing numerical perceptions of group strength will lead to progress in our understanding of how misperceptions can give rise to intergroup conflict.

References

Ahler, D. (2017, January). Online appendix for measuring perceptions of shares of groups. In D. Ahler & G. Sood, *Partisan perceptions dataverse* (Vanderbilt University and Florida State University), Harvard Dataverse, vol. 1. http://dx.doi.org/10.7910/DVN/2JXAYZ

Ahler, D. J., & Sood, G. (forthcoming). The parties in our heads: Misperceptions about party composition and their consequences. *The Journal of Politics*.

Alba, R., Rumbaut, R. G., & Marotz, K. (2005). A distorted nation: Perceptions of racial/ethnic group sizes and attitudes toward immigrants and other minorities. *Social Forces, 84*(2), 901–919.

Ansolabehere, S., Meredith, M., & Snowberg, E. (2013). Asking about numbers: Why and how. *Political Analysis, 21*(1), 48–69.

Barthel, M., Mitchell, A., & Holcomb, J. (2016). Many Americans believe fake news is sowing confusion. Pew Research Center. Retrieved from http://www.journalism.org/2016/12/15/many-americans-believe-fake-news-is-sowing-confusion

Berinsky, A. J., Huber, G. A., & Lenz, G. S. (2012). Evaluating online labor markets for experimental research: Amazon.com's Mechanical Turk. *Political Analysis, 20*(2), 351–368.

Blalock, H. M. (1967). *Toward a theory of minority-group relations*. New York, NY: Wiley.

Bordalo, P., Coman, K., Gennaioli, N., & Shleifer, A. (2016). "Stereotypes." *Quarterly Journal of Economics, 131*(4), 1753–1794.

Bullock, J. G., Gerber, A. S., Hill, S. J., & Huber, G. A. (2013). Partisan bias in factual beliefs about politics. NBER working paper no. 19080. Retrieved from http://www.nber.org/papers/w19080

Campbell, A., Converse, P. E., Miller, W. E., & Stokes, D. E. (1960). *The American voter*. Chicago, IL: University of Chicago Press.

Campbell, D. (1965). Ethnocentric and other altruistic motives. In D. Levine (Ed.), *Symposium on motivation* (pp. 283–311). Lincoln, NE: University of Nebraska Press.

Dancygier, R. M. (2010). *Immigration and conflict in Europe*. New York, NY: Cambridge University Press.

Delli Carpini, M. X., & Keeter, S. (1996). *What Americans know about politics and why it matters*. New York, NY: Yale University Press.

Freeder, S., Lenz, G., & Turney, S. (2016). What goes with what: Reinterpreting the evidence on attitude stability, policy voting, and multi-item issue scales [Working paper]. University of California, Berkeley.

Gennaioli, N., & Shleifer, A. (2010). What comes to mind. *Quarterly Journal of Economics, 125*(4), 1399–1433.

Gilens, M. (1996). Race and poverty in America: Public misperceptions and the American news media. *Public Opinion Quarterly, 60*(4), 515–541.

Gilens, M. (1999). *Why Americans hate welfare: Race, media, and the politics of antipoverty policy*. Chicago, IL: University of Chicago Press.

Gilovich, T., & Savitsky, K. (1996, March/April). Like goes with like: The role of representativeness in erroneous and pseudoscientific beliefs. *Skeptical Inquirer, 20*, 34–40.

Green, D., Palmquist, B., & Schickler, E. (2002). *Partisan hearts and minds: Political parties and the social identities of voters*. New Haven, CT: Yale University Press.

Jackson, B., & Jamieson, K. H. (2007). *UnSpun: Finding facts in a world of disinformation*. New York, NY: Random House.

Kahneman, D. (2011). *Thinking, fast and slow*. New York, NY: MacMillan.

Kahneman, D., & Frederick, S. (2002). Representativeness revisited: Attribute substitution in intuitive judgment. In T. Gilovich, D. Gri, & D. Kahneman (Eds.), *Heuristics of intuitive judgment: Extensions and applications* (pp. 49–81). New York, NY: Cambridge University Press.

Key, V. O. (1949). *Southern politics in state and nation*. New York, NY: Knopf.

Khanna, K., & Sood, G. (2015). Motivated learning or motivated responding? Using incentives to distinguish between the two processes. Paper presented at the annual meeting of the Midwest Political Science Association, San Francisco, CA.

Krogstad, J. M., & Passel, J. S. (2016). 5 facts about illegal immigration in the U.S. Pew Research Center. Retrieved from http://www.pewresearch.org/fact-tank/2015/11/19/5-facts-about-illegal-immigration-in-the-u-s

Lin, C. A. (1998). Uses of sex appeals in prime-time television commercials. *Sex Roles, 38*(5/6), 461–475.

Lippman, W. (1922). *Public opinion*. New Brunswick, NJ: Transaction Publishers.

Luskin, R. C,, Sood, G., & Blank, J. (2013). The waters of Casablanca: Political misinformation (and knowledge and ignorance). Paper presented at the annual meeting of the Midwest Political Science Association, Chicago, IL.

Mendes, E. (2013). Regular soda popular with young, nonwhite, low-income. Gallup. Retrieved from http://www.gallup.com/poll/163997/regular-soda-popular-young-nonwhite-low-income.aspx

Nadeau, R., Niemi, R. G., & Levine, J. (1993). Innumeracy about minority populations. *Public Opinion Quarterly, 57*(3), 332–347.

Petty, R., & Cacioppo, J. (1986). The elaboration likelihood model of persuasion. *Advances in Experimental Social Psychology, 19*, 123–181.

Prior, M., Sood, G., & Khanna, K. (2015). You cannot be serious: The impact of accuracy incentives on partisan bias in reports of economic perceptions. *Quarterly Journal of Political Science, 10*(4), 489–518.

Romer, D., Jamieson, K. H., & Aday, S. (2003). Television news and the cultivation of fear of crime. *Journal of Communication, 53*(1), 88–104.

Ruggiero, V. R. (2012). *Beyond feelings: A guide to critical thinking.* New York, NY: McGraw-Hill.

Sherif, M. (2015). *Group conflict and co-operation: Their social psychology.* New York, NY: Psychology Press.

Sides, J., & Citrin, J. (2007a). European opinion about immigration: The role of identities, interests and information. *British Journal of Political Science, 37*(03), 477–504.

Sides, J., & Citrin, J. (2007b, April). How large the huddled masses? The causes and consequences of public misperceptions about immigrant populations. Paper presented at the annual meeting of the Midwest Political Science Association, Chicago, IL.

Tajfel, H. (1970). Experiments in intergroup discrimination. *Scientific American, 223*(5), 96–102.

Tajfel, H., & Turner, J. C. (2004). The social identity theory of intergroup behavior. In J. Jost & J. Sidanius (Eds.), *Political psychology* (pp. 376–390). New York, NY: Psychology Press.

Thorson, E. A. (2014). Some of my best friends are poor? Income misperceptions and policy attitudes. Paper presented at the annual meeting of the American Political Science Association, Washington, DC.

Tversky, A., & Kahneman, D. (1973). Availability: A heuristic for judging frequency and probability. *Cognitive Psychology, 5*(2), 207–232.

Wong, C. J. (2007). Little and big pictures in our heads: Race, local context, and innumeracy about racial groups in the United States. *Public Opinion Quarterly, 71*(3), 392–412.

Wong, C., Bowers, J., Williams, T., & Simmons, K. D. (2012). Bringing the person back in: Boundaries, perceptions, and the measurement of racial context. *Journal of Politics, 74*(4), 1153–1170.

Yoder, J. D., Christopher, J., & Holmes, J. D. (2008). Are television commercials still achievement scripts for women? *Psychology of Women Quarterly, 32*(3), 303–311.

Dimensions of Visual Misinformation in the Emerging Media Landscape

FIVE

JEFF HEMSLEY AND JAIME SNYDER

W e live in a hybrid media landscape. Both new media like Twitter and Facebook and traditional media like BBC, CNN, and the *New York Times* form assemblages of actors that interact to create content and influence how it flows within and between different media platforms (Chadwick, 2013). The boundaries between mainstream media and social media have blurred. Social media, platforms that enable "people to connect, communicate, and collaborate" (Jue, Marr, & Kassotakis 2009, p. 44), have emerged as a space where individuals can engage in what Castells refers to as *mass self-communication* (2009, p. 55). This is the idea that social media users can broadcast content to their own audiences of social media users, those who opt to follow them or be their friends on platforms like Twitter and Facebook. A by-product of mass self-communication in social media is that through the collective sharing of many users, content can go viral (Nahon & Hemsley, 2013) and reach large audiences in an incredibly short time. The hybridity of the media space means that social media and mainstream media interact. That is, professional journalists sometimes break stories on social media (Vis, 2013), and news organizations both report social media events and occurrences and adapt and integrate social media practices (Chadwick, 2015). Conversely, social media content that goes viral often comprises "derivatives, responses, or copies of content generated by the mass-media producers" (Hemsley & Mason, 2013, p. 146).

The sharing and diffusion of images in social media is ubiquitous.

People share eyewitness photos in times of disaster as a kind of citizen journalism (Liu, Palen, Sutton, Hughes, & Vieweg, 2008); post images of themselves to construct and communicate identity (Nemer & Freeman, 2015; Sorokowska et al., 2016; Uimonen, 2013); and share photos and memes of police brutality (Nahon & Hemsley, 2013), user-generated artworks (Salah et al., 2012), and political humor in the form of photos and other images (Tay, 2015). Photos are the kind of image most frequently shared, but about 30% of images are other kinds of visual content, including graphics, screen captures, and mashups of photos, text, graphs, and other content (Thelwall et al., 2015). Researchers have found that the diffusion of photos is related to attracting new recruits to the Facebook pages of social movements (Gaby & Caren, 2012), and tweets with images are more likely to be retweeted on Twitter (Rogers, 2014). The importance of sharing images on social media cannot be overemphasized. Shared images in social media can be an impetus for users to form new social networks (Salah et al., 2012) and communities of practice (Herrema, 2011).

A growing body of research has focused on the diffusion of misinformation online, especially in social media contexts (Oyeyemi, Gabarron, & Wynn, 2014; Procter et al., 2011; Spiro et al., 2012; Starbird, Maddock, Orand, Achterman, & Mason, 2014) and includes research on *faked* images, such as photos that have been Photoshopped or real images with captions suggesting they are relevant in a current situation (Gupta, Lamba, Kumaraguru, & Joshi, 2013). Research and discussion concerning the sharing and diffusion of visual misinformation, particularly in the form of data or information visualization, however, are lacking. Thus, in this work we focus on the specific subset of images colloquially referred to as "data visualization," "information visualization," or "scientific visualization." We use the phrase "visual artifact" or simply "visualization" to refer to plots, charts, or other data graphics that "display measured quantities by means of the combined use of points, lines, a coordinate system, numbers, symbols, words, shading, and color" (Tufte, 2001, p. 9).

For the purpose of this discussion, "misinformation" simply refers to information that is factually incorrect (Bode & Vraga, 2015). As such, misinformation can lead to people holding misperceptions about the facts. We challenge the common view that instances of visual misinformation in media are solely the result of intentional deception. We argue that there are many ways the creation and dissemination of visual artifacts in our media environments can produce misinformation. We present a categorical schema of the ways visual artifacts contribute to misinformation, from intentional deception to naive interpretation. The framework we provide extends traditional approaches to visual media literacy and encourages new ways of thinking about misinformation and the basis of credibility. By articulating these dimensions of visual misinformation and showing how they interact with the current media landscape, this work contributes to the ways that researchers and policy makers can conceptualize visual misinformation.

The Construction of Credible Visual Artifacts

Our definition of misinformation describes instances in which information is deemed "objectively incorrect." Determining whether a data artifact such as a visualization meets this criterion requires an assignation of credibility, a process by which we ask, Can the image be trusted? Is this visualization true? According to Mathison (2009, p. 181), "The credibility of evidence, the knowledge it generates, is contingent on experience, perception, and social conventions" and is typically established through a combination of coherent presentation, a quality of authenticity and legitimacy, relevance to the viewer, and a sense that the information being represented is in its original context.

In the current data-driven media landscape, the process of evaluating the credibility of visualizations is complicated in a few ways. First, data-driven visual artifacts are being created by a wide range of individuals, including journalists, data scientists, graphic designers, activists, marketers, and consultants. The growing number of people making visualizations is a result of the increasing availability of information sources through open-data initiatives, commercial packaging of sophisticated digital visualization and design tools, and vast online social networks that connect previously siloed communities. Knowing who has created a visualization, including their affiliations and politics, can be a critical aspect of assessing credibility (Mathison, 2009). It can also be challenging, even impossible, to determine the source once an image has entered the social media stream, where it can be incorporated into mashups or framed for new audiences with accompanying text. Second, and related to the first, is the ease with which professional-looking graphics can be generated. The test of authenticity and legitimacy is often reduced to a question of aesthetics: If it looks legitimate (polished, refined, and aesthetically pleasing), then it must be credible (true, accurate, and trustworthy). Given the sophistication of automated tools like Piktochart, Tableau, and Microsoft

Excel, it is increasingly easy to generate a visualization that looks more credible than it actually is, particularly in terms of how well it represents the underlying data.

Third, the situation in which a visualization is viewed can vary greatly from the circumstances in which it was made. What a given visual artifact was intended to mean and what it means at any given moment are dependent on context. Bertin highlights the situated nature of meaning in visual artifacts, explaining, "A graphic is not 'drawn' once and for all; it is 'constructed' and reconstructed until it reveals all the relationships constituted by the interplay of the data. . . . To construct a useful graphic, we must know what has come before and what is going to follow" (1981, p. 16). Visual artifacts created for academic audiences as a means of supporting scientific claims are picked up and modified by journalists and bloggers to explain and communicate current events (e.g., Andrews, 2016). Infographics created by activists and campaign managers are circulated through social media networks as proof of claims against a political candidate or evidence of injustices perpetrated by institutional powers. According to Bertin, the provenance of a visualization and the process of its interpretation are significant aspects of its meaning.

In many ways these issues related to the evaluation of credibility stem from the vernacular aspects of the data visualization practices we are considering here (Viégas & Wattenberg, 2008). A critical aspect of vernacular visual practices is that they arise from lived experience rather than disciplinary expertise (Glassie, 2000; Hubka, 1979). In the context of popular data visualizations, this means that creators may or may not have training in data science, graphic design, visual communication, or programming. Kostelnick and Hassett (2003) point out that verbal language has rules of grammar that can perform a "gatekeeping function," enabling only those initiated in the code to gain access to the information being presented. However, in some contexts, visual design languages tend to be more open to perceptual engagement and individual interpretation, as seen in the widely diverse people who create and use them. When this openness is combined with vernacular conventions related to localized aesthetics and degrees of exposure to evidentiary practices, the process of interpretation and valuation that underlies any assessment of misinformation gets complicated.

In terms of evaluating the credibility, usefulness, robustness, and value of the resulting visual artifacts, we draw attention to the inherent tensions that arise when vernacular visualization design practices intersect with the relatively boundless world of social media. What happens when a scientific image created with the goal of comprehensive objectivity is edited in order to communicate more clearly to a lay audience? As with textual and numeric representations of evidence (Hilgartner, 1990), decisions are made to reduce, simplify, highlight, and transform. Are these mechanisms of misinformation? Or are they important steps in a vernacular design process? In order to unpack these questions, we look more closely at a set of potential mechanisms for misinformation in visual artifacts.

Mechanisms for Misinformation in Visual Artifacts

This discussion of the social construction of credibility hints at several different ways in which visual misinformation can manifest; many of these run counter to the idea that misrepresentation is always intentional. While misinformation can certainly be produced from intentional deception, visual misinformation can also stem from a misalignment between an author's and viewer's vernacular or from an ambiguous context for interpretation. Here we articulate a schema that captures five dimensions of visual misinformation in order to contribute to a growing conversation about the role of images on social media (e.g., Gupta et al., 2013; Tay, 2015; Thelwall et al., 2015) and opens the door for more specific research into the use and sharing of data visualization in our evolving media environment.

Intentional Deception

Purposefully misleading an audience about underlying data represented through a visualization can take a number of forms. Visualization designers typically make a series of decisions at the onset of a project that include how data will be presented and which data within a data set will be shown (Wainer, 2009). Intentionally selecting a visualization format that oversimplifies or overcomplicates relationships in data (Figure 5.1, items a and b), omitting relevant variables in order to bury confounding or contradictory correlations, inappropriately scaling an axis to over- or underemphasize relationships (Figure 5.1, items c and d), or knowingly manipulating data to make certain patterns appear more explicitly in a visualization are all ways in which designers can produce visual misinformation. These manipulations would be considered unethical by most people and if discovered would be met with disapproval.

In Figure 5.1 the example training plot shows a complicated mosaic plot

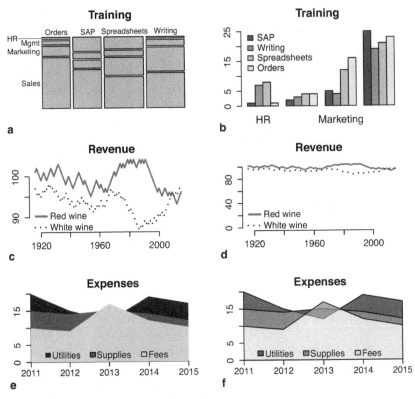

Figure 5.1. Examples of visual misinformation

in item a, while item b uses the same data in an easier-to-understand bar graph. Example revenue plot c shows inappropriate axis scaling that over-emphasizes the relationship, while item d uses the same data but shows the correct relationship. The expenses data plot in item e hides data points in 2013, but border lines and transparency fix this problem in item f. These are example plots only. They do not depict real data and ought not to be thought of as related to each other.

Technical Error

The multistep process of creating a data visualization is potentially complex. Errors can be introduced at any stage of this process, resulting in a visualization that misrepresents data. These errors can be technical or conceptual. They can result from improper data handling, software programming errors, or inappropriate choices regarding the means by which patterns and relationships are highlighted and represented through visual encoding (Fry, 2008).

For example, a typical data visualization process might be described as follows. Assuming the data already exist, the visualization process begins with preparing, or "cleaning," the data. Cleaning data may be as simple as removing nonvalues such as blank cells, NAs, and NULLs, but it might also require converting data types (e.g., text to numeric values), mathematically combining columns, filtering out categories, or other sophisticated statistical or computational manipulations. Once the data are clean, they may still need to be further processed before they can be represented visually. Frequencies, averages, or medians may need to be calculated within categories or time segments; outliers may need to be identified and included, excluded, or highlighted. Technical mistakes can be introduced at any point in the cleaning process; because this process is unique for every dataset, both novices and experts are prone to making errors, although the latter will typically catch and fix problems more quickly.

The next phase in creating a data graphic often involves selecting a type of visualization that fits the data. Errors can be introduced when visualization creators lack technical visual literacy skills or are unaware of the norms and practices of visualization. One might select a complicated mosaic plot, as in Figure 5.1 item a, when a bar graph like the one in item b would be more appropriate. Mosaic plots can be useful for understanding internal proportional relationships but can make other types of comparisons, such as comparing across instances, difficult and thus lead to misperceptions. Errors are also visible when a designer fails to address display issues such as occlusion, which occurs when graphic elements are layered on top of one another in ways that make it difficult to read a chart or graph or, worse, hide observations, resulting in skewed interpretation. The occlusion problem in Figure 5.1 item e is fixed in item f by making the colors somewhat transparent.

Although many of these steps can be supported by computational methods and tools such as R, Tableau, and D3, the output of these applications is only as good as the inputs. More egregious mistakes may be mitigated by the software responding with an error. For example, the statistical analysis and graphing application R will return an error message if a user attempts to use a visual format that does not match the underlying data structure. However, for intermediate-level visualization designers, their mistakes might not always be flagged by error messaging. Moreover, the use of sophisticated tools may imbue technically flawed representations of data with a professional sheen. Studies of fluency effects associated with visual attributes of information suggest it is possible that cognitive processing of such graphics potentially could be associated with tendencies to process information less critically (Alter & Oppenheimer, 2009; Marsh & Yang, this volume).

Viewing the range of technical errors that are possible throughout the data visualization process as an issue of literacy highlights the importance of training designers to be proficient in the basics of data science so that problems are noticed and corrected before graphics are disseminated. An approach to teaching people to see errors earlier and more clearly draws from Liu and Stasko's (2010) work on visual cognition processes, which looks at the interplay between internal cognitive models and external representations. Visualization experts often have a keen awareness of what a graphic *should* look like based on their understanding of the data; they have a strong mental model of data characteristics and patterns. For these individuals, unexpected results often signal possible errors. Training less experienced designers to perform this same type of mental modeling during the data cleaning and preparation phases could result in less error and more accurate visual representations.

Naive Interpretation

Bar charts, pie charts, and line graphs are familiar to many different audiences. Because of their prevalence, they can sometimes be considered uninteresting compared to more complicated-looking alternatives. Diagrams of complex systems such as the 3-D social network in Figure 5.2 can be interesting to look at and aesthetically appealing but extremely challenging to interpret. Extracting information from these types of sophisticated visualizations requires a degree of education in the field of network analysis. Absence of this training can lead to naive interpretations of the relationships being depicted, and those interpretations can be a source of misinformation. The use of complex visualizations in situations with a high likelihood of novice or uninitiated viewers does not reflect the same sort of ethical breach as an intentional misrepresentation of information. Both, however, start from a similar point in the design process. In the case of an overly complex visualization, a designer can avoid the risk of misinformation by considering the needs of his or her audience over aesthetic, theoretical, or technical considerations.

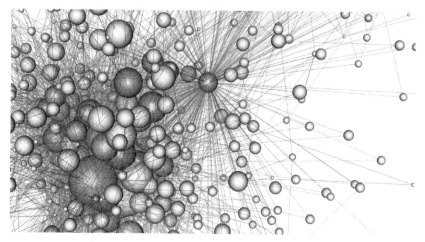

Figure 5.2. Social network and data art

Differences of Conventional Norms

On a related plane, in our discussion of vernacular difference among visualization audiences, another source of visual misinformation relates to the different interpretive and meaning-making conventions that are associated with specific communities of practice. Within the domain of data art (Figure 5.2), visualizations are created and evaluated based on a combination of aesthetic and technical criteria (Pearson, 2011) but are not expected to convey objective representations of information. They are intended to explore the material properties of data and be thought-provoking. On the other hand, scientific visualizations that can look remarkably similar to data art are expected to serve very different sense-making functions and are often evaluated using the criteria of objectivity, reliability, and accuracy. If data art is viewed as scientific evidence or vice versa, conclusions drawn from the visual representation might not be appropriate. In these cases, there is nothing inherently deceptive about the way a visualization is created or presented. The potential for misinformation comes from the perspective from which the viewer approaches the image. Closely associated with this is the context in which a data visualization is presented.

Figure 5.2 presents an example of both a 3-D social network and data art. This visualization depicts Twitter data related to the Occupy Wall Street movement in 2011. Each sphere represents a person, and the links are cases of one person retweeting another. Spheres are darker for users with more followers and sized by how many times that user is retweeted during the movement.

Context of Presentation

Another dimension of potential visual misinformation stems, again, not from the data visualization itself but from the context in which the visualization is presented. The location in which an image is encountered can influence how it is interpreted and how its credibility is assessed. Established news outlets, Twitter accounts, or blogs might lend credibility to a visualization that would otherwise be seen as questionable. This is in part due to assumptions we make about the vetting or review of material that gets posted to these venues. However, in both academic and popular media, visualizations do not always receive the same scrutiny or rigorous review as text-based information (Carpendale, 2008). Further, when a visualization that was generated for a professional publication is adjusted or simplified for a more general media outlet, the changes that are made could introduce elements of misinformation, even though they are possibly intended only to help the visualization communicate to a broader audience or are rendered with the goal of producing a unique or more technically or aesthetically compatible version. Audiences accustomed to seeing simplified information graphics might not think to question the visualization in ways that a professional audience would. In these ways, the context in which the visualization is presented can contribute to an instance of misinformation.

We can group these five dimensions of visual misinformation into two temporal groups: at conception, which includes *intentional deception* and *technical error*, and at interpretation, which includes *naive interpretation*, *differences of conventional norms*, and *context of presentation*. At the conception stage, creators of visual artifacts have a certain level of control over establishing the appearance of credibility. They do this through a combination of design elements, such as a coherent presentation, image quality that promotes a sense of authenticity and legitimacy, relevance to the viewer, and context. For visualization artifacts, context may include text that specifies the source of the data and the creator of the image. Assuming the creator has created an artifact that faithfully represents the data and is error-free, users may still become misinformed during their interpretation of the visualization.

The Spread of Visual Misinformation

Upon posting a visual artifact to a social media site, the author has little control over who sees it. Even when an image is posted with restrictions, the content can be copied and reposted where it may spread; Nahon and Hemsley (2013), for example, discuss Alexandra Wallace, a university student who was asked to leave UCLA after she posted a racist rant video that went viral. Certainly most content that is posted to the web remains obscure (Nahon & Hemsley, 2013), but when visual artifacts do spread, the eventual audience emerges along and around the path of sharing. Individuals exposed to the artifact may opt to share the visualization with their own audiences of followers, any of these followers may again share the artifact with their followers, and so on. The result is that it is possible for the artifact to spread along any number of paths to audiences in different geographic locations with varying levels of education and embedded in diverse cultures. Each of these paths creates a distinct context for credibility.

As users share content they have discovered online, they "can be idiosyncratic, creative, and even resistant" (Kozinets, De Valck, Wojnicki, & Wilner, 2010, p. 73) to that content. They can alter the content in subtle and unsubtle ways such that they are coproducers of the meaning of the artifact for the next generation of audiences who encounter the visualization. There are four ways that users can alter the meaning of content for their audiences: repost as is, include their own text with the repost, alter the artifact and repost it, and repost the content to a different channel where the new context may alter the meaning. Users are influenced in their decision to consume and repost content by who posted it (Huberman & Adamic 2004; Kwak, Lee, Park, & Moon, 2010). This suggests that when some users share content, it can be judged as being more credible than when other users share the same content. Users might think that if someone they admired posted a visualization, it must be relevant or important. Even when users repost a visualization as is, they can lend or detract from an artifact's credibility. We can even refer to some influential users as *opinion leaders* (Katz & Lazarsfeld, 1955). These are active media consumers who interpret the meaning of content for those who are less active consumers. To do this, they may include their own narratives as text posted with the artifacts, or as text or other material posted independently but with a pointer—such as a link—to an artifact. When users include text, their own narration can *frame* an artifact or *prime* the audience (Scheufele & Tewksbury, 2007). The text thus can influence how the audience will interpret the artifact by, for example, putting it in a positive or negative light or providing a point of reference for the audience. Such a point of reference can contextualize the artifact in ways the original author may not have intended. Finally, users can use tools like Photoshop to alter an image and then repost it. In doing so, they may be mixing the artifact with a photo, adding text, or fundamentally altering a graph or plot. The result may be entirely different from what the author intended.

From the discussion above, it should be clear that even when an author creates a visualization that accurately reflects the data and is error-free, the audience itself can alter the meaning and introduce misinformation for downstream audiences. The result can be a bit like the telephone game, in which a group of people sit in a ring and someone whispers a message to their neighbor, who passes the message on to the next person. By the time the message has made its way around the circle, it can be quite different from the original message. Because viral information often crosses educational, geographic, and cultural boundaries, audiences can become misinformed due to differences in conventions and norms. Misinformation can be generated by subtle differences of interpretation, micro-alterations due to being reposted on different platforms, larger intentional edits, or sedimentation, erosion, or reformulation of subtle contextual cues. Understanding the spread of visual misinformation across a social media context involves developing awareness of the ways in which these mechanisms of credibility interact.

Implications and Conclusion

Kirby and Marsden (2006) suggest that what spreads online is what is remarkable; the content must be worth talking about or remarking on. People share things online to start or be part of a conversation (boyd, Golder, & Lotan, 2010). Visual artifacts that spread online are one part of an audience-constructed conversation. Different audiences may have different conversations centered on the same artifact; unlike our telephone game example in which the message moves in a circle, content online can spread more like the branches of a tree. The artifact starts its journey at the trunk but may travel through entirely different branches, each of which may branch again many times. An artifact, then, can be a central part of many conversations, any or all of which may misinform to different degrees and in different ways. Indeed, it seems likely that at least some misinformation will be introduced when a visual artifact spreads widely.

As a starting point for establishing an empirically based understanding of the mechanics of visual misinformation across different communities of practice, we proposed an analytic matrix pairing the dimension of visual misinformation (intentional deception, technical error, naive interpretation, differences of conventional norms, and context of presentation) with Mathison's (2009) factors of credibility (coherent presentation, quality of authenticity and legitimacy, relevance to the viewer, and original context). This framework enables source, context, and content to be considered when mapping the locus and trajectories of visual misinformation. It can help us discern whether certain groups are more prone to relying on context of presentation to determine authenticity and legitimacy, or whether visualizations designed and built using a specific type of software are more likely to be considered credible. The matrix can be useful in detecting rhythms or patterns to the interpretive framing that people bring to data visualizations; an example is whether in a time of crisis or upheaval people are more likely to turn to scientific or pseudo-scientific images to justify, explain, or calm their fears. The multidimensional matrix presented here has the ability to draw relationships across dimensions of misinformation and factors of credibility in terms of specific communities of practice and in relation to how specific artifacts are shared. As an analytical tool, this is especially valuable for social media contexts where the rapid and decentralized dissemination of information produces complex issues around context, authorship, and provenance.

We have argued that in our current media environment, one cannot assume that visual misinformation is solely the result of intentional deception. Our framework includes a categorical schema of different sources of misinformation and provides a matrix that we expect will be useful in analyzing empirical data. The framework extends visual media literacy and encourages new ways of thinking about misinformation as it relates to factors of credibility. We expect that studies done with this framework could provide the basis for visual literacy interventions and education based on empirical data. The framework can also be useful for examining how different dimensions of visual misinformation are more or less likely to spread.

References

Alter, A. L., & Oppenheimer, D. M. (2009). Uniting the tribes of fluency to form a meta-cognitive nation. *Personality and Social Psychology Review, 13*(3), 219–235.

Andrews, R. (2016). Deep ancient water is stopping the Antarctic Ocean from warming. IFL Science. Retrieved from http://www.iflscience.com/environment/deep-ancient-water-stopping-antarctic-ocean-warming.

Bertin, J. (1981). *Graphics and graphic information processing.* (W. J. Berg & P. Scott, Trans.). New York, NY: Walter de Gruyter.

Bode, L., & Vraga, E. K. (2015). In related news, that was wrong: The correction of misinformation through related stories functionality in social media. *Journal of Communication, 65*(4), 619–638.

boyd, d., Golder, S., & Lotan, G. (2010). Tweet, tweet, retweet: Conversational aspects of retweeting on Twitter. In R. H. Sprague Jr. (Ed.), *HICSS-43 Proceedings of the 43nd Hawaii International Conference on System Sciences* (pp. 1–10). Los Alamitos, CA: IEEE Computer Society.

Carpendale, S. (2008). Evaluating information visualizations. In A. Kerren, J. T. Stasko, J-D. Fekete, & C. North (Eds.), *Information visualization: Human-centered issues and perspectives* (pp. 19–45). Berlin, Germany: Springer.

Castells, M. (2009). *Communication power.* New York, NY: Oxford University Press.

Chadwick, A. (2013). *The hybrid media system: Politics and power.* New York, NY: Oxford University Press.

Chadwick, A. (2015). The "social media" maneuver. *Social Media + Society.* Retrieved from http://journals.sagepub.com/doi/10.1177/2056305115578133.

Fry, B. (2008). *Visualizing data: Exploring and explaining data with the Processing Environment.* Sebastopol, CA: O'Reilly.

Gaby, S., & Caren, N. (2012). Occupy online: How cute old men and Malcolm X recruited 400,000 US users to OWS on Facebook. *Social Movement Studies, 11*(3–4), 367–374.

Glassie, H. (2000). *Vernacular architecture.* Bloomington: Indiana University Press.

Gupta, A., Lamba, H., Kumaraguru, P., & Joshi, A. (2013). Faking Sandy: Characterizing and identifying fake images on Twitter during Hurricane Sandy. In *WWW'13 Companion Proceedings of the 22nd International Conference on World Wide Web* (pp. 729–736). New York, NY: Association for Computing Machinery.

Hemsley, J., & Mason, R. M. (2013). Knowledge and knowledge management in the social media age. *Journal of Organizational Computing and Electronic Commerce, 23*(1–2), 138–167.

Herrema, R. (2011). Flickr, communities of practice, and the boundaries of identity: A musician goes visual. *Visual Studies, 26*(2), 135–141.

Hilgartner, S. (1990). The dominant view of popularization: Conceptual problems, political uses. *Social Studies of Science, 20*(3), 519–539.

Huberman, B., & Adamic, L. (2004). Information dynamics in the networked world. *Lecture Notes in Physics, 650 (Complex Networks)*, 371–398.

Hubka, T. (1979). Just folks designing: Vernacular designers and the generation of form. *Journal of Architectural Education, 32*(3) 27–29.

Jue, A. L., Marr, J. A., & Kassotakis, M. E. (2009). *Social media at work: How networking tools propel organizational performance.* San Francisco, CA: Jossey-Bass.

Katz, E., & Lazarsfeld, P. (1955). *Personal influence: The part played by people in the flow of mass communications.* New York, NY: Free Press.

Kirby, J., & Marsden, P. (2006). *Connected marketing.* New York, NY: Routledge.

Kostelnick, C., & Hassett, M. (2003). *Shaping information: The rhetoric of visual conventions.* Carbondale, IL: Southern Illinois University Press.

Kozinets, R. V., De Valck, K., Wojnicki, A. C., & Wilner, S. J. (2010). Networked narratives: Understanding word-of-mouth marketing in online communities. *Journal of Marketing, 74*(2), 71–89.

Kwak, H., Lee, C., Park, H., & Moon, S. (2010). What is Twitter, a social network or a news media? In *WWW'10 Proceedings of the 19th International Conference on World Wide Web* (pp. 591–600). New York, NY: Association for Computing Machinery.

Liu, S. B., Palen, L., Sutton, J., Hughes, A. L., & Vieweg, S. (2008). In search of the bigger picture: The emergent role of on-line photo sharing in times of disaster. In F. Fiedrich & B. Van de Walle (Eds.), *Proceedings of ISCRAM 2008—5th International Conference on Information Systems for Crisis Response and Management.* Information Systems for Crisis Response and Management.

Liu, Z., & Stasko, J. T. (2010). Mental models, visual reasoning, and interaction in information visualization: A top-down perspective. *IEEE Transactions on Visualization and Computer Graphics, 16*(6), 999–1008.

Mathison, S. (2009). Seeing is believing: The credibility of image-based research and evaluation. In S. I. Donaldon, C. A. Christie, & M. M. Mark (Eds.), *What counts as credible evidence in applied research and evaluation practice?* (pp. 181–196). London, England: Sage.

Nahon, K., & Hemsley, J. (2013). *Going viral.* Cambridge, England: Polity Press.

Nemer, D., & Freeman, G. (2015). Empowering the marginalized: Rethinking selfies in the slums of Brazil. *International Journal of Communication, 9*, 1832–1847.

Oyeyemi, S. O., Gabarron, E., & Wynn, R. (2014). Ebola, Twitter, and misinformation: A dangerous combination? *BMJ, 349*, g6178.

Pearson, M. (2011). *Generative art.* Greenwich, CT: Manning.

Procter, R., Vis, F., Voss, A., Cantijoch, M., Manykhina, Y., Thelwall, M., . . . Gray, S. (2011, December 7). Riot rumours: How misinformation spread on Twitter during a time of crisis. *Guardian.* Retrieved from http://www.guardian.co.uk/uk/interactive/2011/dec/07/london-Riots-Twitter.

Rogers, S. (2014, March 10). What fuels a tweet's engagement? [Blog post]. Twitter. Retrieved from https://blog.twitter.com/2014/what-fuels-a-tweets-engagement.

Salah, Almila A., Salah, Alberto A., Buter, B., Dijkshoorn, N., Modolo, D., Nguyen, Q., . . . van de Poel, B. (2012). DeviantArt in spotlight: A network of artists. *Leonardo, 45*(5), 486–487.

Scheufele, D. A., & Tewksbury, D. (2007). Framing, agenda setting, and priming: The evolution of three media effects models. *Journal of Communication, 57*(1), 9–20.

Sorokowska, A., Oleszkiewicz, A., Frackowiak, T., Pisanski, K., Chmiel, A., & Sorokowski, P. (2016). Selfies and personality: Who posts self-portrait photographs? *Personality and Individual Differences, 90*, 119–123.

Spiro, E. S., Fitzhugh, S., Sutton, J., Pierski, N., Greczek, M., & Butts, C. T. (2012). Rumoring during extreme events: A case study of Deepwater Horizon 2010. In *WebSci '12 Proceedings of the 4th Annual ACM Web Science Conference* (pp. 275–283). New York, NY: Association for Computing Machinery.

Starbird, K., Maddock, J., Orand, M., Achterman, P., & Mason, R. M. (2014). Rumors, false flags, and digital vigilantes: Misinformation on Twitter after the 2013 Boston marathon bombing. In M. Kindling & E. Greifeneder (Eds.), *iConference 2014 Proceedings* (pp. 654–662). iSchools.

Tay, G. (2015). Binders full of LOLitics: Political humour, Internet memes, and play in the 2012 US presidential election (and beyond). *European Journal of Humour Research, 2*, 46–73.

Thelwall, M., Goriunova, O., Vis, F., Faulkner, S., Burns, A., Aulich, J., . . . D'Orazio, F. (2015). Chatting through pictures? A classification of images tweeted in one week in the UK and USA. *Journal of the Association for Information Science and Technology, 67*(11), 2575–2586.

Tufte, E. (2001). *The visual display of quantitative information*. Cheshire, CT: Graphics Press.

Uimonen, P. (2013). Visual identity in Facebook. *Visual Studies, 28*(2), 122–135.

Viégas, F. B., & Wattenberg, M. (2008). Timelines, tag clouds, and the case for vernacular visualization. *Interactions, 15*(4), 49–52.

Vis, F. (2013). Twitter as a reporting tool for breaking news: Journalists tweeting the 2011 UK riots. *Digital Journalism, 1*(1), 27–47.

Wainer, H. (2009). *Picturing the uncertain world: How to understand, communicate, and control uncertainty through graphical display*. Princeton, NJ: Princeton University Press.

PART II

Theoretical Effects and Consequences of Misinformation

The Effects of False Information in News Stories

SIX

MELANIE C. GREEN AND JOHN K. DONAHUE

ndividuals rely on news sources for help in understanding current events and making decisions about policies and leaders. An informed citizenry is an important underpinning of democracy. However, sometimes authors of news reports and other forms of communication provide misinformation—incorrect or misleading statements presented as facts. Often, this misinformation is unintentional, but in some cases, the authors intend to deceive either for their own personal benefit or to achieve some other outcome. In either case, damage can occur. The public may form opinions based on the incorrect information, and policy makers may take actions that they might have otherwise avoided. Even if misinformation is discovered and publicized, it is often difficult to correct a wrong idea in the minds of news consumers.

In this chapter, we consider the distinctions between different types of misinformation and examine the psychological processes that make the acceptance of misinformation likely and the correction of misinformation more difficult. When considering the types of misinformation that come from news stories, a formal distinction should be made. Some instances involve unintentional misinformation on the part of the reporter, while other instances happen when the reporter intentionally promotes misinformation. Misinformation that is embedded in a narrative or story may be particularly likely to be retained by news consumers.

Unintentional Misinformation

In the case of unintentional misinformation, errors may occur due to insufficient fact checking or hasty reporting as a result of a desire to get breaking news to audiences quickly. When such errors involve minor details, they may be quickly corrected without consequences, but sometimes these mistakes are significant, such as when reporting the motivations or identities of perpetrators of crimes. The effects of such errors may be magnified if the erroneous reporting is picked up by other media outlets.

Furthermore, sometimes reporters file inaccurate stories because their sources were misinformed or because the sources were lying to them. The *New York Times* relied upon unnamed sources when it broke the story that Hillary Clinton was the direct target of a criminal investigation by two federal inspectors general regarding her use of emails when she was secretary of state (Rieder, 2016). Later, it was revealed that the investigation was not directly aimed at her, and it was not a criminal investigation (Rieder, 2016). Another *Times* story implicitly asked how the government could have missed the fact that, according to unnamed sources, Tashfeen Malik, who engaged in a mass shooting in San Bernadino with her husband, was going to commit a horrendous crime when she had "talked openly on social media" of supporting religious-based violence. Yet, Malik had only expressed her opinions on a private dating site and in emails (Rieder, 2016).

Among stories containing misinformation that had the greatest consequences for America were those filed by *Times* reporter Judith Miller. As part of a series of articles, she cited sources that claimed Iraq had biological and chemical weapons and possibly even nuclear weapons (Miller, 2015). In a strange turnabout, it was the Bush administration that provided her with the sources' testimonies, including that of a former Iraqi chemical engineer (Miller, 2015). Then Miller's articles were cited by administration officials as one of the reasons to go to war with Iraq (Miller, 2015). Eight years after the Iraq War began, the chemical engineer Rafid al-Janabi, code-named Curveball, publicly admitted that he had lied about an Iraqi weapons of mass destruction program (Kinchen, 2011). Janabi stated that he hated Saddam Hussein and in the buildup to the war he saw his chance to have Saddam Hussein removed (Kinchen, 2011). In a review of Judith Miller's book about her perception of her role in the war, the writer says, "She acknowledges being wrong, but not making any mistakes" (McDermott, 2015, p. 6).

Commodity Theory and Unintentional Misinformation

Why might a reporter unintentionally make a mistake in reporting a story? The sources might be misleading him or her, sending up a trial balloon, or perhaps getting back at a perceived enemy. Yet, what psychological factors might be at work, separate from these more practical concerns? Commodity theory, a concept that comes from psychology, may help shed some light. The central premise of commodity theory is that the less available a commodity is, the more it will be sought (Brock, 1968). A commodity is defined as anything useful to the possessor, such as an object or a communication (Brock, 1968). Commodity theory is a series of hypotheses grouped within the categories of scarcity, effort, restriction, and delay (Brock, 1968).

Scarcity is divided into two hypotheses. The first is that desirability for the commodity increases as the perceived number of corecipients declines relative to the potential number of corecipients. Since a communication is considered a commodity, if reporters have a source they trust, the source's desirability should increase if many other reporters want but did not actually have that source. The second hypothesis stemming from scarcity is that the effectiveness of a message will increase as the recipients perceive that few other communicators exist who might deliver the same message (Brock, 1968). In the case of the *New York Times* reporter Judith Miller and the erroneous articles about weapons of mass destruction, she may have valued the messages that Curveball was relaying because there were very few other former Iraqis who would have had any knowledge about Saddam Hussein's weapons program.

Brock's commodity theory also has a component of effort, with one hypothesis being that "a message will increase in effectiveness the greater the perceived effort involved for the communicator, either to conceal the information or to transmit it" (Brock, 1968, p. 249). Judith Miller understood the serious situation for Curveball, compared to more typical unnamed sources on whom the *New York Times* relied, if he had been discovered by the Iraqis talking to German and American intelligence agencies. For this reason, his communication would seem more desirable.

Commodity theory (Brock, 1968) also has the component of restriction, which in part is that a message will increase in effectiveness relative to the quantity of accompanying reasons opposing its disclosure. The fact that the information coming from Curveball might be a significant reason for America going to war with another country should have increased the effectiveness of his communications. Knowing that many politicians, activists, and citizens in general would oppose going to war and any arguments made for that course of action, *New York Times* editors might have actually been more likely to value what Curveball said.

Lastly, the delay hypothesis states that a commodity will increase in desirability the greater the delay in obtaining it. According to Brock (1968, p. 250), "Delay is a further means of conveying unavailableness." This element of commodity theory is applicable to any instance of news reporters relying upon sources, whether the sources are reliable or unreliable. If a reporter has to wait to get the message he or she wants, according to commodity theory this should increase the desirability of that message.

Intentional Misinformation

Another type of misinformation occurs when a news reporter or author intentionally reports false information. In 2004 the chief political correspondent for Fox News posted quotes on the channel's website attributed to John Kerry (Rich, 2004). With a degree of heightened scrutiny that might be expected during an election year, the quotes were noticed and demonstrated to be false (Rich, 2004).

Misinformation may be created for political gain, such as a partisan website creating a false story or rumor about a political opponent, but misinformation can also be propagated for financial gain. Individuals can gain advertising revenues when individuals view particular websites, and so some forms of misinformation have been used to drive web traffic and thus increase profits. A particularly striking case of this type of misinformation emerged during the 2016 U.S. presidential election campaign. Young people in Macedonia created a hub of websites promoting candidate Donald Trump that frequently reported false information, which was then widely shared. According to interviews with the Macedonians, their motivation was to earn money rather than to influence electoral outcomes (Silverman & Alexander, 2016).

In addition to false news stories, purveyors of misinformation have now even gone so far as to create entirely fake news websites. Such websites may have names similar to real news organizations—the made-up "Denver Guardian," for example—but are not real journalistic outlets (Sydell, 2016). These websites may have political goals or may be ways for their proprietors to make money.

One journalist who received widespread attention for his acts of intentional misinformation was *New York Times* reporter Jayson Blair. After he was caught in 2003, the *Times* summarized his actions, such as ostensibly reporting from locations in "Maryland, Texas, and other states, when often he was far away, in New York. He fabricated comments. He concocted scenes. He lifted material from other newspapers and wire services. He selected details from photographs to create the impression he had been somewhere or seen someone, when he had not" (Calame, 2006, p. 12). Similarly, Stephen Glass, a writer for the *New Republic*, was found to have fabricated multiple stories. The motivation for Jayson Blair's and Stephen Glass's lying may be hard to know for certain, but some writers who provide intentional misinformation appear to be motivated by the desire for fame, status, money, or other personal rewards. A more intriguing question is, what sort of effect do these stories continue to have when readers are told afterward that the writer intentionally misinformed them? Would it have changed readers' attitudes about the content of the fabricated stories, knowing that a reporter had lied? We address this issue below, in the section on motivation to correct.

Another form of misinformation occurs when individuals publish nonfiction books, including autobiographies, that state false information. Jonathan Frey's best-selling book about drug addiction, *A Million Little Pieces* (2003), contained stories of events that he later admitted had never occurred. Similarly, the bestseller *Three Cups of Tea* (Mortenson & Relin, 2007), about Greg Mortenson's efforts to build schools in Afghanistan, has come under criticism both for reporting false information (perhaps most importantly, claiming to build schools that apparently do not exist) and for using these false claims to raise money (Krakauer, 2011).

The creation of intentional misinformation is not limited to journalism; the scientific community likewise has experienced cases of falsified scientific publications in fields from psychology to medicine. Problems with these papers have included alterations to the data or, in extreme cases, the reporting of studies that were never actually conducted. Typically such papers are retracted once the deception is discovered. However, the retraction notices are not always effective; such papers often continue to be cited in the popular press and by other scientists who may be unaware of the retraction (Bornemann-Cimenti, Szilagyi, & Sandner-Kiesling, 2016; Sheble, this volume).

Misinformation Acceptance: Psychological Processes

Although individuals may react very differently to the purveyors of intentional versus unintentional misinformation (a careless or misinformed journalist is more easily forgiven than a liar), the mental processes that occur when individuals encounter such information are often similar. Evidence from cognitive psychology, social psychology, and communication research provides insights into how individuals fall prey to misinformation and why this mistaken knowledge is difficult to correct.

False Facts from Fiction

Studies in cognitive psychology suggest that individuals can gain both true and false knowledge from stories, even those explicitly labeled as fiction (Fazio, Dolan, & Marsh, 2015; Fazio & Marsh, 2008; Marsh & Fazio, 2006; Marsh, Meade, & Roediger, 2003; Marsh & Yang, this volume; Prentice, Gerrig, & Bailis, 1997; Wheeler, Green, & Brock, 1999). This body of research has focused on general knowledge, such as the capitals of countries and historical facts, and has shown that individuals rely on information presented in stories even when instructed to correct it for possible misinformation. A key message from this research is the difficulty individuals have in identifying and correcting the information. Warning individuals that the texts may contain errors is not sufficient to reduce their reliance on misinformation, even when they are reading relatively easy texts (Marsh & Fazio, 2006).

Perhaps most striking in this paradigm is that calling attention to possible errors can even have the ironic effect of increasing the use of misinformation (Eslick, Fazio, & Marsh, 2011). In one study (Fazio & Marsh, 2008), researchers highlighted information that might be erroneous in red font, but this information was more—not less—likely to be given as an answer in a later general knowledge test. Similarly, slowing down the presentation of the information increased rather than decreased errors.

What worked? Having individuals mark whether each sentence contained an error reduced suggestibility and the illusion of knowledge (Fazio & Marsh, 2008). Readers appear to have a strong tendency to passively accept the information they read. Strong reminders and active participation in monitoring for errors are needed to overcome this natural acceptance of the text. Unfortunately, such strategies are likely to be difficult or impractical to institute in everyday life; most readers are not going to approach every article or website with a pen in hand, ready to find an error!

Belief Perseverance

A long tradition of research on belief perseverance suggests that individuals frequently retain newly created beliefs even after learning that the information on which those beliefs were based was incorrect. Belief perseverance is particularly likely to occur if individuals have integrated those beliefs into their knowledge structures (Anderson, Lepper, & Ross, 1980; Gilbert, Taforadi, & Malone, 1993; Johnson & Seifert, 1994; Loftus, 1979; Schul & Burnstein, 1985; Skurnik, Yoon, Park, & Schwarz, 2005; Wegner, Coulton, & Wenzlaff, 1985; Wyer & Unverzagt, 1985). That is, typically, individuals not only have learned a piece of information but also may have engaged in elaboration; perhaps they linked the new information to facts they already knew, or they constructed mental models so the new information would make sense as part of their worldviews. Dismantling this network of thoughts is more challenging than simply rejecting a single bit of information, particularly as individuals may not be consciously aware of the extent to which they have integrated a piece of information into their cognitive networks.

Indeed, in the case of political misinformation, individuals may already have well-developed mental models based on their political party affiliations or ideological beliefs. Information consistent with those existing mental models may be readily accepted and difficult to correct.

Narratives

Due to their cause-and-effect structure and potential for deep imaginative engagement, narratives may be a particularly effective way of creating a cognitive network of information. Journalistic information is often presented in a narrative or story form. Narrative has been defined as "a representation of connected events and characters that has an identifiable structure [and] is bounded in space and time" (Kreuter et al., 2007, p. 4); narratives also have been described as "knowledge structures that consist of a sequence of thematically and temporally related events" (Adaval & Wyer, 1998, p. 208). Narratives are a frequent vehicle for misinformation; Lewandowsky and colleagues give examples ranging from personal stories told by parents who believe their child has been harmed by a vaccine to Michael Crichton's novel *State of Fear*, which depicts the state of climate science in a way that is inconsistent with scientific facts (Lewandowsky, Ecker, Seifert, Schwarz, & Cook, 2012).

Information presented in the form of a narrative may be especially likely to lead to belief perseverance. There are several reasons narratives may have these effects. First, narratives are particularly powerful when they create a feeling of being immersed in or transported into the narrative world (Green & Brock, 2000, 2002). In this state, readers' imaginative resources have them feeling removed from their surroundings and completely engaged in the world created by the author. Being transported into a narrative world can have both emotional and persuasive consequences; it inhibits counterarguing and epistemic monitoring, paying attention to the truth status of a narrative (Green & Brock, 2000; Richter, Schroeder, & Wohrmann, 2009; Slater & Rouner, 2002).

Interestingly, the effects of being transported may depend on the type of information conveyed in a story. Research in the "false facts" paradigm, which focuses on tests of specific pieces of general knowledge, finds that transportation is not related to suggestibility (Fazio, Dolan, & Marsh, 2015). However, studies in which attitude-relevant information is conveyed as part of the plot typically do show effects of transportation (see van Laer, de Ruyter, Visconti, & Wetzels, 2014, for a review).

Next, narratives present information in a causal structure (Dahlstrom, 2010) that may be more likely to be retained (Anderson, 1983; Johnson & Seifert, 1994) and encourage integrative processing, which increases the difficulty of correction (Schul & Burnstein, 1985). Furthermore, when a reader discovers that a narrative is false, it may be difficult for him or her to generate an alternative true scenario. People may hear that the description of drug treatment centers in a story they read was incorrect, but they still may not know what actual drug treatment centers are like. Correction is more likely to be successful when a clear alternative exists; the opposite of "he built schools" is "he did not build schools."

Motivation to Correct

Individuals are not always equally likely to try to correct their false beliefs. However, even when individuals are motivated to correct misinformation, they may be unable to do so (Wilson & Brekke, 1994). In one study, we tested moral motivations for belief correction (Green & Donahue, 2011).

Specifically, we provided readers with a journalistic short story. The story we used was a slightly edited version of "Jimmy's World," a Pulitzer Prize–winning story by Janet Cooke (1980) about an eight-year-old heroin addict that was later found to be falsified; Jimmy did not exist (Maraniss, 1981). In some conditions, participants were told after they read the story that it was inaccurate. We varied whether the misinformation was described as intentional (the author made up the story to gain money and fame) or unintentional (a mix-up during the publishing process introduced errors). Readers showed narrative-based attitude changes even when they were informed that the story was intentionally inaccurate. Individuals derogated the deceptive author but were still affected by the story messages. An informal analysis of "false notes" that participants identified in the story suggests that participants may not have been able to figure out which parts of the story were deceptive. Thus, the correction task may have been especially challenging because individuals did not know exactly which story elements or implied beliefs were in error.

In a follow-up study, we extended these effects to examine deceptive narrative advertising (Green & Donahue, 2015). Intentional misinformation by reporters can be analogized to deceptive advertising practices. Many advertising companies and marketing departments of businesses have included fabricated elements in their work (Armstrong, Gurol, & Russ, 1979). The consequences for reporting inaccurate information can lead to public relations problems or even investigations by the government (Adita, 2001). One way that advertisers have been creative in promoting awareness and building an image for a product is by making an ad resemble a news item or documentary in order to increase credibility (Adita, 2001).

In the experiment we conducted (Green and Donahue, 2015), the central issue was whether any backlash readers have toward a business's deceptive marketing department would extend to evaluations of the product being advertised or willingness to purchase the product. The narrative ad used in the experiment was about backpacks made from recycled materials, and the ad was mostly written in a documentary style about the company's founder. We hypothesized that since the advertisement was written in a narrative format, readers might be transported by the story within the ad. This sense of transportation might overcome any objections readers had about purchasing the product, even for those who were told after reading the ad that it was in fact deceptive.

We found that, compared to a control group that was not informed of any deception, participants who were told after having read the ad that the ad was deceptive disparaged the founder of the company and the marketing department that created the advertisement. However, both groups of participants had similar responses in their willingness to buy the product and their evaluations of it. The presence of deception created unfavorable attitudes toward the deceivers, but this motivation did not extend to rejecting the primary message about the product.

Similarly, Appel and Malečkar (2012) demonstrate that even stories labeled as fake can be persuasive. Individuals rated stories labeled "fake" as very low in usefulness and trustworthiness, yet in an experiment, even individuals reading a story labeled as fake showed belief change relative to a control group. This effect was reduced among individuals who were high in need for cognition (enjoyment of thinking) (Cacioppo & Petty, 1982), who presumably were more attentive to the implications of the story label.

A related area of research has explored the conditions under which jurors are willing and able to ignore evidence that is ruled inadmissible. Inadmissible evidence is not necessarily misinformation, but these studies provide insights into the processes that individuals use to correct their beliefs when explicitly instructed to do so. This line of research highlights the important role of motivation in belief correction; findings suggest that jurors are motivated to reach a fair verdict, and thus they may use inadmissible evidence when they believe it will help them find the truth (see Steblay, Hosch, Culhane, & McWethy, 2006, for a review). Kassin and Sommers (1997; Sommers & Kassin, 2001) have found that jurors disregarded inadmissible evidence when the reason for discounting it was that the evidence was unreliable (a wiretap that was very difficult to hear) but not when it represented a procedural violation (an illegally obtained wiretap). Similarly, readers of news articles may fail to correct for misinformation if they are not motivated to do so; they may want to believe that a discredited medical treatment is actually effective, or they may not wish to believe disparaging information about a favored candidate or policy.

More generally, individuals' susceptibility to misinformation may depend on their level of trust in the source or even their feelings of distrust. Distrust appears to lead people to automatically activate alternatives to the communicated information, most likely as a protective mechanism (Schul, Burnstein, & Bardi, 1996; Schul, Mayo, & Burnstein, 2004). Rising skepticism about the media among citizens may not be a positive development in general, but it may have the beneficial effect of reducing acceptance of misinformation.

Implications

Because of the basic psychological effects described here, correcting misinformation is a challenging task. Lewandowsky et al. (2012) and various chapters in this volume offer reviews of current strategies. Further research into strategies that may work effectively for narrative misinformation specifically would be an important next step: How might an erroneous causal chain be replaced with a new story, or incorrect information be untangled from other information? One possibility might be to combat misinformation with detailed or narrative alternatives to help address broader cognitive connections. Efforts to reduce or stop misinformation before it reaches the public also may be an effective way to combat this problem, but the question of who censors it also can raise important ethical questions.

If misinformation becomes frequent in journalism, troubling implications emerge. In the movie *All the President's Men* (Pakula, 1976), based on the eponymous nonfiction book by investigative reporters Carl Bernstein and Bob Woodward (1974), the two submit a minor story that gets published in the *Washington Post* on matters concerning the Nixon administration. When it is revealed that they had been mistaken in this one particular story, their primary source of information, code-named "Deep Throat," tells them that this one inaccurate article could undermine their whole overall objective of bringing to light the significant aspects of President Nixon's misdeeds.

There are other ways by which unintentional misrepresentations can undermine perceptions of the trustworthiness of the media. Grieder (1993) states that the people who appear on TV news shows should talk about the news as if they were providers of facts and not members of an editorial board. Otherwise, the credibility of TV news would diminish among all viewers (Grieder, 1993). If many TV news shows have guests who are misinformed, this conceivably results in viewers also doubting the veracity of those who are not misinformed or deceptive.

Beyond the mistakes by journalists that appear on TV news, recent historical research shows organizations exist to produce intentional misinformation and pass these lies on to unsuspecting members of the media (Rabin-Havt, 2016). A related issue is presented when groups like the Annenberg Public Policy Center's Factcheck.org claim that a politician's statements are not true during an election campaign, and the politician continues to repeat the statements anyway. According to a number of psychologists, hearing that a politician's statement is untrue might not change the views of the person who heard it or read it (Seelye, 2008). Instead, what seems to be important in choosing a candidate is whether the lie fits into narratives that the person already has about the candidates (Seelye, 2008).

In conclusion, the experiments we have presented suggest that unintentional and intentional misinformation written in a narrative style might result in the disparagement of the source of a news article but not change a reader's attitudes about the content of the article, even after he or she has been informed of the misinformation. Beyond having a misinformed public, this increased spread and acceptance of misinformation may have unhealthy consequences for the democratic process.

References

Adaval, R., & Wyer, R. S. (1998). The role of narrative in consumer information processing. *Journal of Consumer Psychology, 7*(3), 207–245.

Adita, R. N. (2001). The psychology of deception in marketing: A conceptual framework for research and practice. *Psychology and Marketing, 18,* 735–761.

Anderson, C. A. (1983). Abstract and concrete data in the perseverance of social theories: When weak data lead to unshakeable beliefs. *Journal of Experimental Social Psychology, 19*(2), 93–108.

Anderson, C. A., Lepper, M. R., & Ross, L. (1980). Perseverance of social theories: The role of explanation in the persistence of discredited information. *Journal of Personality and Social Psychology, 39*(6), 1037–1049.

Appel, M., & Malečkar, B. (2012). The influence of paratext on narrative persuasion: Fact, fiction, or fake? *Human Communication Research, 38*(4), 459–484.

Armstrong, G. M., Gurol, M. N., & Russ, F. A. (1979). Detecting and correcting deceptive advertising. Journal of Consumer Research, 6(3), 237–246.

Bernstein, C., & Woodward, B. (1974). *All the president's men.* New York, NY: Simon & Schuster.

Bornemann-Cimenti H., Szilagyi, I. S., & Sandner-Kiesling, A. (2016). Perpetuation of retracted publications using the example of the Scott S. Reuben Case: Incidences, reasons, and possible improvements. *Science and Engineering Ethics, 22*(4), 1063–1072.

Brock, T. C. (1968). Implications of commodity theory for value change. In A. G. Greenwald, T. C. Brock, & T. M. Ostrom (Eds.), *Psychological foundations of attitudes* (pp. 243–275). New York, NY: Academic.

Cacioppo, J. T., & Petty, R. E. (1982). The need for cognition. *Journal of Personality and Social Psychology, 42,* 116–131.

Calame, B. (2006, June 18). Preventing a second Jayson Blair. *New York Times.*

Cooke, J. (1980, September 28). Jimmy's world; 8-year-old heroin addict lives for a fix. *Washington Post.* Retrieved from https://www.washingtonpost.com/archive/poli

tics/1980/09/28/jimmys-world/605f237a-7330-4a69-8433-b6da4c519120/?utm
_term=.8dd02625e7e0

Dahlstrom, M. F. (2010). The role of causality in information acceptance in narratives: An example from science communication. *Communication Research, 37*(6), 857–875.

Eslick, A. N., Fazio, L. K., & Marsh, E. J. (2011). Ironic effects of drawing attention to story errors. *Memory, 19,* 184–191.

Fazio, L. K., Dolan, P. O., & Marsh, E. J. (2015). Learning misinformation from fictional sources: Understanding the contributions of transportation and item-specific processing. *Memory, 23,* 167–177.

Fazio, L. K., & Marsh, E. J. (2008). Slowing presentation speed increases illusions of knowledge. *Psychonomic Bulletin and Review, 15,* 180–185.

Frey, J. (2003). *A million little pieces.* New York, NY: Random House.

Gilbert, D. T., Taforadi, R. W., & Malone, P. S. (1993). You can't not believe everything you read. *Journal of Personality and Social Psychology, 65,* 221–233.

Green, M. C., & Brock, T. C. (2000). The role of transportation in the persuasiveness of public narratives. *Journal of Personality and Social Psychology, 79,* 701–721.

Green, M. C., & Brock, T. C. (2002). In the mind's eye: Transportation-imagery model of narrative persuasion. In M. C. Green, J. J. Strange, & T. C. Brock (Eds.), *Narrative impact: Social and cognitive foundations* (pp. 315–341). Mahwah, NJ: Lawrence Erlbaum.

Green, M. C., & Donahue, J. K. (2011). Persistence of attitude change in the face of deception: The effect of factual stories revealed to be false. *Media Psychology, 14,* 312–331.

Green, M. C., & Donahue, J. K. (2015, May). Continued willingness to purchase a product after reading a false ad about it. Paper presented at the International Communication Association conference, San Juan, Puerto Rico.

Grieder, W. (1993). *Who will tell the people? The betrayal of American democracy.* New York, NY: Simon and Schuster.

Johnson, H. M., & Seifert, C. M. (1994). Sources of the continued influence effect: When misinformation in memory affects later inferences. *Journal of Experimental Psychology: Learning, Memory, and Cognition, 20,* 1420–1436.

Kassin, S. M., & Sommers, S. R. (1997). Inadmissible testimony, instructions to disregard, and the jury: Substantive versus procedural considerations. *Personality and Social Psychology Bulletin, 23*(10), 1046–1054.

Kinchen, R. (2011, February 20). A liar's bombshell. *Sunday Times* (London).

Krakauer, J. (2011). *Three cups of deceit.* New York, NY: Anchor.

Kreuter, M. W., Green, M. C., Cappella, J. N., Slater, M. D., Wise, M. E., Storey, D., . . . Woolley, S. (2007). Narrative communication in cancer prevention and control: A framework to guide research and application. *Annals of Behavioral Medicine, 33*(3), 221–235.

Lewandowsky, S., Ecker, U. H., Seifert, C. M., Schwarz, N., & Cook, J. (2012). Misinformation and its correction: Continued influence and successful debiasing. *Psychological Science in the Public Interest, 13*(3), 106–131.

Loftus, E. F. (1979). Reactions to blatantly contradictory information. *Memory and Cognition, 7*(5), 368–374.

Maraniss, D. A. (1981, April 16). Post reporter's Pulitzer Prize is withdrawn. *Washington Post*.

Marsh, E. J., & Fazio, L. K. (2006). Learning errors from fiction: Difficulties in reducing reliance on fictional stories. *Memory & Cognition, 34*, 1140–1149.

Marsh, E. J., Meade, M. L., & Roediger, H. L. (2003). Learning facts from fiction. *Journal of Memory and Language, 49*(4) 519–536.

McDermott, T. (2015, April 8). A reporter who made (and was) front-page news tells it again. *New York Times*.

Miller, J. (2015). *A reporter's journey*. New York, NY: Simon and Schuster.

Mortenson, G., & Relin, D. O. (2007). *Three cups of tea: One man's mission to promote peace—one school at a time*. New York, NY: Penguin Books.

Pakula, A. J. (Dir.). (1976). *All the president's men* [Film]. Los Angeles, CA: Warner Brothers.

Prentice, D. A., Gerrig, R. J., & Bailis, D. S. (1997). What readers bring to the processing of fictional texts. *Psychonomic Bulletin & Review, 4*, 416–420.

Rabin-Havt, A. (2016). *Lies, incorporated: The world of post-truth politics*. New York, NY: Random House.

Rich, F. (2004, October 17). Will we need a new "All the President's Men"? *New York Times*.

Richter, T., Schroeder, S., & Wohrmann, B. (2009). You don't have to believe everything you read: Background knowledge permits fast and efficient validation of information. *Journal of Personality and Social Psychology, 96*(3), 538–558.

Rieder, R. (2016, March 17). Cracking down on anonymous sources; "New York Times" announces new rules after embarrassments. *USA Today*.

Schul, Y., & Burnstein, E. (1985). When discounting fails: Conditions under which individuals use discredited information in making a judgment. *Journal of Personality and Social Psychology, 49*(4), 894–903.

Schul, Y., Burnstein, E., & Bardi, A. (1996). Dealing with deceptions that are difficult to detect: Encoding and judgment as a function of preparing to receive invalid information. *Journal of Experimental Social Psychology, 32*, 228–253.

Schul, Y., Mayo, R., & Burnstein, E. (2004). Encoding under trust and distrust: The spontaneous activation of incongruent cognitions. *Journal of Personality and Social Psychology, 86*, 668–679.

Seelye, K. Q. (2008, September 17). Ringing untrue, again and again. *New York Times*. Retrieved from http://www.nytimes.com/2008/09/18/us/politics/18web-seelye.html

Silverman, C., & Alexander, L. (2016, November 3). How teens in the Balkans are duping Trump supporters with fake news. *Buzzfeed News*. Retrieved from http://www.buzzfeed.com/craigsilverman/how-macedonia-became-a-global-hub-for-pro-trump-misinfo

Skurnik, I., Yoon, C., Park, D. C., & Schwarz, N. (2005). How warnings about false claims become recommendations. *Journal of Consumer Research, 31*(4), 713–724.

Slater, M. D., & Rouner, D. (2002). Entertainment-education and elaboration likelihood: Understanding the processing of narrative persuasion. *Communication Theory, 12*(2), 173–191.

Sommers, S. R., & Kassin, S. M. (2001). On the many impacts of inadmissible testimony: Selective compliance, need for cognition, and the overcorrection bias. *Personality and Social Psychology Bulletin, 27*(10), 1368–1377.

Steblay, N., Hosch, H. M., Culhane, S. E., & McWethy, A. (2006). The impact on juror verdicts of judicial instruction to disregard inadmissible evidence: A meta-analysis. *Law and Human Behavior, 30*(4), 469–492.

Sydell, L. (2016, November 23). We tracked down a fake-news creator in the suburbs. Here's what we learned [Radio broadcast]. *All Things Considered.* Washington, DC: National Public Radio. Retrieved from http://www.npr.org/sections/alltechconsidered/2016/11/23/503146770/npr-finds-the-head-of-a-covert-fake-news-operation-in-the-suburbs

van Laer, T., de Ruyter, K., Visconti, L. M., & Wetzels, M. (2014). The extended transportation-imagery model: A meta-analysis of the antecedents and consequences of consumers' narrative transportation. *Journal of Consumer Research, 40*(5), 797–817.

Wegner, D. M., Coulton, G. F., & Wenzlaff, R. (1985). The transparency of denial: Briefing in the debriefing paradigm. *Journal of Personality and Social Psychology, 49*(2), 338–346.

Wheeler, S. C., Green, M. C., & Brock, T. C. (1999). Fictional narratives change beliefs: Replications of Prentice, Gerrig, and Bailis (1997) with mixed corroboration. *Psychonomic Bulletin & Review, 6*, 136–141.

Wilson, T. D., & Brekke, N. (1994). Mental contamination and mental correction: Unwanted influences on judgments and evaluations. *Psychological Bulletin, 116*(1), 117–142.

Wyer, R. S. Jr., & Unverzagt, W. H. (1985). Effect of instructions to disregard information on its subsequent recall and use in making judgments. *Journal of Personality and Social Psychology, 48*(3), 533–549.

SEVEN

Can Satire and Irony Constitute Misinformation?

DANNAGAL G. YOUNG

I n February 2012, the anti-abortion advocate and Republican congressman from Louisiana, John Fleming, shared a news story on his Facebook page. "More on Planned Parenthood, abortion by the wholesale," the congressman captioned the news story, entitled "Planned Parenthood Opens $8 Billion Abortionplex" (2011). The problem, however, was that the article was not real. It was a piece of satire published by the popular satire site the *Onion*. Fleming removed the post but not before his followers (and likely his pride) had suffered the consequences of sharing satirical information as though it were real. Prominent politicians and news organizations are not alone in their misreading of ironic satire. Citizens misread satirical texts on a regular basis, too, as is evident to those who have spent time on social media, where ironic fake news stories are often shared as real by unaware readers.

Satire and Irony: Juxtapositions between the Real and the Ideal

Scholars have conceptualized satire in terms of content, function, and the intention of the author. Test (1991) posits that satire aims at a target, has a spirit of aggression, and issues judgment while eliciting laughter. Colletta (2009) describes satire as "a form that holds up human vices and follies to ridicule and scorn" (p. 859). According to Simpson (2003), satire, a "discursive practice," has several core functions: an aggressive function, as it targets some "object of attack"; a social function, as it serves to bond people together; and an intellectual function, as it "relies upon linguistic creativity" (p. 3). And, in spite of satire's critical and aggressive nature, its fundamental message is one of optimism, as it "rests upon engagement, the satirist and the viewer need to feel that something could possibly change" (Colletta, 2009, p. 859).

One of the most common devices used in the construction of satire is irony. Simpson posits, "It is the concept of *irony*, more than any other device, which tends to be regarded as the central mechanism in the production of satire" (2003, p. 52). Colletta assumes that irony is inherent in satirical texts, as satire's efficacy "relies on the ability of the audience to recognize the irony that is at the heart of its humor" (2009, p. 860). Though scholars disagree on the subtle criteria to categorize irony, most agree that irony as a rhetorical form involves the inversion of meanings, such that what the speaker literally states is not consistent with what he or she actually means (Burgers, van Mulken, & Schellens, 2011). As Henri Bergson explained in 1914, ironic texts juxtapose "the real and the ideal," or "what is and what ought to be" (p. 127).

The Psychological Processing of Irony

Irony is enjoyable, but it is also complex, cognitively taxing, and often misunderstood (Burgers, van Mulken, & Schellens, 2012; LaMarre, Landreville, & Beam, 2009; Pexman, Ferretti, & Katz, 2000). To comprehend ironic texts, listeners engage in multiple stages of information processing and retrieval. Once the text's literal meaning is processed, the listener then inverts that meaning to understand its ironic interpretation (Giora & Fein, 1999). All humor, by definition, involves the juxtaposition of two competing frames of reference. It is through the reconciliation of this incongruity that humor is experienced (Koestler, 1964). The reconciliation of the incongruous elements requires the listener to access and integrate constructs in working memory. Humor's unique construction and the resulting cognitive demands likely account for humor's positive impact on message attention and interest (Markiewicz, 1974; Xenos & Becker, 2009), recall (Schmidt & Williams, 2001), and construct salience (Young, 2006). Additionally, humor—and irony in particular—appear to impose such a high cognitive load on the audience that it may reduce their ability and motivation to counterargue the claims presented within the text (LaMarre, Landerville, Young, & Gilkerson, 2014; Young, 2008).

Although the many powers of humor—to elicit laughter, fuel recall and salience, and disrupt argument scrutiny—all derive from humor's incongruity, it is also incongruity that renders humorous texts fundamentally polysemic, as listeners come away from humorous texts with multiple, often competing, interpretations (Boxman-Shabtai & Shifman, 2014). The problem, of course, is that the meaning of a humorous text is not in the text itself. It is constructed by the listeners as they infer what the author believes ought to be or what the author is describing actually is, hence the assertion that "the use of irony remains a risky strategy" (Burgers et al., 2012, p. 232).

To properly comprehend irony, the listener must recognize the author's ironic intention (Attardo, 2000). According to linguists, irony comprehension is largely determined by the presence and recognition of "irony markers," that is, "meta-communicative clues" (Burgers et al., 2012, p. 231) that "alert the reader to the fact that an utterance is ironic" (Attardo, 2000, p. 7). These markers can include source cues, nonverbal gestures and facial expressions, and strategic placement of punctuation, quotation marks, italics, and emoticons in text (Attardo, 2000). In the absence of visual or textual cues such as these, ironic texts will sometimes include irony markers in the form of exaggerated or absurd details designed to flag to the reader that the text is intended to be read as irony. Research indicates that irony comprehension is significantly enhanced by the presence of such markers (Burgers et al., 2012).

What Is, What Isn't, What Ought to Be, and What Oughtn't

Ironic texts come in many forms, implicitly or explicitly evaluative of some target, more or less complex (see Burgers et al., 2012), but for purposes of explication, let us consider some common forms and techniques of contemporary satire. Fake news sites like the *Onion* generally offer a false version of what "is" to poke fun at what actually is and hence encourage readers to consider what should be. These false versions of reality are heightened using the rhetorical tool of *reductio ad absurdum*, in which the flawed aspects of reality are revealed through the extension of that reality or belief system to its logical yet absurd conclusion. When they are done with ironic satirical intent, such absurdities are presented as though they are true. For the reader to come to a particular moral evaluation of the person or issue targeted by such texts, she or he must recognize that the version of reality being presented is exaggerated and false but has similarities to the actual reality underlying it.

For instance, the *Onion* article mistakenly shared by Congressman Fleming (*Onion*, 2011) offers an *implicitly* evaluative news story that is consistent in valence and argumentation with the criticisms of Planned Parenthood (PP) offered by many conservative politicians and interest groups. Their criticism of PP is predicated on the belief that the organization's central mission is to provide abortions to women. While the *Onion* article does not explicitly state a valence toward the fictional PP project, it does include details that imply valence to the reader. This piece includes several irony markers that signal to the audience that the piece is not real news. First, obviously, is the source. The *Onion* is widely recognized as a popular satire site. However, if a reader were not familiar with the *Onion* as a satire site, several instances of exaggerated language might flag the ironic intent to the reader. These include details like the new "sprawling abortion facility . . . [allowing] the organization to terminate unborn lives with an efficiency never before thought possible," Planned Parenthood adopting a new slogan of "No Life Is Sacred," and PP spokespeople using unlikely language like "We really want abortions to become a regular part of women's lives" (*Onion*, 2011).

The article quotes Planned Parenthood president Cecile Richards as saying, "Although we've traditionally dedicated 97 percent of our resources to other important services such as contraception distribution, cancer screening, and STD testing, this new complex allows us to devote our full attention to what has always been our true passion: abortion." By highlighting the real-life proportion of PP resources dedicated to contraception, cancer screening, and STD testing, the *Onion* marks the belief that the organization's main function is that of abortion provider as incorrect. The reader is thereby encouraged to reconsider the underlying logic of conservative critiques of the organization.

Another common type of contemporary satire comes when a satirist ironically proposes what ought to be. Such texts rely on "explicitly evaluative" irony (Burgers et al., 2011), as they state a clear valence toward an attitude object, often a policy or person. In so doing, the satirist falsely advances a position or policy that is the opposite of what she really believes ought to be done. Here the best-known modern example is the ironic commentary of comedian Stephen Colbert on his show, *The Colbert Report*, which aired on Comedy Central from 2005 to 2015. Colbert used deadpan humor as he articulated political points of view that were the opposite of his own. Playing the part of an arrogant but uninformed conservative pundit, Colbert stated support or opposition to policies and people in ways that highlighted Republican hypocrisy or flaws in conservative logic.

Colbert's statement in ironic support of the death penalty is an example: "Folks, I love capital punishment. It sends a clear message. We as a society think it is depraved to take a human life and to prove it we're going to kill you" (in Lang, 2014). Here the irony is revealed as the viewer follows the satirist's proposed solution to an absurd conclusion. If the viewer is unfamiliar with Colbert as an ironic satirist, the absurdity and hypocrisy of the conclusion should flag her as to the ironic nature of the text and hence serve as an irony marker in itself. As the viewer follows the argument, she is confronted with the question of whether the proposed policy is viable, ideologically consistent, or sound. Most importantly, if the solution is not viable, what does it say about real-world policies and solutions currently under consideration?

It is fair to assume that most individuals in Colbert's audience understood his ironic intent. They were likely familiar with him from his years as a correspondent on *The Daily Show* with Jon Stewart, another liberal-leaning satire program on Comedy Central that aired from 1999 to 2015. But for those missing this source familiarity, the irony markers of exaggeration and hyperbole might still not be enough to flag Colbert's content as ironic. In an experimental setting in which students were assigned to watch segments from Colbert, the researchers LaMarre, Landreville, and Beam (2009) conclude that while most students found Colbert to be funny, conservative students were significantly more likely to believe that Colbert was himself a conservative who was mocking liberals in an exaggerated way. In other words, as described by the authors, these students, likely unfamiliar with the ironic style of Colbert, missed the irony markers and engaged in selective perception, "seeing what they wanted to see" in affirmation of their own ideological perspective.

We would be remiss in our discussion of ironic satire without mentioning the well-known work of Jonathan Swift. In Swift's 1729 essay "A Modest Proposal," he suggests a way to solve the Irish famine, by encouraging Irish families to sell their babies to rich English folk as food. With fewer children to feed and more money in hand, Irish parents would be unburdened (Swift, 1996). Swift's essay is *explicitly* evaluative, as it literally states a positive valence toward this policy. The intended meaning, of course, is the condemnation of Britain's utilitarian approach to social policies in Ireland and the British conceptualization of Ireland's poor as expendable. Given the explicit positive presentation of such an illogical, inhumane, and grotesque proposal, readers at the time were forced to invert Swift's intended meaning and then to draw parallels to other proposals under consideration.

A more recent example of ironic propositions is an online petition authored by Hyperationalist (Jim Ryan) on Change.org in March 2016. The petition, framed as though written by a conservative gun-rights advocate, condemns the Republican Party for planning to hold the Republican National Convention (RNC) at a venue that did not allow "open-carry" firearms. Within a week of its creation, the petition had more than 50,000 signatures (Westcott, 2016). Given the contested GOP primary campaign and the resistance to Donald Trump as the party's nominee, the notion of an RNC full of individuals carrying firearms seems, on its face, unwise at best and deadly at worst. Yet the fake petition, "Recognize Our Constitutional Right to Open Carry Firearms at the Republican National Convention at the Quicken Loans Arena in July 2016," included real quotes from Republican candidates and National Rifle Association leaders stressing the danger of so-called "gun-free zones." As explained by the petition's author, by taking the argument of "dangerous gun-free zones" to its logical conclusion, his goal was to reveal the absurdity of the policy. Ryan contends the petition was a way of forcing conservatives "to be consistent in their beliefs. It was an invitation for them to articulate" why allowing open-carry guns at the RNC was not a good idea. Continuing in his ironic voice, Ryan states, "If everyday Americans 'get' to have protection of armed citizens, then I don't see why GOP doesn't get to have those same 'protections'" (J. Ryan, personal communication, March 31, 2016).

The petition itself is loaded with irony markers in the form of hyperbolic language that would likely signal to the reader that the author was not actually endorsing open carry of firearms at the RNC. Including phrases like "Barack HUSSEIN Obama" and the "basic God-given rights to carry handguns or assault weapons in public" was Ryan's way of winking to the audience to signal that this text was ironic. And while Ryan's goal may have been for readers to consider the many reasons guns at the RNC are actually not a good idea, the way in which the petition was shared likely contributed to people's misreading of it. "I think that the media turned [the petition] into misinformation," he says (J. Ryan, personal communication, March 31, 2016). By covering the petition as a real political act, media outlets cued audiences to see it as real. Meanwhile, those who came to the petition after it was tweeted by gun-rights groups did read it ironically, as the source cue accurately indicated to them that this was a piece of ironic satire.

Misinformation, Disinformation, or Just Not Getting the Joke?

When a reader misses the irony markers and mistakenly reads an ironic text as literal, does that satirical text constitute a form of misinformation? Some conceptualize misinformation as occurring on the part of the audience rather than the message sender or the text (Kuklinski, Quirk, Jerit, Schwieder, & Rich, 2000). Here, misinformation describes wrongly held beliefs on the part of an individual. Other scholars have used both "misinformation" and "disinformation" to describe "wrong or misleading information" (Stahl, 2006). The notable distinction is that disinformation is the spreading of a "known falsehood" in anticipation of audiences believing it is true, whereas misinformation is simply unintentionally misleading (Stahl, 2006, p. 86). Using these definitions, then, misinformation is the accidental spreading of false information, while disinformation is a strategic act on the part of a message producer to deliberately provide inaccurate information intended to shape the views of the audience.

The goal of ironic satire is to implicitly critique some aspects of political or social life in such a way that the listener is forced to ask not only "what is" but also "what ought to be." This consideration of prescriptive arguments can happen only if the reader recognizes a text as ironic and processes it as such. Let us assume that the goal of a satirist is for the audience to interpret the text consistent with the embedded meaning of the author. In other words, true satirists want audiences to read their work as ironic in order for those audiences to see the prescriptive arguments being advanced. If this is true, then a satirist would never intend for a reader to take an ironic text literally. Once people process an ironic text as literal, it ceases to offer the critiques of—and aggression toward—that which it is intended to satirize. Hence, satire and disinformation are mutually exclusive categories.

But what about misinformation? Can satire be *unintentionally* misleading and hence lead readers to hold misperceptions of what is real or ideal? The answer is yes. However, given the goals of true satire, such an outcome ought to be devastating to a satirist. Colletta warns, "If the irony is missed, or the better moral standard is also ironically presented as just another construction, then satire is no longer an effective social critique and may even be misunderstood as an example of the very thing it sets out to critique" (2009, p. 860). Let us assume that a satirist's true intention is to ironically critique society through play and aggression in a way that encourages social or political change. Though she may encourage a temporary misreading of the text before the audience suddenly notes the irony and inverts its meaning, the author ought to go to great lengths to be certain the literal interpretation is not what the reader is left with.

Admittedly, all of this logic is predicated on the idealistic assumption that the author of such works is driven by the artistic, political, and social goals of satire. In reality, contemporary satirists are employed by for-profit entities that are themselves driven by economic and cultural motives. The writers of the *Onion* are not Jonathan Swift, authoring a piece of satirical literature with the goal of changing British policy toward the poor. They are employees of a business—a growing business recently purchased in part by Univision (James, 2016)—whose jobs and future depend on page views, shares, and click-through rates. And yes, while the writers of popular political satire like the *Onion* are surely hoping to successfully critique people and issues, that same content is also what keeps their media enterprise afloat, regardless of whether audiences read it as ironic or literal. Undoubtedly, the goals of satire and the goals of the market are at odds here. A satirist wants a piece to be read ironically to reveal the intended meaning and critique. A for-profit online satire publication will benefit financially when individuals who mistakenly read the irony literally click on and then share that story out of misplaced outrage.

This very tension is at the heart of current critiques of other self-proclaimed satire sites, including *Empire News* and the *Daily Currant*. The *Daily Currant* publishes online fake news stories that have been mistakenly covered as real news by media organizations from Breitbart.com to the *Boston Globe* and the *Washington Post*. Criticism of the *Daily Currant* and of its editor Daniel Barkeley is commonplace—and scathing. *Slate's* Josh Voorhees (2013) describes how the *Drudge Report* was fooled by the *Daily Currant* as a "classic Currant con." *Esquire's* Charles Pierce (2013) hypothesizes that the *Daily Currant* "exists to punk the mainstream media." Writes the *New Republic's* Emmet Rensin (2014), "The Daily Currant is a fake-news site of a different stripe: one entirely devoid of jokes." Rensin suggests that Barkeley's chief goal is to fool people in order to increase page views because "the site's business model as an ad-driven clickbaitgenerator relies on it." To do this, he argues, the site is almost devoid of irony markers that would signal ironic intent to a reader. He notes, "The Daily Currant's headlines don't engage in subtlety so much as fail entirely to signal humorous intention" (Rensin, 2014).

For his part, *Currant* editor Daniel Barkeley insists that he is not hoping to fool media outlets with his stories: "It's not a big score, you know, for us to have a news organization pick it up as real" (in Weinstein, 2013). In fact, argues Barkeley, the lack of cues that might signal satirical intent to the reader is intentional. It is part of his comedic style. He explains, "The reason why we write the articles so close to truth is because that's what we think is funny" (in Weinstein, 2013). Weinstein of the *Daily Caller* describes Barkeley's satire as "subtler" than the *Onion's*: "He tries not to give the joke away in the headline like the *Onion* often does, and it often takes several paragraphs before the reader even realizes what they are reading is a joke, if they realize it at all" (Weinstein, 2013).

In an email exchange Barkeley admits, "There is a responsibility on the part of the message producer to make their comedic intentions clear," but he also places responsibility in the hands of the reader. "No matter how obvious a joke may be, it will always be misinterpreted by some people," he writes. "And for me that misinterpretation is not misinformation. On the contrary, it is usually a sign that the satirist's message has been effective at revealing some sort of truth that certain people cannot accept" (D. Barkeley, personal communication, March 18, 2015). But even if Barkeley is correct about readers' own biases shaping their interpretations, without adequate markers—without context to signal ironic intent—does such a story constitute satire at all? Speaking to this mutual exclusivity of satire and misinformation, the *Washington Post's* Gathman writes (2014), "Satire is meant to expose its subject as wrong: evil, ridiculous, or contradictory. False information presented and consumed as fact spectacularly fails as satire, because it doesn't expose anything."

Satire, Misinformation, and the Courts

The role of irony markers is crucial to the understanding of a satirical text. Indeed, the U.S. judicial system explicitly highlights "context" as the central criterion to determine whether a speech act constitutes satire and hence whether it is to be afforded protections under the First Amendment. Countless cases have come before the U.S. and state courts in which individuals have brought charges of defamation and libel against publications of satirical and ironic work. The courts' judgments in these cases universally protect satirical and ironic speech. In addition to the central role played by context in these decisions, the courts consistently reference "reasonable" interpretations by "reasonable" readers of the text in question.

An example is the Texas Supreme Court's ruling in *New Times, Inc. v. Isaacks* (2004). Here, the court reaffirms that "satire and parody should not be interpreted literally, but must be viewed in context and as they would be interpreted by an objectively reasonable person" (Penrod, 2004, p. 20). In its ruling the court cites the presence of various cues (irony markers) in the story that signal its humorous intent to the reader. The ruling also highlights the publication's history of publishing satirical content (*New Times, Inc. v. Isaacks*, 2004).

In a more recent ruling in a case filed by Joseph Farah and Jerome Corsi against *Esquire* in 2013, the U.S. District Court of Appeals for the District of Columbia protected the rights to satire as free speech. The magazine published a satirical piece suggesting that Corsi's and publisher Farah's new book *Where's the Birth Certificate? The Case That Barack Obama Is Not Eligible to Be President* (2011) had been pulled from the shelves following President Obama's real-life release of his long-form birth certificate. The book had not been pulled from the shelves. However, through implicit evaluative irony, the article suggests that if the authors were operating in pursuit of truth, the release of the birth certificate should be the end of the book (*Farah v. Esquire Magazine*, 2013).

In the opinion, Judge Judith Rogers writes, "Despite its literal falsity, satirical speech enjoys First Amendment protection . . . the 'statement' that the plaintiff must prove false . . . is not invariably the literal phrase published but rather what a reasonable reader would have understood the author to have said." The opinion continues that the First Amendment demands consideration of the context of a given statement, which includes "not only the immediate context of the disputed statements, but also the type of publication, the genre of writing, and the publication's history of similar works" (*Farah v. Esquire Magazine*, 2013).

The Absence of Irony Markers in Digital Spaces

According to the court's definition, a reasonable reader will have some knowledge of the source and will read irony in context. Knowing that an article comes from the *Onion* should signal to most readers that the text is satirical. The problem, however, is that in digital spaces, texts are encountered and processed independent of their source cues. Digital technologies fuel "migratory" behavior of users, in which source loyalty is a thing of the past and à la carte media consumption is the rule (Jenkins, 2006). Individuals scroll through their social media news feeds, encountering friends' posts and links to traditional news articles and satire pieces, all in the same mixed literal and ironic digital space. In 2014 the *Atlantic* announced the "death of the homepage" (Thompson, 2014), citing dramatic declines in homepage traffic as individuals increasingly come to news and entertainment outlets through social media. This shift has profound consequences for media producers and readers alike. Notes Thompson (2014), "Homepages reflect the values of institutions, and Facebook and Twitter reflect the interest of individual readers." By entering a story through the "side door" of social media (LaFrance 2012), users are not reminded of those institutional values that come through a homepage. When encountered through social media, ironic texts become stripped of their institutional context and disseminated independent of those cues that would help a listener process them in keeping with the author's intended meaning.

In an interview with Terry Gross on NPR's *Fresh Air*, Trevor Noah, host of *The Daily Show* on Comedy Central, was asked about controversial tweets he had made a few years prior. "I'm not surprised by the response to any comedy taken out of context," he replies. "Comedy is all about context. If you think about the things you say to your friends or to people you know, if a stranger hears them, they would think you're the most horrible human being in the world" (in Gross & Miller, 2016). Noah then discusses the importance of unique spaces for satire and comedy and the implicit contract that exists between a comic and his or her audience: "This is why comedy has existed for so long in a safe space and that is a comedy club. But now with the change in social media and sharing videos and sound bites, we now live in a world where people are part of conversations that they originally weren't really. You're now overhearing everything that everybody's talking about and you're not part of the conversation" (in Gross & Miller, 2016).

Once protected in dark underground spaces, irony and satire are now disseminated through digital technologies, where they are encountered everywhere by anyone, without the cues necessary to decode them properly. The result is social media companies struggling to regulate and contextualize satirical content across their platforms.

Social Media's Battle with Satire and Fake News

Since the early days of the Internet, online users have found it difficult to "mark" irony, satire, and parody in a way that facilitates appropriate interpretation by the reader. Poe's Law, named after online religion commentator Nathan Poe from a post in 2005, states that "online parodies of religious views are indistinguishable from sincere expressions of religious views" (Aikin, 2013, p. 301). Poe writes in his original post (2005), "Without a winking smiley or other blatant display of humor, it is utterly impossible to parody a Creationist in such a way that *someone* won't mistake it for the genuine article."

Digital technologies empower consumers to create, repurpose, and distribute hybrid media content. Yet the owners of social media platforms seem to be internally conflicted about the nature and extent of this empowerment. Jenkins notes, "Media producers are responding to these newly empowered consumers in contradictory ways, sometimes encouraging change, sometimes resisting what they see as renegade behavior" (2006, p. 19). Twitter's rules for satire and parody accounts require explicit cues to signal the author's intent to the reader. The accounts must clearly state in the "bio" that the account is a "parody" or "fake," "in a way that would be understood by the intended audience." Violations of the policy result in account suspension (Twitter, 2016). In essence, Twitter has codified the use of irony markers across its platform.

Facebook, too, has struggled to find effective ways to deal with satirical content. In August 2014, in response to "feedback that people wanted a clearer way to distinguish satirical articles from others" (Stark, 2014), Facebook temporarily labeled links to satirical articles as "Satire." In essence, the social media platform was providing the irony markers that are absent from digital spaces. After several months, however, the satire tag disappeared. Instead, in January 2015, Facebook embarked on a mission to crowd-source the concept of "context." This new feature allowed users to hide and report "fake news stories" to Facebook. With its announcement to "show fewer hoaxes" in users' news feeds, the social media company explained that posts including links to stories receiving numerous reports as "fake" would "get reduced distribution in News Feeds" (Owens & Weinsberg, 2015). In anticipation of criticism of censorship, Facebook explained that this process would not affect distribution of truly "satirical" content: "We've found from testing that people tend not to report satirical content intended to be humorous, or content that is clearly labeled as satire. This type of content should not be affected by this update" (Owens & Weinsberg, 2015).

According to the *Daily Currant*'s Barkeley, the months following the change did affect distribution of his content through Facebook. Instead of a satire tag, Barkeley laments, "Facebook opted for a mechanism that effectively bans any form of satire that may be mistaken for reality" (D. Barkeley, personal communication, May 3, 2015). Barkeley notes that referral traffic from Facebook to his site dropped by 95% from January into March 2015. While Barkeley calls this proof of "a clear act of censorship," Facebook would likely see this as confirmation that more readers were categorizing Barkeley's stories as fake than funny.

Within a few months of the algorithm change, referral traffic to Barkeley's site returned to normal, suggesting that either more users were recognizing his content as satire or that Facebook was being less restrictive in its distribution algorithm (D. Barkeley, personal communication, May 3, 2016). In February 2016 Facebook introduced a new set of "reaction" emojis to allow users to choose emoticons to communicate responses of "love," "ha-ha," "wow," "sad," and "angry." The emojis not only give users more options to express discrete emotional responses but also provide data that Facebook can use to curate individual newsfeeds. Arguably, stories that receive numerous "ha-has" will be considered successful attempts at humor or satire.

Conclusion

In a rapidly changing information environment, distinguishing fact from fiction becomes increasingly complicated. The nature of digital spaces, with their user-generated content and side doors to entry, renders these distinctions problematic. Understanding the role of irony markers and context in the psychological processing of irony can help people think about ways to address these misunderstandings. Popular social media sites have identified various ways to integrate irony markers in ways designed to combat the problem of misinformation across their platforms. Twitter requires the explicit labeling of a source as parody or irony, hence providing the irony markers at the level of the source. Facebook uses collective user-response data to confirm the humorous reading of a particular post, thereby capturing the extent to which readers of a post are able to identify irony markers within it. Neither of these methods will stop individual users from misreading ironic posts, and both methods likely exist more for legal protections than user protection. However, they do illustrate a sense on the part of these entities that satire and misinformation are two distinct forms of content. Satire and irony are clearly marked and as such are privileged and protected forms of speech that users are expected to read accurately. Misinformation lacks the cues that would facilitate accurate reading by the audience and therefore is not only "not protected" but also actively shut down across these platforms.

Scholars and media executives wrestling with these questions must consider the tensions between the goals of satire and the goals of for-profit online content. If the goal of satire is to critique some aspects of political or social life, then the true satirist will work to be accurately interpreted by the audience. A literal interpretation of an ironic text fails to produce the kind of critique or dialogue that makes satire satirical at all. The deliberate downplaying or outright exclusion of irony markers that would be recognized by a reasonable reader should be taken as an indication that the author's claims of satirical intent are dubious at best.

References

Aikin, S. F. (2013). Poe's Law, group polarization, and argumentative failure in religious and political discourse. *Social Semiotics, 23*(3), 301–317.

Attardo, S. (2000). Irony markers and functions: Towards a goal-oriented theory of irony and its processing. *Rask, 12*(1), 3–20.

Bergson, H. (1914). *Laughter: An essay on the meaning of the comic.* New York, NY: Macmillan.

Boxman-Shabtai, L., & Shifman, L. (2014). Evasive targets: Deciphering polysemy in mediated humor. *Journal of Communication, 64*(5), 977–998.

Burgers, C., van Mulken, M., & Schellens, P. J. (2011). Finding irony: An introduction of the verbal irony procedure (VIP). *Metaphor and Symbol, 26*(3), 186–205.

Burgers, C., van Mulken, M., & Schellens, P. J. (2012). Type of evaluation and marking of irony: The role of perceived complexity and comprehension. *Journal of Pragmatics, 44*(3), 231–242.

Colletta, L. (2009). Political satire and postmodern irony in the age of Stephen Colbert and Jon Stewart. *Journal of Popular Culture, 42*(5), 856–874.

Corsi, J. (2011). *Where's the birth certificate? The case that Barack Obama is not eligible to be president.* Washington, DC: WND Books.

Farah v. Esquire Magazine. (2013). 12-7055. U.S. Ct. App. D.C. Circuit.

Gathman, C. (2014, September 12). Why people fall for dumb Internet hoaxes. *Washington Post.* Retrieved from https://www.washingtonpost.com/news/the-intersect/wp/2014/09/12/why-people-fall-for-dumb-internet-hoaxes

Giora, R., & Fein, O. (1999). Irony: Context and salience. *Metaphor and Symbol, 14*(4), 241–257.

Gross, T., & Miller, D. (2016, February 18). Under apartheid, Trevor Noah's mom taught him to face injustice with humor. In T. Gross (Producer), *Fresh Air* [Radio program]. Philadelphia, PA: National Public Radio. Retrieved from http://www.npr.org

James, M. (2016, January 19). It's no joke: Univision buys a stake in the Onion. *Los Angeles Times*. Retrieved from http://www.latimes.com/entertainment/envelope /cotown/la-et-ct-univision-onion-20160119-story.html

Jenkins, H. (2006). *Convergence culture: Where old and new media collide*. New York, NY: NYU Press.

Koestler, A. (1964). *The act of creation*. New York, NY: Arkana.

Kuklinski, J. H., Quirk, P. J., Jerit, J., Schwieder, D., & Rich, R. F. (2000). Misinformation and the currency of democratic citizenship. *Journal of Politics, 62*(3), 790–816.

LaFrance, A. (2012). Coming in the side door: The value of homepages is shifting from traffic-driver to brand. *Nieman Journalism Lab, 22*, 2012.

LaMarre, H. L., Landreville, K. D., & Beam, M. A. (2009). The irony of satire: Political ideology and the motivation to see what you want to see in *The Colbert Report. International Journal of Press/Politics, 14*(2), 212–231.

LaMarre, H. L., Landreville, K. D., Young, D., & Gilkerson, N. (2014). Humor works in funny ways: Examining satirical tone as a key determinant in political humor message processing. *Mass Communication and Society, 17*(3), 400–423.

Lang, B. (2014, April 3). Stephen Colbert loves capital punishment [Video]. *The Wrap*. Retrieved from http://www.thewrap.com/stephen-colbert-loves-capital-punish ment-video/.

Markiewicz, D. (1974). Effects of humor on persuasion. *Sociometry, 37*, 407–422.

New Times, Inc. v. Isaacks. 146 S.W.3d 144 (Tex. Ct. App. 2004).

Onion. Planned Parenthood opens $8 billion abortionplex. (2011, May 18). Retrieved from http://www.theonion.com/article/planned-parenthood-opens-8-billion-abor tionplex-20476

Owens, E., & Weinsberg, U. (2015, January 20). News feed FYI: Showing fewer hoaxes. *Facebook Newsroom*. Retrieved from http://newsroom.fb.com/news/2015/01/news -feed-fyi-showing-fewer-hoaxes

Penrod, G. (2004). Texas high court finds strong protection for satire, parody. *News Media and the Law, 28*(4), 20.

Pexman, P. M., Ferretti, T. R., & Katz, A. N. (2000). Discourse factors that influence online reading of metaphor and irony. *Discourse Processes, 29*(3), 201–222.

Pierce, C. (2013, May 3). Things in Politico that make me want to guzzle antifreeze, part the infinity. *Esquire*. Retrieved from http://www.esquire.com/news-politics/poli tics/a18382/the-day-in-humor/.

Poe, N. (2005, August 10). Poe's law [Forum comment]. Retrieved from http://www .christianforums.com/threads/big-contradictions-in-the-evolution-theory.1962 980/page-3#post-17606580

Rensin, E. (2014, June 5). The great satirical-news scam of 2014. *New Republic*. Retrieved from https://newrepublic.com/article/118013/satire-news-websites-are -cashing-gullible-outraged-readers

Schmidt, S. R., & Williams, A. R. (2001). Memory for humorous cartoons. *Memory & Cognition, 29*(2), 305–311.

Simpson, P. (2003). *On the discourse of satire: Toward a stylistic model of satirical humor*. Amsterdam, Netherlands: John Benjamins.

Stahl, B. (2006). On the difference or equality of information, misinformation, and disinformation: A critical research perspective. *Informing Science, 9*, 83–96.

Stark, C. (2014, August 17). Facebook testing "satire" tags for sites like the Onion. *Mashable*. Retrieved from http://mashable.com/2014/08/17/facebook-satire-tag /#k1ToaJCYiSqz

Swift, J. (1996). *A modest proposal and other satirical works*. New York, NY: Dover. (Original work published 1729)

Test, G. A. (1991). *Satire: Spirit and art*. Gainesville, FL: University Press of Florida.

Thompson, D. (2014, May 15). What the death of homepages means for the future of news. *Atlantic*. Retrieved from http://www.theatlantic.com/business/archive/2014 /05/what-the-death-the-homepage-means-for-news/370997

Twitter. (2016). Parody, commentary, and fan account policy. Retrieved from https:// support.twitter.com/articles/106373#

Voorhees, J. (2013, May 3). The Daily Currant strikes again, dupes Drudge. Slate.com. Retrieved from http://www.slate.com/blogs/the_slatest/2013/05/03/drudge _fooled_by_the_daily_currant_satirical_story_about_bloomberg_s_trip.html

Weinstein, J. (2013, March 12). Meet the man who fools the news industry. *Daily Caller*. Retrieved from http://dailycaller.com/2013/03/12/meet-the-man-who-fools-the -news-industry

Westcott, L. (2016, March 29). Man behind GOP convention open-carry petition wanted to start gun control conversation. *Newsweek*. Retrieved from http://www .newsweek.com/gop-convention-open-carry-petition-441808

Xenos, M. A., & Becker, A. B. (2009). Moments of Zen: Effects of The Daily Show on information seeking and political learning. *Political Communication, 26*(3), 317–332.

Young, D. G. (2006). Late-night comedy and the salience of the candidates' caricatured traits in the 2000 election. *Mass Communication & Society, 9*(3), 339–366.

Young, D. G. (2008). The privileged role of the late-night joke: Exploring humor's role in disrupting argument scrutiny. *Media Psychology, 11*(1), 119–142.

EIGHT

Media and Political Misperceptions

BRIAN E. WEEKS

An accurately informed public is a hallmark of a thriving democracy. The benefits of an informed citizenry are vast, ranging from increased participation in the political process to more reliable opinions on political issues and increased tolerance for marginalized groups (Delli Carpini & Keeter, 1996). *Misperceptions*, however, may jeopardize these democratic virtues. Political misperceptions are individual beliefs about politics, public affairs, or social issues that are inaccurate when compared to the best available standard of evidence (Kuklinski, Quirk, Jerit, Schwieder, & Rich, 2000). These incorrect beliefs are troubling and can pose a threat to democracy by reshaping citizens' political judgments, including their support for public policies and political candidates (Gilens, 2001; Hochschild & Levine Einstein, 2014; Thorson, 2016; Weeks & Garrett, 2014).

Individuals increasingly encounter false or deceptive information in their media environments, and such exposure can affect citizens' beliefs, as evident by the significant numbers of Americans who are misinformed about a variety of political issues (e.g., Ramsay, Kull, Lewis, & Subias, 2010). Given this trend, it is necessary to examine the dynamics of mediated misinformation and how it can lead to political misperceptions. To address this need, I focus in this chapter on some of the key theoretical mechanisms through which media contribute to a politically misinformed public. In particular, I investigate four important stages in the process of media influence on political misperceptions: the key ways individuals come to be exposed to mediated political misinformation, how the content of media facilitates inaccurate political beliefs, information processing strategies that can encourage biased perceptions, and the democratic consequences of misperceptions. For each stage, the extent of empirical evidence is reviewed and key unanswered questions are posed for future research. Taken together, the four steps in this chain more clearly illuminate how people are exposed to misinformation, how and why that information leads to false beliefs, and the implications for the political process.

Exposure to Misinformation in the Media

Before individuals can hold misperceptions about politics, they must first be exposed to misinformation. Although such exposure can occur in unmediated interpersonal contexts (DiFonzo, 2008; Southwell & Yzer, 2007), misinformation in media content is widespread, particularly problematic, and likely to mislead (Southwell & Thorson, 2015). Although the mainstream media and general Internet use can increase awareness of political falsehoods (Weeks & Southwell, 2010), this section focuses on two important factors that enhance the likelihood of exposure to political misinformation in both mass and social media: news selection bias toward like-minded partisan media, and online social network characteristics.

Media Choice and Misinformation

The Internet provides nearly unlimited choice in political media content, allowing people the opportunity to craft news environments that reflect and reinforce their attitudes and biases (Bennett & Iyengar, 2008). Although individuals do not entirely avoid news outlets that challenge their political views (Garrett, Carnahan, & Lynch, 2013; Weeks, Ksiazek, & Holbert, 2016), when given the choice, they prefer media that offer content that affirms their ideologies (Iyengar & Hahn, 2009; Stroud, 2011). This tendency to engage in selective exposure has a number of implications for the extent to which individuals encounter false or misleading political information, as well as for their beliefs.

When media consumers select political news outlets that reflect their existing worldviews, they are prone to encounter outlet-favored misperceptions—those false or misleading claims that benefit a preferred political party, favor a supported candidate or issue, or disparage or damage the opposing side (Garrett, Weeks, & Neo, 2016). Numerous media outlets, including websites and cable television networks, promote misinformation as a way to either gain political advantage or attract larger audience shares (Jamieson & Cappella, 2008; Silverman, 2015). Feldman, Maibach, Roser-Renouf, and Leiserowitz (2012) found coverage of global warming on Fox News to be more dismissive of climate change (a position generally more consistent with that of Republicans than that of Democrats) and to feature climate change doubters more often than did other cable networks. Similarly, early media coverage of the Iraq war beginning in 2003 differed drastically across media outlets and often exhibited a lack of objectivity (Aday, Livingston, & Hebert, 2005).

Although exposure to inaccurate information in mainstream media may be consequential (Weeks & Southwell, 2010), it is the use of partisan media that bears particularly strong associations with awareness of and belief in ideologically consistent political misperceptions. Notable examples include inaccurate beliefs about the existence of weapons of mass destruction (WMDs) in Iraq (Kull, Ramsay, & Lewis, 2003), the inclusion of "death panels" in U.S. health care reform (Meirick, 2013), controversies surrounding a New York City mosque (Garrett, Nisbet, & Lynch, 2013), and issues and policies surrounding elections (Ramsay et al., 2010). Importantly, the relationship between media use and beliefs is not limited to use of conservative news outlets, as growing evidence suggests that use of liberal news media promotes misperceptions that reflect well on liberals or poorly on conservatives (Garrett et al., 2016; Meirick & Bessarabova, 2016; Ramsay et al., 2010). Thus, there is not clear asymmetry in the link between liberals' or conservatives' like-minded partisan news use and misperceptions.

Although partisan news is associated with increased exposure to and belief in ideologically consistent misperceptions, recent work has begun to explore how exposure to misinformation in partisan news affects beliefs. There are several possible ways in which partisan media could promote misperceptions. First, partisan news media can shield individuals from evidence by omitting facts in their coverage. Second, these outlets may create confusion and misunderstanding regarding evidence and expert conclusions. Third, partisan media may reduce the credibility of experts who are key sources for determining fact from fiction by criticizing or marginalizing their work. Conservative news use was associated with decreased trust in scientists that was subsequently related to misperceptions about global warming (Hmielowski, Feldman, Myers, Leiserowitz, & Maibach, 2014). And finally, partisan media may promote misperceptions through selective rejection of evidence, even when audience members are knowledgeable of the facts. Garrett et al. (2016) find support for this final possibility, as partisan news users held inaccurate personal beliefs despite being aware of expert consensus on the issues. This suggests that partisan news users are not unaware of or confused about the facts; rather, partisan media may provide cues that suggest people should reject those facts when they are inconsistent with the particular ideology.

Partisan media may also facilitate further exposure to misinformation by creating reinforcing spirals in which users encounter misinformation that reinforces and strengthens their beliefs, which subsequently increases the likelihood they will seek out and encounter more attitude-consistent misinformation (Feldman, Myers, Hmielowski, & Leiserowitz, 2014; Slater, 2007). Regardless of the precise mechanism through which exposure to misinformation in partisan news affects beliefs, future research needs to analyze content within these outlets to better answer questions about the extent to which partisan media promote misinformation and how they do so.

Online Social Networks

Online social networks, including friends, family, and contacts within social networking sites like Facebook and Twitter, are another important source of political misinformation. Despite the promise of politically diverse environments, political networks online are often homogeneous (Himelboim, McCreery, & Smith, 2013) and thus can encourage exposure to misinformation. Politically homogeneous groups often share beliefs, opinions, and values; this suggests that individuals are more likely to disseminate political information and misinformation online that reflects well on the group (Rojecki & Meraz, 2016). Information that is highly relevant to such groups is often shared within the networks to endorse content, to ensure that others see it, and to persuade others (Southwell, 2013; Weeks, Ardévol-Abreu, & Gil de Zúñiga, 2015). Because people trust information received through close social ties, misinformation can spread rapidly within and between groups online, resulting in widespread exposure (Friggeri, Adamic, Eckles, & Cheng, 2014). A recent study found that political misinformation on Twitter tended to circulate within "echo chambers" of politically homogeneous groups, facilitating exposure of those within the network (Shin, Jian, Driscoll, & Bar, 2016). Misinformation shared from peers is particularly problematic, as it is more likely to be believed and subsequently reshared, creating a reinforcing process that increases overall exposure to the false claims (Garrett, 2011).

The Internet and online social networks in particular may also facilitate exposure to misinformation through the various algorithms used to filter and generate content. Some social networking sites and search engines like Facebook and Google use algorithms to determine, based on past behavior, what political content individuals see on a site (Bakshy, Messing, & Adamic, 2015). There is concern these algorithms can create "filter bubbles" in which people are primarily exposed to information that is consistent with their political beliefs as determined by their online interactions (Pariser, 2011). This raises the possibility that algorithms may increase exposure to attitude-consistent political misinformation, which people are more prone to believe, through their use of social networking sites (Bode & Vraga, 2015) or online search behaviors (Weeks & Southwell, 2010). Software robots, or simply "bots," may introduce individuals to political misinformation. Bots often appear as credible social media accounts and are hard to detect but can spread inaccurate information through a high volume of social media posts and fake news stories (Ferrara, Varol, Davis, Menczer, & Flammini, 2016). Understanding how users are exposed to political misinformation via algorithms and the consequences of such exposure is a promising and relatively untapped avenue of research.

Media Content and Political Misperceptions

Although objectivity and balance are journalistic norms, the presentation of misleading or false claims in mass or social media may also facilitate political misperceptions. This section reviews how journalists' reporting of news stories containing misinformation, including their strict adherence to objectivity, can lead individuals astray. In addition, the changing nature of truth online is also examined.

Journalistic Norms and Misperceptions

Journalists have long pursued the goal of being objective and unbiased in their reporting. While this is seemingly a worthy pursuit, Bennett (2012) argues that journalists' endeavors to remain objective create a problematic paradox in that they can result in more bias and a greater likelihood that the news will misinform audiences. Bennett (2012) acknowledges that journalists seek to be fair and balanced in their reporting, but he notes that in doing so, they ultimately provide equal time to two sides of an argument or issue (even when one side presents more accurate or factually based evidence) and tend to remain steadfast in their ostensible neutrality in reporting. Political elites invested in a particular campaign or issue have a strong motivation to spin the truth to their advantage (Jackson & Jamieson, 2007), and the strict use of objective reporting can provide these political figures a legitimized outlet for spreading false information (Bennett, 2012).

The typical political news story simply provides quotes from both sides of the argument, and the reporter does not intervene between the two parties (Pingree, Brossard, & McLeod, 2014). The problem is that for many political stories there is a right and wrong answer. One such story is the claim that Barack Obama was not born in the United States. Obama produced a legitimate birth certificate, and the evidence clearly indicates that he was born in Hawaii. Yet mainstream media outlets frequently reported on and gave ample time and space to those who challenged the legitimacy of the birth certificate (Pew Research Center, 2011). This adherence to ostensible balance allowed politicians and those who opposed Obama a platform to spin the facts and propagate misinformation. Lawrence and Schafer (2012) find a similar pattern in their investigation of news coverage surrounding Sarah Palin's false claim that a proposed health care bill included "death panels." Their analyses indicate that in many instances journalists simply reported both sides of the claim and failed to step in to clearly identify the truth. In doing so, these stories provided unwarranted credibility to blatantly false information.

This type of "he said/she said" political coverage is problematic and can lead to political misperceptions. It is not limited to news stories, either. Politicians use candidate debates to spin their respective sides of an issue and are often able to disseminate misinformation in these forums without challenges from journalists or moderators (Maurer & Reinemann, 2006). Although reporters are hesitant to engage in it because of fears of being labeled biased, journalistic adjudication, in which journalists intervene and offer additional fact checking and analyses, can be quite effective in minimizing political misperceptions (Jamieson & Waldman, 2003; Pingree et al., 2014). Pingree and colleagues (2014) offer experimental evidence that journalistic adjudication can simultaneously decrease misperceptions and increase the perceived quality of news, suggesting that such interventions are not seen as biased by the audience. Although in its infancy, research into understanding how adjudication of political facts during initial reporting can diminish misperceptions better than post hoc corrections promises to be fruitful moving forward.

Online "Truths" and Political Facts

Part of the difficulty in adjudicating facts is that in the contemporary political environment, many facts are considered to be politically determined. There is often little agreement on what is an objective fact, and partisans on different sides of an argument or issue hold different truths (Kuklinski, Quirk, Schwieder, & Rich, 1998). Some argue that politics are by nature ambiguous and political events are open to several, oftentimes conflicting, interpretations that create disagreements about the truth (Uscinski & Butler, 2013). Republicans and Democrats were equally able to accurately report that Iraq did not have weapons of mass destruction prior to the U.S. invasion in 2003. Yet these partisans' interpretations of why WMDs were not found differed dramatically; Democrats reported that WMDs did not exist, and Republicans claimed that they were moved, destroyed, or not yet found (Gaines, Kuklinski, Quirk, Peyton, & Verkuilen, 2007). Thus, the truth about Iraq and WMDs was open to interpretation and to some degree politically determined.

In many ways the Internet has accelerated people's notion that the truth is relative. As Kata (2012) argues, the Internet has facilitated a postmodern paradigm of truth in which expert consensus is delegitimized and personal values and experiences are tantamount to scientific evidence. Within this new paradigm, Kata notes, everyone is considered an expert and truth is "flattened," as each perspective and view of the facts is represented as legitimate, with evidence from legitimate experts considered one of multiple opinions (2012, p. 3779). The changing nature of what is considered true is problematic in terms of misperceptions, as people are increasingly exposed to online discussions and debates about what is true. If grossly inaccurate evidence, personal experiences, or the words of charlatans are presented and considered alongside evidence from scientific consensus without consideration of validity based on evidence, it becomes more difficult for people to determine which information is legitimate and true. Furthermore, online postmodern discourses often shift the standards of evidence to suit participants' arguments, making it more likely that people will become confused about the facts and ultimately misinformed (Edy & Risley-Baird, 2016).

Biased Information Processing

Once people are exposed to misinformation, it is processed and sometimes used to form beliefs. However, humans are prone to a number of psychological biases that increase the chances of believing inaccurate claims encountered in the media. In this section I review the empirical findings regarding these biases as they relate to political misperceptions, paying particular attention to the roles of motivated reasoning, social identities, and memory errors.

Motivated Reasoning

Inaccurate political claims that people encounter in the media are not always considered in an even-handed manner. Instead, individuals often process this information through partisan or ideological lenses that can ultimately lead to inaccurate beliefs. The theory of partisan-motivated reasoning suggests that individuals tend to defend their prior dispositions, which leads them to evaluate political claims in a way that is consistent with their existing attitudes, beliefs, or opinions (Taber & Lodge, 2006). Attitude-consistent information is often deemed more convincing and valid than is information that challenges one's prior attitudes and beliefs. As a result, inaccurate claims that align with individuals' political party affiliations or ideologies are more likely to be believed than are claims that challenge their worldviews. There is abundant evidence supporting this contention, as individuals are more likely to hold attitude-consistent misperceptions about a range of political topics, including claims about political and policy issues (Garrett & Weeks, 2013; Jerit & Barabas, 2012; Meirick, 2013; Nyhan & Reifler, 2010) and individual politicians (Miller, Saunders, & Farhart, 2015; Pasek, Stark, Krosnick, & Tompson, 2016; Weeks & Garrett, 2014).

Motivated reasoning can also affect how people respond to corrections to misinformation. While journalists use both mainstream and social media to fact-check claims (Coddington, Molyneux, & Lawrence, 2014; Graves, Nyhan, & Reifler, 2016), if people are motivated to defend their prior worldviews, corrections to attitude-consistent misinformation are often viewed with greater skepticism (Lewandowsky, Ecker, Seifert, Schwarz, & Cook, 2012). When presented with corrective information, people may attempt to counterargue the evidence (Lewandowsky et al., 2012), denigrate the source (Nisbet, Cooper, & Garrett, 2015), or reinterpret the facts (Gaines et al., 2007), all of which can lead to rejection of the corrective message and even a strengthening of the misperception, that is, a backfire effect (Garrett & Weeks, 2013; Nyhan & Reifler, 2010). However, this is not to suggest that individuals always process misinformation and corrections through a motivated lens. In fact, there is mounting evidence that exposure to corrections can successfully overcome misinformation and lead to more accurate political beliefs (Berinsky, 2017; Bode & Vraga, 2015; Nyhan & Reifler, 2015; Pingree et al., 2014; Thorson, 2016; Weeks, 2015). It is clear that corrections work in some circumstances but not others. What is not apparent is why or how corrections succeed or fail when one is attempting to challenge partisan-based claims. This is a critical question that must be answered in order to design more consistently successful fact-checking messages.

Social Identities and Intergroup Bias

Individuals' social identities or group memberships related to race, religion, gender, or age (among other factors) can bias processing of misinformation encountered in mass and social media, leading to misperceptions. Humans have a tendency to categorize themselves based on attributes they share with other individuals and to distinguish themselves from individuals and groups they perceive as different. Media exposure can highlight group differences and facilitate the categorization process, leading people to hold prototypical or stereotypical mental representations of dissimilar groups (Hogg & Reid, 2006). Garrett and colleagues (2013) argue that stereotypical representations can be triggered by contextual information in mass media that increases perceptions of out-group members as threatening, and such perceptions can ultimately lead to increased acceptance of false negative information about members of that group. The researchers find support for this argument in a study in which false claims that a Muslim American religious leader sympathized with terrorists were more likely to be believed when participants were shown photographs of the leader in traditional Arab clothing than when he was wearing a Western-style business suit (Garrett et al., 2013). Similarly, inaccurate statements about 2008 presidential candidates Barack Obama and John McCain were more readily accepted when each candidate's race and age were emphasized, suggesting that social categories affect beliefs (Kosloff, Greenberg, Schmader, Dechesne, & Weise, 2010). Finally, racial stereotypes have been found to bias beliefs; individuals who held stereotypical perceptions of blacks were more likely to endorse the false claim that Obama was born outside of the United States (Pasek et al., 2015).

Memory Errors

Failures in human memory can facilitate political misperceptions. Human memory is notoriously unreliable, and errors of memory can lead individuals to hold inaccurate perceptions based on discredited or corrected misinformation, even when they acknowledge that the information is not true (Ecker, Lewandowsky, & Tang, 2010). Often termed the "continued influence effect," reliance on misinformation when forming beliefs occurs because the corrective information does not entirely eliminate the false information from memory that continues to be cognitively accessible and can subsequently affect people's beliefs and attitudes (Johnson & Seifert, 1994). In this way the continued influence of misinformation is similar to the effect on jurors who incorporate tainted evidence into their verdicts; the information is still stored in memory and used in evaluations, even if people report knowing it is false (Ecker et al., 2010). In a political context, corrected misinformation can have continued effects on people's attitudes toward the target of the misinformation. Thorson (2016) has demonstrated that individuals exposed to misinformation about a politician updated their beliefs after being exposed to a subsequent correction, but they used the discredited misinformation in forming their attitudes toward the politician. More specifically, individuals exposed to the corrected information held more negative evaluations of the candidates compared to those of a control group (Thorson, 2016). Other studies have similarly found that individuals hold more negative opinions of politicians when positive information about the individuals is shown to be false (Cobb, Nyhan, & Reifler, 2013). Taken together, the studies suggest that misinformation in the media can affect beliefs even when the information is known to be false. Because memory errors are difficult to overcome, political operatives may use them to their advantage by knowingly spreading misinformation about their opponents, with the idea that it can be influential even if it is not believed.

Consequences of Exposure to Political Misinformation

If a knowledgeable citizenry is considered by many to be a necessary condition for democratic success (Delli Carpini & Keeter, 1996), then it is critical to assess whether exposure to misinformation in the media has political consequences. It is apparent that political misperceptions matter on normative grounds. The volume of political deception and the diminishing value of facts in the political process make it more difficult to have meaningful debates about the real policy issues facing the country (Jamieson, 2015). If opposing sides of a political argument cannot agree on the facts upon which deliberative discussion is to be based, democracy suffers. Furthermore, being accurately informed about politics has democratic benefits, as knowledgeable citizens are more politically tolerant and more interested in politics, hold more stable attitudes, have greater confidence in their ability to participate in the process, and are more likely to actually be involved (Delli Carpini, 2000). Misperceptions jeopardize these values and, consequently, democratic progress (Delli Carpini & Keeter, 1996).

Yet misperceptions pose more than normative threats to democratic outcomes. There is evidence they can have direct consequences on a variety of political outcomes and behaviors (Ramsay et al., 2010). Misinformed individuals hold markedly different preferences about political policies than do accurately informed people; thus public opinion on issues can be swayed by misinformation (Delli Carpini & Keeter, 1996; Gilens, 2001; Kuklinski et al., 2000). Hochschild and Levine Einstein (2014) highlight this possibility in the context of global warming, as significant proportions of individuals who are misinformed about global warming oppose policies intended to mitigate climate change. The polarization of beliefs about pressing political issues is troubling, reflects larger ideological divides, and may make it more difficult to enact legislation that addresses the issues (Hart & Nisbet, 2012).

It is also clear that misperceptions contribute to citizens' perceptions of and support for politicians. Weeks and Garrett (2014) examine voters' exposure to and belief in a series of false claims about the 2008 presidential candidates. They find that believing false negative claims about a candidate significantly reduced the likelihood of voting for that candidate, even beyond the influence of partisanship. In other words, the more misinformation people believed about a candidate, the less likely they were to vote for that candidate. Thorson (2016) notes that exposure to misinformation about a candidate, even when corrected, reduced support for that candidate. Though this link has been observed, it is necessary for future work to investigate how misperceptions factor into citizens' evaluations of candidates and politicians.

Misperceptions can affect democratic outcomes, and citizens' increasing exposure to misinformation via mass and social media exacerbates the problem and highlights the need for corrective messages intended to overcome misperceptions. While research suggests that media-based corrections can at times lead to more accurate beliefs (Berinsky, 2015; Bode & Vraga, 2015; Nyhan & Reifler, 2015; Pingree et al., 2014; Thorson, 2016; Weeks, 2015), it is not clear what the best strategy is to mitigate the effects of false beliefs. Lewandowsky and colleagues (2012) outline several promising approaches, including repeatedly emphasizing the facts and not the misinformation, providing alternative explanations for the events, and affirming individuals' worldviews. Images and visuals that highlight the strength of evidence for or against a particular claim also hold promise as means to use media to challenge false information (Dixon, McKeever, Holton, Clarke, & Eosco, 2015), but more work is needed. Identifying and testing various corrective strategies continues to be one of the most important areas of misperception research moving forward.

Conclusion

Political misperceptions are prevalent in American politics and pose a challenge to democratic ideals. Although misinformation can spread through interpersonal communication, mass and social media facilitate widespread exposure to political falsehoods. I have examined how the media's influence on political misperceptions unfolds by reviewing research at four stages of this process—how people are exposed to misinformation in the media, how media content creates misperceptions, the psychological biases that can encourage false beliefs, and the consequences of political misperceptions. Although this account does not explain every factor in the process leading to inaccurate political beliefs, it does provide a theoretically based explanation for how mediated misinformation affects people and the nation politically and why it is necessary to investigate and understand the phenomenon.

References

Aday, S., Livingston, S., & Hebert, M. (2005). Embedding the truth: A cross-cultural analysis of objectivity and television coverage of the Iraq war. *International Journal of Press/Politics, 10,* 3–21.

Bakshy, E., Messing, S., & Adamic, L. (2015). Exposure to ideologically diverse news and opinion on Facebook. *Science, 348,* 1130–1132.

Bennett, W. L. (2012). *The politics of illusion* (9th ed.). New York, NY: Longman.

Bennett, W. L., & Iyengar, S. (2008). A new era of minimal effects? The changing foundations of political communication. *Journal of Communication, 58,* 707–731.

Berinsky, A. J. (2017). Rumors and health care reform: Experiments in political misinformation. *British Journal of Political Science, 47*(2), 241–262.

Bode, L., & Vraga, E. K. (2015). In related news, that was wrong: The correction of misinformation through related stories functionality in social media. *Journal of Communication, 65,* 619–638.

Cobb, M. D., Nyhan, B., & Reifler, J. (2013). Beliefs don't always persevere: How political figures are punished when positive information about them is discredited. *Political Psychology, 34,* 307–326.

Coddington, M., Molyneux, L., & Lawrence, R. G. (2014). Fact checking the campaign: How political reporters use Twitter to set the record straight (or not). *International Journal of Press/Politics, 19,* 391–409.

Delli Carpini, M. X. (2000). In search of the informed citizen: What Americans know about politics and why it matters. *Communication Review, 4,* 129–164.

Delli Carpini, M. X., & Keeter, S. (1996). *What Americans know about politics and why it matters.* New Haven, CT: Yale University Press.

DiFonzo, N. (2008). *The watercooler effect: A psychologist explores the extraordinary power of rumors.* New York, NY: Penguin Group.

Dixon, G. N., McKeever, B. W., Holton, A. E., Clarke, C., & Eosco, G. (2015). The power of a picture: Overcoming scientific misinformation by communicating weight-of-evidence information with visual exemplars. *Journal of Communication, 65,* 639–659.

Ecker, U. K. H., Lewandowsky, S., & Tang, D. T. W. (2010). Explicit warnings reduce but do not eliminate the continued influence of misinformation. *Memory & Cognition, 38,* 1087–1100.

Edy, J. A., & Risley-Baird, E. E. (2016). Misperceptions as political conflict: Using Schattschneider's conflict theory to understand rumor dynamics. *International Journal of Communication, 10,* 2596–2615.

Feldman, L., Maibach, E. W., Roser-Renouf, C., & Leiserowitz, A. (2012). Climate on cable: The nature and impact of global warming coverage on Fox News, CNN, and MSNBC. *International Journal of Press/Politics, 17,* 3–31.

Feldman, L., Myers, T. A., Hmielowski, J. D., & Leiserowitz, A. (2014). The mutual reinforcement of media selectivity and effects: Testing the reinforcing spirals framework in the context of global warming. *Journal of Communication, 64*(4), 590–611.

Ferrara, E., Varol, O., Davis, C., Menczer, F., & Flammini, A. (2016). The rise of social bots. *Communications of the ACM, 59*(7), 96–104.

Friggeri, A., Adamic, L., Eckles, D., & Cheng, J. (2014). Rumor cascades. In *ICWSM-11 Proceedings of the Eighth International AAAI Conference on Weblogs and Social Media* (pp. 101–110). Palo Alto, CA: Association for the Advancement of Artificial Intelligence.

Gaines, B. J., Kuklinski, J. H., Quirk, P. J., Peyton, B., & Verkuilen, J. (2007). Same facts, different interpretations: Partisan motivation and opinion on Iraq. *Journal of Politics, 69,* 957–974.

Garrett, R. K. (2011). Troubling consequences of online political rumoring. *Human Communication Research*, 37, 255–274.

Garrett, R. K., Carnahan, D., & Lynch, E. (2013). A turn toward avoidance? Selective exposure to online political information, 2004–2008. *Political Behavior*, 35, 113–134.

Garrett, R. K., Nisbet, E. C., & Lynch, E. K. (2013). Undermining the corrective effects of media-based political fact checking? The role of contextual cues and naïve theory. *Journal of Communication*, 63, 617–637.

Garrett, R. K., & Weeks, B. E. (2013). The promise and peril of real-time corrections to political misperceptions. In *CSCW '13 Proceedings of the 16th ACM Conference on Computer Supported Cooperative Work* (pp. 1047–1058). New York, NY: Association for Computing Machinery.

Garrett, R. K., Weeks, B. E., & Neo, R. (2016). Driving a wedge between evidence and beliefs: How online ideological news exposure promotes political misperceptions. *Journal of Computer-Mediated Communication*, 21, 331–348.

Gilens, M. (2001). Political ignorance and collective policy preferences. *American Political Science Review*, 95, 379–396.

Graves, L., Nyhan, B., & Reifler, J. (2016). Understanding innovations in journalistic practice: A field experiment examining motivations for fact–checking. *Journal of Communication*, 66, 102–138.

Hart, P. S., & Nisbet, E. C. (2012). Boomerang effects in science communication: How motivated reasoning and identity cues amplify opinion polarization about climate mitigation policies. *Communication Research*, 39, 701–723.

Himelboim, I., McCreery, S., & Smith, M. (2013). Birds of a feather tweet together: Integrating network and content analyses to examine cross-ideology exposure on Twitter. *Journal of Computer-Mediated Communication*, 18, 40–60.

Hmielowski, J. D., Feldman, L., Myers, T. A., Leiserowitz, A., & Maibach, E. (2014). An attack on science? Media use, trust in scientists, and perceptions of global warming. *Public Understanding of Science*, 23(7), 866–883.

Hochschild, J., & Levine Einstein, L. (2014). "It isn't what we don't know that gives us trouble, it's what we know that ain't so": Misinformation and democratic politics. *British Journal of Political Science*, 45, 467–475.

Hogg, M. A., & Reid, S. A. (2006). Social identity, self-categorization, and the communication of group norms. *Communication Theory*, 16, 7–30.

Iyengar, S., & Hahn, K. S. (2009). Red media, blue media: Evidence of ideological selectivity in media use. *Journal of Communication*, 59, 19–39.

Jackson, B., & Jamieson, K. H. (2007). *Unspun: Finding facts in the world of disinformation*. New York, NY: Random House.

Jamieson, K. H. (2015). Implications of the demise of "fact" in political discourse. *Proceedings of the American Philosophical Society*, 159, 66–84.

Jamieson, K. H., & Cappella, J. N. (2008). *Echo chamber: Rush Limbaugh and the conservative media establishment*. Oxford, England: Oxford University Press.

Jamieson, K. H., & Waldman, P. (2003). *The press effect: Politicians, journalists, and the stories that shape the political world*. New York, NY: Oxford University Press.

Jerit, J., & Barabas, J. (2012). Partisan perceptual bias and the information environment. *Journal of Politics*, 74, 672–684.

Johnson, H. M., & Seifert, C. M. (1994). Sources of the continued influence effect: When misinformation in memory affects later inferences. *Journal of Experimental Psychology: Learning, Memory, & Cognition, 20*, 1420–1436.

Kata, A. (2012). Anti-vaccine activists, web 2.0, and the postmodern paradigm. An overview of tactics and tropes used online by the anti-vaccination movement. *Vaccine, 30*, 3778–3689.

Kosloff, S., Greenberg, J., Schmader, T., Dechesne, M., & Weise, D. (2010). Smearing the opposition: Implicit and explicit stigmatization of the 2008 U.S. presidential candidates and the current U.S. president. *Journal of Experimental Psychology, 139*, 383–398.

Kuklinski, J. H., Quirk, P. J., Jerit, J., Schwieder, D., & Rich, R. F. (2000). Misinformation and the currency of democratic citizenship. *Journal of Politics, 62*, 790–816.

Kuklinski, J. H., Quirk, P. J., Schwieder, D., & Rich, R. F. (1998). Just the facts, ma'am: Political facts and public opinion. *Annals of the American Academy of Political and Social Science, 560*, 143–154.

Kull, S., Ramsay, C., & Lewis, E. (2003). Misperceptions, the media, and the Iraq War. *Political Science Quarterly, 118*, 569–598.

Lawrence, R. G., & Schafer, M. L. (2012). Debunking Sarah Palin: Mainstream news coverage of "death panels." *Journalism, 13*, 766–782.

Lewandowsky, S., Ecker, U. K. H., Seifert, C. M., Schwarz, N., & Cook, J. (2012). Misinformation and its correction: Continued influence and successful debiasing. *Psychological Science in the Public Interest, 13*, 106–131.

Maurer, M., & Reinemann, C. (2006). Learning versus knowing: Effects of misinformation in televised debates. *Communication Research, 33*, 489–506.

Meirick, P. C. (2013). Motivated misperception? Party, education, partisan news, and belief in "death panels." *Journalism & Mass Communication Quarterly, 90*(1), 39–57.

Meirick, P. C., & Bessarabova, E. (2016). Epistemic factors in selective exposure and political misperceptions on the right and left. *Analyses of Social Issues and Public Policy, 16*(1), 36–68.

Miller, J. M., Saunders, K. L., & Farhart, C. E. (2016). Conspiracy endorsement as motivated reasoning: The moderating roles of political knowledge and trust. *American Journal of Political Science, 60*(4), 824–844.

Nisbet, E. C., Cooper, K. E., & Garrett, R. K. (2015). The partisan brain: How dissonant science messages lead conservatives and liberals to (dis)trust science. *Annals of the American Academy of Political and Social Science, 658*, 36–66.

Nyhan, B., & Reifler, J. (2010). When corrections fail: The persistence of political misperceptions. *Political Behavior, 32*, 303–330.

Nyhan, B., & Reifler, J. (2015). *Estimating fact-checking's effects: Evidence from a long-term experiment during campaign 2014.* Washington, DC: American Press Institute.

Pariser, E. (2011). *The filter bubble: What the Internet is hiding from you.* New York, NY: Penguin Press.

Pasek, J., Stark, T. H., Krosnick, J. A., & Tompson, T. (2015). What motivates a conspiracy theory? Birther beliefs, partisanship, liberal-conservative ideology, and anti-black attitudes. *Electoral Studies, 40*, 482–489.

Pew Research Center. (2011, May 3). *Too much coverage: Birth certificate, royal wedding.* Retrieved from http://www.people-press.org/2011/05/03/too-much-coverage-birth-certificate-royal-wedding

Pingree, R. J., Brossard, D., & McLeod, D. M. (2014). Effects of journalistic adjudication on factual beliefs, news evaluations, information seeking, and epistemic political efficacy. *Mass Communication & Society, 17,* 615–638.

Ramsay, C., Kull, S., Lewis, E., & Subias, S. (2010). *Misinformation and the 2010 election: A study of the US electorate.* College Park, MD: Program on International Policy Attitudes.

Rojecki, A., & Meraz, S. (2016). Rumors and factitious informational blends: The role of the web in speculative politics. *New Media & Society, 18,* 25–43.

Shin, J., Jian, L., Driscoll, K., & Bar, F. (2016). Political rumoring on Twitter during the 2012 US presidential election: Rumor diffusion and correction. *New Media & Society.* Advance online publication. https://dx.doi.org/10.1177/1461444816634054

Silverman, C. (2015). *Lies, damn lies, and viral content. How news websites spread (and debunk) online rumors, unverified claims, and misinformation* [Tow/Knight Report]. New York, NY: Tow Center for Digital Journalism.

Slater, M. D. (2007). Reinforcing spirals: The mutual influence of media selectivity and media effects and their impact on individual behavior and social identity. *Communication Theory, 17*(3), 281–303.

Southwell, B. G. (2013). *Social networks and popular understanding of science and health: Sharing disparities.* Baltimore, MD: Johns Hopkins University Press.

Southwell, B. G., & Thorson, E. A. (2015). The prevalence, consequence, and remedy of misinformation in mass media systems. *Journal of Communication, 65,* 589–595.

Southwell, B. G., & Yzer, M. C. (2007). The roles of interpersonal communication in mass media campaigns. *Communication Yearbook, 31,* 419–462.

Stroud, N. J. (2011). *Niche news: The politics of news choice.* New York, NY: Oxford University Press.

Taber, C. S., & Lodge, M. (2006). Motivated skepticism in the evaluation of political beliefs. *American Journal of Political Science, 50,* 755–769.

Thorson, E. (2016). Belief echoes: The persistent effects of corrected misinformation. *Political Communication, 33*(3), 460–480.

Uscinski, J. E., & Butler, R. W. (2013). The epistemology of fact checking. *Critical Review, 25,* 162–180.

Weeks, B. E. (2015). Emotions, partisanship, and misperceptions: How anger and anxiety moderate the effect of partisan bias on susceptibility to political misinformation. *Journal of Communication, 65,* 699–719.

Weeks, B. E., Ardévol-Abreu, A., & Gil de Zúñiga, H. (2015). Online influence? Social media use, opinion leadership, and political persuasion. *International Journal of Public Opinion Research.* Advance online publication. https://dx.doi.org/10.1093/ijpor/edv050

Weeks, B. E., & Garrett, R. K. (2014). Electoral consequences of political rumors: Motivated reasoning, candidate rumors, and vote choice during the 2008 U.S. presidential election. *International Journal of Public Opinion Research, 26,* 401–422.

Weeks, B. E., Ksiazek, T. B., & Holbert, R. L. (2016). Partisan enclaves or shared media experiences? A network approach to understanding citizens' political news environment. *Journal of Broadcasting and Electronic Media, 60,* 248–268.

Weeks, B., & Southwell, B. (2010). The symbiosis of news coverage and aggregate online search behavior: Obama, rumors, and presidential politics. *Mass Communication & Society, 13,* 341–360.

Misinformation and Science

NINE Emergence, Diffusion, and Persistence

LAURA SHEBLE

I n science, misinformation sometimes arises and spreads from scientific fraud, such as the purposeful publication of studies based on fabricated ("invented") or false (prejudicially selected) data and misleading claims (Bornmann, 2013; Fang, Steen, & Casadevall, 2012; Gross, 2016). In other circumstances, misinformation about scientific findings may arise as reports of study results are shared with different audiences (Hilgartner, 1990), or as novel yet preliminary study results are broadcast widely and later turn out to be false (Schwartz, Woloshin, & Baczek, 2002). When the findings of scientific studies have direct implications in domains that intersect with powerful vested interests, such as those related to climate change (Farrell, 2016; Oreskes, 2004), tobacco products (Cummings, Brown, & O'Connor, 2007), and the pharmaceutical industry (Barnes & Bero, 1998; Lundh, Sismondo, Lexchin, Busuioc, & Bero, 2012), systematic campaigns, and even conspiracies (Cummings et al., 2007) may influence public perceptions and cast doubt on research findings even when there is a broad consensus within science.

More mundane circumstances also lead to the emergence, diffusion, and persistence of misinformation within science. Such circumstances may be associated with the passage of time, such as outdated information, or originate in accidental misrepresentations (Nguyen & Ho-Pham, 2012), misinterpretations (Cooper & Rosenthal, 1980), or overinterpretations of research (e.g., Henrich, Heine, & Norenzayan, 2010). Limitations associated with research tools and practices can also generate inaccuracies (e.g., Fidler, Burgman, Cumming, Buttrose, & Thomason, 2006). The conservative nature of science, and the resistance of specialists within a field to accept findings contrary to established beliefs, highlight the need for the accumulation of evidence in support of new ideas and the persistence of established but potentially suboptimal beliefs (e.g., Genuis, 2005). Biases such as publication bias (Sterling, 1959), also referred to as "the file drawer problem" (Rosenthal, 1979), can also introduce misinformation.

As indicated above, there is the potential for misinformation to enter the science system in a wide variety of circumstances that range from cases of outright fraud to attempts to communicate research findings to broader audiences by journalists and others. Misinformation may persist within science, thereby influencing subsequent work as well as spreading and swaying beliefs in the public sphere. Once purportedly scientific misinformation enters public discourse, misperceptions of scientific knowledge and their effects may be difficult to counter. The misperceptions may be aggravated by the presentation of falsely "balanced" expert testimony (e.g., Thorson, this volume; Weeks, this volume), argumentation from vocal science dissidents (Jones, 2002), and laypersons' approaches to evaluations of science (e.g., Horlick-Jones, Walls, & Kitzinger, 2007). Professional contexts such as clinical medicine, in which the decisions of health care providers would ideally be informed by the best available scientific evidence, are challenged by lags in synthesis and diffusion of relevant evidence (Antman, Lau, Kupelnick, Mosteller, & Chalmers, 1992). Direct-to-physician (DTP) and direct-to-consumer (DTC) advertising by vested interests such as pharmaceutical and medical-device companies may further heighten challenges to the application of unbiased science-based evidence to application contexts (Boudewyns et al., this volume).

After a brief overview of networks, diffusion, and consensus formation in science, the remainder of this chapter focuses on contexts in which "scientific" misinformation arises and spreads: cases of scientific misconduct such as fraudulent research, everyday research practices, issues related to replication and systematic biases in research, and popularization and other types of audience-oriented translations.

Networks, Diffusion, and Consensus

Network studies focus on relationships. The relationships may be among people, ideas, organizations, semantic concepts (e.g., Cappella, Ophir, &

Sutton, this volume), and other types of entities. Network studies are conducted to examine how, to what extent, or with whom people, ideas, organizations, and other elements of society relate or interact. The relationships of interest may be direct, as in the case of friendship, or indirect, such as when people are connected based on affiliation with a common organization. Networks, often represented in network diagrams, consist of nodes (also called "vertices") and edges (also called "ties" or "links"). Edges represent relationships between nodes. For example, edges between author nodes may indicate sharing, flow, or exchange of information or other goods between authors. Studies of ideas might foreground similarity in meaning between concepts presented in a collection of documents and therefore depict the containers of those concepts, documents, or groups of words with nodes and assign edges to indicate similarity between concepts represented by the nodes.

Knowledge Networks

It is possible to view knowledge as a complex heterogeneous network of concepts and ideas distilled from human experience in the world. Within this network, only the small portion that emerged according to and in the context of accepted standards and norms of research fields is considered scientific (or more broadly, scholarly) knowledge. Scientific knowledge is represented in forms that are more or less fixed—in the language used to describe studies (Darian, 2003; Hyland, 2004); embedded in the instruments and other technologies used to sense, measure, and analyze (Latour & Woolgar, 1986; see also Bazerman, 2009); and in the text, visuals, and other recordings used to communicate, store, and preserve findings and interpretations of them (Bazerman, 1988; Pepe, Mayernik, Borgman, & Van de Sompel, 2010). People, though essential to science knowledge networks generally, may be foregrounded as communicators or creators of ideas or occluded and only indirectly represented by work to which they contributed.

In the context of networks of scientific knowledge, research fields are an important level of aggregation. Research fields consist of scientists or scholars who are focused on a common set of problems and draw on a common knowledge base. The culture of a research field guides research processes and decisions and defines research standards. The members of a research field constitute the primary audience for whom a scientist publishes and have the expertise necessary to assess critically a scientist's work (Kuhn, 1970). Members of a research field are typically tightly linked in relatively cohesive networks rich in social, intellectual, and other ties. Though such dense interest-based networks imply a level of homogeneity, recent research suggests there may be more optimal degrees of social, cognitive, and perhaps other types of distance or difference for tasks such as paper and grant evaluations (Wang & Sandström, 2015).

Diffusion of Innovations

Network studies of diffusion focus on how innovations—ideas, technologies, methods, conventions, and so on—are communicated and spread from person to person across social systems over time (Rogers, 2003). To an extent, homogeneity among actors in a network ensures effective communication (Rogers, 2003) and therefore greater potential for an idea to diffuse with greater fidelity, as does greater codification of knowledge. Heterogeneity, on the other hand, is important for introducing ideas (Granovetter, 1983), overcoming deficit thinking (Medin, Bennis, & Chandler, 2010), and developing novel combinations of ideas (e.g., Upham, Rosenkopf, & Ungar, 2010). As an innovation diffuses across increasingly heterogeneous contexts, the essential elements are kept intact and others are translated, transformed (Carlile, 2004; Latour & Woolgar, 1986), and edited (Sahlin & Wedlin, 2008) to fit use contexts.

Whether an innovation diffuses is not necessarily an indication of the quality or efficacy of that idea. It is possible for innovations that would be effective to fail and for innovations that are not especially effective to be widely adopted (Abrahamson, 1991). Diffusion may occur through mimesis, with new ideas adopted or rejected based on observations of decisions of others with whom the potential adopter identifies or whom she or he seeks to emulate (DiMaggio & Powell, 1983). Further, whether a given idea or set of ideas is taken up may depend on factors such as the availability of resources, participation of high-status intellectual leaders, structural conditions that provide access to key resources and micromobilization contexts, and the ability of proponents to frame ideas "in ways that resonate with the concerns of those who inhabit an intellectual field" (Frickel & Gross, 2005, p. 207).

Though concerns internal to research fields may be of primary interest to many, science does not function as a closed system; members of research fields typically maintain many relationships that may influence allegiances and priorities (Chubin, 1976), including memberships or affiliations with publishing bodies, professional associations, employing institutions, funding bodies, and practice constituencies. Individual experiences more broadly inevitably influence decisions. Scientists inhabit different types of institutions as well, including academic, governmental, nongovernmental, and, increasingly, private institutions (Halpern & Berlin, 2005; Pray & Naseem, 2003), each with its own traditions and culture.

Consensus Formation and Consensus

In any given area of research, consensus—the joint or deliberative agreement on a proposition—can occur only after careful accumulation and evaluation of evidence (Beatty & Moore, 2010). In some respects, processes of consensus formation may be viewed as the inverse of diffusion, with distant, contesting beliefs coalescing around a broadly shared agreement through the convergence of findings and integration of evidence from several lines of inquiry. Broad scientific consensuses are often recognized as gold standards that can be used to judge whether any given statement or object informs or misinforms. However, standards and norms associated with how science is practiced and what is accepted as scientific knowledge remain unfixed and are subject to change over time.

Once established, widely held consensual beliefs may in themselves contribute to the emergence of misinformation, given that established beliefs may be resistant to modification in light of emerging lines of evidence from new research. A study by Genuis (2005) chronicles one such example, that of the causal link between human infection with *Helicobacter pylori* and stomach ulcers. Though the first study that established an etiological link between a spiral bacteria (later to be renamed *Helicobacter pylori*) and stomach ulcers was published in 1984 in the *Lancet* (Marshall & Warren, 1984), it was not until 10 years later that the association between the bacterium and peptic ulcers was formally confirmed in a National Institutes of Health (NIH) consensus statement and not until the 2000s that eradication of *H. pylori* emerged as a standard treatment for peptic ulcer. Subsequently, *H. pylori* has been designated an infectious disease that is a cause—and the most important risk factor—for not only peptic ulcer but also gastric (stomach) cancer (Sugano et al., 2015).

As the lag between research and treatment—or professional practice—in the case of *H. pylori* and peptic ulcer illustrates, science does not operate in a closed system. Though members of a research field may be the primary evaluators of accumulating evidence from studies within a research field, additional research and related efforts are required to translate find-ings to other contexts. In some cases, studies of a given problem may con-tinue well beyond the point of scientific consensus. This is particularly true when a problem is publicly contested or perceived to be relevant to powerful vested interests. Notable examples of such ongoing lines of post-consensus research have been documented for climate change (Oreskes, 2004; Shwed & Bearman, 2010), the health risks associated with tobacco use (Cummings et al., 2007), and the fabricated link between childhood measles, mumps, rubella (MMR) vaccines and autism (Godlee, Smith, & Marcovitch, 2011; Kaplan, this volume; Shwed & Bearman, 2010).

Research Misconduct and Questionable Research Practices

As Gross (2016) and others have pointed out, there is at least anecdotal evidence that acts considered to be research misconduct in contemporary science practice have been around for quite some time. Newton, for ex-ample, adjusted the measurements he presented in *Principia* to support the law of universal gravitation. Newton ensured that the presented data matched the expected theoretical values of the supported concepts at a high level of precision (Westfall, 1973). At the time of Newton, however, the practice of science and expectations for scientists differed from cur-rent practices.

In the U.S. literature, definitions of research misconduct published by the Office of Research Integrity (ORI, n.d.), currently a division of the Department of Health and Human Services (HHS), and by the National Science Foundation (NSF) Office of Inspector General (OIG) (NSF, 2002) are widely used. Both identify three research misconduct behaviors: fab-rication of research, falsification of research, and plagiarism. The NSF Re-search Misconduct code defines falsification, fabrication, and plagiarism as follows:

(1) *Fabrication* means making up data or results and recording or reporting them.
(2) *Falsification* means manipulating research materials, equipment, or pro-cesses, or changing or omitting data or results such that the research is not accurately represented in the research record.
(3) *Plagiarism* means the appropriation of another person's ideas, processes, re-sults, or words without giving appropriate credit. (NSF, 2002, p. 237)

Especially egregious examples of data fabrication by researchers in-clude that by John Darsee, once a medical researcher at Harvard, later

Emory, who specialized in cardiology, and Diederik Stapel, a psychology researcher at Tilburg University in the Netherlands. Darsee contributed to at least 83 published papers and abstracts over 14 years (through 1981) that were later retracted because they were based on fabricated data. In the following decade, misinformation presented in these papers persisted and was further diffused; Darsee's papers were cited more than 300 times, primarily in a positive context (Kochan & Budd, 1992). Stapel, similarly prolific, contributed to at least 125 papers between 1994 and 2011, 55 of which were found to have been based on fabricated and falsified data (Markowitz & Hancock, 2014). As these examples demonstrate, it is possible for researchers to continue to publish fraudulent research for years and for this research to continue to influence subsequent studies even after the fraud has been highly publicized.

Falsification, in contrast to fabrication, involves manipulating research materials originally obtained through the process of research such that the actual research is misrepresented. As noted, Stapel both falsified and fabricated data. In addition to text and numeric data, other types of research materials are sometimes falsified. Images were manipulated to support a 2014 *Nature* study led by Haruko Obokata that claimed to present an easy way to make stem cells (Pollack, 2014). Plagiarism, in contrast to fabrication and falsification, introduces misinformation through misrepresenting the source of information.

While widespread agreement on the extent and severity of misinformation in science has yet to emerge, recent studies (e.g., Fanelli, 2009; Fang et al., 2012; Seife, 2015) suggest that the problem may be more severe than once assumed (Chubin, 1985; Gross, 2016; Merton, 1957) and may be increasing. In an examination by Fang and colleagues (2012) of 2,047 retracted biomedical publications, a tenfold increase in the number of occurrences of fraud or suspected fraud from 1975 to approximately 2011 was found. The majority of publications (67%) were retracted for some form of research misconduct, including 43% for use of fabricated or falsified data. As noted by the authors, one would expect retraction data to underestimate the actual rate of fraud since some proportion is not detected or is detected but not systematically reported in peer-reviewed literature (Fang et al., 2012).

Research by Seife (2015) and estimates based on survey data further support the suggestion that misinformation in science is likely greater than retraction studies indicate. According to estimates from a systematic review and meta-analysis of survey studies (Fanelli, 2009), 1.97% of researchers surveyed admitted to having fabricated, falsified, or modified data at least once; and approximately 14.12% indicated knowing of a colleague who had. More than one third (33.7%) admitted to having committed other questionable research practices, such as selective publication of results or concealing conflicts of interest, and 72% indicated knowing of colleagues who had committed these other types of questionable research practices. Problems are compounded when misinformation introduced by research misconduct becomes further entrenched and disseminated by subsequent studies that build on the initial fraudulent research (Kochan & Budd, 1992).

A better understanding of research misconduct and its effects can be developed by examining not only the prevalence, distribution, causes, and characteristics of research misconduct in broad studies but also individual cases, such as Andrew Wakefield and colleagues' 1998 *Lancet* paper, in which the authors used fraudulent data to fabricate a link between childhood MMR vaccines and autism (Godlee et al., 2011). The paper exemplifies the dangerous consequences even a single misinforming paper can have when presented as science. In 2004, six years after the initial publication, Wakefield's ten coauthors issued a "retraction of interpretation," but it was not until 2010, twelve years after initial publication, that a retraction of the paper in full was issued. Though it was later revealed that Wakefield stood to gain financially from the paper's reported findings (Deer, 2011), and he eventually lost his license to practice medicine, reverberations of the false claims made in the publication, which were amplified by subsequent media reports, have been linked to decreased vaccination rates (Godlee et al., 2011) and have necessitated costly expenditures on follow-up research and corrective public information campaigns (Lewandowsky, Ecker, Seifert, Schwarz, & Cook, 2012).

Efforts aimed at increasing the transparency of research, such as the EQUATOR network (http://www.equator-network.org), and other goals of the open science movement more broadly (Levin, Leonelli, Weckowska, Castle, & Dupré, 2016) may counter misinformation in science to an extent, although studies such as that by Seife (2015) suggest there are opportunities to develop more robust and encompassing approaches to mitigate the introduction of misinformation in science contexts. Seife (2015) examines publications associated with clinical trials that, following U.S. Food and Drug Administration (FDA) inspections, were determined to warrant regulatory action, indicated by an "official action indicated" (OAI) classification, because of noncompliance with FDA regulations. Of 644 inspections in 2013, 2% received OAI classifications for issues such as research misconduct, improper reporting of adverse events, and failure to follow research protocols. Of 101 clinical trials that received an OAI classification, 68 had one or more associated peer-reviewed publications, for a total of 95 publications. Of these, OAI documentation was presented in enough detail to determine the type of problems identified by inspections for 57 trials and an associated 78 publications. Further analysis showed that only 3 of the 78 publications mentioned conditions or practices identified in the inspections that led to the OAI classification. No subsequent corrections, retractions, expressions of concern, or other comments mentioning the issues identified in inspections were found (Seife, 2015).

While a cultural shift to open science, motivated by interests such as improving the integrity, accessibility, assessibility, and interpretability of research development, products, and practices, may contribute to the mitigation of misinformation in science, so too might research on the adverse career impacts of misconduct. Research misconduct affects not only the scientists directly responsible but also their broader social circles. Publication of fraudulent research negatively affects the broader body of work by researchers associated with a retracted paper, including that of collaborators at a distance of up to four degrees of separation (Lu, Jin, Uzzi, & Jones, 2013). On a related note, Mongeon and Lariviere (2016) find that first and last authors of retracted studies were most affected and that adverse effects were greater for studies retracted for research misconduct than those retracted due to error.

Mundane Misinformation in Science

Less nefarious circumstances also lead to the emergence, diffusion, and persistence of misinformation within science. Such circumstances may include those in which there are more ambiguous norms of behavior (Chubin, 1985; Leahey, Entwisle, & Einaudi, 2003) and greater variation in research practices (e.g., Leahey et al., 2003). Similarly, accidental misrepresentations, misinterpretations, and overinterpretations of research, limitations associated with research tools, mistakes, insufficient training, lack of knowledge, and shortcuts may contribute to systematic biases and other patterns of misinformation in the research record.

Disciplinary differences in research training programs and the extent to which training draws on codified versus tacit knowledge may influence the degree of variation in practice and perceived ambiguity (Polanyi, 1966;

Whitley, 2000). Knowledge that has been codified has been selected, reduced in complexity, and translated or possibly transformed with the intent of helping others focus attention on what is important and necessary to be able to perform a set of activities. Tacit knowledge, conversely, refers to knowledge that exists in situ; that which is important remains embedded in a broader context. When a group or individual must learn procedural knowledge that is primarily tacit, it is often helpful for people to be enmeshed in the experience such as through visiting and working with others, though such experiences and what is learned through them will differ across individuals and over time.

Tacit knowledge has been and continues to be important across many facets of science (e.g., Collins, 1974; Polanyi, 1966). In many fields, very specific practical information such as that related to fine-grained aspects of field and laboratory procedures (Collins, 1974) and data editing (Leahey et al., 2003) traditionally has been passed from person to person or gleaned from available cues in the environment. Similarly, organization of computer interfaces and default values in data-analysis software might informally guide researchers' choices. Three examples of everyday practices that have the potential to systematically introduce bias and inaccuracies into the research record include reading and evaluation of primary research reports in the context of literature review (Cooper & Rosenthal, 1980), co-opting references from other material read, and opting to use default values in data-analysis packages without making a considered and informed choice among possible values.

Cooper and Rosenthal (1980) ran an experiment to compare researcher assessments of the findings of past research when using statistical versus traditional review procedures. Researchers who used statistical procedures were able to more accurately describe and make inferences from past research in the aggregate and more likely to engage with the actual findings of research studies. Researchers who used traditional methods, on the other hand, were more likely to rely on what the report authors said they did than on what they actually did. These findings are congruent with qualitative research by Bazerman (1988), who found that, when reading physics papers, readers tended not to review mathematics equations in detail unless moved to do so for a specific reason. Under normal reading circumstances, readers tended to trust the author and likely, implicitly, the peer-review system, which is expected to identify and prevent publication of mistakes.

Mistakes and shortcuts taken when reviewing past research, presumably to expedite processes associated with developing research projects or writing papers, can introduce bias as well. For example, when a researcher uses "induced citations," those adopted from reference lists of published papers (Braun, Glänzel, & Schubert, 2010), the scientist is far removed from the actual study findings and relies not even on what the authors of the cited work said they did (as Cooper and Rosenthal [1980] found in the case of traditional literature reviews) but rather on what someone else said they did. Leistedt and Linkowski (2016) take a more critical view of induced citations and describe this practice as "citation plagiarism," a subcategory of plagiarism and therefore presumably research misconduct. Such co-opting of references from other publications is believed to be relatively common and widespread (Ball, 2002; Liang, Zhong, & Rousseau, 2014; Simkin & Roychowdhury, 2003).

Tool design and use may contribute to or reinforce misinformation. As discussed by Costello and Osborne (2005), principal components analysis (PCA) is the default choice for factor analysis (FA) in popular data analysis packages such as SPSS and SAS. Though technically one might differentiate between PCA and FA based on how variance is handled by each technique, it is not unusual for authors to describe PCA as a type of FA in peer-reviewed literature. A lack of distinction between the analysis techniques likely is reinforced when analysts interact with statistical packages that frame PCA in the context of FA. Whether these software tools contribute to the potentially flawed understanding of these different techniques and whether or to what extent this negatively influences research are open questions.

Replication and Bias

Headlines in popular news media (e.g., Ioannidis, 2015) and prestigious science journals such as *Science* (e.g., Open Science Collaboration, 2015) alike proclaim that we know less than we thought we did, and, potentially, a sizable proportion of what we think we know is false or will not hold up under scrutiny. The "replication crisis," or failure to produce concordant findings in replications of research studies, has emerged as a major concern in some fields (Makel & Plucker, 2014), including psychology (Pashler & Wagenmakers, 2012) and preclinical medicine (Begley & Ellis, 2012), because the inability to replicate previous research suggests that published research evidence is less robust and reliable than generally presumed.

One of the largest and highest-profile replication studies to date was published by the Open Science Collaboration (2015), an international team of scientists who replicated 100 studies published in three prestigious psychology journals (*Journal of Personality & Social Psychology: Social*; *Journal of Experimental Psychology: Learning, Memory, & Cognition*; and *Psychological Science*). The team was able to reproduce findings from only 36% of the published studies. Furthermore, findings that were reproduced tended to have smaller effects than those reported in the original studies.

Systematic biases in publication—or more broadly, the research reporting system—are thought to contribute to the lack of reproducibility of research. Publication bias (Rosenthal, 1979; Sterling, 1959), generally defined as the lack of representativeness of published research compared to all research, and preferential evaluations of some research, most commonly that which is statistically significant (e.g., Fanelli, 2011, 2012; Sterling, 1959), contribute to this problem. Publication bias occurs in large part because authors choose not to publish studies they perceive as less significant, statistically and otherwise. While publication bias has received the most attention in fields such as psychology (e.g., Rothstein, Sutton, & Borenstein, 2005), other forms of bias also contribute to misinformation (Chavalarias & Ioannidis, 2010), including citation bias, the preferential selection of references to support a perspective or claim. Greenberg (2009), in a study of citations in NIH grant applications, argues that citation bias lends unfounded scientific authority to more preliminary research findings, thereby contributing to establishment of "scientific facts" without consideration of all available evidence, let alone an appropriate level of evidence. More specifically, Greenberg (2009) observes that grant writers tended to preferentially select research that supported their proposed research and neglect or distort contrary research findings.

Popularization and Popular Debates of Science

Misinformation that emerges within science may spread to other spheres of society, including interested communities in the general public and in professional practice and policy, potentially with profound and irreversible effects (e.g., Ludwig, Hilborn, & Walters, 1993). Misinformation about scientific findings may arise as reports of study results are translated and transformed (Carlile, 2004)—necessarily imperfectly and incompletely—to share with different audiences. Typically, we think of such cases as occurring as scientific results are shared across boundaries with and between more general audiences (e.g., Hilgartner, 1990; Ladle, Jepson, &

Whittaker, 2005), though specialists also may draw on popular science literature (e.g., Paul, 2004) or reinterpret historical texts based on new knowledge or circumstances.

In a study of the process of popularization, Hilgartner (1990) examined changes in how a broad estimate of the relationship between diet/nutrition and cancer presented in the highly publicized review *Causes of Cancer* (Doll & Peto, 1981) was represented in popular, scientific, and professional media. Across contexts, there was the tendency to simplify the estimate such that it was represented as more certain and precise than indicated in the original report. Ladle and colleagues (2005) found similar distortions in 26 of 29 secondary media reports of a 2004 *Nature* study on the potential effects of global warming on distributional ranges and extinctions of animal and plant species (Thomas et al., 2004). The news media tended to indicate more severe consequences over a shorter time span than the original study did. The original study by Thomas and colleagues, as summarized by Ladle and colleagues, estimates that "given a number of key assumptions and under 'moderate' climate change scenarios, between fifteen and thirty-seven per cent of the 1103 species considered within the study would be 'committed to extinction' by 2050" (Ladle et al., 2005, p. 232). In contrast, 21 of 29 media reports indicate that "over a million species would go extinct due to global warming by 2050" (Ladle et al., 2005, p. 232).

In related research, Littell (2008) observes similar patterns of distortion in how results of a trial intervention were reported in reviews; Brown (2008) found that the "Freshman 15," a health myth and shorthand phrase widely used in popular media that suggests students tend to gain about 15 pounds in their first year of college, was generally impervious to scientific evidence, which indicates college freshmen gain an average of about 5 pounds. Brown's study (2008) extends previous work by Antman and colleagues (1992) in which recommended treatments for myocardial infarction presented in textbooks and traditional literature reviews were compared with results based on systematic syntheses of the scientific evidence via cumulative meta-analysis. Those authors found that though cumulative meta-analyses revealed the availability of relatively new treatments that reduced the risk of dying, the majority of clinical experts who wrote traditional reviews and textbooks lagged behind, sometimes by 10 years or more, and continued to recommend treatments that either were less effective or, though once standard treatment, had been shown to be harmful (Antman et al., 1992; Chalmers, Hedges, & Cooper, 2002). The clear implication of Antman and colleagues' study was that some patients received suboptimal care and had more negative outcomes than what would have been available with state-of-the-art treatment options. Accordingly, health care providers who relied on memory, outdated treatments archived in aging medical documents, unsystematic research reviews written by eminent but biased authors, and their professional practice networks were misinformed.

Conclusion

We rely on the findings of scientific studies to develop treatments that we expect to extend and improve people's quality of life, to estimate the severity of global threats such as climate change, and to inform decision making in an increasing variety of political, professional, and personal contexts. Given that decisions in all of these circumstances have potentially irreversible consequences (e.g., Ludwig, Hilborn, & Walters, 1993), it is imperative that these decisions be based on not only the best information available but also the best information that can be produced. If science is to inform rather than misinform, we must evaluate knowledge derived from science based on both products and practices of research.

Yet uncertainty, curiosity, and lack of knowledge drive scientific inquiry. Lack of knowledge, in combination with curiosity, enables researchers to formulate new questions and step into the unknown, grounded in findings and discoveries of their predecessors, training in the norms and practices of research communities and with the instrumental and procedural tools that allow questions to be shaped into systematic studies that define, measure, analyze, and abstract knowledge from that which can be sensed, theorized, and encountered. Ultimately, the findings of any given study, no matter how seemingly accurate or robust, are marked by at least a degree of uncertainty, which can be considered in the context of the best available advice that can be derived from the accumulating networks of scientific knowledge.

The integrity of scientific information is compromised through accidental misrepresentations of data, misinterpretation and overinterpretation of past findings within the science system, and scientific information's translation into other social and cultural contexts. Science that once informed may later misinform when knowledge and understandings are refined, disproved, or otherwise changed. Practices associated with reading, writing, and publishing contribute to scientific misinformation, as can the materials, tools, practices, and methods through which scientific knowledge is produced. Finally, if we understand the production of scientific information to be embedded in social, cultural, political, and value-laden systems, we must take bias, perspective, and context into account when evaluating scientific evidence and the extent to which any given representation informs or misinforms. While it can be disconcerting to emphasize shortcomings of how science is currently conducted and the extent to which scientific knowledge informs decision making by professionals, policy makers, and interested publics, a better understanding of misinformation in science may potentially lead us to more effective strategies to prevent, identify, and mitigate effects of practices that introduce misinformation into science systems and undermine science and our trust in scientific information.

References

Abrahamson, E. (1991). Managerial fads and fashions: The diffusion and rejection of innovations. *Academy of Management Review, 16*(3), 586–612.

Antman, E. M., Lau, J., Kupelnick, B., Mosteller, F., & Chalmers, T. C. (1992). A comparison of results of meta-analyses of randomized control trials and recommendations of clinical experts: Treatments for myocardial infarction. *Journal of the American Medical Association, 268*(2), 240–248.

Ball, P. (2002). Paper trail reveals references go unread by citing authors. *Nature, 420,* 594.

Barnes, D. E., & Bero, L. A. (1998). Why review articles on the health effects of passive smoking reach different conclusions. *Journal of the American Medical Association, 279*(19), 1566–1570.

Bazerman, C. (1988). *Shaping written knowledge: The genre and activity of the experimental article in science.* Madison, WI: University of Wisconsin Press.

Bazerman, C. (2009). How does science come to speak in the courts? Citations, intertexts, expert witnesses, consequential facts, and reasoning. *Law & Contemporary Problems, 72,* 91–120.

Beatty, J., & Moore, A. (2010). Should we aim for consensus? *Episteme, 7,* 198–214.

Begley, C. G., & Ellis, L. M. (2012). Drug development: Raise standards for preclinical cancer research. *Nature, 483,* 531–533.

Bornmann, L. (2013). Research misconduct: Definitions, manifestations and extent. *Publications, 1,* 87–98.

Braun, T., Glänzel, W., & Schubert, A. (2010). On sleeping beauties, princes, and other tales of citation distributions. *Research Evaluation, 19*(3), 195–202.

Brown, C. (2008). The information trail of the "Freshman 15": A systematic review of a health myth within the research and popular literature. *Health Information and Libraries Journal, 25*(1), 1–12.

Carlile, P. R. (2004). Transferring, translating, and transforming: An integrative framework for managing knowledge across boundaries. *Organization Science, 15*(5), 555–568.

Chalmers, I., Hedges, L. V., & Cooper, H. (2002). A brief history of research synthesis. *Evaluation and the Health Professions, 25*(1), 12–37.

Chavalarias, D., & Ioannidis, J. P. A. (2010). Science mapping analysis characterizes 235 biases in biomedical research. *Journal of Clinical Epidemiology, 63,* 1205–1215.

Chubin, D. E. (1976). The conceptualization of scientific specialties. *Sociological Quarterly, 17*(4), 448–476.

Chubin, D. E. (1985). Misconduct in research: An issue of science policy and practice. *Minerva, 23*(2), 175–202.

Collins, H. M. (1974). The TEA set: Tacit knowledge and scientific networks. *Science Studies, 4*(2), 165–185.

Cooper, H. M., & Rosenthal, R. (1980). Statistical versus traditional procedures for summarizing research findings. *Psychological Bulletin, 87,* 442–449.

Costello, A. B., & Osborne, J. W. (2005). Best practices for exploratory factor analysis: Recommendations for getting the most from your analysis. *Practical Assessment, Research, & Evaluation, 10*(7). Retrieved from http://pareonline.net/getvn.asp?v=10&n=7

Cummings, K. M., Brown, A., & O'Connor, R. (2007). The cigarette controversy. *Cancer Epidemiology Biomarkers & Prevention, 16*(6), 1070–1076.

Darian, S. (2003). *Understanding the language of science.* Austin, TX: University of Texas Press.

Deer, B. (2011). How the case against the MMR vaccine was fixed. *BMJ, 342,* 342c5347.

DiMaggio, P. J., & Powell, W. W. (1983). The iron cage revisited: Institutional isomorphism and collective rationality in organizational fields. *American Sociological Review, 48*(2), 147–160.

Doll, R., & Peto, R. (1981). The causes of cancer: Quantitative estimates of avoidable risks of cancer in the United States today. *Journal of the National Cancer Institute, 66*(6), 1192–1308.

Fanelli, D. (2009). How many scientists fabricate and falsify research? A systematic review and meta-analysis of survey data. *PLoS ONE, 4*(5), e5738.

Fanelli, D. (2011). Negative results are disappearing from most disciplines and countries. *Scientometrics, 90,* 891–904.

Fanelli, D. (2012). Positive results receive more citations, but only in some disciplines. *Scientometrics, 94,* 701–709.

Fang, F. C., Steen, R. G., & Casadevall, A. (2012). Misconduct accounts for the majority of retracted scientific publications. *Proceedings of the National Academy of Sciences, 109*(42), 17028–17033.

Farrell, J. (2016). Corporate funding and ideological polarization about climate change. *Proceedings of the National Academy of Science, 113*(1), 92–97.

Fidler, F., Burgman, M. A., Cumming, G., Buttrose, R., & Thomason, N. (2006). Impact of criticism of null-hypothesis significance testing on statistical reporting practices in *Conservation Biology. Conservation Biology, 20*(5), 1539–1544.

Frickel, S., & Gross, N. (2005). A general theory of scientific/intellectual movements. *American Sociological Review, 70*(2), 204–232.

Genuis, S. K. (2005). Published literature and diffusion of medical innovation: Exploring innovation generation. *Canadian Journal of Information & Library Science, 29*(1), 27–54.

Godlee, F., Smith, J., & Marcovitch, H. (2011). Clear evidence of falsification of data should now close the door on this damaging vaccine scare. *BMJ, 342,* bmj.c7452.

Granovetter, M. S. (1983). The strength of weak ties: A network theory revisited. *Sociological Theory, 1*(1), 201–233.

Greenberg, S. A. (2009). How citation distortions create unfounded authority: Analysis of a citation network. *BMJ, 339,* b2680.

Gross, C. (2016). Scientific misconduct. *Annual Review of Psychology, 67,* 693–711.

Halpern, S. D., & Berlin, J. A. (2005). Beyond conventional publication bias: Other determinants of data suppression. In H. R. Rothstein, A. J. Sutton, & M. Borenstein (Eds.), *Publication bias in meta-analysis: Prevention, assessment, and adjustments* (pp. 303–317). West Sussex, England: Wiley.

Henrich, J., Heine, S. J., & Norenzayan, A. (2010). The WEIRDest people in the world? *Behavioral and Brain Sciences, 33*(2/3), 61–83.

Hilgartner, S. (1990). The dominant view of popularization: Conceptual problems, political uses. *Social Studies of Science, 20*(3), 519–539.

Horlick-Jones, T., Walls, J., & Kitzinger, J. (2007). Bricolage in action: Learning about, making sense of, and discussing issues about genetically modified crops and food. *Health, Risk, and Society, 9*(1), 83–103.

Hyland, K. (2004). *Disciplinary discourses: Social interactions in academic writing.* Ann Arbor, MI: University of Michigan Press.

Ioannidis, J. P. A. (2005). Why most published research findings are false. *PLoS ONE, 2*(8), e124.

Ioannidis, J. (2015, August 28). Psychology experiments are failing the replication test—for good reason. *Guardian.* Retrieved from https://www.theguardian.com/commentisfree/2015/aug/28/psychology-experiments-failing-replication-test-findings-science

Jones, W. E. (2002). Dissident versus loyalist: Which scientists should we trust? *Journal of Value Inquiry, 36,* 511–520.

Kochan, C. A., & Budd, J. M. (1992). The persistence of fraud in the literature: The Darsee case. *Journal of the American Society for Information Science, 43*(7), 488–493.

Kuhn, T. S. (1970). *Structure of scientific revolutions* (2nd ed.). Chicago, IL: University of Chicago Press.

Ladle, R., Jepson, P., & Whittaker, R. (2005). Scientists and the media: The struggle for legitimacy in climate change and conservation science. *Interdisciplinary Science Reviews, 30,* 231–240.

Latour, B., & Woolgar, S. (1986). *Laboratory life: The construction of scientific facts.* Princeton, NJ: Princeton University Press.

Leahey, E., Entwisle, B., & Einaudi, P. (2003). Diversity in everyday research practice: The case of data editing. *Sociological Methods & Research, 32,* 64–89.

Leistedt, S. J., & Linkowski, P. (2016). Fraud, individuals, and networks: A biopsycho-social model of scientific frauds. *Science & Justice, 56,* 109–112.

Levin, N., Leonelli, S., Weckowska, D., Castle, D., & Dupré, J. (2016). How do scientists define openness? Exploring the relationship between open science policies and research practice. *Bulletin of Science, Technology & Society, 36*(2), 128–141.

Lewandowsky, S., Ecker, U. K. H., Seifert, C. M., Schwarz, N., & Cook, J. (2012). Misinformation and its correction: Continued influence and successful debiasing. *Psychological Science in the Public Interest, 13*(3), 106–131.

Liang, L., Zhong, Z., & Rousseau, R. (2014). Scientists' referencing (mis)behavior revealed by the dissemination network of referencing errors. *Scientometrics, 101,* 1973–1986.

Littell, J. H. (2008). Evidence-based or biased? The quality of published reviews of evidence-based practices. *Children & Youth Services Review, 30*(11), 1299–1317.

Lu, S. F., Jin, G. Z., Uzzi, B., & Jones, B. (2013). The retraction penalty: Evidence from the *Web of Science. Scientific Reports, 3,* 3146.

Ludwig, D., Hilborn, R., & Walters, C. (1993). Uncertainty, resource exploitation, and conservation: Lessons from history. *Ecological Applications, 3*(4), 547–549.

Lundh, A., Sismondo, S., Lexchin, J., Busuioc, O. A., & Bero, L. A. (2012). Industry sponsorship and research outcome. *Cochrane Database of Systematic Reviews, 12,* MR000033.

Makel, M. C., & Plucker, J. A. (2014). Facts are more important than novelty: Replication in the education sciences. *Educational Research, 20*(10), 1–13.

Markowitz, D. M., & Hancock, J. T. (2014). Linguistic traces of a scientific fraud: The case of Diederik Stapel. *PLoS ONE, 9*(8), e105937.

Marshall, B. J., & Warren, J. R. (1984). Unidentified curved bacilli in the stomach of patients with gastritis and peptic ulceration. *Lancet, 323*(8390), 1311–1315.

Medin, D., Bennis, W., & Chandler, M. (2010). Culture and the home-field disadvantage. *Perspectives on Psychological Science, 5*(6), 708–713.

Merton, R. K. (1957). Priorities in scientific discovery: A chapter in the sociology of science. *Sociological Review, 22,* 635–659.

Mongeon, P., & Lariviere, V. (2016). *Journal of the Association for Information Science & Technology, 67*(3), 535–542.

National Science Foundation (NSF). (2002). Office of Inspector General. NSF Research Misconduct, 45 C.F.R. § 689. Retrieved from https://www.nsf.gov/oig/_pdf/cfr/45-CFR-689.pdf

Nguyen, T. V., & Ho-Pham, L. T. (2012, October 11). Misquotation of percent body fat [Reader comment]. *PLoS ONE.* Retrieved from http://journals.plos.org/plosone/article/comments?id=10.1371%2Fjournal.pone.0033308

Open Science Collaboration. (2015). Estimating the reproducibility of psychological science. *Science, 349*(6251), aac4716.

Oreskes, N. (2004). Science and public policy: What's proof got to do with it? *Environmental Science & Policy, 7,* 369–383.

ORI. *See* U.S. Office of Research Integrity (ORI).

Pashler, H., & Wagenmakers, E-J. (2012). Editors' introduction to the special section on replicability in psychological science: A crisis of confidence? *Perspectives on Psychological Science, 7*(6), 528–530.

Paul, D. (2004). Spreading chaos: The role of popularizations in the diffusion of scientific ideas. *Written Communication, 21*(1), 32–68.

Pepe, A., Mayernik, M., Borgman, C. L., & Van de Sompel, H. (2010). From artifacts to aggregations: Modeling scientific life cycles on the semantic web. *Journal of the Association for Information Science & Technology, 61*, 567–582.

Polanyi, M. (1966). *The tacit dimension.* Garden City, NY: Doubleday.

Pollack, A. (2014, July 2). Stem cell research papers are retracted. *New York Times.* Retrieved from http://www.nytimes.com/2014/07/03/business/stem-cell-research-papers-are-retracted.html

Pray, C. E., & Naseem, A. (2003). *The economics of agricultural biotechnology research* (ESA working paper no. 03-07). Rome, Italy: Food and Agriculture Organization of the United Nations, Agriculture and Economic Development Analysis Division.

Rogers, E. M. (2003). *Diffusion of innovations* (5th ed.). New York, NY: Free Press.

Rosenthal, R. (1979). The file drawer problem and tolerance for null results. *Psychological Bulletin, 86,* 638–641.

Rothstein, H. R., Sutton, A. J., & Borenstein, M. (Eds.). (2005). *Publication bias in meta-analysis: Prevention, assessment and adjustments.* West Sussex, England: Wiley.

Sahlin, K., & Wedlin, L. (2008). Circulating ideas: Imitation, translation, and editing. In R. Greenwood, C. Oliver, R. Suddaby, & K. Sahlin (Eds.), *The Sage handbook of organizational institutionalism* (pp. 218–242). Thousand Oaks, CA: Sage.

Schwartz, L. M., Woloshin, S., & Baczek, L. (2002). Media coverage of scientific meetings: Too much, too soon? *Journal of the American Medical Association, 287*(21), 2859–2863.

Seife, C. (2015). Research misconduct identified by the US Food and Drug Administration: Out of sight, out of mind, out of the peer-reviewed literature. *JAMA Internal Medicine, 175*(4), 567–577.

Shwed, U., & Bearman, P. S. (2010). The temporal structure of scientific consensus formation. *American Sociological Review, 75*(6), 817–840.

Simkin, M. V., & Roychowdhury, V. P. (2003). Read before you cite! *Complex Systems, 14*(3), 269–274.

Sterling, T. D. (1959). Publication decisions and their possible effects on inferences drawn from tests of significance—or vice versa. *Journal of the American Statistical Association, 54*(285), 30–34.

Sugano, K., Tack, J., Juipers, E. J., Graham, D. Y., El-Omar, E. M., Miura, S., . . . Malfertheiner, P. (2015). Kyoto global consensus report on *Helicobacter pylori* gastritis. *Gut, 64,* 1353–1367.

Thomas, C. D., Cameron, A., Green, R. E., Bakkenes, M., Beaumont, L. J., Collingham, Y. C., . . . Williams, S. E. (2004). Extinction risk from climate change. *Nature, 427*(6970), 145–148.

Upham, S. P., Rosenkopf, L., & Ungar, L. H. (2010). Innovating knowledge communities: An analysis of group collaboration and competition in science and technology. *Scientometrics, 83*(2), 525–554.

U.S. Office of Research Integrity (ORI). (N.d.) Definition of research misconduct. Retrieved from https://ori.hhs.gov/definition-misconduct

Wakefield, A. J., Murch, S. H., Anthony, A., Linnell, J., Casson, D. M., Malik, M., . . . Walker-Smith, J. A. (1998). RETRACTED: Ileal-lymphoid-nodular hyperplasia, non-specific colitis, and pervasive developmental disorder in children. *Lancet*, *351*(9103), 637–641.

Wang, Q., & Sandström, U. (2015). Defining the role of cognitive distance in the peer review process with an explorative study of a grant scheme in infection biology. *Research Evaluation*, *24*(3), 271–281.

Westfall, R. S. (1973). Newton and the fudge factor. *Science, 179,* 751–758.

Whitley, R. (2000). *The intellectual and social organization of the sciences* (2nd ed.). Oxford, England: Oxford University Press.

Doing the Wrong Things for the Right Reasons

TEN How Environmental Misinformation
Affects Environmental Behavior

ALEXANDER MAKI, AMANDA R. CARRICO,
AND MICHAEL P. VANDENBERGH

The world is dealing with environmental problems of unprecedented scope and complexity, particularly as a result of the rapidly escalating threat of climate change, as Intergovernmental Panel on Climate Change (IPCC) findings have shown (Pachauri & Meyer, 2014). Pressing environmental problems such as climate change and access to clean water are difficult to solve for a number of reasons. They are often global in scale, require coordination between innumerable parties, involve complex risks that are difficult to estimate, and entail future outcomes that are hard for people to appreciate in the present. These challenges are further exacerbated by a lack of the basic knowledge people need to make choices to minimize the impact on the environment and, in some cases, their own immediate well-being. Uncertain or inaccurate beliefs about issues such as climate change or water use can induce people to engage in environmentally harmful actions, including inefficient use of energy, water-wasting behaviors, and failure to support effective environmental policies. In a nation as large and energy-intensive as the United States, even seemingly minor behaviors and trivial knowledge gaps can translate into significant impacts. For example, the widespread yet inaccurate belief in the necessity of letting a car idle to warm up the engine before driving in the winter results in unnecessary carbon emissions in the United States comparable to the annual emissions of Jamaica (Carrico, Padgett, Vandenbergh, Gilligan, & Wallston, 2009). Similarly, people systematically underestimate the potential benefits of energy-efficient products, leading some to wrongly focus on actions like turning off lights rather than on high-impact energy- and water-saving actions (Attari, DeKay, Davidson, & Bruine de Bruin, 2010).

The extent to which individuals' beliefs about environmental issues are accurate is vitally important, given the myriad ways in which individual behaviors influence environmental outcomes (Dietz, Gardner, Gilligan, Stern, & Vandenbergh, 2009; Vandenbergh, Barkenbus, & Gilligan, 2008). In this chapter we examine how people's common misperceptions of the environmental impact of energy- and water-use behaviors influence behavioral choices and environmental outcomes. We first discuss how misinformation fits within traditional theories of environmental behavior change, and we examine common misperceptions that lead to unnecessary resource use and related environmental problems. We next discuss promising but understudied misunderstandings, such as people's beliefs about food waste, a topic that has received increased attention in recent years and implicates both energy and water use. Finally, we review the empirical evidence for the effectiveness of efforts to correct misperceptions and highlight effective approaches to addressing misperceptions that target mass audiences, including strategies such as informational campaigns, social influence interventions such as normative feedback, and policy recommendations such as carbon labeling of consumer products. Correcting common misperceptions surrounding energy and water use could be an integral part of a successful strategy to reduce their consumption in the United States and across the world.

The Role of Information in Theories of Environmental Behavior

Environmental misinformation can take many forms. It can be intentional or accidental. Companies that produce energy may intentionally downplay the role of dirty fuels in environmental problems such as climate change. Alternatively, people may accidently spread environmental misinformation, like those who perpetuate misunderstandings about when cars should be turned off to reduce idling and limit unnecessary carbon emissions (Carrico et al., 2009). Environmental misinformation can vary from general misunderstandings like those about the causes of climate change to specific myths such as hot water killing more bacteria than cold water during handwashing (Carrico, Spoden, Wallston, & Vandenbergh, 2013).

Misinformation and its perpetuation can occur for various reasons. Evidence suggests that people tend to remember and believe previously heard misinformation (Gilbert, Tafarodi, & Malone, 1993; Southwell & Thorson, 2015), meaning that once misinformation is initially spread, it can be difficult to counteract. People tend to overestimate the extent to which others engage in harmful behaviors, a kind of skepticism that has been called "pluralistic ignorance" (Prentice & Miller, 1993; Taylor, 1982). Environmental misinformation can be perpetuated because of motivated reasoning (Hart & Nisbet, 2012; Kunda, 1990), that is, seeking out information that allows one to retain his or her viewpoints or way of life. This convenient misinformation is believed in part because it allows people the opportunity to continue to engage in behaviors that are harmful to the environment but that benefit them, such as driving cars and traveling by airplane. In the late 1990s many people in the United States believed that hydropower, solar, and nuclear supplied most of the energy in the country, when coal and oil were actually the largest energy sources (National Environmental Education & Training Foundation, 1999). This kind of myth allows people to downplay feelings of guilt or concern that may arise from energy use.

The Role of Misinformation in Theories of Environmental Behavior

Environmental information or misinformation has relevance to day-to-day behaviors and choices. However, the importance of information as a factor in the adoption of behaviors and, by extension, as a point of leverage for changing behavior has been disputed by many behavioral scientists (e.g., Steg, Perlaviciute, & van der Werff, 2015; Steg & Vlek, 2009). Some behavioral models do propose that knowledge plays an important role as a driver of environmental behavior and policy support. The A-B-C model (Guagnano, Stern, & Dietz, 1995), the information-motivation-behavioral skills model (Fisher, Fisher, Bryan, & Misovich, 2002), and motivated reasoning approaches (Hart & Nisbet, 2012; Whitmarsh, 2011) all propose a central role for environmental knowledge when trying to understand and influence people's environmental intentions and behaviors. These models, by natural extension, then, consider how and when environmental misinformation leads to harmful action or inaction. However, many models are less prepared to offer insights into the role of environmental misinformation in environmental behavior, or they bypass information altogether. The theory of reasoned action or theory of planned behavior (Ajzen, 1985; Fishbein & Ajzen, 1975) and the value-belief-norm theory (Stern, Dietz, Abel, Guagnano, & Kalof, 1999), commonly used models in the environmental behavior change literature, traditionally focus on attitudes (such as "using energy is good/bad"), values (including altruistic beliefs), or related cognitions, but they less directly consider whether people have accurate beliefs or knowledge. Likewise, theories emphasizing the importance of social norms often downplay the importance of knowledge, instead finding that observations of others' behaviors or others' expectations of one's own behavior can often drive environmental actions (Cialdini, Reno, & Kallgren, 1990; Schultz, Nolan, Cialdini, Goldstein, & Griskevicius, 2007).

This disagreement may be, in part, due to the common assertion that knowledge is a necessary but insufficient condition for behavior change (Steg et al., 2015; Steg & Vlek, 2009), suggesting that "the information-deficit model" (Gross, 1994) may be useful to an extent, but motivation or some kind of action-orienting belief is required for people to change their behavior. Thus, researchers have focused on other types of cognition when trying to understand and predict environmental behaviors and policy support, such as perceived social norms, self-efficacy, or general attitudes (Ajzen, 1985; Fishbein & Ajzen, 1975). However, some evidence exists to the contrary; knowledge can sometimes be a significant and even strong predictor of environmental actions. Meta-analytic research quantifying the relationship between knowledge and environmental behavior has found that awareness of an environmental problem, one type of knowledge, is a significant predictor of environmental intentions and behavior (Bamberg & Möser, 2007). Knowledge more generally has been found to be a predictor of environmental behaviors such as recycling, energy conservation, and efficient travel choices (Stern, 1999). Recent meta-analytic work has found small to medium relationships between subjective climate change knowledge, objective climate change knowledge, and belief in climate change (Hornsey, Harris, Bain, & Fielding, 2016).

Behavior change intervention research has found that information-based behavior change efforts can be effective. Providing people with information about wind energy made them more supportive of wind energy compared to those assigned to a control condition (Bidwell, 2016). Meta-analytic work has found that supplying households with information such as energy-saving tips indeed has a positive effect on environmental behavior (Delmas, Fischlein, & Asensio, 2013; Osbaldiston & Schott, 2012;

Zelezny, 1999). However, there is also reason to believe that the type and timing of the delivery of information can make a difference. For example, it may be best to combine information-based interventions with other approaches, such as those that elicit changes in motivation or make a behavior easier or cheaper (Delmas et al., 2013; Osbaldiston & Schott, 2012; Stern, 1999). This would seem to support the information-deficit model, but the literature does suggest that change in knowledge in itself can be sufficient in some cases. Given these findings, it is important to acknowledge that the role of information in behavior change is decidedly more nuanced than is often portrayed, and misperceptions of environmental facts may be important contributors to harmful environmental actions and policies.

Environmental Misinformation and Its Consequences

We know that people often misunderstand environmental issues, and researchers have explored instances of environmental misinformation in relation to a number of environmental issues and behaviors. In this section, we discuss the most common areas where research on environmental misinformation exists, including energy efficiency, belief in anthropogenic climate change, water use, and corporate advertising ("greenwashing").

Energy Myths and Behavior

A growing body of literature has demonstrated that incomplete information or outdated perceptions frequently lead individuals to make choices that are inconsistent with their own economic well-being and with the goal of environmental preservation. In the household, people often perceive curtailment behaviors (Gardner & Stern, 2002), such as turning off lights or unplugging electronic devices, to be more effective at conserving energy than they actually are (Attari et al., 2010). Likewise, people tend to underestimate the effect that purchasing energy-efficiency devices and materials has on energy savings, such as buying efficient appliances and light bulbs or installing new insulation in their homes (e.g., Attari et al., 2010; Gardner & Stern, 2008). Even though research suggests that the highest-impact actions to reduce energy use are through purchasing energy-efficient appliances, only 16% of individuals know the energy rating of the appliances in their homes (Yohanis, 2012). Similarly, smart meters are increasingly common in homes across the country, and although their installation is an important step toward improving the efficiency of the electricity grid, individuals in only about one third of households accurately understand what a smart meter is and does (Raimi & Carrico, 2016). In fact, nearly one quarter of respondents in a recent survey reported that they thought a smart meter is an intelligence test (Raimi & Carrico, 2016). People also struggle to understand their energy bills; one study found that only 27% of participants were able to successfully answer three questions about the contents of a hypothetical energy bill (Southwell, Murphy, DeWaters, & LeBaron, 2012).

Other examples of common misinformation in an energy context abound. Unnecessary idling of cars is a surprisingly prevalent source of carbon emissions in the United States. When asked how long it makes sense to idle cars when hoping to save gas, reduce air pollution, or prevent vehicle wear and tear, people estimated that people should idle their cars anywhere from two and a half to four minutes (Carrico et al., 2009). In reality, car idling should last no more than 30 seconds to have the maximum positive effect on gas savings, carbon emissions, or car wear and tear. This misperception leads to annual U.S. carbon emissions on par with the entire emissions of the country of Jamaica. The link between hot water use and the energy required to heat the water means people's incorrect beliefs that hot water helps kill bacteria during handwashing could similarly lead to large reductions in carbon emissions if corrected (Carrico et al., 2013).

Water Myths and Behavior

Misunderstandings also abound in the water efficiency area. People overestimate the positive effects of water-use-curtailment behaviors such as turning off the water while brushing teeth and reducing shower length, and they underestimate the effect of purchasing water-efficient devices such as toilets, showerheads, and washing machines (Attari, 2014). Even though flushing of toilets tends to be the largest residential water use inside the home (up to 27%; Mayer et al., 1999), people tend to be ignorant of the importance of reduced toilet flushing. This could partially be a function of motivated reasoning, as people often hold a number of social and personal concerns about not flushing the toilet, including their dislike of the smell and potential embarrassment (Lute, Attari, & Sherman, 2015). Over 60% of U.S. residents surveyed report flushing their toilets on every use (Lute, Attari, & Sherman, 2015), indicating a behavior that has a large effect on water conservation and thus is worthy of targeting.

Belief in Global Warming

Many people hold misconceptions about the existence and causes of climate change (Leiserowitz, 2005; Leiserowitz, Maibach, Roser-Renouf, Feinberg, & Howe, 2013). Climate change is a complex phenomenon, and so in some ways it is no surprise that people do not completely understand it. In the United States, 60% to 70% of Americans believe that climate change is taking place (Weber & Stern, 2011); there is evidence that Democrats remained relatively stable in their beliefs while Republicans tended to become more skeptical about climate change (Hornsey et al., 2016; McCright & Dunlap, 2000, 2003; Weber & Stern, 2011). These findings highlight the importance of the political context when trying to understand climate change beliefs, making it a somewhat different, more politicized issue than other types of environmental misinformation.

Sources of climate change misinformation include news reports and the media more generally (Huertas & Adler, 2012; Huertas & Kriegsman, 2014), meteorology and weather reports specifically (Maibach et al., 2016; Stenhouse et al., 2014), and even textbooks and other classroom materials used in the U.S. educational system (Román & Busch, 2015). People consistently underestimate the overwhelming scientific consensus about the existence of climate change, with only 47% of respondents in 2008 stating that most scientists think global warming is happening (Leiserowitz et al., 2013). This is troubling, given that the perception of scientific consensus surrounding climate change is a gateway belief that leads people to espouse anthropogenic climate change (van der Linden, Leiserowitz, Feinberg, & Maibach, 2015). All of this misinformation surrounding climate change makes it difficult to ensure accurate climate change beliefs in the public; makes it less likely that people will change their individual behaviors that contribute to climate change, such as home energy use and transportation decisions; and creates a political stalemate that decreases the likelihood of effective public and private policies (Vandenbergh & Gilligan, 2015).

It is important to acknowledge, however, that some research suggests that knowledge is not necessarily a driver of beliefs or attitudes about climate change. Highly knowledgeable individuals are not more likely to believe in anthropogenic global warming (AGW) but, rather, more likely to hold extreme views that tend to conform to their political affiliations. For example, scientifically literate conservatives in the United States tend to be more extreme in their skepticism of AGW, whereas liberals tend to be more extreme in their belief in and concern about AGW (Kahan et al., 2012; Raimi & Leary, 2014). However, as a whole, the literature does suggest that in some cases knowledge deficits and misunderstandings surrounding climate change can be a significant barrier to changing environmental behaviors and policies linked to climate change.

Greenwashing

At an institutional level, research shows that companies sometimes misrepresent their environmental efforts; doing so is often called "greenwashing" (Laufer, 2003). There are reasons to believe that green branding and perhaps greenwashing are effective only for people who already care about environmental issues, suggesting that some people are motivated to believe dubious company reports of sustainability efforts (Gromet, Kunreuther, & Larrick, 2013; Magnier & Schoormans, 2015). Even though some companies are making genuine strides in how they create and brand sustainable products, such as improved product packaging (Bech-Larsen, 1996; Esslinger, 2011), greenwashing actions by even a minority of companies may lead to confusion over which products are truly more sustainable and may even decrease trust in both legitimate and illegitimate company sustainability efforts and products (Chen & Chang, 2013).

Food-Waste Myths and Behaviors

We have covered some of the more common environmental areas in which we know misinformation exists and is being perpetuated. There is much more to learn, though, as many potentially important misunderstandings may exist undetected or underdetected in other domains of environmental behavior. Food waste is an issue that is fraught with misinformation but has received relatively little attention from researchers or policy makers. Food involves a variety of environmental issues, including energy use, water use, and carbon emissions, as well as social justice issues. We already have some idea where food-waste myths may exist. Despite their ubiquitous nature, food labels are commonly misunderstood (e.g., Wansink & Wright, 2006). People often believe that food labels such as "use by" and "sell by" dates indicate not peak quality but instead general food quality, optimal taste, or even health safety (Gunders, 2012). People also often misunderstand the carbon footprints of their meals, sometimes believing that eating a meal plus a sustainable food product can produce a lower carbon footprint than eating just the meal alone without the additional sustainable food product (Gorissen & Weijters, 2016). Future research should further explore where myths exist surrounding food waste and how to correct them.

Correcting Environmental Misperceptions

How can misinformation be corrected? Research has found that simple informational approaches to adjusting environmental misperceptions can sometimes be effective (Bullock, 2015; Delmas et al., 2013; Inskeep & Attari, 2014). This includes providing tips on the most energy-intensive home behaviors and giving people real-time information on how much energy they use in their homes; these are called "feedback information interventions" (Karlin, Zinger, & Ford, 2015). Education efforts, such as through classes or workshops, can be used to address environmental misinformation, though these strategies often focus on more intensive, in-depth supplying of knowledge and thus can take longer to produce changes in knowledge (Zelezny, 1999).

Social influence approaches are a potent method of overcoming misperceptions and information barriers more broadly. In some cases, social norms could be considered a type of information that conveys how common a given behavior is ("descriptive norm"), how correct or appropriate a behavior is ("injunctive norm"), or sometimes both considerations at once (Cialdini et al., 1990; Sherif, 1936). Messages such as signs in national parks or in hotel rooms can highlight different types of norms to induce people to change their behavior (Burchell, Rettie, & Patel, 2013; Cialdini et al., 2006; Cialdini et al., 1990; Goldstein, Cialdini, & Griskevicius, 2008). Research has found that messages highlighting how common the theft of petrified wood is from national forests are less effective at decreasing theft than are messages that only state that it is wrong to steal petrified wood (Cialdini et al., 2006).

Information can correct social norm misperceptions surrounding environmental behaviors, fixing pluralistic ignorance; people sometimes think that only a few people care about environmental issues, when in fact most people do care (Monin & Norton, 2003; Prentice & Miller, 1993).

Feedback-information interventions can even be crafted to highlight social norms in ways that influence people to change their environmental behaviors; particular success has been achieved using these interventions in the home energy conservation area (e.g., Abrahamse & Steg, 2013; Delmas et al., 2013; Ferraro, Miranda, & Price, 2011; Osbaldiston & Schott, 2012). Home energy–use information provided on bills by the company OPower has revealed that just learning about how one's household energy use compares to the neighbors' can lead to sustained energy reductions in the 2% to 4% range (Allcott, 2011; Ayres, Raseman, & Shih, 2013).

Policy approaches, beyond individual behavior–change interventions, could go a long way toward stopping the creation and spread of environmental misinformation. Carbon labeling of consumer products can help make the carbon footprints of materials more transparent, thus correcting misperceptions about the carbon effects of various products (Cohen & Vandenbergh, 2012; Upham, Dendler, & Bleda, 2011). Another area would be updating federal, state, and local government disclosures and recommended behaviors on topics such as handwashing and food waste handling; updating the information could counteract currently perpetuated misinformation on these topics but also potentially affect the environmental behaviors of countless individuals and organizations across the country.

It is important to acknowledge that many behavior change interventions and policies may not be attempts to correct environmental misinformation but may nevertheless prove effective at changing underlying behaviors. Use of behavioral cues or policy nudges to adjust default settings such as those of thermostats and encourage certain choices can be effective at changing environmental behaviors (e.g., Johnson & Goldstein, 2003; Osbaldiston & Schott, 2012; Thaler & Sunstein, 2009), as can changes in physical home infrastructure to make desired actions easier (Brothers, Krantz, & McClannahan, 1994; Gibson, 1977; Osbaldiston & Schott, 2012). However, it is currently unclear whether these interventions could actually affect environmental beliefs or misperceptions indirectly, an important topic worthy of future consideration.

Conclusion

Knowledge is a crucial factor in addressing environmental problems. Misinformation, whether intentionally or accidently perpetuated, can drive people to engage in harmful environmental behaviors that implicate problems such as climate change and access to quality water. Correcting misperceptions could have a substantial effect on a wide range of environmental issues, including climate policy, individual energy and water efficiency, travel behavior, and even food waste. A variety of interventions and policies could help correct misperceptions; among these are access to correct information, informational feedback on people's behavior, social norm information, and labeling on products. Despite what we currently know about environmental misinformation and effective interventions to address misperceptions, we still have a great deal to learn about misinformation in understudied environmental areas and the most potent environmental behavior change interventions that can correct those misperceptions.

References

Abrahamse, W., & Steg, L. (2013). Social influence approaches to encourage resource conversation: A meta-analysis. *Global Environmental Change, 23*, 1773–1785.

Ajzen, I. (1985). From intentions to actions: A theory of planned behavior. In J. Kuhl & J. Beckman (Eds.) *Action-control: From cognition to behavior* (pp. 11–39). Heidelberg, Germany: Springer.

Allcott, H. (2011). Social norms and energy conservation. *Journal of Public Economics, 95*, 1082–1095.

Attari, S. Z. (2014). Perceptions of water use. *Proceedings of the National Academy of Sciences, 111*, 5129–5134.

Attari, S. Z., DeKay, M. L., Davidson, C. I., & Bruine de Bruin, W. (2010). Public perceptions of energy consumption and savings. *Proceedings of the National Academy of Sciences, 107*, 16054–16059.

Ayres, I., Raseman, S., & Shih, A. (2013). Evidence from two large field experiments that peer comparison feedback can reduce residential energy use. *Journal of Law, Economics, & Organization, 29*, 992–1022.

Bamberg, S., & Möser, G. (2007). Twenty years after Hines, Hungerford, and Tomera: A new meta-analysis of psycho-social determinants of pro-environmental behaviour. *Journal of Environmental Psychology, 27*, 14–25.

Bech-Larsen, T. (1996). Danish consumers' attitudes to the functional and environmental characteristics of food packaging. *Journal of Consumer Policy, 19*, 339–363.

Bidwell, D. (2016). The effects of information on public attitudes toward renewable energy. *Environment and Behavior, 48*, 743–768.

Brothers, K. J., Krantz, P. J., & McClannahan, L. E. (1994). Office paper recycling: A function of container proximity. *Journal of Applied Behavior Analysis, 27*, 153–160.

Bullock, G. (2015). Independent labels? The power behind environmental information about products and companies. *Political Research Quarterly, 68*, 46–62.

Burchell, K., Rettie, R., & Patel, K. (2013). Marketing social norms: Social marketing and the "social norm approach." *Journal of Consumer Behaviour, 12*, 1–9.

Carrico, A. R., Padgett, P., Vandenbergh, M. P., Gilligan, J., & Wallston, K. A. (2009). Costly myths: An analysis of idling beliefs and behavior in personal motor vehicles. *Energy Policy, 37,* 2881–2888.

Carrico, A. R., Spoden, M., Wallston, K. A., & Vandenbergh, M. P. (2013). The environmental cost of misinformation: Why the recommendation to use elevated temperatures for handwashing is problematic. *International Journal of Consumer Studies, 37,* 433–441.

Chen, Y., & Chang, C. (2013). Greenwash and green trust: The mediation effect of green consumer confusion and green perceived risk. *Journal of Business Ethics, 114,* 489–500.

Cialdini, R. B., Demaine, L. J., Sagarin, B. J., Barrett, D. W., Rhoads, K., & Winter, P. L. (2006). Managing social norms for persuasive impact. *Social Influence, 1,* 3–15.

Cialdini, R. B., Reno, R. R., & Kallgren, C. A. (1990). A focus theory of normative conduct: Recycling the concept of norms to reduce littering in public places. *Journal of Personality and Social Psychology, 58*(6), 1015–1026.

Cohen, M. A., & Vandenbergh, M. P. (2012). The potential role of carbon labeling in a green economy. *Energy Economics, 34,* S53–S63.

Delmas, M. A., Fischlein, M., & Asensio, O. I. (2013). Information strategies and energy conservation behavior: A meta-analysis of experimental studies from 1975 to 2012. *Energy Policy, 61,* 729–739.

Dietz, T., Gardner, G. T., Gilligan, J., Stern, P. C., & Vandenbergh, M. P. (2009). Household actions can provide a behavioral wedge to rapidly reduce US carbon emissions. *Proceedings of the National Academy of Sciences, 106,* 18452–18456.

Esslinger, H. (2011). Sustainable design: Beyond the innovation-driven business model. *Journal of Product Innovation Management, 28,* 401–404.

Ferraro, P. J., Miranda, J. J., & Price, M. K. (2011). The persistence of treatment effects with norm-based policy instruments: Evidence from a randomized environmental policy experiment. *American Economic Review, 101,* 318–322.

Fishbein, M., & Ajzen, I. (1975). *Belief, attitude, intention, and behavior.* Reading, MA: Addison-Wesley.

Fisher, J. D., Fisher, W. A., Bryan, A. D., & Misovich, S. J. (2002). Information-motivation-behavioral skills model-based HIV risk behavior change. *Health Psychology, 21,* 177–186.

Gardner, G. T., & Stern, P. C. (2002). *Environmental problems and human behavior.* Boston, MA: Pearson.

Gardner, G. T., & Stern, P. C. (2008). The short list: The most effective actions U.S. households can take to curb climate change. *Environment Magazine, 50,* 12–24.

Gibson, J. J. (1977). The theory of affordances. In R. Shaw & J. Bransford (Eds.), *Perceiving, acting, and knowing: Toward an ecological psychology* (pp. 67–82). Hillsdale, NJ: Erlbaum.

Gilbert, D. T., Tafarodi, R. W., & Malone, P. S. (1993). You can't not believe everything you read. *Journal of Personality and Social Psychology, 65,* 221–223.

Goldstein, N. J., Cialdini, R. B., & Griskevicius, V. (2008). A room with a viewpoint: Using social norms to motivate environmental conversation in hotels. *Journal of Consumer Research, 35,* 472–482.

Gorissen, K., & Weijters, B. (2016). The negative footprint illusion: Perceptual bias in sustainable food consumption. *Journal of Environmental Psychology, 45*, 50–65.

Gromet, D. M., Kunreuther, H., & Larrick, R. P. (2013). Political ideology affects energy-efficiency attitudes and choices. *Proceedings of the National Academy of Sciences, 110*, 9314–9319.

Gross, A. G. (1994). The roles of rhetoric in the public understanding of science. *Public Understanding of Science, 3*, 3–23.

Guagnano, G. A., Stern, P. C., & Dietz, T. (1995). Influences on attitude-behavior relationships: A natural experiment with curbside recycling. *Environment and Behavior, 27*, 699–718.

Gunders, D. (2012). Wasted: How America is losing up to 40 percent of its food from farm to fork to landfill. Washington, DC: National Resources Defense Council.

Hart, P. S., & Nisbet, E. C. (2012). Boomerang effects in science communication: How motivated reasoning and identity cues amplify opinion polarization about climate mitigation policies. *Communication Research, 39*, 701–723.

Hornsey, M. J., Harris, E. A., Bain, P. G., & Fielding, K. S. (2016). Meta-analyses of the determinants and outcomes of belief in climate change. *Nature Climate Change, 6*(6), 622–626.

Huertas, A., & Adler, D. (2012). *Is News Corp. failing science? Representations of climate science on Fox News Channel and in the Wall Street Journal opinion pages.* Cambridge, MA: Union of Concern Scientists Publications.

Huertas, A., & Kriegsman, R. (2014). *Science or spin? Assessing the accuracy of cable news coverage of climate science.* Cambridge, MA: Union of Concern Scientists Publications.

Inskeep, B. D., & Attari, S. Z. (2014). The water short list: The most effective actions U.S. households can take to curb water use. *Environment: Science and Policy for Sustainable Development, 56*, 4–15.

Johnson, E. J., & Goldstein, D. (2003). Do defaults save lives? *Science, 302*, 1338–1339.

Kahan, D. M., Peters, E., Wittlin, M., Slovic, P., Ouellette, L. L., Braman, D., & Mandel, G. (2012). The polarizing impact of science literacy and numeracy on perceived climate change risks. *Nature Climate Change, 2*, 732–735.

Karlin, B., Zinger, J. F., & Ford, R. (2015). The effects of feedback on energy conservation: A meta-analysis. *Psychological Bulletin, 141*, 1205–1227.

Kunda, Z. (1990). The case for motivated reasoning. *Psychological Bulletin, 108*, 480–498.

Laufer, W. S. (2003). Social accountability and corporate greenwashing. *Journal of Business Ethics, 43*, 253–261.

Leiserowitz, A. (2005). American risk perceptions: Is climate change dangerous? *Risk Analysis, 25*, 1433–1442.

Leiserowitz, A., Maibach, E., Roser-Renouf, C., Feinberg, G., & Howe, P. (2013). *Climate change in the American mind: Americans' global warming beliefs and attitudes in April, 2013.* New Haven, CT: Yale Project on Climate Change Communication.

Lute, M. L., Attari, S. Z., & Sherman, S. J. (2015). Don't rush to flush. *Journal of Environmental Psychology, 43*, 105–111.

Magnier, L., & Schoormans, J. (2015). Consumer reactions to sustainable packaging:

The interplay of visual appearance, verbal claim, and environmental concern. *Journal of Environmental Psychology, 44,* 53–62.

Maibach, E., Perksins, D., Francis, Z., Myers, T., Engblom, A., Yona, B., & Seitter, K. (2016). *A 2016 national survey of American Meteorological Society member views on climate change: Initial findings.* Fairfax, VA: Center for Climate Change Communication.

Mayer, P. W., DeOreo, W. B., Opitz, E. M., Kiefer, J. C., Davis, W. Y., Dziegielewski, B., & Nelson, J. O. (1999). *Residential end uses of water.* Denver, CO: AWWA Research Foundation and American Water Works Association.

McCright, A. M., & Dunlap, R. E. (2000). Challenging global warming as a social problem: An analysis of the conservative movement's counter-claims. *Social Problems, 47,* 499–522.

McCright, A. M., & Dunlap, R. E. (2003). Defeating Kyoto: The conservative movement's impact on US climate change policy. *Social Problems, 50,* 348–373.

Monin, B., & Norton, M. I. (2003). Perceptions of a fluid consensus: Uniqueness bias, false consensus, false polarization, and pluralistic ignorance in a water conservation crisis. *Personality and Social Psychology Bulletin, 29,* 559–567.

National Environmental Education & Training Foundation. (1999). *Environmental readiness for the 21st century.* Washington, DC: EPA. Retrieved from nepis.epa.gov /Exe/ZyPURL.cgi?Dockey=400007C5.TXT

Osbaldiston, R., & Schott, J. P. (2012). Environmental sustainability and behavioral science: A meta-analysis of proenvironmental behavior experiments. *Environment and Behavior, 44,* 257–299.

Pachauri, R. K., & Meyer, L. A. (Eds.). (2014). *Climate change 2014: Synthesis report. Contribution of working groups I, II, and III to the fifth assessment report of the Intergovernmental Panel on Climate Change.* Geneva, Switzerland: Intergovernmental Panel on Climate Change. Retrieved from http://www.ipcc.ch/pdf/assessment-report/ar5 /syr/SYR_AR5_FINAL_full_wcover.pdf

Prentice, D. A., & Miller, D. T. (1993). Pluralistic ignorance and alcohol use on campus: Some consequences of misperceiving the social norm. *Journal of Personality and Social Psychology, 64,* 243–256.

Raimi, K. T., & Carrico, A. R. (2016). Understanding and beliefs about smart energy technology. *Energy Research & Social Science, 12,* 68–74.

Raimi, K. T., & Leary, M. R. (2014). Belief superiority in the environmental domain: Attitude extremity and reactions to fracking. *Journal of Environmental Psychology, 40,* 76–85.

Román, D., & Busch, K. C. (2015). Textbooks of doubt: Using systemic functional analysis to explore the framing of climate change in middle-school science textbooks. *Environmental Education Research, 22*(8), 1158–1180.

Schultz, P. Wesley, Nolan, J. M., Cialdini, R. B., Goldstein, N. J., & Griskevicius, V. (2007). The constructive, destructive, and reconstructive power of social norms. *Psychological Science, 18,* 429–434.

Sherif, M. (1936). *The psychology of social norms.* Oxford, England: Harper.

Southwell, B. G., Murphy, J. J., DeWaters, J. E., & LeBaron, P. A. (2012). *Americans' perceived and actual understanding of energy* (Peer-reviewed report no. RR-0018-1208).

Research Triangle Park, NC: RTI International. Retrieved from https://www.rti .org/sites/default/files/resources/rr-0018-1208-southwell.pdf

Southwell, B. G., & Thorson, E. A. (2015). The prevalence, consequence, and remedy of misinformation in mass media systems. *Journal of Communication, 65*, 589–595.

Steg, L., Perlaviciute, G., & van der Werff, E. (2015). Understanding the human dimensions of a sustainable energy transition. *Frontiers in Psychology, 6*, 805.

Steg, L., & Vlek, C. (2009). Encouraging pro-environmental behaviour: An integrative review and research agenda. *Journal of Environmental Psychology, 29*, 309–317

Stenhouse, N., Maibach, E., Cobb, S., Ban, R., Bleistein, A., Croft, P., . . . Leiserowitz, A. (2014). Meteorologists' views about global warming: A survey of American Meteorological Society professional members. *Bulletin of the American Meteorological Society, 97*, 1029–1040.

Stern, P. C. (1999). Information, incentives, and proenvironmental consumer behavior. *Journal of Consumer Policy, 22*, 461–478.

Stern, P. C., Dietz, T., Abel, T. D., Guagnano, G. A., & Kalof, L. (1999). A value-belief-norm theory of support for social movements: The case of environmentalism. Paper 1. Bellingham, WA: Huxley College on the Peninsulas Publications. Retrieved from http://cedar.wwu.edu/cgi/viewcontent.cgi?article=1000&context=hcop_facpubs

Taylor, D. G. (1982). Pluralistic ignorance and the spiral of silence: A formal analysis. *Public Opinion Quarterly, 46*, 311–335.

Thaler, R. H., & Sunstein, C. R. (2009). *Nudge: Improving decisions about health, wealth, and happiness.* London, England: Penguin Books.

Upham, P., Dendler, L., & Bleda, M. (2011). Carbon labeling of grocery products: Public perceptions and potential emission reductions. *Journal of Cleaner Production, 19*, 348–355.

Vandenbergh, M. P., Barkenbus, J., & Gilligan, J. A. (2008). Individual carbon emissions: The low-hanging fruit. *UCLA Law Review, 55*, 1701–1758.

Vandenbergh, M. P., & Gilligan, J. A. (2015). Beyond gridlock. *Columbia Journal of Environmental Law, 40*, 217–303.

van der Linden, S. L., Leiserowitz, A. A., Feinberg, G. D., Maibach, E. W. (2015). The scientific consensus on climate change as a gateway belief: Experimental evidence. *PLoS ONE, 10*, e00184489.

Wansink, B., & Wright, A. O. (2006). "Best if used by..." How freshness dating influences food acceptance. *Journal of Food Science, 71*, S354–S357.

Weber, E. U., & Stern, P. C. (2011). Public understanding of climate change in the United States. *American Psychologist, 66*, 315–328.

Whitmarsh, L. (2011). Skepticism and uncertainty about climate change: Dimensions, determinants, and change over time. *Global Environmental Change, 21*, 690–700.

Yohanis, Y. G. (2012). Domestic energy use and householders' energy behaviour. *Energy Policy, 41*, 654–665.

Zelezny, L. C. (1999). Educational interventions that improve environmental behaviors: A meta-analysis. *Journal of Environmental Education, 31*, 5–14.

PART III   **Solutions and Remedies for Misinformation**

Misinformation and Its Correction

ELEVEN

Cognitive Mechanisms and Recommendations for Mass Communication

BRIONY SWIRE AND ULLRICH ECKER

n 2007 a man in the United Kingdom posted a photograph on his website of a "mummified fairy" that he created as an April Fools prank. After receiving 20,000 visitors to the site in one day, he explicitly revealed that he had fabricated the scenario, yet many accused him of covering up the truth and vehemently insisted that the fairy was real (BBC, 2007). This anecdote highlights a valid concern to mass communicators: regardless of how ridiculous information seems, once it is in the public sphere it can take on a life of its own and may never be fully retractable.

It has become a societal norm that the media and the Internet provide vast quantities of information, placing the onus on the individual to sort fact from fiction. However, individuals have limited time, cognitive resources, and motivation to understand complex topics such as scientific findings and political developments, and misconceptions are commonplace. Once inaccurate beliefs are formed, they are remarkably difficult to eradicate (Ecker, Lewandowsky, Swire, & Chang, 2011). Even after people receive clear and credible corrections, misinformation continues to influence their reasoning; in cognitive psychology, this is known as the *continued influence effect* of misinformation (Johnson & Seifert, 1994; Lewandowsky, Ecker, Seifert, Schwarz, & Cook, 2012). The mummified fairy is a benign example, but the ramifications can be serious. Belief in misinformation can adversely impact decision making, and the continued influence effect has real-world implications in areas as disparate as education, health, and the economy.

One prominent example is the misconception that the measles, mumps, rubella (MMR) vaccine causes autism. This falsehood has been repeatedly and convincingly disputed in the media and by the scientific community over the years since the original myth was disseminated in a fraudulent article. Despite these debunking efforts, the myth has led to a drop in vaccination rates and an increase in vaccine-preventable disease (Poland & Spier, 2010). The economic burden of 16 measles outbreaks in the United States in 2011 alone has been estimated at somewhere between $2.7 million and $5.3 million (Ortega-Sanchez, Vijayaraghavan, Barskey, & Wallace, 2014). Thus, developing evidence-based recommendations on how to adequately communicate corrections and minimize reliance upon inaccurate information not only is important for individual decision making but also has ramifications for society as a whole.

The most important recommendation for traditional mass media such as newspaper and television as well as more recent technologies such as Twitter that have essentially transformed ordinary citizens into would-be journalists is to take greater care to ensure that information is correct to begin with. However, this is not always realistic due to the fast pace of modern information consumption and dissemination and the fact that ordinary citizens are not bound by rules of journalistic integrity. Social media thus make an ideal breeding ground for the propagation and transmission of misinformation. This is exemplified by the role of social media in disseminating rumors about the Boston Marathon bombing in 2013; a well-intentioned Reddit thread was created to help find the perpetrators, yet the accusation of an innocent, deceased Brown University student subsequently went viral (Guzman, 2013). Information shared through social media is usually disseminated, without fact checking, based merely on its potential to elicit emotional responses or support a personally motivated argument (Peters, Kashima, & Clark, 2009).

As the above examples illustrate, continued influence of misinformation can have wide-ranging, unexpected, and potentially costly outcomes. Accordingly, it is important to develop strategies useful to individuals who interact with traditional mass communication and social media systems in both professional and private capacities to mitigate the potential for harm from such influences. The remainder of this chapter focuses on cognitive mechanisms and theories accounting for the continued influence of misinformation. In particular, we will discuss what drives belief in inaccurate information, why certain individuals are predisposed to refrain from belief change even in the face of good corrective evidence, and how corrections can be designed to maximize impact. We provide six practical recommendations based upon current knowledge of cognitive processes. We first discuss theoretical accounts for the continued influence effect, such as mental models, dual processing theory, the necessity of co-activation of misinformation and new information, and the impact of the information's source. We then discuss individual predispositions to the continued influence effect, in particular a person's worldview and skepticism.

Mental Models

When people initially encounter information, a situational model of integrated memory representations is built, and this model is continuously updated as new information becomes available and relevant (Bower & Morrow, 1990). If the required changes are small, they can be integrated into the situational model incrementally (Bailey & Zacks, 2015), but if a larger change is required, a more global update that involves discarding the old mental model and creating a new one is necessary (Kurby & Zacks, 2012). However, even if there are sufficient cognitive resources to notice a difference between one's mental model and the current environment, people are often quite inadequate at assimilating new information or mapping it onto existing memory representations (van Oostendorp, 2014). It is possible that the continued influence effect occurs when people update information incrementally but in fact a global update is called for. Reliance on inaccurate information is less likely when there is an alternative to replace the inaccurate information in a person's mental model, as a readily available alternative explanation facilitates global updating (Ecker, Lewandowsky, Cheung, & Maybery, 2015).

A classic paradigm for studying the continued influence effect entails presenting participants with fictitious scenarios involving the retraction of an event cause. One common example is a narrative in which negligent storage of gas cylinders is initially held responsible for starting a warehouse fire, and their presence is retracted shortly thereafter (Johnson & Seifert, 1994; Wilkes & Leatherbarrow, 1988). If participants are explicitly queried about the gas cylinders, they typically acknowledge the gap in their understanding (i.e., a gap in their mental event model) created by the earlier retraction and correctly state that there were none. However, when answering inferential reasoning questions regarding the event—such as "What was the cause of the explosions?"—participants often still rely upon the outdated information. This indicates that people prefer to have an inaccurate over an incomplete event model, which can lead to reliance upon discredited information even after receiving an explicit correction (Ecker, Lewandowsky, & Apai, 2011).

Recommendation 1: Provide Factual Alternatives

One of the most effective methods of correcting misinformation is to provide an alternative factual cause or explanation to facilitate switching out the inaccurate information in an individual's initial situation model. For example, if people are told that it was not gas cylinders that caused a warehouse fire but that there was evidence of arson, people are dramatically less likely to rely upon the original inaccurate information (Ecker, Lewandowsky, & Tang, 2010; Johnson & Seifert, 1994). The alternative explanation effectively plugs the model gap left by the retraction. The alternative ideally should have the same explanatory relevance as the misinformation it replaces, and it is important that it be plausible; in fact, if the new information is more plausible and easier to understand than the original, updating is even more efficient (Baadte & Dutke, 2012).

In the real world, providing an alternative explanation to ameliorate reliance upon inaccurate information can be problematic, as often there is no available substitute; sometimes all that can be said about a piece of misinformation is that it is not true. For example, if a person is accused of a crime, he might simply turn out to be not guilty without an alternative suspect being readily available. The lack of adequate alternatives can have profound ramifications. The ongoing rumors regarding missing Malaysian Airlines flight MH370, which disappeared over the Indian Ocean in 2014, have proven difficult to retract. In the absence of unequivocal evidence regarding what happened to the plane, traditional and social media were rife with speculation that the plane was hijacked by terrorists or crashed by a suicidal pilot (e.g., Quest, 2016). Arguably, belief in the hijacking speculation has been difficult to shift because a convincing factual alternative has not been available.

Dual Process Theory: Strategic and Automatic Memory Processes

The notion that retractions create gaps in mental models is useful in understanding the continued influence effect. Invalidated information is not simply deleted from memory because memory does not work like a whiteboard, and retractions do not simply erase misinformation. To explain why corrections to misinformation are used during reasoning, some theorists have focused on the memory processes governing information retrieval in which a common assumption is that there are two separate types of memory retrieval, strategic and automatic (Yonelinas, 2002).

Strategic memory processes are effortful and allow for the controlled recollection of the information's contextual details. Similar to the metadata of a computer file, contextual details include information about the information itself. This includes qualities such as the information's spatiotemporal context of encoding, source, and veracity (Frithsen & Miller, 2014). A person's ability to use strategic memory processes efficiently will depend on factors such as effort, motivation, age, and the length of time since encoding (e.g., Herron & Rugg, 2003). In contrast, automatic processes are fast and relatively acontextual; they serve to quickly provide an indication of memory strength or familiarity with an item or notion (Zimmer & Ecker, 2010).

Automatic retrieval processes can contribute to misinformation effects in two ways. First, the evaluation of a statement's veracity is influenced by its familiarity; this is problematic, as information can be accepted as true just because it seems familiar. When increased familiarity gives the illusion that information is valid, this is known as the *illusory truth effect* (e.g., Begg, Anas, & Farinacci, 1992). Second, when questioned about an event or otherwise cued, a person can automatically retrieve retracted misinformation from memory without any accompanying contextual details and potentially without recalling that the information has been retracted (cf. Ayers & Reder, 1998; Ecker et al., 2010). To illustrate, it has been argued that once misinformation has been encoded and then retracted, a "negation tag" is linked to the original memory representation, as in "Flight MH370 was hijacked—*NOT TRUE*" (Gilbert, Krull, & Malone, 1990). When queried about the topic, fast automatic memory processes might simply retrieve the familiar claim, while strategic memory processes are required to retrieve the negation tag and dismiss the familiar statement as untrue. If strategic memory processes are not engaged, familiar claims are likely to be judged as true even after plausible retractions (Dechene, Stahl, Hansen, & Wanke, 2010).

Recommendation 2: Boosting Retrieval of the Retraction, Not Familiarity of the Myth

The extent to which people engage their strategic memory processes can be actively encouraged, and this can reduce misinformation effects. Ecker et al. (2010) found that presenting participants with a pre-exposure warning detailing the continued influence effect greatly reduced reliance on misinformation, and the warning was as effective as providing a factual alternative. The authors argue that warnings not only allowed individuals to more effectively tag misinformation as false when encoding its retraction but also boosted later recall of the retraction, the negation tag (Ecker et al., 2010). The effect of warnings was investigated mainly for theoretical reasons; providing a pre-exposure misinformation warning will not be a viable option in most real-world settings. However, any incentive to engage in strategic memory processes should be useful, such as boosting source monitoring (Lindsay & Johnson, 1989; Poole & Lindsay, 2002).

Enhancing recollection is one way of reducing reliance on misinformation, but circumventing the inflation of a misconception's familiarity is potentially another way. This involves minimizing unnecessary explicit repetition of misinformation. An educational pamphlet using a "myth-busting" format that repeats the myth before indicating that it is false ("Flight MH370 was hijacked—FALSE") can boost the familiarity of the misconception, potentially increasing the risk that misconceptions are later mistakenly remembered as being true. The misremembering of myths as facts is demonstrated by Skurnik, Yoon, Park, and Schwarz (2005) as well as by Peter and Koch (2016). In both these studies, participants misremembered the originally false statements as true more often than they misremembered originally true statements as false. Swire, Ecker, and Lewandowsky (2016) found that retracting myths and affirming facts led to comparable belief change initially—belief reduction for myths, belief increase for facts—but that belief change was less sustained with myths over the course of a week. In other words, misinformation began to be "rebelieved," while fact belief remained stable. Thus, where possible, communicators should focus on the facts and minimize explicit repetition of a myth if the retraction does not provide adequate information to allow people to revise their understanding.

Co-Activation of Misconception and Corrective Facts

Despite the theoretically motivated suggestion to avoid myth repetition, for practicality, corrections usually do require repetition of the myth; the question then becomes how best to execute the repetition. As discussed previously, presentation of factual alternative information is conducive to successful mental-model revision. Beyond that, several theoretical accounts have proposed that the *co-activation* of inaccurate knowledge and newly encoded factual information facilitates knowledge revision. Co-activation is believed to increase the likelihood that individuals will notice discrepancies between originally held misconceptions and factual evidence and update their knowledge accordingly (Kendeou & van den Broek, 2007).

After a correction, the outdated and new information may coexist in memory and both can be activated by relevant cues (cf. Ayers & Reder, 1998). Thus, to efficiently update and revise knowledge, it is crucial to provide a sufficient amount and quality of factual information, and, ideally, for the correction to explain the reasons the misconception is wrong (Seifert, 2002). Adding adequate detail to the new, accurate information can systematically strengthen the correction by slowly decreasing interference from the outdated information (Kendeou, Smith, & O'Brien, 2013). This effect of detail illustrates how, when ample factual information is available, misinformation can be used as an educational tool (Bedford, 2010).

Recommendation 3: Refutations of Misinformation as an Educational Tool

A *refutation* involves not only a statement that the misconception is false but also a comprehensive explanation as to why it is incorrect (Hynd, 2001). The efficacy of refutations has primarily been investigated in the field of education and has often focused on the updating of scientific misconceptions held by students in a classroom. A meta-analysis of 70 studies by Guzzetti, Snyder, Glass, and Gamas (1993) indicates that corrections were most successful when they included sufficient explanation of why misconceptions were false and why the facts are true. Other educational strategies aimed at reducing reliance on misinformation, such as class discussions, demonstrations, and nonrefutational texts that simply present the correct information without descriptions of the misconceptions, are often successful in the short term but not after a delay (Guzzetti, 2000).

It has been argued that one reason for the relative success of the refutation at promoting belief change is that, by design, it increases the likelihood of the old and new information being co-activated in memory (Kowalski & Taylor, 2009). It follows that when a myth is debunked, its repetition seems acceptable, despite the potential myth-familiarity boost, as long as the repetition serves to highlight a discrepancy between a misconception and factual evidence, thus promoting co-activation; the focus of the intervention can be shifted promptly from the myth to the factual evidence; and the target audience has the necessary resources—in particular the time and motivation—to engage with the provided materials and sees the information source as credible, as would ideally be the case in a classroom setting.

Retraction Source Credibility

People often do not have the time or inclination to be experts in all fields, so most knowledge, to a degree, is reliant upon accepting what others claim to be true. Thus, people hold many opinions and beliefs about events and causal relations without having relevant involvement or expertise. For example, trust in climate scientists is a predictor of whether an individual acknowledges that climate change is anthropogenic (Mase, Cho, & Prokopy, 2015). In general, high-credibility sources are more persuasive than low-credibility sources (Eagly & Chaiken, 1993), and the less one's prior knowledge about a topic, the more influential source credibility becomes (Jung, Walsh-Childers, & Kim, 2016). The two core factors of source credibility discussed in the literature are expertise, the extent to which the source is capable of providing accurate information, and trustworthiness, the perception that the source is willing to provide information that the source herself believes to be accurate (Pornpitakpan, 2004). A source can independently have varying degrees of these two qualities; a doctor may have a high degree of perceived expertise, but if found to be paid by pharmaceutical companies may have relatively low perceived trustworthiness.

When it comes to retracting inaccurate information or belief change, intriguingly, trustworthiness seems to play a much larger role than expertise (McGinnes & Ward, 1980). Guillory and Geraci (2013) investigated the credibility of retraction sources by presenting participants with a story about a politician who was witnessed taking a bribe. The allegation was later retracted by people with varying degrees of trustworthiness and expertise. The authors found that trustworthiness was integral to the success of the retraction, and expertise was not. It should be noted that the way expertise was operationalized in this study was more akin to "involvement in an event" than to expertise in its perhaps more common meaning, "possessing relevant knowledge." Ecker and Antonio (2016) replicated Guillory and Geraci's (2013) main finding with a more traditional interpretation of expertise and also found an effect of trustworthiness but not expertise on the efficacy of retractions.

Recommendation 4: Building Credibility

The ability to successfully correct misinformation appears to depend more on sources' perceived honesty and integrity than on their expertise. This means that Leonardo DiCaprio's 2016 Oscar speech correcting climate-change misconceptions (Goldenberg, 2016) could be more effective than an expert communication. Paek, Hove, Jeong, and Kim (2011) found that YouTube videos created by viewers' peers had more impact in terms of attitude change than videos created by a nonprofit organization. This means that social media can be an effective vehicle for influencing others, and Facebook or Twitter posts may have more influence on friends' opinions than expert advice does.

Ideally, and ethically, science communicators should aim to combine high trustworthiness with high expertise. The quality and accuracy of the presented information will influence how the source itself is perceived; perceptions are influenced by factors such as the information's presentation and plausibility, and whether it is supported by good examples (Jung et al., 2016; Metzger, 2007). In general, perception of a source seems to be an iterative process, and the more high-quality information a source releases, the greater the level of perceived credibility. In mass communications in particular, basing claims on evidence, adequately referencing the evidence, and presenting data in an easily accessible way to minimize misinterpretations—and doing this consistently—will build credibility and thus contribute to a greater efficacy of corrections (Gigerenzer, Gaissmaier, Kurz-Milcke, Schwartz, & Woloshin, 2007).

Worldview

If an individual holds a strong belief that is fundamental to his identity, even the most credible source may not be able to shift it. A person's ideology often influences how information is sought out and evaluated; if the information runs counter to one's prior beliefs, it is likely to be ignored or more critically appraised (Wells, Reedy, Gastil, & Lee, 2009). This is known as *motivated reasoning* (Kunda, 1990). Motivated reasoning can be compounded by the formation of ideological echo chambers in which information is exchanged primarily among people with similar viewpoints, such that corrections are less likely to reach the target audience (Barbera, Jost, Nagler, Tucker, & Bonneau, 2015). This is fostered by social media platforms, where misinformation tends to circulate more quickly than associated corrections (Shin, Jian, Driscoll, & Bar, 2016).

Even if a correction reaches the misinformed target audience, simply providing the correct information is ineffective, as continued reliance on misinformation is likely when the misinformation conforms to a person's existing belief system and the correction does not (Lewandowsky, Stritzke, Oberauer, & Morales, 2005). Retracting misinformation that runs counter to a person's worldview can, ironically, even strengthen the to-be-corrected misinformation, a phenomenon known as the *worldview backfire effect*; this has been demonstrated in correcting misinformation surrounding contentious issues such as climate change (Hart & Nisbet, 2012) and vaccine safety (Nyhan & Reifler, 2015). Worldview biases are particularly difficult to overcome, as even neutral coverage of an issue can lead to polarization (Jerit & Barabas, 2012).

Recommendation 5: Provide Worldview- or Self-Affirming Corrections

If a correction is about a contentious topic or politically sensitive subject matter, in order to reduce perceived threat, it is beneficial to frame the correction such that it is congruent with the person's values (Kahan, 2010). Conservatives are more likely to accept anthropogenic climate science if it is presented as a business opportunity for the nuclear industry (Feygina, Jost, & Goldsmith, 2010). In line with the effects of source credibility, worldview congruence can potentially be conveyed through the appropriate choice of messenger. Callaghan and Schnell (2009) found that attitudes toward gun control were affected by the way the information was framed but also by the source of the message. Participants who were presented an argument regarding the impacts of crime and violence were 19% more likely to support gun control measures if the message came from a *New York Times* journalist than if it was presented without a source. People also seem less defensive about counterattitudinal information when their self-worth is strengthened. Cohen, Aronson, and Steele (2000) demonstrate this effect of self-affirmation: participants who had been instructed to write about personal qualities that made them feel good about themselves were subsequently more likely to respond positively to evidence that challenged their beliefs regarding the death penalty.

Skepticism

Skepticism is not a form of evidence denial driven by motivated reasoning, but an awareness of potential hidden agendas and a desire to accurately understand the evidence at hand (Mayo, 2015). Skepticism can reduce misinformation effects, as it leads to the allocation of more cognitive resources to the task of weighing the veracity of both the misinformation and the correction. People rely less on misinformation when given the tasks of checking facts, looking for inconsistencies, and correcting inaccuracies as they read a text (Rapp, Hinze, Kohlhepp, & Ryskin, 2014). The increased deliberation over the accuracy of information is often instigated when the information counters an individual's worldview (Taber & Lodge, 2006). To illustrate, Lewandowsky et al. (2005) found that a greater degree of skepticism led to better discounting of retracted real-world news reports; DiFonzo, Beckstead, Stupak, and Walders (2016) found that individuals with greater dispositional skepticism tended to believe inaccurate rumors to a lesser extent. The ability to maintain doubt, question evidence, and scrutinize the original data—even when it aligns with one's worldview—is conducive to avoiding reliance on misinformation, but doing so is a difficult task. Thus, honing the skill of knowing when to trust evidence can potentially have great benefits.

Recommendation 6: Fostering Skepticism

Skepticism is a quality that can be encouraged and even temporarily induced; a negative mood can increase skepticism and improve accuracy in detecting deceitful communications (Forgas & East, 2008). There is also a growing movement suggesting that evidence-based evaluation and critical thinking should formally be taught in schools. Schmaltz and Lilienfeld (2014) suggest that activities such as asking students to identify pseudoscience on campus and in the media could highlight the plethora of falsifiable claims in the public sphere. Alternatively, the authors recommend activities in which students create their own pseudoscience to demonstrate and experience the ease with which anecdotal evidence or "psychobabble" can be fabricated. Even examining real-world false advertising cases can be educational; examples to study might include the Federal Trade Commission's fining Lumosity $2 million for claiming its brain training program could protect against cognitive impairment (Rusk, 2016) and fining Dannon $21 million for claiming its yogurt could prevent the flu (Lordan, 2010). Lastly, the ability to question *causal illusions*—the perception that one event caused another when in fact they are unrelated—can also be taught, and a better understanding about the probability of an outcome, the probability of a cause, and cause-outcome coincidences can help promote skepticism (Matute et al., 2015).

Conclusion

Assessing the accuracy of information can be a difficult task. In today's fast-paced society, mass communication and social media play key roles in the sharing and receiving of current events. In reality, people generally do not have time to investigate each claim they encounter in depth; therefore, providing quality information is essential. In the aftermath of Brexit (Britain's exit from the European Union) and the 2016 U.S. presidential election campaign, events around which the political landscapes of the United States and Britain were rife with misinformation and fake news (Barthel, Mitchell, & Holcomb, 2016; McCann & Morgan, 2016), the ability to correct inaccuracies has rarely seemed more pertinent. The six recommendations we have provided can serve as guidelines for mass communication as to how best to retract the plethora of misinformation in the public sphere. However, it is important to note that no corrective technique can reduce belief to base level, as if the misinformation was never previously mentioned. And even if people do shift their opinions and acknowledge that information they previously believed to be true is incorrect, they are unlikely to change their voting preferences or feelings toward political candidates (Swire, Berinsky, Lewandowsky, & Ecker, 2016). Given what we know about misinformation and its correction, communicators thus hold a great deal of responsibility to ensure that the information initially released is as accurate as possible.

References

Ayers, M. S., & Reder, L. M. (1998). A theoretical review of the misinformation effect: Predictions from an activation-based memory model. *Psychonomic Bulletin & Review, 5,* 1–21.

Baadte, C., & Dutke, S. (2012). Learning about persons: The effects of text structure and executive capacity on conceptual change. *European Journal of Psychology of Education, 28,* 1045–1064.

Bailey, H. R., & Zacks, J. M. (2015). Situation model updating in young and older adults: Global versus incremental mechanisms. *Psychology and Aging, 30,* 232–244.

Barbera, P., Jost, J., Nagler, J., Tucker, J., & Bonneau, R. (2015). Tweeting from left to right: Is online political communication more than an echo chamber? *Psychological Science, 26,* 1531–1542.

Barthel, M., Mitchell, A., & Holcomb, J. (2016) Many Americans believe fake news is sowing confusion. Pew Research Center. Retrieved from http://www.journalism.org/2016/12/15/many-americans-believe-fake-news-is-sowing-confusion

BBC. (2007, April 1). Fairy fool sparks huge response. Retrieved from http://news.bbc.co.uk/2/hi/uk_news/england/derbyshire/6514283.stm

Bedford, D. (2010). Agnotology as a teaching tool: Learning climate science by studying misinformation. *Journal of Geography, 109,* 159–165.

Begg, I. M., Anas, A., & Farinacci, S. (1992). Dissociation of processes in belief: Source recollection, statement familiarity, and the illusion of truth. *Journal of Experimental Psychology: General, 121,* 446–458.

Bower, G. H., & Morrow, D. G. (1990). Mental models in narrative comprehension. *Science, 247,* 44–48.

Callaghan, K. C., & Schnell, F. (2009). Who says what to whom: Why messengers and citizen beliefs matter in social policy framing. *Journal of Social Science, 46,* 12–28.

Cohen, G. L., Aronson, J., & Steele, C. M. (2000). When beliefs yield to evidence: Reducing biased evaluation by affirming the self. *Personality and Social Psychology Bulletin, 26,* 1151–1164.

Dechene, A., Stahl, C., Hansen, J., & Wanke, M. (2010). The truth about the truth: A meta-analytic review of the truth effect. *Personality and Social Psychology Review, 14,* 238–257.

DiFonzo, N., Beckstead, J. W., Stupak, N., & Walders, K. (2016). Validity judgments of rumors heard multiple times: The shape of the truth effect. *Social Influence, 11,* 22–39.

Eagly, A. H., & Chaiken, S. (1993). *The psychology of attitudes.* Fort Worth, TX: Harcourt Brace Jovanovich College Publishers.

Ecker, U. K. H., & Antonio, L. (2016). *Source credibility and the continued influence effect.* Unpublished manuscript.

Ecker, U. K. H., Lewandowsky, S., & Apai, J. (2011). Terrorists brought down the plane!—No, actually it was a technical fault: Processing corrections of emotive information. *Quarterly Journal of Experimental Psychology, 64,* 283–310.

Ecker, U. K. H., Lewandowsky, S., Cheung, C. S. C., & Maybery, M. T. (2015). He did it!

She did it! No, she did not! Multiple causal explanations and the continued influence of misinformation. *Journal of Memory and Language, 85*, 101–115.

Ecker, U. K. H., Lewandowsky, S., Swire, B., & Chang, D. (2011). Correcting false information in memory: Manipulating the strength of misinformation encoding and its retraction. *Psychonomic Bulletin & Review, 18*, 570–578.

Ecker, U. K. H., Lewandowsky, S., & Tang, D. T. W. (2010). Explicit warnings reduce but do not eliminate the continued influence of misinformation. *Memory & Cognition, 38*, 1087–1100.

Feygina, I., Jost, J. T., & Goldsmith, R. E. (2010). System justification, the denial of global warming, and the possibility of "system-sanctioned change." *Personality and Social Psychology Bulletin, 36*, 326–338.

Forgas, J. P., & East, R. (2008). On being happy and gullible: Mood effects on skepticism and the detection of deception. *Journal of Experimental Social Psychology, 44*, 1362–1367.

Frithsen, A., & Miller, M. B. (2014). The posterior parietal cortex: Comparing remember/know and source memory tests of recollection and familiarity. *Neuropsychologia, 61*, 31–44.

Gigerenzer, G., Gaissmaier, W., Kurz-Milcke, E., Schwartz L. M., & Woloshin S. (2007). Helping doctors and patients make sense of health statistics. *Psychological Science in the Public Interest, 8*, 53–96.

Gilbert, D. T., Krull, D. S., & Malone, P. S. (1990). Unbelieving the unbelievable: Some problems in the rejection of false information. *Journal of Personality and Social Psychology, 59*, 601.

Goldenberg, S. (2016, February 29). How Leonardo DiCaprio became one of the world's top climate change champions. *Guardian*. Retrieved from http://www.theguardian.com/environment/2016/feb/29/how-leonardo-dicaprio-oscar-climate-change-campaigner

Guillory, J. J., & Geraci, L. (2013). Correcting erroneous inferences in memory: The role of source credibility. *Journal of Applied Research in Memory and Cognition, 2*, 201–209.

Guzman, M. (2013). After Boston, still learning. *Quill, 101*, 22–25.

Guzzetti, B. J. (2000). Learning counter-intuitive science concepts: What have we learned from over a decade of research? *Reading & Writing Quarterly, 16*, 89–98.

Guzzetti, B. J., Snyder, T. E., Glass, G. V., & Gamas, W. S. (1993). Promoting conceptual change in science: A comparative meta-analysis of instructional interventions from reading education and science education. *Reading Research Quarterly, 28*, 117–159.

Hart, P. S., & Nisbet, E. C. (2012). Boomerang effects in science communication: How motivated reasoning and identity cues amplify opinion polarization about climate mitigation policies. *Communication Research, 39*, 701–723.

Herron, J. E., & Rugg, M. D. (2003). Strategic influences on recollection in the exclusion task: Electrophysiological evidence. *Psychonomic Bulletin & Review, 10*, 703–710.

Hynd, C. R. (2001). Refutational texts and the change process. *International Journal of Educational Research, 35*, 699–714.

Jerit, J., & Barabas, J. (2012). Partisan perceptual bias and the information environment. *Journal of Politics, 74*, 672–684.

Johnson, H. M., & Seifert, C. M. (1994). Sources of the continued influence effect: When misinformation in memory affects later inferences. *Journal of Experimental Psychology: Learning, Memory, and Cognition, 20,* 1420–1436.

Jung, E. H., Walsh-Childers, K., & Kim, H. S. (2016). Factors influencing the perceived credibility of diet-nutrition information web sites. *Computers in Human Behavior, 58,* 37–47.

Kahan, D. (2010). Fixing the communications failure. *Nature, 463,* 296–297.

Kendeou, P., Smith, E. R., & O'Brien, E. J. (2013). Updating during reading comprehension: Why causality matters. *Journal of Experimental Psychology: Learning, Memory, and Cognition, 39,* 854–865.

Kendeou, P., & van den Broek, P. (2007). The effects of prior knowledge and text structure on comprehension processes during reading of scientific texts. *Memory & Cognition, 35,* 1567–1577.

Kowalski, P., & Taylor, A. K. (2009). The effect of refuting misconceptions in the introductory psychology class. *Teaching of Psychology, 36,* 153–159.

Kunda, Z. (1990). The case for motivated reasoning. *Psychological Bulletin, 108,* 480–498.

Kurby, C. A., & Zacks, J. M. (2012). Starting from scratch and building brick by brick in comprehension. *Memory & Cognition, 40,* 812–826.

Lewandowsky, S., Ecker, U. K. H., Seifert, C. M., Schwarz, N., & Cook, J. (2012). Misinformation and its correction: Continued influence and successful debiasing. *Psychological Science in the Public Interest, 13,* 106–131.

Lewandowsky, S., Stritzke, W. G. K., Oberauer, K., & Morales, M. (2005). Memory for fact, fiction, and misinformation: The Iraq War 2003. *Psychological Science, 3,* 190.

Lindsay, D. S., & Johnson, M. K. (1989). The eyewitness suggestibility effect and memory for source. *Memory & Cognition, 17,* 349–358.

Lombrozo, T. (2007). Simplicity and probability in causal explanation. *Cognitive Psychology, 55,* 232–257.

Lordan, B. (2010). Dannon agrees to drop exaggerated health claims for Activia yogurt and DanActive dairy drink. Federal Trade Commission. Retrieved from https://www.ftc.gov/news-events/press-releases/2010/12/dannon-agrees-drop-exaggerated-health-claims-activia-yogurt

Mase, A. S., Cho, H., & Prokopy, L. S. (2015). Enhancing the Social Amplification of Risk Framework (SARF) by exploring trust, the availability heuristic, and agricultural advisors' belief in climate change. *Journal of Environmental Psychology, 41,* 166–176.

Matute, H., Blanco, F., Yarritu, I., Diaz-Lago, M., Vadillo, M., & Berberia, I. (2015). Illusions of causality: How they bias our everyday thinking and how they could be reduced. *Frontiers in Psychology, 1,* 1–13.

Mayo, R. (2015). Cognition is a matter of trust: Distrust tunes cognitive processes. *European Review of Social Psychology, 26,* 283–327.

McCann, K., & Morgan, T. (2016) Nigel Farage: £350 million pledge to fund the NHS was "a mistake." *The Telegraph* (London). Retrieved from http://www.telegraph.co.uk/news/2016/06/24/nigel-farage-350-million-pledge-to-fund-the-nhs-was-a-mistake

McGinnes, E., & Ward, C. (1980). "Better liked than right": Trustworthiness and expertise in credibility. *Personality and Social Psychology Bulletin, 6,* 67–472.

Metzger, M. J. (2007). Making sense of credibility on the web: Models for evaluating online information and recommendations for future research. *Journal of the American Society for Information Science and Technology, 58*, 2078–2091.

Nyhan, B., & Reifler, J. (2015). Does correcting myths about the flu vaccine work? An experimental evaluation of the effects of corrective information. *Vaccine, 33*, 459–464.

Ortega-Sanchez, I. R., Vijayaraghavan, M., Barskey, A. E., & Wallace, G. S. (2014). The economic burden of sixteen measles outbreaks on United States public health departments in 2011. *Vaccine, 32*, 1311–1317.

Paek, H. J., Hove, T., Jeong, H., & Kim, M. (2011). Peer or expert? The persuasive impact of YouTube public service announcement producers. *International Journal of Advertising, 30*, 161–188.

Peter, C., & Koch, T. (2016). When debunking scientific myths fails (and when it does not): The backfire effect in the context of journalistic coverage and immediate judgments as prevention strategy. *Science Communication, 38*, 3–25.

Peters, K., Kashima, Y., & Clark, A. (2009). Talking about others: Emotionality and the dissemination of social information. *European Journal of Social Psychology, 39*, 207–222.

Poland, G. A., & Spier, R. (2010). Fear, misinformation, and innumerates: How the Wakefield paper, the press, and advocacy groups damaged the public health. *Vaccine, 28*, 2361–2362.

Poole, D. A., & Lindsay, D. S. (2002) Reducing child witnesses' false reports of misinformation from parents. *Journal of Child Psychology, 81*, 117–40.

Pornpitakpan, C. (2004). The persuasiveness of source credibility: A critical review of five decades' evidence. *Journal of Applied Social Psychology, 34*, 243–281.

Quest, R. (2016, March 7). MH370: Did the pilots do it? CNN. Retrieved from http://www.cnn.com/2016/03/07/asia/mh370-quest-pilots

Rapp, D. N., Hinze, S. R., Kohlhepp, K., & Ryskin, R. A. (2014). Reducing reliance on inaccurate information. *Memory & Cognition, 42*, 11–26.

Rusk, M. (2016). Lumosity to pay $2 million to settle FTC deceptive advertising charges for its "brain training" program. Federal Trade Commission. Retrieved from https://www.ftc.gov/news-events/press-releases/2016/01/lumosity-pay-2-million-settle-ftc-deceptive-advertising-charges

Schmaltz, R., & Lilenfeld, S. (2014) Hauntings, homeopathy, and the Hopkinsville Goblins: Using pseudoscience to teach scientific thinking. *Frontiers in Psychology, 5*, 1–5.

Seifert, C. M. (2002). The continued influence of misinformation in memory: What makes a correction effective? *Psychology of Learning and Motivation: Advances in Research and Theory, 41*, 265–292.

Shin, J., Jian, L., Driscoll, K., & Bar, F. (2016). Political rumoring on Twitter during the 2012 US presidential election: Rumor diffusion and correction. *New Media and Society.* Advance online publication.

Skurnik, I., Yoon, C., Park, D. C., & Schwarz, N. (2005). How warnings about false claims become recommendations. *Journal of Consumer Research, 31*, 713–724.

Swire, B., Berinsky, A., Lewandowsky, S., & Ecker, U. K. H. (2017). Processing political misinformation — Comprehending the Trump phenomenon. *Royal Society Open Science*, 4, 160802.

Swire, B., Ecker, U. K. H., & Lewandowsky, S. (in press). The role of familiarity in correcting inaccurate information. *Journal of Experimental Psychology: Learning, Memory, and Cognition*.

Taber, C. S., & Lodge, M. (2006). Motivated skepticism in the evaluation of political beliefs. *American Journal of Political Science*, 50, 755–769.

van Oostendorp, H. (2014). The ambivalent effect of focus on updating mental representations. In D. N. Rapp & J. L. Braasch (Eds.), *Processing inaccurate information and applied perspectives from cognitive science and the educational sciences* (pp. 223–244). Cambridge, MA: MIT Press.

Wells, C., Reedy, J., Gastil, J., & Lee, C. (2009). Information distortion and voting choices: The origins and effects of factual beliefs in initiative elections. *Political Psychology*, 30, 953–969.

Wilkes, A. L., & Leatherbarrow, M. (1988). Editing episodic memory following the identification of error. *Quarterly Journal of Experimental Psychology: Human Experimental Psychology*, 52, 165–183.

Yonelinas, A. P. (2002). The nature of recollection and familiarity: A review of 30 years of research. *Journal of Memory and Language*, 46, 441–517.

Zimmer, H. D., & Ecker, U. K. H. (2010). Remembering perceptual features unequally bound in object and episodic tokens: Neural mechanisms and their electrophysiological correlates. *Neuroscience & Biobehavioral Reviews*, 34, 1066–1079.

How to Counteract Consumer Product Misinformation

TWELVE

GRAHAM BULLOCK

In 2011 the U.S. Department of Transportation and the Environmental Protection Agency (EPA) finalized a new label for all passenger vehicles sold in the United States (EPA, 2016b). The labels include information about each vehicle's fuel economy (miles per gallon, gallons per 100 miles, and annual fuel costs) but also its greenhouse gas and smog emissions. The emissions data are presented in simple-to-read, graphical 1–10 ratings, with 10 clearly labeled as best (California Air Resources Board, n.d.). Beginning in 2013, a car shopper could evaluate both the environmental performance and financial costs associated with driving different vehicles and make a well-informed decision about them (EPA, 2016b)—except, it turns out, if the buyer was comparing any one of 64 Audi and Volkswagen models, including Jettas, Beetles, and Passats, made between 2009 and 2015 (Gates, Ewing, Russell, & Watkins, 2016).

The Volkswagen company admitted in 2015 to installing software designed to generate inaccurate results on required emissions tests. The "defeat device" turned on equipment in the car engine to reduce emissions when it was being tested. During normal operations of the car, the software disengaged the equipment, improving the car's performance and fuel economy but also causing a significant increase in emissions (Gates et al., 2016). The West Virginia University researchers who discovered the discrepancy found the actual emissions of the VW Jetta they tested to be 15 to 35 times more than the EPA's standard (Kretchmer, 2015). The EPA reports that nitrogen oxide (NOx) emitted by vehicles with the devices installed are up to 40 times higher than the government's standard (EPA, 2016a). Given that NOx is a major contributor to smog and its related environmental and health effects, the incorrect emissions readings mean that the smog ratings reported on the cars' labels are incorrect (California Air Resources Board, n.d.). Not only did Volkswagen break the law by using such software, as defeat devices are explicitly banned in the Clean Air Act, but also it actively misled consumers by reporting incorrect data and claiming that its vehicles are ecofriendly (EPA, 2015; Shepardson, 2016).

The Volkswagen case is an excellent example of misinformation and even disinformation, as it represents an intentional effort to deceive. In the context of environmental claims, it also represents a clear case of greenwashing, which Delmas and Burbano (2011, p. 66) define as an "act of misleading consumers regarding the environmental practices of a company (firm-level greenwashing) or the environmental benefits of a product or service (product-level greenwashing)." It is not the first or only such case, in the context of either automobiles or defeat devices. Complaints about the devices date back to 1972, when the EPA issued a letter to all auto manufacturers selling cars in the United States saying that they must report the use of defeat devices to the agency (EPA, 1973). In 1974, Volkswagen paid $120,000 to settle an EPA complaint for not disclosing two temperature-sensing switches that disabled its vehicles' pollution controls (Beene, 2015). Since 1974 the EPA has brought charges against several other major auto companies, including General Motors, Ford, Chrysler, and Honda, for similar use of devices to circumvent emission controls (Beene, 2015; Gallucci, 2015).

Defeat devices have been found in other types of consumer products as well. An Australian consumer advocacy group discovered in 2010 that LG installed a circumvention device in two of its refrigerator models that turns on energy-saving modes when it detects that the refrigerator's temperature has been set for test conditions (Singer, 2010). In a settlement with the U.S. Department of Energy (DOE), the company agreed to remove the products from the ENERGY STAR program, modify them to improve energy efficiency, and reimburse consumers for their higher energy bills (DOE, 2008).

These examples raise important questions about misinformation in the context of consumer products: How do consumers, government regulators, nonprofit advocates, and private-sector competitors identify and counteract product misinformation? What are the strengths and limitations of regulatory mechanisms? How might existing mechanisms be improved? I address these questions by first presenting a conceptual framework outlining five primary mechanisms for counteracting misinformation that builds on insights from the academic literature. I then analyze six types of institutions that utilize the mechanisms to protect the interests of consumers and combat misinformation in the marketplace. The institutions include for-profit companies such as Yelp and Walmart, nonprofit organizations such as the Consumers Union and the Council of Better Business Bureaus, and government agencies such as the Federal Trade Commission and the Consumer Product Safety Commission. The chapter concludes with a discussion of ways in which a more aggressive, holistic, and creative approach to counteracting misinformation about consumer products can complement existing institutions.

Mechanisms to Address Consumer Misinformation

The literature on misinformation is too vast to summarize in one short chapter. Instead, in this section I present a parsimonious framework that builds on two particularly relevant sources from the literature. The first is an article by Glaeser and Ujhelyi (2010) that outlines three primary mechanisms government policy might use to prevent or respond to misleading advertising about particular types of products, such as medicines, cigarettes, and foods. The first option is banning or taxing advertising on the products. Bans can include outright and partial bans, both of which have been used extensively. For example, the Pure Food and Drug Act of 1906 completely banned false or misleading labels and packages of any food or drugs, while the Public Health Cigarette Smoking Act of 1969 banned the advertising of cigarettes on any television or radio broadcast (CDC, 2012; Glaeser & Ujhelyi, 2010).

The second option is to tax the profits or sales of products that are associated with misinformation. The payments required by tobacco litigation settlements, for example, are the equivalent of more than $200 billion of sales taxes over 25 years. Television advertisements for prescription drugs are subject to a $41,390 fee per ad for advisory review (Glaeser & Ujhelyi, 2010). The City of Berkeley, California, instituted a first-in-the-nation tax on sugar-sweetened beverages in 2014 (Lochner, 2015).

The third mechanism is counteradvertising, which Glaeser and Ujhelyi (2010) define as an effort to present an alternative viewpoint regarding a particular product. Examples include public health campaigns and associated advertisements (e.g., public service announcements about counterfeit medicines), labeling and disclosure requirements (e.g., nutrition labels), and health warnings on products (e.g., surgeon general's warnings on cigarettes explaining the dangers of smoking) (FDA, 2013; Glaeser & Ujhelyi, 2010). Within this arena are specific corrective efforts intended to counter misstatements in advertising. For example, Aikin et al. (2015 and 2017) experimentally tested the effects of corrective advertising. In both studies, authors found that corrective advertising can indeed counteract at least some of the effects of misinformation in prescription drug advertisements.

To these three mechanisms to counteract misinformation described by Glaeser and Ujhelyi (2010)—bans or taxes on misleading advertising, taxes on products associated with misinformation, and counteradvertisements—I would add two more. The first is education of either buyers or sellers about the nature and effects of misinformation that goes beyond counteradvertising about individual products. This mechanism includes self-regulation efforts by firms and marketers that emphasize codes of conduct and best practices (International Chamber of Commerce, n.d.). The second entails partial or complete bans on products that are associated with misinformation. While rare, classic examples include the prohibition of alcohol or drugs such as marijuana and cocaine. Promoters of the products seldom mention all their effects. Given the severity of some effects, many advocates have argued that complete bans on their sale and distribution are justified; the temperance advocates of the early 20th century who were responsible for Prohibition are a case in point (Blocker, 2006). Hanson (2003) argues that bans are a necessary tool for regulators under certain conditions of consumer ignorance, market failures, and undesirable externalities (consequences of an economic activity experienced by a third party unrelated to the original action).

Agents to Implement Available Mechanisms

Given these mechanisms, we can ask who should implement them. Many assume the answer is government regulators, but the range of actors who can and do play important roles in counteracting misinformation extends beyond the public sector. Bullock (2011) outlines six types of actors that participate in monitoring and regulating initiatives designed to provide information to the public, and all but one are primarily nongovernmental in nature. They include for-profit and nonprofit organizations that facilitate market transactions in which all parties have access to relevant information ("market facilitators"), filter out low-quality products and poorly performing companies ("market editors"), collate product reviews and evaluations from consumers ("democratic organizers"), evaluate products and companies based on specialized knowledge and/or particular interests ("experts and advocates"), and bring together organizations that assess the quality of products and companies ("club coordinators"). Only the sixth type of actor explicitly includes government agencies that have legislative mandates from elected officials to protect consumers from fraud ("the people's representatives"). I describe the types of actors in more detail by outlining the methods they use and analyzing their strengths and limitations.

Providing Relevant Information: The Role of Market Facilitators

Market facilitators are in many ways the first line of defense against misinformation. They reduce transaction costs associated with collecting information about products and reduce information asymmetries between sellers and buyers (Bakos, 1998; Liang & Huang, 1998). If well designed, marketplaces, and in particular, electronic marketplaces, can "lower the buyers' cost to obtain information about the price and product features of seller offerings as well as the sellers' cost to communicate information about their prices and product characteristics" (Bakos, 1998, p. 39). Internet-based technologies can improve information sharing and lower search costs for consumers, enabling them to compare products by prices and features and verify claims made by sellers (Bakos, 1998). For example, buyers encountering products being advertised as the lowest price option or the only option with a certain feature can quickly check resources such as Amazon or Google Shopping to confirm whether these claims are indeed true. Personalized recommendation engines and comparison matrices for shopping sites can also reduce search costs for buyers, enable in-depth product assessments, and improve the quality of purchase decisions (Häubl & Trifts, 2000). But even brick-and-mortar retailers can provide information services to consumers. Shelf labels at electronics retailers such as Best Buy list the attributes and prices of similar products so shoppers can compare available products more easily.

In terms of the counteraction mechanisms outlined above, market facilitators are utilizing a form of counteradvertising to combat misinformation. They are not taxing or banning either advertisements or products; instead they are providing information to consumers that can counteract the effects of misleading information from some sellers. The strengths of this approach are the low transaction costs and significant benefits it provides to consumers. While retailers often mark up the prices of products they sell well above wholesale prices, many consumers are willing to pay for the added choice and convenience of the one-stop shopping experience the retailers provide.

Implementing market facilitation does not require an act of Congress but can be done by a single firm. A significant limitation of the market facilitator approach, however, is its dependence on consumers to actively compare and analyze claims of competing companies and brands. Many consumers do not have the knowledge, skills, or time to systematically and accurately make the comparisons, particularly when the differences between products are highly technical and nuanced, although still very important (Ben-Shahar & Schneider, 2014).

Filtering Out Poor Performance: The Role of Market Editors

Market editors take the role of market facilitators to the next level, going beyond merely presenting comparable information to actively editing out certain products or companies from the range of choices that consumers consider. Retailers and government procurement offices can directly filter product offerings that do not meet certain quality or price standards they establish. Walmart announced it would not sell household cleaning and personal care products with any of ten hazardous chemicals, and it directed its suppliers to phase out their use of these chemicals (Koch, 2013). Building on executive orders by Presidents Clinton and Bush, President Obama used a similar strategy when he signed Executive Order 13693, which required federal agencies to purchase products whenever practicable that are certified by approved environmental certifications, including Energy Star, EPEAT, BioPreferred, WaterSense, Safer Choice, and SmartWay. Target has developed a scoring system that penalizes—through less marketing support and poor shelf location—products that contain any one of more than 1,000 listed hazardous chemicals (Howland, 2015).

These policies are examples of decision or choice editing, which comes out of the field of behavioral economics. Choice editing can include partial or complete bans on products within a decision context, as the Walmart and executive order examples demonstrate, or it can utilize penalties—

a form of tax—that disincentivize the production of particular products, as exemplified by the Target scoring system (Maniates, 2010). Over time, choice editing combats misinformation by eliminating or penalizing products that are not as safe, high-quality, or environmentally friendly as alternative products. Even if the makers of alternative products have not explicitly claimed superior characteristics, the companies remaining in the marketplace benefit from consumers' default assumption that they are better.

The primary advantage of market editing is that it does not depend on busy consumers to evaluate products and companies themselves; rather, it places that responsibility on institutional decision makers who are better positioned to judge products (Hickman, 2007). Because they are involved in many more market transactions than their customers, market editors can utilize their market position and economies of scale to monitor and discourage opportunistic behavior by sellers to defraud unsuspecting consumers (Bailey, 1994). A major limitation of market editing, however, is the potential for backlash by consumers and policy makers who view such efforts as unnecessarily restrictive. Another limitation is the dependence on market intermediaries such as retailers and vendors who may not be willing to threaten their relations with manufacturers by engaging in such unilateral actions.

Collating Consumer Opinions:
The Role of Democratic Organizers

For those interested in a less heavy-handed approach, an alternative is the collation of consumer product evaluations. A host of organizations has emerged to provide this service for companies; among them are Yotpo.com, Feefo.com, and PowerReviews.com. Ratings and reviews by PowerReviews.com appear on Google Shopping pages; the organization works with more than 1,000 companies to "generate and syndicate reviews to drive traffic, increase sales, and create actionable insights" (PowerReviews, n.d.). Epinions.com, which paid reviewers to provide their product insights, was an early mover in this space, but competitors discovered such payments were not necessary, as many consumers are willing to provide their reviews for free (Goldman, 2014). Opinion aggregators have emerged in specific categories, such as TripAdvisor for travel and Yelp for restaurants, as well as in particular issue areas such as Green washing.org with its consumer ratings of environmental claims and Fortune's Best Companies to Work For with its surveys of employees about their companies' employment practices.

Online democratic organizers enable the voice of the people to inform shoppers' decision making and combat misinformation from sellers. They rely on "the wisdom of crowds," a phrase popularized by James Surowiecki (2004); he posits that "the many are smarter than the few," particularly when they hold a diversity of opinions, are not influenced by other people, have specialized and decentralized knowledge, and can aggregate their knowledge. Surowiecki (2004) documents many cases when crowds have held more accurate opinions than individual experts, underscoring the value of aggregated consumer reviews in the context of product misinformation. Unlike bans or taxes, these reviews serve the function of counteradvertising when a seller makes claims that consumers find to be inaccurate. Studies have shown that reviews do indeed influence consumers' purchasing intentions, although this effect depends on not only the quality and quantity of the reviews but also the type of product and the consumers' level of involvement with it (Park, Lee, & Han, 2007; Sen & Lerman, 2007; Zhu & Zhang, 2010).

Surowiecki (2004) also notes that crowds can be greatly misinformed when certain conditions (such as the input from a diverse array of sources or unbiased aggregation of knowledge in a way that reflects different viewpoints) are not met; this situation constitutes a major limitation of democratic organizing. If reviewers' knowledge is not sufficiently diversified, independent, specialized, and aggregated, they are not likely to identify important forms of misinformation. Furthermore, consumer reviews are often faked, gamed, and incentivized by unscrupulous sellers, adding another layer of misinformation that requires buyers to beware (Stone, 2015).

Providing Specialized Evaluations: The Role of Experts and Advocates

Specialized knowledge may be the right antidote when consumer reviews are flawed. Experts and advocates can utilize their domain-specific knowledge to independently evaluate the validity of claims made by advertisers in ways that the average consumer cannot. Similar to retailers and market editors, they may also have more time, resources, and motivation than consumers to evaluate products and services. Consumers Union, a nonprofit organization founded in 1936, perhaps best embodies this approach

(Silber, 1983). Its more than 100 testing experts evaluate thousands of products every year in its 50 laboratories and on its automotive testing track (Consumers Union, 2016a, 2016b). It then publishes its test results in its magazine, *Consumer Reports*, and on its website, complete with five-level graphical ratings and product reviews. Many other public, private, and civil society organizations have pursued similar information-based strategies to combat marketplace fraud by developing ratings or lists of acceptable or unacceptable products or companies and encouraging consumers to use them to guide their choices (Bullock, 2011; Conroy, 2007). The evaluations may be developed by experts trained in a particular area or advocates with a relevant agenda. Examples include certifications, seals of approval, ratings, and boycott lists created by organizations such as Greenpeace, Good Housekeeping, the EPA, and JD Power.

While based on the opinions of experts or advocates and not on those of individual consumers, this approach is also a form of counteradvertising. It relies on consumers' perceptions of the credibility and legitimacy of the organizations publishing the information and on the demand for the information, which in general is high (De Maeyer & Estelami, 2011). A study by inPowered and Nielsen in 2013–2014 found that 85% of consumers surveyed regularly or occasionally sought out trusted expert content in third-party articles and reviews when considering purchases, and 67% agreed that an endorsement from an unbiased expert made them more likely to consider a purchase (Bradley, 2014). Using an experimental design, the researchers also discovered that expert content increases brand familiarity, affinity, and purchase intent significantly more than branded content and user reviews (Bradley, 2014).

The perceived influence of expert opinions can translate into an effective incentive for firms to publish misinformation about their brands, as these organizations often evaluate specific claims made about product performance. For example, Consumers Union concluded in 2016 that 43% of the 65 sunscreens it tested failed to meet their own SPF label claims (Arensberg, 2016). A 2015 study lends weight to the validity of *Consumer Reports* assessments compared to aggregated consumer ratings, as it finds that consumer ratings are less scientifically rigorous, do not predict resale prices as well, and favor more expensive products and premium brands (Langhe, Fernbach, & Lichtenstein, 2015). Despite their added technical rigor, though, organizations publishing product information may not necessarily live up to their potential. Those that do cannot subject every product on the market to systematic testing, as their time and money are limited. Thus they are likely to miss at least some fraudulent claims that they do not have the resources to evaluate.

Organizing Collective Assessments: The Role of Club Coordinators

A solution to the dilemma for consumer advocacy organizations is to divide and conquer the crowded landscape of product claims, or at least to communicate and coordinate their respective strategies among themselves. This approach is based on the concept of a club that confers membership only on those who meet certain standards and requirements. In the context of green product claims, for example, the Global Ecolabelling Network (GEN) and the ISEAL Alliance act as coalitions of "ecolabels" that meet a set of standards that member firms have collectively set for themselves (GEN, n.d.; ISEAL, n.d.). In battling product misinformation, the Council of Better Business Bureaus (CBBB) is one of the best examples of club coordinators—organizations that establish such clubs and enforce their standards. The CBBB, established in 1912 as the National Vigilance Committee, is the umbrella organization for local Better Business Bureaus in the United States and Canada (CBBB, n.d.a). The local chapters must meet nine performance and accountability standards established by the CBBB, including 67 specific requirements relating to their finances, governance, technology, and operations (CBBB, 2013). A committee of the CBBB, made up of "experienced BBB CEOs, is charged with overseeing operations of the 113 BBBs across the U.S. and Canada, and is responsible for setting and enforcing standards so that BBBs are reviewed and held accountable by their peers" (CBBB, 2013). The chapters provide grades of local businesses based on such factors as a history of complaints from consumers, size and type of business, time in business, transparency, licensing, government actions, and advertising practices (CBBB, n.d.c). The chapters also accredit businesses that pay regular fees and meet a certain set of standards (CBBB, n.d.b).

The local organizations thus utilize a mix of consumer reviews and their own knowledge-based assessments to evaluate businesses. Like other types of institutions, they rely on counteradvertising and lack the power to ban or tax businesses.

A club-based approach has several advantages. It provides a useful monitoring and enforcement function of organizations purporting to represent consumers' interests. In 2013 the CBBB expelled its Los Angeles chapter for failing to ensure the eligibility of companies for accreditation and employing extortion-type pay-to-play practices, rewarding paying members with higher grades than nonpaying members (CBBB, 2013; Tuttle, 2013). While disturbing, such practices are much less likely to be detected in organizations that are not members of clubs like the BBB. Firms may also pay more attention to ratings issued by organizations that are members of clubs, particularly if the ratings are likely to propagate through their networks. Due to their economies of scale and broader perspectives, club coordinators can serve other functions as well. The CBBB runs several consumer education programs and facilitates discussions with industries on improving efforts to self-regulate advertising and eliminate misinformation.

However, club coordinators face important limitations as well. Coordination can be costly and difficult—it took two years for the LA chapter to be expelled—and is no guarantee of effectiveness or high standards. Many commentators have complained that the BBB model does not represent the interests of consumers, does not resolve consumers' complaints, and is plagued by conflicts of interest (Ellis & Hicken, 2015; Fisher, Garrett, Arnold, & Ferris, 1999; Tugend, 2013; Tuttle, 2013). In fact, a lowest-common-denominator effect may occur in which the organizations with the lowest standards determine the requirements for the whole network.

Regulating the Market: The Role of the People's Representatives

The sixth type of actor that works to counteract misinformation is government. Public agencies exist at local, state, federal, and international levels and include consumer protection services, attorney general offices, independent commissions, and intergovernmental networks such as the International Consumer Protection and Enforcement Network (ICPEN, n.d.; USA.gov, n.d.a). Often charged with broad legislative mandates that extend beyond issues associated with misinformation, government agencies are tasked by elected officials to represent the concerns and interests of consumers and the general public. Two of the most important of these institutions are the Federal Trade Commission (FTC), established by Congress in 1914 (FTC, n.d.a), and the Consumer Product Safety Commission (CPSC), created by Congress in 1972 (CPSC, 2011). In order to protect consumers and stop "unfair, deceptive or fraudulent practices in the marketplace," the FTC conducts investigations, files lawsuits against companies and individuals, develops marketplace rules and guidelines, and implements education programs for both consumers and businesses (FTC, n.d.b). The CPSC, in order to protect "children and families from unreasonable risks of injuries or death associated with consumer products," monitors hazards associated with consumer products under its jurisdiction; contributes to the development of voluntary and mandatory safety standards; enforces compliance with those standards through recalls, litigation, and other methods; and educates the public about relevant consumer product safety issues (CPSC, 2015a).

Government institutions thus utilize a range of mechanisms to counteract misinformation. Their standards development and enforcement actions include bans and fines on advertising and products, while their educational initiatives incorporate different forms of counteradvertisements and are oriented toward buyers and sellers. Settlement of an FTC lawsuit against LifeLock required the company to pay $100 million for falsely advertising its services and failing to secure consumers' personal information (FTC, 2015). The FTC has also banned nearly 300 companies and individuals from engaging in mortgage assistance and debt-relief operations for prematurely charging fees or misleading people about their results (FTC, 2016). The CSPC has banned certain amounts of six types of phthalates (potentially toxic chemicals) in children's toys and child-care items (CPSC, 2015b). It maintains public online databases of product recalls and product complaints submitted by consumers (CPSC, n.d.a; USA .gov, n.d.b). Both agencies run consumer and business education programs such as the FTC's IdentityTheft.gov (FTC, n.d.a) and the CPSC's online Safety Education Centers (CPSC, n.d.b).

The strengths of a governmental approach are its multipronged nature and ability to leverage the power of official agencies that can exert real power over firms and markets through due process. While consumers, businesses, and advocacy groups can bring lawsuits against fraudulent firms, they do not have the authority to enforce bans and fines that public institutions do. Government agencies are limited by the resources appropriated to them by legislatures, however, and by the interests of political appointees. Public interest groups criticized the FTC under the Bush administration, for example, for not adequately protecting consumers from business practices resulting in rising cable bills and credit card fees (Hart, 2009).

Alternative Approaches

Although each has its limitations, the six types of actors described above have an impressive record of combating misinformation. In 2014 Better Business Bureaus processed and closed 873,208 consumer complaints (CBBB, 2014), and in 2015 the Federal Trade Commission returned $49.8 million to consumers from fraudulent companies (FTC, 2016). For seven years, however, all of these actors failed to identify the misinformation provided by Volkswagen about emission controls in its vehicles. Consumers, retailers, experts, club coordinators, and regulators were all fooled by a repeat offender and a device that has more than 30 years of precedents. Commentators have convincingly asserted that the VW emissions case is only the tip of the iceberg and that other manufacturers are guilty of similar deceptions (Archer, 2015; Trigg, 2015). Consumers may therefore be legitimately dubious about product claims they encounter in the marketplace. Indeed, multiple surveys have shown declining levels of trust in brands and the information they provide (Rozdeba, 2016). In 2016, nearly a third of consumers expressed little or no trust in advertisements they find on Facebook, an increase of 10% from 2014 (Vizard, 2016).

A more aggressive, creative, and persuasive approach may be necessary to build consumer confidence in information in the marketplace. Existing mechanisms and institutions, while extensive, may be too underfunded, piecemeal, and disconnected to effectively and comprehensively combat misinformation to the extent the public desires. A more effective approach should have three primary goals: greater transparency about product claims generally, stronger monitoring of fraudulent claims specifically, and more extensive awareness among consumers and producers of claims. Consumer frustration with misinformation begins with the inability to evaluate the validity of the hundreds of claims encountered every day. A typical box of toothpaste might state "clinically proven" or "9 out of 10 dentists recommend" but provide no evidence backing up the claims (Mushnick, 2006). Requiring manufacturers to support their claims can ameliorate consumers' frustration and enable easier monitoring and detection of claims that do not hold up to scrutiny. If buyers and sellers are then more effectively educated about cases of misinformation, the former will be better equipped to differentiate between truthful and untruthful product claims and the latter will be less likely to engage in deceptive behavior.

These goals can be accomplished through three key innovations in efforts to combat misinformation. The first is a comprehensive database of product information that would serve as a one-stop shop for buyers and sellers. The current ecosystem of databases is fragmented, confusing, and poorly designed; each public agency hosts multiple databases (recalls.gov, saferproducts.gov, ftccomplaintassistant.gov, etc.) that are not as user-friendly or effective as they could be. Requiring manufacturers to list and support *all* claims they make and *all* information they provide about their products in a single database would radically increase the transparency—and ultimately the value—of product claims. The database would include links to studies of product efficacy and definitions of terms they are using, such as "natural" or "sustainable," and would be publicly accessible via both a website and an Application Programming Interface (API). The website could be administered by the FTC, which would collaborate extensively on its design with businesses, nongovernmental organizations, and other government agencies.

The second innovation is an annual report on the state of consumer products in the United States that would summarize the status of efforts to combat misinformation and fraud in marketplaces typically accessible to U.S. consumers. The FTC, CSPC, BBB, Consumers Union, and other organizations all issue their own impact and performance reports, but they present an incomplete and fragmented perspective on the overall quality of information being provided to consumers about the products they buy. A key component of a single, comprehensive report would be independent and systematic research assessing the extent of misinformation that to date has been undetected and unaddressed by existing institutions and mechanisms. A rigorous, regular, well-publicized, and holistic synthesis of those efforts that honestly and objectively assesses progress made in the fight against misinformation could greatly enhance the public's trust in market transactions.

The third innovation would capitalize on this report through an extensive education program about product misinformation more generally. It would include two primary components. A "Responsible Marketer" certification program would certify individuals and businesses engaged in any form of advertising. The certification would go beyond existing programs such as the American Marketing Association's Professional Certified Marketer accreditation and require extensive knowledge of the history of consumer fraud, best and worst practices in the advertising industry, and the ethics of marketing (American Marketing Association, n.d.). A certificate would be mandatory for any firm that does business with the government or sells or buys advertising over the airwaves. Another educational component would be a "Smart Consumer" module to incorporate into high school civics courses. The module would explore the history of citizen and government efforts to combat consumer fraud and the fruits of those labors. It would educate students about the importance of individuals taking action in the marketplace, and in the process it would build student skills and confidence as engaged citizens and consumers (McGregor, 1999). It could complement and be incorporated into existing state curricula that require financial literacy components for consumer education, which have been shown to have positive effects on consumer competencies (Bernheim, Garrett, & Maki, 2001; Council for Economic Education, 2016; Langrehr, 1979).

These three innovations—a nationwide product database, an annual report on the state of the nation's products, and a two-pronged education program designed for consumers and marketers—would complement the important work that consumers, manufacturers, retailers, advocates, and policy makers are already doing to counteract product misinformation. They would provide a platform for coordinating and integrating those efforts as well as educating the public about them. They would also help build the political will to appropriate more resources and dedicate more attention to combating fraudulent and misleading practices. While it is likely impossible to fully eradicate misinformation from the marketplace, these strategies could greatly reduce it and in the process significantly improve product quality, economic transactions, and consumer confidence.

References

Aikin, K. J., Betts, K. R., O'Donoghue, A. C., Rupert, D. J., Lee, P. K., Amoozegar, J. B., & Southwell, B. G. (2015). Correction of overstatement and omission in direct-to-consumer prescription drug advertising. *Journal of Communication, 65*(4), 596–618.

Aikin, K. J., Southwell, B. G., Paquin, R. S., Rupert, D. J., O'Donoghue, A. C., Betts, K. R., & Lee, P. K. (2017). Correction of misleading information in prescription drug television advertising: The roles of advertisement similarity and time delay. *Research in Social and Administrative Pharmacy, 13*, 378–388.

American Marketing Association. (N.d.). AMA's Professional Certified Marketer (PCM®). Retrieved June 15, 2016, from https://www.ama.org/events-training/Certification/Pages/default.aspx

Archer, G. (2015, September 21). VW's cheating is just the tip of the iceberg. *Transport & Environment*. Retrieved from http://www.transportenvironment.org/publications/vw%E2%80%99s-cheating-just-tip-iceberg

Arensberg, C. (Producer). (2016, May 17). Burn notice: Consumer Reports investigates sunscreen claims. *CBS this morning* [Television broadcast]. New York: NY: CBS News. Retrieved from http://www.cbsnews.com/news/consumer-reports-which -sunscreens-live-up-to-product-claims-keep-skin-safe

Bailey, K. D. (1994). *Typologies and taxonomies: An introduction to classification techniques.* Thousand Oaks, CA: Sage.

Bakos, Y. (1998). The emerging role of electronic marketplaces on the Internet. *Communications of the ACM, 41*(8), 35–42.

Beene, R. (2015, September 24). VW emissions "defeat device" isn't the first. *Autoweek.* Retrieved from http://autoweek.com/article/car-news/vw-emissions-defeat -device-isnt-first

Ben-Shahar, O., & Schneider, C. E. (2014). *More than you wanted to know: The failure of mandated disclosure.* Princeton, New Jersey: Princeton University Press.

Bernheim, B. D., Garrett, D. M., & Maki, D. M. (2001). Education and saving: The long-term effects of high school financial curriculum mandates. *Journal of Public Economics, 80*(3), 435–465.

Blocker, J. S. (2006). Did prohibition really work? Alcohol prohibition as a public health innovation. *American Journal of Public Health, 96*(2), 233–243.

Bradley, D. (2014, March 25). Study: Consumers prefer credible, third-party content over branded content. *PR Week.* Retrieved from http://www.prweek.com/article /1286769/study-consumers-prefer-credible-third-party-content-branded-content

Bullock, G. (2011). *Green grades: The popularity and perceived effectiveness of information-based environmental governance strategies* (Doctoral dissertation). University of California, Berkeley, CA. Retrieved from http://search.proquest.com.ezproxy.lib .davidson.edu/docview/892713398/abstract/13B97E4A36531119FAD/1?account id=10427

California Air Resources Board. (N.d.). Understand the smog rating. *DriveClean.* Retrieved June 2, 2016, from http://www.driveclean.ca.gov/Know_the_Rating/Un derstand_the_Smog_Rating.php

CDC. *See* U.S. Centers for Disease Control and Prevention (CDC).

Conroy, M. E. (2007). *Branded! How the certification revolution is transforming global corporations.* Gabriola Island, Canada: New Society Publishers.

Consumer Product Safety Commission (CPSC). (2011). *2011–2016 U.S. Consumer Product Safety Commission strategic plan.* Retrieved from http://www.cpsc.gov//Page Files/123374/2011strategic.pdf

Consumer Product Safety Commission (CPSC). (2015a). *2014 Annual report to the president and Congress.* Retrieved from http://www.cpsc.gov//Global/About-CPSC/Re ports/Annual-Reports/FY14AnnualReport.pdf

Consumer Product Safety Commission (CPSC). (2015b, July 7). Phthalates. Retrieved from https://www.cpsc.gov/en/Business—Manufacturing/Business-Education /Business-Guidance/Phthalates-Information

Consumer Product Safety Commission (CPSC). (N.d.a). About SaferProducts.gov. Retrieved June 14, 2016, from http://www.saferproducts.gov/About.aspx.

Consumer Product Safety Commission (CPSC). (N.d.b). Safety education centers. Retrieved June 14, 2016, from http://www.cpsc.gov/en/Safety-Education/Safety -Education-Centers

Consumers Union. (2016a). Our mission. Retrieved from http://www.consumerreports
.org/cro/about-us/index.htm

Consumers Union. (2016b). What's behind the ratings. Retrieved from http://www
.consumerreports.org/cro/about-us/whats-behind-the-ratings/index.htm

Council for Economic Education. (2016). *Survey of the states: Economic and personal finance education in our nation's schools.* Retrieved from http://www.councilforeconed
.org/wp/wp-content/uploads/2014/02/2014-Survey-of-the-States.pdf

Council of Better Business Bureaus (CBBB). (2013, March 12). *Better Business Bureau expels Los Angeles organization for failure to meet standards.* Retrieved from http://
www.bbb.org/council/news-events/news-releases/20131/03/better-business
-bureau-expels-los-angeles-organization-for-failure-to-meet-standards

Council of Better Business Bureaus (CBBB). (2014). *Impact report 2014.* Retrieved from
https://www.bbb.org/globalassets/local-bbbs/council-113/media/annual-reports
/2014-annual-reports/cbbb_ar_2014_b.pdf

Council of Better Business Bureaus (CBBB). (N.d.a). About. Retrieved June 13, 2016,
from http://www.bbb.org/council/about/council-of-better-business-bureaus

Council of Better Business Bureaus (CBBB). (N.d.b). Get accredited. Retrieved June 13,
2016, from http://www.bbb.org/council/for-businesses/about-bbb-accreditation

Council of Better Business Bureaus (CBBB). (N.d.c). Overview of BBB rating. Retrieved
June 13, 2016, from http://www.bbb.org/council/overview-of-bbb-grade

Delmas, M. A., & Burbano, V. C. (2011). The drivers of greenwashing. *California Management Review, 54*(1), 64–87.

De Maeyer, P., & Estelami, H. (2011). Consumer perceptions of third party product
quality ratings. *Journal of Business Research, 64*(10), 1067–1073.

Ellis, B., & Hicken, M. (2015, September 30). Slammed by the government, A-rated
by the Better Business Bureau. CNN Money. Retrieved from http://money.cnn
.com/2015/09/30/news/better-business-bureau/index.html

EPA. *See* U.S. Environmental Protection Agency (EPA).

FDA. *See* U.S. Food and Drug Administration (FDA).

Federal Trade Commission (FTC). (2015, December 17). LifeLock to pay $100 million to
consumers to settle FTC charges it violated 2010 order. Retrieved from https://
www.ftc.gov/news-events/press-releases/2015/12/lifelock-pay-100-million-con
sumers-settle-ftc-charges-it-violated

Federal Trade Commission (FTC). (2016, May 25). FTC bans hundreds of mortgage assistance and debt relief operations. Retrieved from https://www.consumer.ftc.gov
/blog/ftc-bans-hundreds-mortgage-assistance-and-debt-relief-operations

Federal Trade Commission (FTC). (N.d.a). IdentityTheft.gov. Retrieved June 14, 2016,
from https://www.identitytheft.gov

Federal Trade Commission (FTC). (N.d.b). Our history. Retrieved June 13, 2016, from
https://www.ftc.gov/about-ftc/our-history

Federal Trade Commission (FTC). (N.d.c). What we do. Retrieved June 13, 2016, from
https://www.ftc.gov/about-ftc/what-we-do

Fisher, J. E., Garrett, D. E., Arnold, M. J., & Ferris, M. E. (1999). Dissatisfied consumers
who complain to the Better Business Bureau. *Journal of Consumer Marketing, 16*(6),
576–589.

Gallucci, M. (2015, September 23). Volkswagen scandal 2015: VW not the first auto-maker to adopt "defeat devices" and override emissions controls. *International Business Times*. Retrieved from http://www.ibtimes.com/volkswagen-scandal-2015-vw-not-first-automaker-adopt-defeat-devices-override-2110859

Gates, G., Ewing, J., Russell, K., & Watkins, D. (2016, June 1). Explaining Volkswagen's emissions scandal. *New York Times*. Retrieved from http://www.nytimes.com/interactive/2015/business/international/vw-diesel-emissions-scandal-explained.html

Glaeser, E. L., & Ujhelyi, G. (2010). Regulating misinformation. *Journal of Public Economics*, 94(3–4), 247–257.

Global Ecolabelling Network (GEN). (N.d.). What is GEN? Retrieved April 1, 2017, from http://www.globalecolabelling.net/about/gen-the-global-ecolabelling-network

Goldman, E. (2014, March 12). Epinions, the path-breaking website, is dead: Some lessons it taught us. *Forbes*. Retrieved from http://www.forbes.com/sites/ericgoldman/2014/03/12/epinions-the-path-breaking-website-is-dead-some-lessons-it-taught-us

Hanson, R. (2003). Warning labels as cheap-talk: Why regulators ban drugs. *Journal of Public Economics*, 87(9–10), 2013–2029.

Hart, K. (2009, April 15). Georgetown law professor tapped to lead FTC's Consumer Protection Division. *Washington Post*. Retrieved from http://www.washingtonpost.com/wp-dyn/content/article/2009/04/14/AR2009041402853.html

Häubl, G., & Trifts, V. (2000). Consumer decision making in online shopping environments: The effects of interactive decision aids. *Marketing Science*, 19(1), 4–21.

Hickman, L. (2007, October 25). Does the consumer really know best? *Guardian*. Retrieved from http://www.theguardian.com/environment/2007/oct/25/ethicalliving.lifeandhealth1

Howland, D. (2015, September 29). Target broadens its list of problematic chemicals in consumer goods. Retail Dive. Retrieved from http://www.retaildive.com/news/target-broadens-its-list-of-problematic-chemicals-in-consumer-goods/406414

International Chamber of Commerce. (N.d.). *Self-regulation*. Retrieved June 15, 2016, from http://www.iccwbo.org/advocacy-codes-and-rules/areas-of-work/marketing-and-advertising/self-regulation

International Consumer Protection and Enforcement Network (ICPEN). (N.d.). Who we are. Retrieved from http://www.icpen.org/for-consumer-experts/who-we-are

ISEAL. (N.d.). Membership. Retrieved from http://www.isealalliance.org/our-members

Koch, W. (2013, September 12). Wal-Mart announces phase-out of hazardous chemicals. *USA TODAY*. Retrieved from http://www.usatoday.com/story/news/nation/2013/09/12/walmart-disclose-phase-out-toxic-chemicals-products-cosmetics/2805567

Kretchmer, H. (2015, October 13). The man who discovered the Volkswagen emissions scandal. BBC News. Retrieved from http://www.bbc.com/news/business-34519184

Langhe, B. D., Fernbach, P. M., & Lichtenstein, D. R. (2015). Navigating by the stars: Investigating the actual and perceived validity of online user ratings. *Journal of Consumer Research*, ucv047.

Langrehr, F. W. (1979). Consumer education: Does it change students' competencies and attitudes? *Journal of Consumer Affairs*, 13(1), 41–53.

Liang, T.-P., & Huang, J.-S. (1998). An empirical study on consumer acceptance of products in electronic markets: A transaction cost model. *Decision Support Systems*, 24(1), 29–43.

Lochner, T. (2015, November 19). Berkeley: First-in-nation soda tax begins to show results. *Mercury News*. Retrieved from http://www.mercurynews.com/news/ci_29137613/berkeley-first-nation-soda-tax-begins-show-results

Maniates, M. (2010). Editing out unsustainable behavior. In L. Starke & L. Mastny. (Eds.) *State of the world 2010* (pp. 119–126). New York, NY: W. W. Norton.

McGregor, S. (1999). Towards a rationale for integrating consumer and citizenship education. *Journal of Consumer Studies and Home Economics*, 23(4), 207–211.

Mushnick, P. (2006, March 12). Don't trust those toothpaste ads. *New York Post*. Retrieved from http://nypost.com/2006/03/12/dont-trust-those-toothpaste-ads

Park, D.-H., Lee, J., & Han, I. (2007). The effect of on-line consumer reviews on consumer purchasing intention: The moderating role of involvement. *International Journal of Electronic Commerce*, 11(4), 125–148.

PowerReviews. (N.d.). About. Retrieved June 10, 2016, from http://www.powerreviews.com.

Rozdeba, D. (2016, January 4). Lies and the declining trust In brands. *Branding Strategy Insider*. Retrieved from http://www.brandingstrategyinsider.com/2016/01/lies-and-the-declining-trust-in-brands.html

Sen, S., & Lerman, D. (2007). Why are you telling me this? An examination into negative consumer reviews on the web. *Journal of Interactive Marketing*, 21(4), 76–94.

Shepardson, D. (2016, March 29). U.S. FTC sues Volkswagen over diesel advertising claims. *Thomson Reuters*. Retrieved from http://sustainability.thomsonreuters.com/2016/03/30/u-s-ftc-sues-volkswagen-over-diesel-advertising-claims

Silber, N. I. (1983). *Test and protest: The influence of Consumers Union*. Teaneck, NJ: Holmes & Meier.

Singer, M. (2010, March 17). Green fridge labelled a fraud. *Sydney Morning Herald*. Retrieved from http://www.smh.com.au/environment/green-fridge-labelled-a-fraud-20100316-qclx.html

Stone, Z. (2015, December 9). A surprisingly large amount of Amazon reviews are fake. *The Hustle*. Retrieved from http://thehustle.co/a-surprisingly-large-number-of-amazon-reviews-are-scams-the-hustle-investigates

Surowiecki, J. (2004). *The wisdom of crowds*. New York, NY: Little, Brown.

Trigg, T. (2015, September 30). Why the VW #Dieselgate is only the tip of the iceberg, part 1 [Blog post]. *Scientific American*. Retrieved from http://blogs.scientificamerican.com/plugged-in/why-the-vw-dieselgate-is-only-the-tip-of-the-iceberg-part-1

Tugend, A. (2013, November 15). Sizing up the Better Business Bureau, and its rivals on the Internet. *New York Times*. Retrieved from http://www.nytimes.com/2013/11/16/your-money/sizing-up-the-better-business-bureau-and-its-rivals.html

Tuttle, B. (2013, March 19). Why the Better Business Bureau should give itself a bad grade. *Time*. Retrieved from http://business.time.com/2013/03/19/why-the-better-business-bureau-should-give-itself-a-bad-grade

USA.gov. (N.d.a). Filing a consumer complaint. Retrieved June 13, 2016, from https://www.usa.gov/consumer-complaints

USA.gov. (N.d.b). Recalls.gov. Retrieved June 14, 2016, from http://www.recalls.gov

U.S. Centers for Disease Control and Prevention (CDC). (2012, November 15). Selected actions of the U.S. Government regarding the regulation of tobacco sales, marketing, and use. *Smoking and Tobacco Use.* Retrieved from http://www.cdc.gov /tobacco/data_statistics/by_topic/policy/legislation

U.S. Department of Energy (DOE). (2008, November 14). DOE reaches agreement with LG Electronics, USA, on refrigerator energy matter. Retrieved from https://www .energystar.gov/ia/partners/manuf_res/PressRelease_DOE_LG_SettlementAgree ment.pdf

U.S. Environmental Protection Agency (EPA). (1973, July 23). EPA refers investigation of Volkswagen to Justice. Retrieved from http://www.autosafety.org/sites /default/files/imce_staff_uploads/VW%20Defeat%20Device%20EPA%20Prosecu tion%207-23-73%20Pr.pdf

U.S. Environmental Protection Agency (EPA). (2015, November 13). Laws and regulations related to Volkswagen violations. Policies and guidance. Retrieved from https://www.epa.gov/vw/laws-and-regulations-related-volkswagen-violations.

U.S. Environmental Protection Agency (EPA). (2016a, February 9). Frequent questions about Volkswagen violations. Policies and guidance. Retrieved from https://www .epa.gov/vw/frequent-questions-about-volkswagen-violations

U.S. Environmental Protection Agency (EPA). (2016b, April 1). Fuel economy and environment labels: Basic information. Retrieved from https://www3.epa.gov /carlabel/basicinformation.htm

U.S. Food and Drug Administration (FDA). (2013, September 3). *Educational resources: Counterfeit medicine.* Retrieved from http://www.fda.gov/Drugs/ResourcesForYou /Consumers/BuyingUsingMedicineSafely/CounterfeitMedicine/ucm106262 .htm#print_psa

Vizard, S. (2016, June 8). Consumer trust in brands on social media falls as line between marketing and non-commercial blurs. *Marketing Week.* Retrieved from https://www.marketingweek.com/2016/06/08/consumer-trust-in-brands-on -social-media-falls-as-line-between-marketing-and-non-commercial-blurs

Zhu, F., & Zhang, X. (M). (2010). Impact of online consumer reviews on sales: The moderating role of product and consumer characteristics. *Journal of Marketing, 74*(2), 133–148.

| THIRTEEN | # A History of Fact Checking in U.S. Politics and Election Contexts |

SHANNON POULSEN AND DANNAGAL G. YOUNG

The existence of an informed and engaged citizenry is fundamental to democratic theory. Although theorists disagree on the nature and necessary extent of citizens' information and engagement, even conservative models assume that for democracy to work and for citizens to hold elected leaders accountable, citizens must be informed in some fashion. Delli Carpini and Keeter (1997, p. 61) note, "The more citizens are passingly informed about the issues of the day, the behavior of political leaders, and the rules under which they operate, the better off they are, the better off *we* are." While political scientists have written for decades about the problem of uninformed citizens, over the past two decades scholars have become increasing concerned about *misinformed* citizens, "people who hold inaccurate factual beliefs, and do so confidently" (Kuklinski, Quirk, Jerit, Schwieder, & Rich, 2000, p. 792).

Regardless of how one conceptualizes the duty of citizens to get informed and correct their misperceptions, the mechanism through which citizens achieve these goals remains the same: a vibrant, resourced journalistic enterprise that delivers accurate information, highlights and corrects inaccuracies made by elites and public officials, and actively plays the role of arbiter of the truth. Although this is the role people expect news organizations to play, the extent to which these organizations have tried—or been able—to exercise this role has evolved over the years. The past three centuries have brought with them fundamental changes in the economics, routines, and norms of journalism as well as changes in campaign dynamics and media technologies. As a result, the very nature of the pursuit of political truths, and who is responsible for that pursuit, have gone through myriad iterations, among them the routinization of independent fact-checking organizations.

The Pursuit of Facts and Truth in Early American Newspapers

In the early days of journalism in the United States, partisan newspapers provided important factual information explicitly for party members (Schudson, 2013). With the introduction of the telegraph in the 1840s, newspapers found a quick and easy, albeit notoriously unreliable, way to share information between cities. Wire services like the Associated Press were created to share basic facts of newsworthy events using telegraph lines that ran parallel to the railroads (Schudson, 1981). Newspapers big and small began relying on wire services as sources of news content.

The story structure that took shape through the wire services was the "inverted pyramid" style of news that journalism students are still taught today. In part due to the telegraph's reputation as an unreliable technology as well as in order to standardize news production and dissemination, reporters placed the important facts of a story up front: who, what, when, where, then why and how. This practice indirectly foreshadowed the rise in objectivity in journalism, as the inverted pyramid led with facts as opposed to opinion (Shaw, 1967).

The move toward mass production of newspapers in the United States did not occur until the late 19th century, as industrialization moved citizens away from their agrarian homesteads into urban areas. It was at this time that tools of mass production brought down the cost of printing newspapers. Meanwhile, the influx of population in urban centers facilitated cheap, efficient distribution of the medium, contributing to newspapers' economic success in the early 20th century (Blumler & Kavanagh, 1999). The mass appeal of nonpartisan information for everyone helped newspapers maximize demand—and hence circulation.

Although the telegraph, mass production, and wide circulation of newspapers paved the way for objective journalism, it was not until the aftermath of "yellow journalism" in the 1880s that objectivity became a stated journalistic goal (Schudson, 1981). New tools of mass production and the ease of distribution facilitated such a boom in newspaper circulation that publishers were able to drop the price of their product substantially, knowing that huge advertising revenues would sustain the papers. Dropping prices raised circulation even more, increasing the potential for profit. Two newspaper magnates in particular capitalized on this important moment: William Randolph Hearst of the *New York Journal* and Joseph Pulitzer of the *New York World*.

The competition between Hearst and Pulitzer shaped the manner in which stories were covered and reported at the turn of the 20th century. To fuel mass demand, the Hearst and Pulitzer papers covered sensational stories of crime, bloodshed, drama, and scandal, with full-color illustrations and cartoons. The publishers encouraged reporters to cover the news in wild and colorful ways. The sensationalized stories not only exaggerated the truth but sometimes did not tell the truth at all (Campbell, 2001). As the Cuban revolution of 1895 brought with it reports of Spanish abuses against Cuban citizens, Hearst's and Pulitzer's newspapers covered alleged Spanish atrocities in ways that seemed to goad the United States into involvement in the Spanish-American War.

The phenomenon of sensationalized and often dubious reporting was later named "yellow journalism," after the "yellow kid" cartoon that was featured in Pulitzer's *New York World* until the cartoon was purchased by Hearst. Among elite journalists, scholars, and politicians, yellow journalism was met with contempt. Senator Edward Wolcott of Colorado once said, in reference to Hearst's and Pulitzer's news, "It knows no party, no honor, no virtue, and appeals only to the low and the base. It calls itself journalism, but its name is Pander and its color is yellow" (in Campbell, 2001, p. 28). Stemming in part from a dramatic boycott by libraries and universities as well as regret on the part of Pulitzer himself, the era of yellow journalism faded in the early 1900s as newspaper publishers sought to reach mass audiences without the sensationalism of the past (Blumler & Kavanagh, 1999; Matheson, 2000; Schudson, 2013).

The flagrant exaggeration of information during the period of yellow journalism, combined with the rise of tabloid newspapers in the United States, pushed the American Society of Newspaper Editors (ASNE) to create a set of ethics for journalists in 1923 (ASNE, 2011, n.d.; Teel, 2015). The canons were designed to shape professional norms of newspaper reporting. Among them are responsibility, sincerity, truthfulness, and accuracy, as responses to the yellow journalism of the late 1800s (Teel, 2015).

According to the ASNE, responsibility requires that any methods of attracting new readers must consider the public welfare. Newspapers are responsible for publishing information that benefits the community through the public attention it garners: "A journalist who uses his power for any selfish or otherwise unworthy purpose is faithless to a high trust" (ASNE, n.d.).

The canon encompassing sincerity, truthfulness, and accuracy reads, "By every consideration of good faith, a newspaper is constrained to be truthful. It is not to be excused for lack of thoroughness, or accuracy within its control, or failure to obtain command of these essential qualities" (ASNE, n.d.). The goal of newspaper reporting, according to ASNE, is clear: to seek the truth and to do so in a way that is exhaustive.

During this same era, a new form of journalism was emerging, starting in the milieu of magazines—that of muckraking (Tichi, 2004). With the growth in industry and manufacturing, progressives became increasingly concerned about the unethical practices of businesses in their dealings with employees and consumers. Writers like Ida Tarbell and Upton Sinclair wrote detailed investigative exposés on aspects of corrupt and dangerous business practices previously hidden from view (Wilson, 2015). President Theodore Roosevelt coined the term "muckraker" in his description of the progressive writers as those who only focused on raking up "muck."

The legacy of muckrakers is strong and has shaped public expectations of the kind of journalism necessary to keep citizens informed about the otherwise unseen aspects of politics and business. In the latter half of the 20th century, new terms arose to describe the practice of uncovering facts and the truth in political reporting; in the 1970s, the journalism industry began to embrace the concepts "watchdog" and "accountability." Watchdog journalists were those who protected democracy by being "suspicious of all intruders" (Donohue, Tichenor, and Olien, 1995, p. 116), for example, the detailed investigation of the Watergate scandal by the *Washington Post* that brought about the resignation of Richard Nixon in 1974 (Schudson, 2013).

Pressures Affecting Journalists' Pursuit of Facts and Truth

Most journalists over the past fifty years have sought to serve the canons of responsibility, accuracy, truthfulness, and sincerity. Yet, due to a variety of commercial, political, and technological factors, numerous obstacles and constraints have limited journalists' ability to adhere to these established goals (Blumler & Kavanagh, 1999). Chief among these factors are market deregulation and its resulting pressure on news as a commercial enterprise, the professionalization of politics and campaigns, media fragmentation, digital technologies, and the changing role of the audience.

Deregulation and Commercial Pressures

Starting in the Reagan era in the United States, existing antitrust policies and efforts toward media regulation were significantly loosened (Holt, 2011). Reagan urged faith in the market to guide Americans, as the market would serve as the best regulator of business. The Federal Trade Commission (FTC) under Reagan's Republican administration challenged mergers a quarter as often as it did under President Carter. Schechter (1990, p. 499) notes, "This extraordinary cutback in merger enforcement took place during a period of phenomenal merger activity—a merger mania perhaps unprecedented in U.S. economic history." For media industries, the regulatory changes meant the growth of newspaper chains and media conglomerates, giant corporate entities with multiple holdings, all designed to generate profits for shareholders (Holt, 2011). The policies of deregulation, which grew with the Telecommunications Act of 1996 under President Clinton, were controversial. FCC Commissioner Nicholas Johnson called this period of deregulation and synergy "the annihilation of competition" (in Holt, 2011, p. 3). Holt finds that "the unchecked corporate power that spread across industrial lines created a media environment that was beneficial to private, not public interests" (2011, p. 4).

Deregulation plays a central role in our consideration of the pressures and constraints on modern journalistic practice because of how the economics of news shifted in response. With deregulation came increasing pressures on all categories of media content to generate profits. Network newsrooms, previously protected from expectations of profit, were now expected to perform in terms of ratings and profits just as the network's entertainment offerings were (Baym, 2010). Journalism, particularly accountability journalism, is a time- and resource-consuming practice. Accountability or watchdog journalism takes time and money to perform properly. Relationships between journalists and sources must be established, cultivated, and maintained. Journalists must have the freedom to dedicate time to fostering those relationships without the burden of imminent production deadlines. Accountability journalism also requires educated, experienced journalists who are practiced in their craft, and such journalists are more expensive to have on a payroll.

Meanwhile, pressures for ratings have shaped news routines in ways that undermine rather than serve the goals of quality journalism. Commercial goals of increasing audience size while cutting costs have increased pressure on reporters to cover breaking stories first, focus on what viewers want rather than what citizens need, and make political coverage entertaining by highlighting personalities, drama, and conflict (Downie & Kaiser, 2002). The pressure to be the first organization to break a story has encouraged some editors and news directors to release stories that are not adequately vetted (Blumler & Kavanagh, 1999; Ricchiardi, 1998). Blumler and Kavanagh write that "time for political and journalistic reflection and judgment is squeezed" (1999, p. 213). The race to publication comes at the cost of verification.

In addition to being underreported because of temporal pressures, information that might benefit democracy now competes with other types of journalism for network resources and the attention of the public (Blumler & Kavanagh, 1999). Specialized news beats such as sports or entertainment provide stories that interest viewers and receive more institutional support than do drier subjects like politics and international affairs.

When news organizations do cover politics, commercial pressures continue to affect the content. Horse-race coverage, "campaign news emphasizing who is ahead or behind" (Mutz, 1995), presents political campaigns through the lens of a sporting event highlighting competition, strategy, and polling data. Such coverage tends to be processed and remembered easily by audiences (Robinson & Clancey, 1985). Compared to reporting on abstract issues or policy debates, covering an election solely as a competition is easy and exciting. But horse-race coverage is unlikely to increase citizen understanding of policy debate, and it has been associated with voter cynicism (Jamieson & Cappella, 1997).

Finally, in response to commercial pressures, news organizations are increasingly investing in online media platforms and new technologies. While such platforms could enhance the distribution of accountability journalism, it takes skilled individuals to gather and report the news. Unfortunately, research suggests that organizations are making such investments while eliminating personnel, a strategy that that is actually reducing the amount of quality reporting (Fenton, 2010; Lee-Wright, 2010). In sum, writes Fenton (2011, p. 64), "The depreciation of the current business model together with increasing commercial pressures is, as a result, devaluing the pursuit of news journalism that is in the public interest and impacting in particular on original newsgathering and investigative reporting as well as on local news."

The Professionalization of Politics

Modern political life in the United States is a professionalized and ritualized practice. Campaigns are developed and run by teams of professional political operatives and polling organizations. The content, tone, and messaging of campaigns or parties are determined almost exclusively by teams of public relations experts whose allegiances are more to outcome than ideology. These "new professionals," as Mancini has called them (1999, p. 234), "do not have an exclusive relationship with one party or leader; like all members of modern professions, they offer their technical knowledge to whom-ever needs it and has the resources to pay for it."

Corporate communication machines are driven by the need to maximize visibility, shape the news agenda in their candidates' favor, and encourage news media to adopt frames that offer constructions of issues and events that best serve their clients, not citizens. Their strategic efforts aimed at persuasion and victory constantly put outcome ahead of purpose. Mancini, in the spirit of Habermas, writes, "Professionalism substitutes for citizenship, and instrumental behavior substitutes for behaviors based on civil values" (1999, p. 242).

The problem from a democratic standpoint is that journalists must rely on political entities for information (Schudson, 2013). But if campaigns are machines driven by the pursuit of victory at all cost, the information they provide—in both scope and content—is unlikely to help journalists in their pursuit of truth. When considering how the professionalization of politics affects accountability journalism and citizens' access to facts, it is crucial to recognize the synergy between the commercial pressures afflicting the practice of journalism and the rise of these "new political professionals" (Mancini, 1999).

With pressures of time and money in the newsroom, journalists become more vulnerable to the schemes and rhetoric of political communication machines. The mere existence of the video news release (VNR) is emblematic of this dangerous dynamic. So-called VNRs are fully produced news packages created by corporations or political groups to be aired on local news broadcasts as though they are actual news (Harmon & White, 2001). Less tangible but no less harmful is the appearance of political operatives and pundits on news programming to talk about the news. The individuals are provided talking points issued by their campaign machinery, often rife with assertions and dubious statistics. Yet these purported pundits can reasonably assume that most of their claims will go unchallenged by the journalist interviewers.

Why do their claims go unchallenged? In an effort to avoid charges of selection bias, reporters are encouraged to cover "both sides" of a story. Yet when one side actually *is* more true than another and journalists strive to treat both sides equally, the result is further muddying of the truth. Schudson characterizes objectivity as the norm that "guides journalists to separate facts from values and to report only the facts" (2001, p. 150). Meanwhile, political machines know that journalists' time and resources are so scarce that even with a desire to challenge the information presented, they have little chance of being afforded the opportunity to engage in the kind of research needed to do so.

Technological Changes and the Perils of Choice

Changes in cable and digital technologies over the past thirty years have indirectly affected the scope and reach of accountability journalism. Media fragmentation, the explosion in media outlets through cable and the Internet, means that citizens have myriad outlets from which they can choose to seek out news—or not. Work by Prior (2005) indicates that with increasing media choice, citizens who are more interested in entertainment than news can drop out of news audiences altogether, thereby reducing their political knowledge and participation rates compared to the politically interested.

Individuals with the requisite political interest to seek out political information in this fragmented media landscape can choose attitude-confirming information from highly partisan outlets online or on television (MSNBC on the left and FOX news on the right). An electorate composed of voters who seek out only the versions of facts that comport with their existing worldviews is normatively concerning, as it is prone to increased political polarization (Stroud, 2011).

The rise in digital technologies in the 2000s empowered citizens, "the people formerly known as the audience" (Rosen, 2006), to become message producers as well as consumers. Citizen journalism is a way people can bear witness to events—often tragedies or moments of crisis—as they unfold (Allan, 2009). While there have long been camera-wielding witnesses to historical events, the capacity of smartphones to capture moments and of the Internet to distribute content has turned citizen journalism into a staple of contemporary news.

Yet, the debate over the extent to which traditional news gatekeepers ought to cover citizen journalism is a contentious one. Laypeople, unlike journalists, are not formally trained. They may not search for multiple perspectives in a story, contextualize conflicts, or attempt to challenge their own cognitive biases in constructing stories. At the same time, raw perspectives might offer something new and important to the marketplace of ideas—perhaps something that challenges the existing political order in a way that is democratically healthy.

With so many avenues for access to information flow, the agenda-setting and gatekeeping roles of traditional news organizations are shrinking. Blumler and Kavanagh write, "Centripetal communication is, to some extent, retreating" (1999, p. 221). While the trajectory seems to be, on its face, democratically healthy, infinite voices actively constructing and reconstructing their own versions of reality can lead to disparate—often conflicting—sets of facts.

The Rise of Fact-Checking Organizations

The sweeping changes in media regulation, campaign professionalization, and media technologies have hindered the ability, and in some cases the motivation, of traditional journalists to check for factual accuracy. In the late 1980s, a growing void in mainstream journalistic practice became increasingly apparent, most notably during the U.S. presidential election of 1988.

The general election campaign between Massachusetts governor Michael Dukakis and Vice President George H. W. Bush is remembered as overwhelmingly negative, as "the most negative presidential campaign since 1964" (Devlin, 1989, p. 394). But perhaps no political ad encapsulates the perceived dirtiness of the 1988 election as much as the Bush campaign's "revolving door" ad against Michael Dukakis. The ad, designed to depict Dukakis as soft on crime, shows in black and white what appear to be dozens of dangerous prisoners entering and leaving a prison through a revolving door. As the narrator is heard saying Dukakis's "revolving-door prison policy gave weekend furloughs to first-degree murderers not eligible for parole," the text "268 Escaped" flashes on screen. The number falsely implies that 268 first-degree murderers not eligible for parole escaped, when in reality 268 prisoners in the entire furlough program escaped (Devlin, 1989). It is important to note that just weeks prior, a pro-Bush political action committee aired an ad about convicted murderer Willie Horton being granted "weekend passes" from prison on Dukakis's watch; the ad describes Horton having kidnapped, raped, and stabbed a young white woman during one such weekend (Jamieson, 1992). Since Dukakis was already trailing Bush in the polls by the time these ads aired in fall of 1988, their impact on public opinion is unclear (Sides, 2016). However, the response of the press at the time was troubling. The Horton ad, despite its racially charged and factually inaccurate allegations, successfully shifted the campaign discourse as journalists jumped on the Horton story. But their coverage did not challenge or assess the accuracy of the ad's claims. Instead, the press furthered the Republicans' anti-Dukakis agenda, even adopting the ad's choice of framing and wording in subsequent press coverage of the Horton case (Jamieson, 1992).

It is no accident, then, that journalists responded to the notorious 1988 campaign with an increase in accountability journalism and new formal efforts aimed at checking the accuracy of political advertising claims (Schudson, 2013). In the aftermath of the campaign, journalists made a choice to become "referees," formally evaluating and calling out the accuracy of political claims (Ansolabehere & Iyengar, 1995). The *Los Angeles Times* first conducted formal "ad watches," created to educate readers about political advertisements, in the context of California Senate races. Soon, ad watches were found on television news as well.

At the Annenberg School for Communication at the University of Pennsylvania, Professor Kathleen Hall Jamieson worked with CNN journalists to develop a formal "visual grammar" to help TV viewers become critical consumers of misleading political ads (Cappella & Jamieson, 1994). The ad watch showed misleading political advertisements in a smaller screen within the broadcast to create distance for the audience and signal that the ad was not being aired but commented upon. Research indicates that exposure to ad watches shaped viewers' perceptions of the ad's source, fairness, and importance but did not affect their perceptions of an ad's target (Cappella & Jamieson, 1994).

With the advent of the Internet, information became easier to gather, access, and disseminate, contributing to a steep increase in fact-checking activities from 2000 to 2012 (Graves & Glaiyser, 2012). In 2003, the former Associated Press and *Wall Street Journal* correspondent Brooks Jackson and Kathleen Hall Jamieson at the Annenberg Public Policy Center launched the nonpartisan, nonprofit organization Factcheck.org as a "'consumer advocate' for voters that aims to reduce the level of deception and confusion in U.S. politics" (Factcheck.org, n.d.). The organization capitalized on Internet technologies to gather and spread fact checks by sourcing information across various databases. Once FactCheck.org was established as a year-round project, events outside of political elections began to be corrected as well (Graves & Glaiyser, 2012). Currently, most fact-checking organizations continue their effects and research year-round.

With the advent of the Internet, no longer did news organizations have to dedicate print space to fact checking. Instead, some began to create online companion sites dedicated exclusively to the verification of political claims. In 2007 the *Tampa Bay Times* began Politifact.com, a nonpartisan fact-checking site that rates the accuracy of claims with its trademarked "Truth-O-Meter," which rates statements from "true" to "pants on fire" (Adair & Drobnic Holan, 2013). The claims checked by Politifact.com are typically claims made by prominent national figures. However, PolitiFact has companion state sites that partner with local broadcast stations to analyze claims made at the state and local levels as well. The *Washington Post* began a Fact Checker column in 2008. Due to its popularity, the column became a permanent part of the Sunday print edition of the *Washington Post* in 2011.

New Fact-Checking Tools

As Internet technologies grew, fact-checking organizations began to capitalize on new ways to correct misleading claims. The technologies allowed citizens to contribute information, and fact-checking organizations relied on the input of citizens with crowd-sourced fact-checking efforts. Sites like NewsTrust's TruthSquad, WikiFact-Check, and Truth Goggles from MIT's Media Lab utilize citizen input to help gather evidence and provide corrective information (Garrett & Weeks, 2013; Graves & Glaiyser, 2012).

The speed of digital technologies contributed to the creation of real-time fact-checking organizations such as Hypothes.is (Garrett & Weeks, 2013). Users of Hypothes.is can hover their cursors over claims made in a text-based online news story and in real time see corrective information that verifies claims made within the stories they are reading. Such fact-checking innovations would be impossible without the interactivity and interconnectedness of digital technologies.

But the same interactivity and interconnectedness also have contributed to the spread of the very misinformation that fact checks are designed to debunk. Social media allow the opportunity for misinformation to be spread instantly within and between social circles. New organizations like Truthy (Truthy.indiana.edu) and SRSR (pronounced "sourcer") have emerged specifically to check claims made through social media channels (Garrett & Weeks, 2013). As every new platform becomes a dissemination tool for misinformation, a new technology is created to combat the obfuscation of truth. Videolyzer is a tool designed as a response to the spread of misinformation through online videos. It empowers viewers to rate the accuracy and bias of online videos while they are being viewed (Garrett & Weeks, 2013).

The presence of and reliance on independent fact-checking organizations has only increased. The *Milwaukee Journal Sentinel* reporter Cary Spivak (2011) notes that the elections in 2010 "featured fact-checking on steroids." By 2012 political campaigns were widely considered to be the most fact-checked in history after a steady increase from 2004 and 2008 (Graves & Glaiyser, 2012). While Internet technologies have contributed to the growth of fact-checking organizations, the speed and ease of information access has also contributed to the growth and spread of misinformation. Fewer resources are required to find information online, but false information can be just as easily accessed and shared. It is the aim of fact-checking organizations, through their ongoing efforts, to thwart the power and influence of misinformation across digital platforms.

Current Fact-Checking Practices

Fact checking remains a central part of accountability journalism. The Duke University reporters' lab, under the direction of Bill Adair, founder of PolitiFact.org, compiles a list of fact-checking organizations, active and inactive, from around the world, among them 24 active organizations in the United States alone. However, fact checking obviously faces challenges in today's saturated media market. People must actively choose to expose themselves to corrective information. As the information is potentially counterattitudinal, people may not selectively seek it at the rate necessary for a healthy and informed democratic society.

In order to appeal to viewers, fact-checking organizations have expanded the formats and delivery mechanisms used for their content. Most fact-checking organizations use social media accounts to meet journalists and citizens where they are. By 2016 PolitiFact.com was tweeting links to its articles to its 261,000 Twitter followers throughout the day (PolitiFact, 2016). Fact-checking organizations have also explored novel ways to make fact-checking information more interesting and appealing to more citizens than just journalists. In 2010 Factcheck.org expanded to include a companion site, FlackCheck.org, to deliver corrective information in a clever, entertaining video format to appeal to less politically engaged citizens.

The spread of corrective information is not limited to independent fact-checking organizations. News organizations increasingly are using the language and customs of independent fact-checking entities. The *New York Times* website features a page of 2016 election fact checks performed by its own journalists (*New York Times*, 2016). National Public Radio (NPR) has an ongoing "Politics: Fact Check" page on its website (NPR, n.d.). The expanded type and volume of fact checking are perhaps in part a result of the demand by consumers.

A survey found that 77% of an NPR audience sample said they were very interested in fact checks (Stencel, 2016). Even though people may not choose to expose themselves to counterattitudinal information, the survey results suggest that the public has an interest in fact checking. How is there is an interest in fact checking but a desire to avoid cognitive dissonance? Consumers are interested in reading corrections of opposing viewpoints rather than having their own views challenged. Indeed, the increase in partisan fact-checking organizations—those that check the claims of the other side—confirms this trend (Graves & Glaiyser, 2012). Graves and Glaiyser (2012) warn that biased so-called fact-checking organizations like Media Matters hide under the same language as nonpartisan fact-checking organizations but are merely designed to contradict claims by one side over the other.

Conclusion

The quality of journalism and the pursuit of truth depend largely on the commercial, social, and technological changes of the times. Partisan newspapers that had delivered meeting time and date information to political parties were transformed by the invention of the telegraph and the advent of urbanization. The news became subjected to competition and responded with sensationalized narratives using semifactual information. The resulting inaccuracies led to the creation of a journalism code of ethics intended to pressure journalists into proper information sharing. Later, deregulation forced journalism to submit to market forces. With limits on resources and demand for ratings and profit, journalists' ability and motivation to fully report accurate information was compromised. Without accountability journalism, politicians and parties played fast and loose with the facts. It was with the advent of digital technologies that new, independent fact-checking organizations began to reestablish the standards for how journalists could hold public figures accountable for their claims.

Looking ahead, what role will these independent and journalistic fact-checking organizations play in future campaigns? The sheer number of fact-checking organizations and rising consumer interest in fact checking indicate that scholars should expect the field to expand. There are new enterprises proposed almost daily seeking to adapt to changing political landscapes and commercial pressures. Timothy Egan (2016) of the *New York Times* proposes, "The Presidential Debate Commission should do what any first-grader with Google access can do, and call out lies before the words hit the floor." Real-time fact checking would force candidates to confront false information immediately.

As professional politicians and parties adapt to and try to circumvent the "truth squads," fact checking may lose its influence in political discourse. In an interview with the *Toronto Star* (Ward, 2016), FactCheck .org's Jamieson describes the 2016 presidential election as occurring in "an effectively fact-free world" with the candidacy of Republican Donald Trump. "He makes so many misstatements so often that the [fact-checking] process can't continue to work," she explains. But that is not for lack of trying. In fact, the sheer volume of misstatements emerging from Trump's campaign are in part what has rendered him seemingly impervious to attack. "You just don't have enough news time to correct all," Jamieson continues. In light of Trump's electoral victory, fact checking in 2016 was apparently offset by campaign spin. Clearly, the need for fact checking that is instant, accessible, and trusted is more salient than ever. PolitiFact's Adair said in 2012, "Whether the fact has actually died or is just on its death bed, I think . . . it's a great time to be in the fact-checking business, because there are just so many questions about what's accurate and what's not" (NPR, 2012). Moving forward, the question of whether political fact checking will successfully serve democracy depends primarily on how citizens choose to use it.

References

Adair, B. & Drobnic Holan, A. (2013, November 1). The principles of PolitiFact, PunditFact, and the Truth-O-Meter. PolitiFact. Retrieved from http://www.politifact.com/truth-o-meter/article/2013/nov/01/principles-politifact-punditfact-and-truth-o-meter

Allan, S. (2009). *Citizen journalism: Global perspectives.* New York, NY: Peter Lang.

American Society of News Editors (ASNE). (2011, October 24). Code of Ethics or Canons of Journalism (1923). Ethics Codes Collection, Illinois Institute of Technology. Retrieved from http://ethics.iit.edu/ecodes/node/4457

American Society of News Editors (ASNE). (N.d.). ASNE statement of principles. Retrieved on December 27, 2016, from http://asne.org/content.asp?pl=24&sl=171&contentid=171

Ansolabehere, S., & Iyengar, S. (1995). *Going negative: How attack ads shrink and polarize the electorate.* New York, NY: Free Press.

Baym, G. (2010). *From Cronkite to Colbert: The evolution of broadcast news.* St. Paul, MN: Paradigm.

Blumler, J. G., & Kavanagh, D. (1999). The third age of political communication: Influences and features. *Political Communication, 16*(3), 209–230.

Campbell, W. J. (2001). *Yellow journalism: Puncturing the myths, defining the legacies.* Westport, CT: Greenwood.

Cappella, J. N., & Jamieson, K. H. (1994). Broadcast adwatch effects a field experiment. *Communication Research, 21*(3), 342–365.

Delli Carpini, M. X., & Keeter, S. (1997). *What Americans know about politics and why it matters.* New Haven, CT: Yale University Press.

Devlin, L. P. (1989). Contrasts in presidential campaign commercials of 1988. *American Behavioral Scientist (1986–1994), 32*(4), 389.

Donohue, G. A., Tichenor, P. J., & Olien, C. N. (1995). A guard dog perspective on the role of media. *Journal of Communication, 45*(2), 115–132.

Downie, L. Jr., & Kaiser, R. G. (2002). *The news about the news: American journalism in peril.* New York, NY: Random House.

Egan, T. (2016, June 9). Lord of the lies. *New York Times.* Retrieved from http://www.nytimes.com/2016/06/10/opinion/lord-of-the-lies.html

FactCheck.org. (N.d.). Our mission. Retrieved from http://www.factcheck.org/about/our-mission

Fenton, N. (Ed.). (2010). *New media, old news: Journalism and democracy in the digital age.* London, England: Sage.

Fenton, N. (2011). Deregulation or democracy? New media, news, neoliberalism, and the public interest. *Continuum, 25*(1), 63–72.

Garrett, R. K., & Weeks, B. E. (2013, February). The promise and peril of real-time corrections to political misperceptions. In *CSCW '13 Proceedings of the 2013 Conference on Computer Supported Cooperative Work* (pp. 1047–1058). New York, NY: Association for Computing Machinery.

Graves, L., and Glaiyser, T. (2012). *The fact-checking universe in 2012.* Washington, DC: New America Foundation.

Harmon, M. D., & White, C. (2001). How television news programs use video news releases. *Public Relations Review, 27*(2), 213–222.

Holt, J. (2011). *Empires of entertainment: Media industries and the politics of deregulation 1980–1996.* New Brunswick, NJ: Rutgers University Press.

Jamieson, K. H. (1992). *Dirty politics.* New York, NY: Oxford University Press.

Jamieson, K. H., & Cappella, J. N. (1997). Setting the record straight: Do ad watches help or hurt? *Harvard International Journal of Press/Politics, 2*(1), 13–22.

Kuklinski, J. H., Quirk, P. J., Jerit, J., Schwieder, D., & Rich, R. F. (2000). Misinformation and the currency of democratic citizenship. *Journal of Politics, 62*(3), 790–816.

Lee-Wright, P. (2010). Culture shock: New media and organizational change in the BBC. In N. Fenton (Ed.), *New media, old news: Journalism and democracy in the digital age* (pp. 71–86). London, England: Sage.

Mancini, P. (1999). New frontiers in political professionalism. *Political Communication, 16*(3), 231–245.

Matheson, D. (2000). The birth of news discourse: Changes in news language in British newspapers, 1880–1930. *Media, Culture, and Society, 22*, 559.

Mutz, D. C. (1995). Effects of horse-race coverage on campaign coffers: Strategic contributing in presidential primaries. *Journal of Politics, 57*(4), 1015–1042.

National Public Radio (NPR). (2012, April 29). *The death of facts in an age of truthiness.* Retrieved from http://www.npr.org/2012/04/29/151646558/if-a-fact-dies-in-the-forest-will-anyone-believe-it

National Public Radio (NPR). (N.d.). Politics: Fact check. Retrieved on December 27, 2016, from http://www.npr.org/sections/politics-fact-check

New York Times. (2016). Fact checks of the 2016 election. Retrieved from http://www.nytimes.com/interactive/2016/us/elections/fact-check.html?_r=0

PolitiFact.org. (2016, May 24). PolitiFact Twitter feed. Retrieved from https://twitter.com/PolitiFact?ref_src=twsrc%5Egoogle%7Ctwcamp%5Eserp%7Ctwgr%5Eauthor

Prior, M. (2005). News v. entertainment: How increasing media choice widens gaps in political knowledge and turnout. *American Journal of Political Science, 49*(3): 594–609.

Ricchiardi, S. (1998). Standards are the first casualty. *American Journalism Review, 20*(2), 30–35.

Robinson, M. J., & Clancey, M. (1985). Teflon politics. In M. J. Robinson & A. Ranney (Eds.), *The mass media in campaign '84.* Washington, DC: American Enterprise Institute.

Rosen, J. (2006, June 27). The people formerly known as the audience. *Press Think.* Retrieved from http://archive.pressthink.org/2006/06/27/ppl_frmr.html

Schechter, R. E. (1990). A retrospective on the Reagan FTC: Musings on the role of an administrative agency. *Administrative Law Review, 42*, 489–517.

Schudson, M. (1981). *Discovering the news: A social history of American newspapers.* New York, NY: Basic Books.

Schudson, M. (2001). The objectivity norm in American journalism. *Journalism: Theory, Practice, and Criticism, 2*(2), 149–170.

Schudson, M. (2013). Reluctant stewards: Journalism in a democratic society. *Daedalus, 142*(2), 159–176.

Shaw, D. L. (1967). News bias and the telegraph: A study of historical change. *Journalism and Mass Communication Quarterly*, *44*(1), 3.

Sides, J. (2016, January 6). It's time to stop the endless hype of the "Willie Horton" ad. *Washington Post*. Retrieved from https://www.washingtonpost.com/news/monkey-cage/wp/2016/01/06/its-time-to-stop-the-endless-hype-of-the-willie-horton-ad

Spivak, C. (2010, December). The fact-checking explosion. *American Journalism Review*. Retrieved from http://ajrarchive.org/Article.asp?id=4980

Stencel, M. (2016, March 22). Public radio listeners want more fact-checking in election coverage. Reporters Lab. Retrieved from https://reporterslab.org/public-radio-listeners-want-fact-checking-election-coverage

Stroud, N. J. (2011). *Niche news: The politics of news choice*. New York, NY: Oxford University Press.

Teel, L. R. (2015). *Reporting the Cuban Revolution: How Castro manipulated American journalists*. Baton Rouge, LA: LSU Press.

Tichi, C. (2004). *Exposés and excess: Muckraking in America, 1900/2000*. Philadelphia, PA: University of Pennsylvania Press.

Ward, O. (2016, May 24). Donald Trump is a fact checker's nightmare. *The Star* (Toronto). Retrieved from https://www.thestar.com/news/world/2016/05/24/donald-trump-is-a-fact-checkers-nightmare.html

Wilson, H. S. (2015). *McClure's Magazine and the muckrakers*. Princeton, NJ: Princeton University Press.

CHAPTER 14

Comparing Approaches to Journalistic Fact Checking

EMILY A. THORSON

n April 2016, during an interview on Fox News, presidential hopeful Donald Trump suggested that Japan should arm itself with nuclear weapons. Three months later, Hillary Clinton referenced Trump's suggestion in a speech. Trump responded by denying he had ever said such a thing and accusing Clinton of making a false accusation (Yglesias, 2016). In covering Trump's denial, journalists were faced with a choice: Should they directly address his inconsistency, or should they simply present his statement along with Clinton's?

Journalists who cover politics often face choices like this, and an active normative debate has emerged over how factual disputes should be addressed by the media (Greenhouse, 2012; Kessler, 2016; Sullivan, 2012). As political campaigns have entered what some journalists have taken to calling a "post-truth" age characterized by an indifference to factual accuracy (Fallows, 2012, Rainey, 2012), three competing perspectives have come to dominate this debate. The first views journalists as arbiters, holding that reporters themselves should adjudicate factual claims and carefully state (if possible within an article) when a claim is false. The second outsources this job to other institutions either within media outlets like the *Washington Post*'s "Fact Checker" column or outside of it like the independent FactCheck.org or Politifact.com. The third, colloquially known as the "he-said, she-said" approach, does not require that journalists adjudicate facts. Instead, it holds that journalists should simply report on each side's remarks and leave it to readers to determine which side is more convincing. Although this description is to some extent an oversimplification of the nuanced positions of journalists and scholars (Graves & Glaisyer, 2012; Rosen, 2010), it provides a useful structure for formulating empirically testable hypotheses.

All three of these approaches were on display after Paul Ryan's speech at the 2012 Republican National Convention. Ryan made several statements that were misleading or, in several circumstances, factually inaccurate (Cooper, 2012). Most notably, he claimed that a General Motors plant in his hometown of Janesville, Wisconsin, was closed under Obama's administration. The plant actually closed while George W. Bush was in office. The Associated Press article headlined "Ryan takes factual shortcuts in speech" corrected Ryan's false claims outright (Woodward & Gillum, 2012). *USA Today* partnered with FactCheck.org to debunk Ryan's statements (Farley, Jackson, Kiely, Robertson, & Finley, 2012). An article in the *Washington Examiner* took the third approach, simply repeating an Obama spokesperson's response that "if Paul Ryan was Pinocchio his nose would be back in Janesville right now" (Gehrke, 2012).

These responses illustrate the three approaches examined in this chapter: journalistic adjudication, outsourcing to fact checkers, and the he-said, she-said approach. Using a controlled experiment, I examine how each of these corrective strategies affects citizens' belief in the misinformation, their evaluations of the political actors involved in the news story, and their trust in media.

The results suggest that while fact checking and journalistic arbitration are both effective at fully correcting a false claim even among partisans inclined to believe it, he-said, she-said is only partially successful. In addition, politicians are not punished for merely making accusations. However, they are evaluated more negatively, even by members of their own parties, when their claims are successfully debunked by journalists or fact checkers. Finally, while the evidence supports journalists' intuition that playing an active role in correcting false claims can increase perceptions of bias, exposure to fact checking may also produce a small "halo effect" that leads readers to evaluate other media outlets more positively. The halo effect is absent when the claim is corrected via the he-said, she-said approach.

Effects of Fact Checking

In this chapter I address an ongoing journalistic debate over how to address dubious claims made by political actors: by offering an explicit correction (either in the journalist's own voice or in referencing a fact-checking organization), or by adopting a he-said, she-said approach that gives equal weight to both sides. Writing in the *Atlantic Monthly*, James Fallows (2012) exhorts journalists to choose the former by taking an active role in helping readers arbitrate between claims: "Reporters are happiest, safest-feeling, and most comfortable when in the mode of he-said, she-said. But when significant political players are willing to say things that flat-out are not true—and when they're not slowed down by demonstrations of their claims' falseness—then reporters who stick to he-said, she-said become accessories to deception." The assumption implicit in Fallows's remarks, and indeed the assumption underlying much of the debate over how active a role journalists should play in fact checking, is that journalistic adjudication is more effective than the he-said, she-said approach at correcting misperceptions.

Pingree, Brossard, and McLeod (2014) show that journalistic adjudication can be effective at altering factual beliefs in a nonpartisan fact check, although they do not directly test adjudication against the he-said, she-said approach to fact checking. Thus, the first hypothesis empirically tests whether arbitration by journalists or fact-checking institutions is more successful than the he-said, she-said approach at reducing misperceptions.

H1: Corrections issued by a newspaper or fact-checking institution are more effective than the he-said, she-said approach at reducing misperceptions.

In addition to affecting readers' factual beliefs, corrections may have downstream effects if politicians who make such false claims are punished by voters for attempting to mislead the public. Currently, the evidence suggests that politicians do believe that public fact checks reflect negatively on them (Nyhan & Reifler, 2015). This is a normatively important question; if politicians do not suffer any consequences from making false claims, then they have an enormous strategic incentive to continue doing so.

It is important to distinguish the potential effect of making an accusation from that of making a false accusation. Intuitively one might expect that a politician who makes a false claim will be punished. However, cross-national research on political corruption suggests that politicians are not always punished for unethical behavior. Whether a politician suffers electoral consequences for her malfeasance is highly dependent on partisanship; perceptions of corruption affect evaluations less if the politician is of a person's own party (Anderson & Tverdova, 2003).

Time magazine's Michael Scherer (2012) expresses a similar thought about American politics: "The vast majority of the American voting public long ago demonstrated their willingness to simultaneously forgive fibs told by their own team and express umbrage at the deception offered by the other team." The second hypothesis empirically tests Scherer's claim, predicting that politicians will be punished for making an accusation when that accusation is shown to be false.

H2: False accusations will lower candidate evaluations more than accusations that are not fact checked.

One reason for journalists' reluctance to implement the arbitration model of fact checking is the concern that such an approach could threaten the public's belief in their objectivity, especially if a correction favors one party over another. Public opinion data suggest that journalists' worries are not baseless. Indeed, public perceptions of biased news media increased in the 2000s (Ladd, 2012). One of the factors contributing to this increase may be the ongoing debate over fact checking, as it makes the general topic of bias more salient for the public (Watts, Domke, Shah, & Fan, 1999). Given the strong observational and experimental evidence for a hostile media effect in which partisans see the media as biased against their own interests (Gunther & Schmitt, 2004; Vallone, Ross, & Lepper, 1985), it seems reasonable to expect that issuing corrections may exacerbate this effect. The same concern is relevant for fact-checking organizations that struggle to maintain credibility in the face of criticism from both sides.

At the same time, however, the proliferation of political misinformation over recent years has intensified public calls for journalistic activism in adjudicating between competing factual claims. The public's frustration with he-said, she-said reporting is exemplified by the response of *New York Times* readers to a column published by its public editor Arthur Brisbane in January 2012. Brisbane wrote that he was "looking for reader input on whether and when *New York Times* news reporters should challenge 'facts' that are asserted by newsmakers they write about" (Brisbane, 2012). Public response, on the *Times* website and elsewhere, was immediate and incensed. Graves (2012) found that of the 265 comments made in the three hours before the *Times* shut down commenting, "exactly two (discounting obvious sarcasm) disagreed with the proposition that reporters should challenge suspect claims made by politicians." Margaret Sullivan, another public editor of the *New York Times*, describes the growing pushback from readers: "Simply put, false balance is the journalistic practice of giving equal weight to both sides of a story, regardless of an established truth on one side. And many people are fed up with it. They don't want to hear lies or half-truths given credence on one side, and shot down on the other. They want some real answers" (Sullivan, 2012, para. 3).

The next hypothesis directly addresses journalists' concerns over taking a more forceful approach to correcting false claims.

H3. When a correction issued by a newspaper runs counter to a person's political predispositions, the newspaper is perceived as more biased than when the correction is in the he-said, she-said format.

In the final hypothesis, given the public demand for journalists to take a more active role, one might expect that even if a correction decreases trust in a particular outlet, it might increase trust in media more generally by providing evidence that news media are capable of adjudicating competing factual claims.

H4. When journalists actively arbitrate factual claims, it will raise evaluations of media more generally.

Design

A total of 606 people were recruited via Amazon's Mechanical Turk for a 5 (misinformation format) × 2 (congeniality of misinformation) between-subjects design. The five misinformation formats were as follows:

1. Newspaper correction (misinformation corrected by the newspaper itself)
2. Fact-check correction (misinformation corrected by a fact-checking organization)
3. Campaign correction (misinformation corrected by a political campaign)
4. Uncorrected misinformation (misinformation with no correction)
5. No misinformation (article did not contain the misinformation)

The "congeniality of misinformation" refers to whether the misinformation reinforced or countered the participant's existing political attitudes.

Participants first answered a short series of demographic questions, including age, education, and political interest. Overall, the sample was relatively young (78% under the age of 40) and more Democratic (66%) than Republican (33%). Subjects who did not immediately identify with a party answered a series of branching questions until they could be sorted into either leaning Democratic or leaning Republican.

Next, all participants read a news article, ostensibly from the *Iowa Ledger*, about an Iowa congressional race. The article provided background information about the race and focused on one of the candidates, John McKenna. Half the participants were told that John McKenna was of the same party as they were, and the other half were told that he was a member of the opposing party. The article read by each group was identical except for one paragraph. The version read by the uncorrected-misinformation and corrected-misinformation groups contained a paragraph describing an accusation made by Eric Hall, McKenna's opponent:

> The campaign has heated up in recent weeks. On Sunday, Hall accused McKenna of accepting campaign donations from a convicted felon named Daniel Elsio. Elsio, who ran the largest drug ring in Iowa while McKenna was mayor, was convicted of first-degree murder in 2010. According to Hall, McKenna accepted over $10,000 from Elsio. Hall commented that "McKenna's corrupt behavior shows that he and other [Democrats/Republicans] can't be trusted to do what's best for Iowa citizens."

In the newspaper correction and fact-check correction conditions, the paragraph was followed immediately by a correction:

> However, further investigation of the campaign donation records by [journalists at the *Iowa Ledger*/the independent fact-checking organization GetTheFacts.org] has shown no record of any donation from Elsio to McKenna's campaign. Campaigns are required to disclose the names of all individuals who contribute $200 or more in an election cycle, and [the *Ledger*/GetTheFacts.org] did not find Elsio's name listed.

The correction issued from the campaign was substantively similar but attributed the fact check to McKenna's campaign:

> However, McKenna's campaign has released a statement stating that there is no record of any donation from Elsio to their campaign. Campaigns are re-

quired to disclose the names of all individuals who contribute $200 or more in an election cycle, and McKenna's campaign stated that Elsio's name is not listed.

After reading the two articles, all participants completed a two-minute distractor task in which they looked for differences between two photos. Next, subjects answered a series of questions measuring their attitudes toward the candidates. Evaluations of John McKenna were measured with six questions that included a feeling thermometer and several trait assessments (α = .89). Evaluations of Eric Hall were measured with five questions (α = .83).

Subjects then completed a manipulation check in which they were asked a series of questions assessing their memory of material in the article: "You read a newspaper story about an ongoing congressional race. Knowing what you know now, please tell us which of these statements are true." They were presented with five statements about the article. Two of the five statements referred to the donations. They were highly correlated (p < .001) and combined into a single measure assessing whether the respondent believed that McKenna had accepted the donations.

Finally, participants answered questions about four different news outlets: *USA Today*, CNN, GetTheFacts.org, and the *Iowa Ledger*. For each outlet, they indicated their overall opinions about the outlet through a feeling thermometer, the extent to which they thought the outlet could be trusted to get the facts right, and perceived partisan bias (i.e., whether they believed it generally favored the Democrats or Republicans). For each outlet, the first two measures were significantly correlated (p < .001) and so were combined to form an overall evaluation measure.

Results

Effectiveness of Corrections

The first hypothesis compares the effectiveness of three approaches to correcting misinformation. Those who never saw the misinformation were generally skeptical of the donation claim, with an average belief of 1.7 on a 0 to 4 scale. In comparison, those who never saw the correction were much more certain that the claim was true, with an average belief of 3.2. In order for the correction to be deemed successful, it must lower belief in misinformation back to the levels of those who never saw the misinforma-

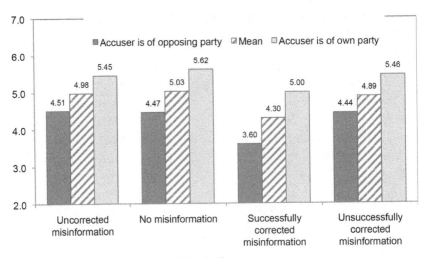

Figure 14.1. Evaluations of accuser (Eric Hall)

tion. Both the newspaper and fact-check conditions succeeded in reverting levels of belief; those who read a correction issued by the newspaper or by a fact-checking organization were as skeptical of the misinformation as those who never saw it in the first place. However, the correction issued by the campaign—the he-said, she-said correction—was much less successful. Although it did significantly reduce belief compared to the misinformation-only condition, it was also significantly higher than the no-misinformation condition ($F = 21.8$, $p < .001$).

When Politicians Are Punished

Figure 14.1 shows evaluations of Eric Hall, the candidate who accused John McKenna of accepting campaign contributions from a convicted felon. Evaluations are measured on a scale of 1 (very unfavorable) to 10 (very favorable). This analysis combines the fact-checking correction and newspaper correction conditions, since both were equally successful at correcting the misinformation.

H2 predicts that politicians will be punished for making accusations only if the claim is perceived as false. This hypothesis is supported. Eric Hall does not suffer from making a negative claim; those who read the accusation without the correction evaluated him no differently than those who did not (i.e., those in the no-misinformation condition). However, those who learned that the accusation was false evaluated Hall significantly more negatively than those in the no-misinformation condition

(F = 13.4, p < .001). It is worth noting that this cost is not incurred in the campaign correction condition. In the campaign correction condition, even people of the opposing party did not punish Hall for making the claim. The he-said, she-said approach thus fails to correct the misinformation but also fails in changing attitudes toward the accuser.

When Media Are Rewarded

H3 directly addresses journalists' concern that when they explicitly arbitrate between competing claims, they are seen as more biased than when they employ the he-said, she-said approach. Figure 14.2 shows the perceived bias of the *Iowa Ledger*, the newspaper that ostensibly published the article read by all participants. Participants were asked to indicate whether the *Iowa Ledger* favored one party over the other. Responses were recoded based on participants' own party on a 0 to 4 scale such that a 0 indicated a belief that the outlet strongly favored one's own party and a 4 indicated a belief that the outlet strongly favored the opposing party.

The results suggest that journalists' intuitions are correct. When journalists arbitrate between factual claims, perception of bias is highly dependent on whose claim they falsify. When a newspaper declares that a Republican candidate made a false claim, Republicans see the paper as

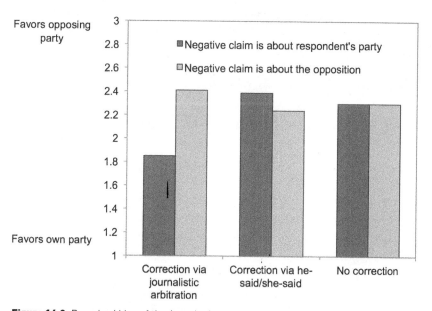

Figure 14.2. Perceived bias of the *Iowa Ledger*

biased toward Democrats, and vice versa. On the other hand, correcting false claims via the he-said, she-said approach does not have a similar effect on perceptions of bias. Indeed, it is not significantly different than simply not correcting the misinformation at all.

H4 predicts that there might also be a positive effect of journalistic arbitration. Over the past few years, citizens have been vocal in demanding that newspapers correct false claims made by politicians. H4 predicts that people will reward the media for taking a stand. Specifically, it predicts that compared to the he-said, she-said approach, when journalists explicitly arbitrate between false claims, it will have a positive impact on evaluations of media more generally.

Traditional media trust questions often follow a format similar to that employed by Gallup's ongoing poll: "In general, how much trust and confidence do you have in the mass media—such as newspapers, TV, and radio—when it comes to reporting the news fully, accurately, and fairly?" (Gallup, n.d.). However, this measure may be problematic given the widely differing definitions that citizens may have of "mass media." Some people may interpret the question as asking about the media available to the American public in general, while others may interpret it as a question about their own media use.

Given this potential problem, the mass media evaluation measure was constructed from questions about two news outlets: CNN and *USA Today*. The evaluation of mass media comprised feeling thermometers on CNN and *USA Today* as well as questions of whether each outlet could be trusted to get the facts right. The questions formed a highly reliable measure (α = .85). CNN and *USA Today* were chosen because they are media outlets familiar to most Americans. In addition, neither is frequently cited as a partisan news outlet (in contrast to, for example, Fox News or the *New York Times*), so there is less potential for ceiling or floor effects to hide shifts in attitudes.

When no correction is issued, media are rated at 6.14. When the correction is in the he-said, she-said format, the rating is 6.04, not a significant difference. However, subjects who read a correction issued by the *Iowa Ledger* evaluated the mass media more positively, at 6.49. The difference is weakly significant ($p < .1$), suggesting that journalistic arbitration can potentially raise evaluations of media more generally—and is unlikely to lower them.

It is also worth noting that there is not a significant interaction between journalistic arbitration and congeniality, suggesting that the increase in mass media evaluations is not driven by partisans who read about their own candidate's exoneration and as a result have more positive attitudes toward mass media.

Conclusion

I address an ongoing debate in journalism by bringing to bear empirical evidence specifically designed to answer questions raised by the media's increasing focus on political misinformation. The results are both encouraging and discouraging. One pattern reoccurs throughout the findings, the enduring effect of partisanship on shaping attitudes and opinions. Partisans are more likely to believe ill of the opposing party. They are less likely to accept corrections when the opposition is the one accused of wrongdoing, and they are more likely to believe that a newspaper is biased when its correction contradicts their own views.

However, the results also suggest that citizens' opinions are shaped by more than just their party identification. Journalistic arbitration and fact checking are extremely effective at correcting misinformation, even when the accused candidate is of the opposing party. In addition, politicians are punished for lying equally by members of the opposing party and members of their own party. Finally, exposure to active fact checking by journalists raises evaluations of mass media, and this effect is not conditional on partisanship.

One potential limitation of these findings is that the false claim was relatively minor and the candidates were unknown to the subjects. To what extent is this stylized version of misinformation generalizable to real-world false claims? Past work on misinformation has tended to focus on contested claims that play a major role in the political landscape, such as President Obama's birthplace, the causes of 9/11, and the existence of weapons of mass destruction in Iraq (Nyhan & Reifler, 2010). These issues, while important, are in some ways very different from the misinformation with which journalists struggle on an everyday basis. Recent dialogues about fact checking have revolved around facts that are more transient yet also important to citizens' political decision making, such as when a GM plant closed, what percentage of federal funding to Planned Parenthood goes to abortions, the requirements of a new welfare program, or whether a candidate supported a particular bill.

This chapter sheds light on important normative questions in journalism. Discussing the controversies around voter fraud in 2012 elections,

Sam Sifton, an editor at the *New York Times*, places himself firmly on the side of the he-said, she-said camp: "There's a lot of reasonable disagreement on both sides. It's not our job to litigate it in the paper. We need to state what each side says" (in Sullivan, 2012, para. 16). The evidence I present here shows that whether Sifton's approach is the right one depends on the end goal. If the goal is preserving the paper's presumed status as unbiased, Sifton's approach is the right one. Adjudicating sides can have the negative consequence of increasing perceptions of bias. But is being perceived as unbiased the goal to which journalists should aspire? Muñoz-Torres points out that this goal has its own ethical problems: "The principle of ever presenting opposing views as equally valid amounts to stating implicitly that all opinions possess the same value as truth-claims" (2012, 576). And indeed, my research shows empirical evidence that Muñoz-Torres's observation is correct. When corrections are presented in the he-said, she-said format, they are perceived as far less credible and the effects of the misinformation persist.

The results also show other positive consequences for journalistic arbitration beyond increased effectiveness in correcting false claims. Most notably, when claims are successfully corrected, the politicians who made the false claim are punished, even by members of their own party. This finding suggests that politicians who lob false accusations at their opponents can suffer serious consequences for doing so, as long as the media do their part to actively discredit those accusations. Journalists face a difficult task, and decisions about how and when to correct misleading claims are rarely black and white. Nonetheless, if media justify their behavior in terms of educating the public, then the evidence suggests that they are better able to achieve this goal by actively interrogating the facts they supply to their consumers.

References

Anderson, C. J., & Tverdova, Y. V. (2003). Corruption, political allegiances, and attitudes toward government in contemporary democracies. *American Journal of Political Science*, 47(1), 91–109.

Brisbane, A. (2012, January 12). Should the Times be a truth vigilante? *New York Times*. Retrieved from http://publiceditor.blogs.nytimes.com/2012/01/12/should-the-times-be-a-truth-vigilante

Cooper, M. (2012, August 20). Fact-checking Ryan's convention speech. *New York Times*. Retrieved from http://thecaucus.blogs.nytimes.com/2012/08/30/in-ryan-critique-of-obama-omissions-help-make-the-case

Fallows, J. (2012, August 29). Bit by bit it takes shape: Media evolution for the "post-truth" age. *Atlantic*. Retrieved from http://www.theatlantic.com/politics/archive/2012/08/bit-by-bit-it-takes-shape-media-evolution-for-the-post-truth-age/261741

Farley, R., Jackson, B., Kiely, E., Robertson, L., & Finley, B. (2012, August 30). Fact check: Paul Ryan at the RNC. *USA Today*. Retrieved from http://usatoday30.usatoday.com/news/politics/story/2012-08-30/paul-ryan-fact-check-republican-convention/57432326/1

Gallup. (N.d.) Media Use and Evaluation. Retrieved from http://www.gallup.com/poll/1663/media-use-evaluation.aspx.

Gehrke, J. (2012, August 29). Obama camp: Paul Ryan is a liar. *Washington Examiner*. Retrieved from http://washingtonexaminer.com/obama-camp-paul-ryan-is-a-liar/article/2506445#.UG2s0ZjA_2U

Graves, L. (2012, January 18). Digging deeper into the *New York Times*' fact-checking faux pas. Nieman Journalism Lab. Retrieved from http://www.niemanlab.org/2012/01/digging-deeper-into-the-new-york-times-fact-checking-faux-pas

Graves, L., & Glaisyer, T. (2012). The fact-checking universe in spring 2012. New America Foundation. Retrieved from http://newamerica.net/publications/policy/the_fact_checking_universe_in_spring_2012

Greenhouse, L. (2012, July 14). Challenging 'he said, she said' journalism. *Nieman Reports*. Retrieved from http://nieman.harvard.edu/reportsitem.aspx?id=102769

Gunther, A., & Schmitt, K. (2004). Mapping boundaries of the hostile media effect. *Journal of Communication, 54*(1), 55–70.

Kessler, G. (2016, May 7). Few stand in Trump's way as he piles up the Four-Pinocchio whoppers. *Washington Post*. Retrieved from https://www.washingtonpost.com/politics/few-stand-in-trumps-way-as-he-piles-up-the-four-pinocchio-whoppers/2016/05/07/8cf5e16a-12ff-11e6-8967-7ac733c56f12_story.html

Ladd, J. M. (2012). *Why Americans hate the media and how it matters*. Princeton, NJ: Princeton University Press.

Muñoz-Torres, J. R. (2012). Truth and objectivity in journalism. *Journalism Studies, 13*(4), 566–582.

Nyhan, B., & Reifler, J. (2010). When corrections fail: The persistence of political misperceptions. *Political Behavior, 32*, 202–330.

Nyhan, B., & Reifler, J. (2015). The effect of fact-checking on elites: A field experiment on US state legislators. *American Journal of Political Science, 59*(3), 628–640.

Pingree, R. J., Brossard, D., & McLeod, D. M. (2014). Effects of journalistic adjudication on factual beliefs, news evaluations, information seeking, and epistemic political efficacy. *Mass Communication and Society, 17*(5), 615–638.

Rainey, J. (2012, September 10). Paul Ryan, the credit rating, and "post-truth politics." *Los Angeles Times*. Retrieved from http://articles.latimes.com/2012/sep/10/news/la-paul-ryan-post-truth-politics-20120910

Rosen, J. (2012, June 22). Fixing the ideology problem in our political press. *Pressthink*. Retrieved from http://archive.pressthink.org/2010/06/22/reply_ambinder.html

Scherer, M. (2012, August 10). Why deceit is everywhere in the 2012 campaign. *Time*.

Retrieved from http://swampland.time.com/2012/08/10/why-deceit-is-every where-in-the-2012-campaign

Sullivan, M. (2012, September 15). He said, she said, and the truth. *New York Times*. Retrieved from http://www.nytimes.com/2012/09/16/public-editor/16pubed.html

Vallone, R. P., Ross, L., & Lepper, M. R. (1985). The hostile media phenomenon: Biased perception and perceptions of media bias in coverage of the Beirut massacre. *Journal of Personality and Social Psychology, 47*, 577–585.

Watts, M., Domke, D., Shah, D. V., & Fan, D. P. (1999). Elite cues and media bias in presidential campaigns: Explaining public perceptions of a liberal press. *Communication Research, 26*(2), 144–175.

Woodward, C., & Gillum, J. (2012, August 30). Fact check: Ryan takes factual shortcuts in speech. Associated Press. Retrieved from http://news.yahoo.com/fact -check-ryan-takes-factual-shortcuts

Yglesias, M. (2016, June 2). CNN has finally figured out how to cover Donald Trump's constant lying. *Vox*. Retrieved from http://www.vox.com/2016/6/2/11841074 /trump-cnn-chyron

The Role of Middle-Level Gatekeepers in the Propagation and Longevity of Misinformation

JEFF HEMSLEY

The past few decades have transformed the media landscape and challenged important theoretical concepts such as gatekeeping (Gans, 1979; Shoemaker & Vos, 2009; Vos, 2015; White, 1950). In this chapter I leverage two views of gatekeeping to explore the role of gatekeepers in the propagation and longevity of misinformation. The first, the *network gatekeeping theory* (Barzilai-Nahon, 2008, 2009), starts from the assumption that in a networked media environment, information may flow over myriad paths to reach audiences who have more media choices than ever before. The result is a dynamic, competitive media environment in which the audience, as a result of its collective media choices, constitutes the gatekeeper. Thus, the role of gatekeeper is not binary—one is or is not—but rather exists on a continuum where some gatekeepers have more control over information flows than others, depending on how successful they are in building and maintaining an audience. The second view, the *curated flows framework* (Thorson & Wells, 2015), accepts that gatekeepers exist on a continuum and suggests that an emerging element of gatekeeping behavior is curating content by actively finding, selecting, remixing, and reposting it. Within this framework, *curation logics* are the incentives and norms that gatekeepers face and that inform their curation decisions.

In this work, I focus on *middle-level gatekeepers*, those with one or two orders of magnitude more followers than the typical user but far fewer than media elites such as Fox News, Huffington Post, and the *Guardian*. I argue that the curation logics used by middle-level gatekeepers can be significantly different from those of media elite, and, further, that middle-level gatekeeping curation logics play an important role in the propagation and longevity of misinformation. Finally, I suggest that while these gatekeepers can keep misinformation alive, even in the face of corrected information, their effect is limited due to the myriad paths by which information flows in a networked media space. This work contributes to the literature around misinformation and gatekeeping by exploring the concept of middle-level gatekeepers and their relationship to misinformation.

Media gatekeepers are often seen as powerful editors working within traditional media. In this view, gatekeepers exercise a certain level of control over the flow of information in society by selecting, from a vast sea of content, a set of storylines that are published and disseminated broadly across society (Shoemaker & Vos, 2009). The published stories become part of the audience's social reality, inform its members' worldviews, and can, when consumed by large national audiences, even inform a national identity (Sunstein, 2001). The stories a gatekeeper decides not to select for publication remain unseen by the gatekeeper's audience and may never become part of the social reality of the audience. The ability to select messages the audience sees, thus shaping members' worldviews, is at the heart of gatekeeping power. For example, by disregarding stories that may challenge societal elites, gatekeepers facilitate the acceptance of the status quo by limiting alternative worldviews (Lukes, 2005; Nahon, 2016). Likewise, by selecting highly credible and verified stories for publication, gatekeepers can build and maintain a reputation for integrity and trustworthiness.

With the low cost of sharing content on social media sites (Shirky, 2009), the power of traditional gatekeepers has diminished. People can select and broadcast content into their own networks in what Walther and colleagues (2011, p. 21) refer to as "masspersonal communication" and Castells (2009, p. 55) dubs "mass self-communication." This many-to-many communication can result in messages that go *viral*, a "social information flow process where many people simultaneously forward a specific information item . . . and where the message spreads beyond their own networks to different, often distant networks, resulting in a sharp acceleration in the number of people who are exposed to the message" (Nahon & Hemsley, 2013, p. 16). Because viral events flow through interconnected and distributed networks, the events can circumvent traditional mass media gatekeepers by limiting their ability to filter out messages whose credibility is suspect. Important examples include the spread of misinformation about disease (Morozov, 2009; Oyeyemi, Gabarron, & Wynn, 2014), disasters (Gupta, Lamba, Kumaraguru, & Joshi, 2013; Maddock et al., 2015; Spiro et al., 2012; Starbird, Maddock, Orand, Achterman, & Mason, 2014), and riots (Procter, Vis, & Voss, 2011).

Although viral content produced by ordinary citizens is overshadowed by content produced by traditional media outlets (Klotz, 2010), viral content can be influential—for example, in shaping people's views toward political candidates (English, Sweetser, & Ancu, 2011)—even when viewers assign low credibility scores to the content and its producers (Ancu, 2010).

The concept of masspersonal communication suggests that in a hyper-networked world, "we are all gatekeepers" (Shoemaker & Vos, 2009, p. 33). That is, all users have the capacity to engage in the process of gatekeeping by selecting some information to share while withholding other information. Of course, most people have relatively few followers. Thus, while collectively users have the potential to construct influential viral events that reach millions of people, any one individual's impact on information flows in the global, national, and even specialized online communities is often trivial. Certainly, some have larger audiences than others, and the distribution of the number of followers actors have tends to be highly skewed. That is, a few actors have many times more followers than the average person. On Twitter the distribution resembles the power law illustrated in Figure 15.1 (Java, Song, Finin, & Tseng, 2007; Kwak, Lee, Park, & Moon, 2010), as do the blogosphere (Adamic et al., 2000; Drezner & Farrell, 2008), website communities (Hindman, 2008; Hindman, Tsioutsiouliklis, & Johnson, 2003), and other social networks (Barabási, 2002; Watts, 2004). Thus, while almost anyone can act as a gatekeeper, some actors have more influence over the flow of information than others do.

People tend to focus on those gatekeepers with the most followers, or largest audiences, under the assumption that they have the most influence over informing their audiences' worldviews. This reflects scholarship that suggests the news ecology is still disproportionally dominated by large institutional players (Thorson & Wells, 2015), whether in terms of online discussions around the news (Baden & Springer, 2014) or in terms of what spreads in social media (Burgess & Green, 2009; Kwak et al., 2010). The nature of the power-law distribution of followers, however, suggests there is a kind of middle class, or middle level of gatekeepers. In Figure 15.1, the area between the dotted lines along the power-law curve is intended to

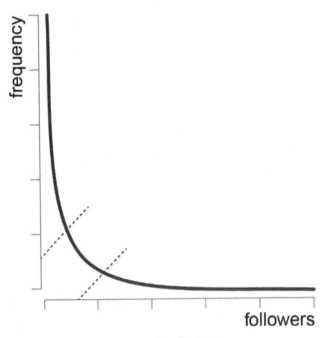

Figure 15.1. Example of power-law distribution

indicate approximate rather than quantified boundaries. An example of a middle-level gatekeeper might be a reasonably well-known academic or political pundit who has a blog or Twitter account with thousands, maybe tens of thousands, of followers interested in the topic area for which she is known.

Middle-level gatekeepers can be influential in a number of ways. Relatively unknown political blogs can influence political and journalism elites who read them (Drezner & Farrell, 2008), have an impact on agenda setting and political participation (Wallsten, 2010; Woodly, 2008), and shape political learning and deliberation (Lawrence, Sides, & Farrell, 2010). News organizations even employ select accounts on Twitter as news sources (Moon & Hadley, 2014). Middle-level gatekeepers also scan and interact with blogs of higher and lower status, highlighting and discussing interesting information (Drezner & Farrell, 2008) that can then "bubble up" to more and more prominent gatekeepers, occasionally reaching mainstream media (Nahon & Hemsley, 2013). Finally, middle-level gatekeepers perform an important bridging function (Barzilai-Nahon, 2008). That is, as a by-product of having many more followers than the average user, they have significantly larger audience reach and are in a position to link clusters of people who may otherwise be connected only tenuously or not at all. This means that through bridging, middle-level gatekeepers can facilitate the flow of information from one part of the network to another.

Middle-level gatekeepers also engage in *information curation practices*. That is, they actively find, select, remix, and repost content from larger media gatekeepers (Thorson & Wells, 2015). In the process of curating information, middle-level gatekeepers make decisions that facilitate or constrain information flows. Certainly, this is similar to the way people have traditionally thought about the gatekeeping role. However, the curation logics, the incentives and norms that inform curation decisions (Thorson & Wells, 2015), may be quite different for middle-level gatekeepers than for those at the top or those further down the power-law curve. While journalistic curation logics may be dominated by values, bias, and the political and profit forces at play, nonjournalists may face different incentives and operate under different norms. Likewise, middle-level gatekeepers in different topic areas (e.g., politics vs. entertainment) may use different curation logics. Apart from journalistic curation logics, Thorson and Wells (2015) identify four additional logics: algorithmic, personal, social, and strategic. Algorithmic curation depends on computer-driven filtering and selection, while personal curation reflects an individual's selection and filter decision criteria for consumption. Social curation logics are the incentives and norms that individuals consider when sharing in their own social networks, as in sharing for the purpose of identity performance. Strategic curation logics reflect a purposive agenda, such as a political pundit selecting only stories that support his point of view. This differs from journalistic curation logics, in which the norms may be to present various sides of a story, even to the extent of providing falsely balanced opposing viewpoints (Thorson, this volume; Weeks, this volume). One or more of these curation logics may be at play for any given gatekeeper. It should be noted that while Thorson and Wells (2015) offer these different curation logics as a conceptual framework, the ideas are new and have not been applied in empirical work.

To bring this back to misinformation, let us consider a hypothetical blogger named Henry, who is a middle-level gatekeeper. Henry writes about politics and leans substantially to the right, though for this discussion the ideological direction (right or left) is less important than how ideology may affect Henry's curation logics. He operates like an opinion leader (Katz & Lazarsfeld, 1955), not a journalist whose curation logics include a norm to pursue objectivity (Weeks, this volume). That means

Henry is less interested in presenting a balanced view than in influencing others by providing commentary and opinions on news stories. Therefore, his curation choices will be strategic. Such choices have been borne out in research results showing that political bloggers are more likely to link to and write about content that supports their ideological stances (Nahon & Hemsley, 2014). Thus, if Henry is against the Affordable Care Act (ACA), commonly called Obamacare, and reads from Fox News that health care reform would create death panels (Meirick, 2013), the story would provide fodder for his blog. By writing about "death panels" Henry would propagate misinformation as a result of his strategic curation logics. Partisan bias effects due to motivated reasoning suggest that Henry has little motivation to examine claims with which he agrees (Bullock, Gerber, Hill, & Huber, 2013), and the concept of strategic curation suggests that he may even draw from less credible sources, provided they support his ideological stance. If Henry later read a story from Associated Press that debunks death panels, he has little if any incentive to post a retraction. Doing so would not support his strategic narrative. He does, however, have an incentive to keep readers on his site and, accordingly, may periodically link back to his own death panel story, resulting in misinformation periodically resurfacing and spreading in networks.

Henry writes in a social, networked environment of readers and other bloggers. Bloggers with similar ideologies and informational interests tend to interact and link to each other by quoting and commenting on each other's posts (Schmidt, 2007). Over time this results in clusters of "communities of blogging practices" in which social norms emerge that influence how Henry uses his blog as a tool for information, identity, and relationship management (Schmidt, 2007). These communities can evolve into echo chambers where actors who share the same viewpoint propagate and discuss the same story, and the repeated information will tend to intensify their ideologically similar viewpoints (Jasny, Waggle, & Fisher, 2015). The discussion will likely be limited to ideologically similar bloggers since clusters of right- and left-leaning blogs rarely link across ideological lines (Adamic & Glance, 2005), and when they do, they tend to simply negate the other's view without addressing the substance of the position (Hargittai, Gallo, & Kane, 2008). People within ideologically similar clusters also engage in practices of inclusion and exclusion of others, such as discrediting an outsider's information sources (Edwards, 2013). Thus, misinformation within an ideological cluster can be reinforced, and challenges to it can be suppressed.

Social curation logics may also plan a role in the content choices of bloggers in these clusters. That is, bloggers may select stories that fit into the discussion in order to be part of the group. They may also avoid posting contrary views if they feel that doing so could jeopardize their standing in the community, or they may compete for status and audiences by creating posts more frequently and of higher quality, by linking to respected sources, or, depending on the community, by framing content in more extreme and polarizing ways. Barzilai-Nahon (2008, 2009) suggests that in our networked environment, the role of gatekeeper is a dynamic one in which gatekeepers need to compete with others in order to grow or even maintain their audience. It is reasonable to assume that Henry is motivated to maintain or grow his audience, which could involve competing with other bloggers in his community. Competition for status and audience may require overlapping social and strategic curation logics. If Henry gained attention for his posts on death panels, he might then seek out new stories to discuss, or post new commentary on old stories, in an effort to keep the social discussion going while also trying to gain more followers.

In the discussion above, it should be clear that Henry, a middle-level gatekeeper embedded in a social blogging community, faces numerous incentives and behaves within the norms of his community. Thus, he will use overlapping curation logics when selecting and posting content, and these logics can result in the propagation and longevity of misinformation. Algorithmic curation logics can reinforce this effect. When Henry searches for new stories on death panels, search engines may order the results based partly on what sources he has read in the past. Thus, conservative sites like Fox News, *National Review*, and Red State will come up before liberal sources like NPR, *Mother Jones*, and Daily Kos. So while NPR, *Mother Jones*, and Daily Kos may all be running stories debunking death panels, Henry is more likely to run into and post about stories that support his existing ideas.

The example uses a blogger to think about how the curation logics of middle-level gatekeepers can propagate misinformation, but similar mechanics can come into play on Twitter and other platforms. There are political hashtags for conservative and liberal discussions on Twitter (e.g., #TCOT and #P2, respectively) for which actors are not bound to journalistic curation logics and may use other logics to achieve their desired goals. As in Henry's case, these goals could be for the participant to become ideologically influential, participate socially in discussions with like-minded others, or both. Like Twitter, Instagram supports discussion streams with hashtags, but the fundamental unit is an image, not text, and most discussions occur within the comments sections of posts. Middle-level gatekeepers on Instagram create and curate content that they post into hashtag streams. They are adept at creating visual mashups, such as photos or other graphics with text overlaid, that form the center of a discussion on Instagram and are shared across social media. Two accounts, @beingliberal and @always.right, could be considered examples of highly ideological middle-level gatekeepers on Instagram. Like middle-level gatekeepers on Twitter and in the blogosphere, these actors may employ curation logics that do not emphasize objectivity, and thus the gatekeepers may be sources of, and propagate, misinformation.

Another important point to consider is that even individuals with a few followers use various curation logics to select and share information in their own social networks. The difference is that middle-level gatekeepers have more followers, giving them much greater reach and influence than the typical user. Since the role of a gatekeeper in a networked environment is a dynamic one (Barzilai-Nahon, 2008, 2009), it is possible that middle-level gatekeepers are more active media consumers, producers, and curators than typical users. The dynamic nature of gatekeepers suggests that those in middle levels have cultivated appealing reputations, at least among their audiences. So, while typical users can also spread misinformation, they just don't have the same reach or influence as middle-level gatekeepers.

On a larger scale, middle-level gatekeepers do not have as much influence or impact on information propagation as mainstream media and other elite gatekeepers do. Research has shown that most content that spreads online consists of copies or derivatives of content generated by mass-media producers (Asur, Huberman, Szabo, & Wang, 2011; Burgess & Green, 2009; Crane & Sornette, 2008; Hindman, 2008; Kwak et al., 2010). With respect to misinformation, the important differentiation is that middle-level gatekeepers face a different set of norms and incentives that influence the kind of curation logics they employ, and these logics appear to be more likely to propagate and repropagate misinformation within clusters of actors. Because of their reach and social positions in clusters, middle-level gatekeepers have the potential to be key actors who keep misinformation alive in echo chambers.

Despite their influential structural positions in the network, the ability of middle-level gatekeepers to keep small population segments misinformed is limited. Audiences have access to a variety of online and offline information sources. The nature of the audience power law means that the same people who might follow a middle-level gatekeeper also follow, for example, Fox News, CNN, or both and any of a wide variety of others that range from close personal contacts to the largest media conglomerates. Eventually, users may be exposed to corrected information along the myriad paths through which information can flow to them, but this depends on their own personal curation logics.

References

Adamic, L., & Glance, N. (2005). The political blogosphere and the 2004 US election: Divided they blog. In *LinkKDD '05 Proceedings of the 3rd International Workshop on Link Discovery* (pp. 36–43). New York, NY: Association for Computing Machinery.

Adamic, L. A., Huberman, B. A., Barabási, A.-L., Albert, R., Jeong, H., & Bianconi, G. (2000). Power-law distribution of the World Wide Web. *Science, 287*(5461), 2115.

Ancu, M. (2010). Viral politics: The credibility and effects of online viral political messages. In M. McKinney & M. Banwart (Eds.), *Communication in the 2008 U.S. election: Digital natives elect a president.* New York, NY: Peter Lang Publishing.

Asur, S., Huberman, B. A., Szabo, G., & Wang, C. (2011). Trends in social media: Persistence and decay. In *ICWSM-11 5th International AAAI Conference on Weblogs and Social Media.* Palo Alto, CA: Association for the Advancement of Artificial Intelligence.

Baden, C., & Springer, N. (2014). Com(ple)menting the news on the financial crisis: The contribution of news users' commentary to the diversity of viewpoints in the public debate. *European Journal of Communication, 29*(5), 529–548.

Barabási, A.-L. (2002). *Linked: The new science of networks.* New York, NY: Basic Books.

Barzilai-Nahon, K. (2008). Toward a theory of network gatekeeping: A framework for exploring information control. *Journal of the American Society for Information Science and Technology, 59*(9), 1493–1512.

Barzilai-Nahon, K. (2009). Gatekeeping: A critical review. *Annual Review of Information Science and Technology, 43,* 433–478.

Bullock, J. G., Gerber, A. S., Hill, S. J., & Huber, G. A. (2013). *Partisan bias in factual beliefs about politics.* Washington, DC: National Bureau of Economic Research.

Burgess, J., & Green, J. (2009). *YouTube: Online video and participatory culture.* New York, NY: Polity Press.

Castells, M. (2009). *Communication power.* New York, NY: Oxford University Press.

Crane, R., & Sornette, D. (2008). Robust dynamic classes revealed by measuring the response function of a social system. *Proceedings of the National Academy of Sciences, 105*(41), 15649.

Drezner, D., & Farrell, H. (2008). The power and politics of blogs. *Public Choice, 134*(1/2), 15–30.

Edwards, A. (2013). (How) do participants in online discussion forums create "echo chambers"?: The inclusion and exclusion of dissenting voices in an online forum about climate change. *Journal of Argumentation in Context, 2*(1), 127–150.

English, K., Sweetser, K. D., & Ancu, M. (2011). YouTube-ification of political talk: An examination of persuasion appeals in viral video. *American Behavioral Scientist, 55*(6), 733–748.

Gans, H. J. (1979). *Deciding what's news: A study of CBS evening news, NBC nightly news, Newsweek, and Time.* Evanston, IL: Northwestern University Press.

Gupta, A., Lamba, H., Kumaraguru, P., & Joshi, A. (2013). Faking Sandy: Characterizing and identifying fake images on Twitter during Hurricane Sandy. In *WWW'13 Companion Proceedings of the 22nd International Conference on World Wide Web* (pp. 729–736). New York, NY: Association for Computing Machinery.

Hargittai, E., Gallo, J., & Kane, M. (2008). Cross-ideological discussions among conservative and liberal bloggers. *Public Choice, 134*(1), 67–86.

Hindman, M. (2008). *The myth of digital democracy.* Princeton, NJ: Princeton University Press.

Hindman, M., Tsioutsiouliklis, K., & Johnson, J. A. (2003). Googlearchy: How a few heavily-linked sites dominate politics on the web. In *Annual meeting of the Midwest Political Science Association* (vol. 4, pp. 1–33).

Jasny, L., Waggle, J., & Fisher, D. R. (2015). An empirical examination of echo chambers in US climate policy networks. *Nature Climate Change, 5*(8), 782–786.

Java, A., Song, X., Finin, T., & Tseng, B. (2007). Why we Twitter: Understanding microblogging usage and communities. In *Proceedings of the 9th WebKDD and 1st SNA-KDD 2007 Workshop on Web Mining and Social Network Analysis* (pp. 56–65). New York, NY: Association for Computing Machinery.

Katz, E., & Lazarsfeld, P. (1955). *Personal influence: The part played by people in the flow of mass communications.* New York, NY: Free Press.

Klotz, R. J. (2010). The sidetracked 2008 YouTube Senate campaign. *Journal of Information Technology & Politics, 7*(2), 110.

Kwak, H., Lee, C., Park, H., & Moon, S. (2010). What is Twitter, a social network or a news media? In *WWW'10 Proceedings of the 19th International Conference on World Wide Web* (pp. 591–600). New York, NY: Association for Computing Machinery.

Lawrence, E., Sides, J., & Farrell, H. (2010). Self-segregation or deliberation? Blog readership, participation, and polarization in American politics. *Perspectives on Politics, 8*(1), 141–157.

Lukes, S. (2005). *Power: A radical view* (2nd ed.). New York, NY: Palgrave Macmillan.

Maddock, J., Starbird, K., Al-Hassani, H., Sandoval, D. E., Orand, M., & Mason, R. M. (2015). Characterizing online rumoring behavior using multi-dimensional signatures. In *CSCW '15 Proceedings of the 18th ACM Conference on Computer Supported Cooperative Work & Social Computing* (pp. 228–241). New York, NY: Association for Computing Machinery.

Meirick, P. C. (2013). Motivated misperception? Party, education, partisan news, and belief in "death panels." *Journalism & Mass Communication Quarterly, 90*(1), 39–57.

Moon, S. J., & Hadley, P. (2014). Routinizing a new technology in the newsroom: Twitter as a news source in mainstream media. *Journal of Broadcasting & Electronic Media, 58*(2), 289–305.

Morozov, E. (2009, April 25). Swine flu: Twitter's power to misinform. *Foreign Policy.*

Retrieved from http://foreignpolicy.com/2009/04/25/swine-flu-twitters-power-to
-misinform/

Nahon, K. (2016). Where there is social media there is politics. In A. Bruns, G. Enli,
E. Skogerbo, A. O. Larsson, & C. Christensen (Eds.), *Routledge companion to social
media and politics* (pp. 39–55). New York, NY: Routledge.

Nahon, K., & Hemsley, J. (2013). *Going viral*. Cambridge, England: Polity Press.

Nahon, K., & Hemsley, J. (2014). Homophily in the guise of cross-linking political blogs
and content. *American Behavioral Scientist, 58*(10), 1294–1313.

Oyeyemi, S. O., Gabarron, E., & Wynn, R. (2014). Ebola, Twitter, and misinformation:
A dangerous combination? *BMJ, 349*, g6178.

Procter, R., Vis, F., & Voss, A. (2011). Riot rumours: How misinformation spread on
Twitter during a time of crisis. *Guardian*. Retrieved from http://www.guardian
.com/uk/interactive/2011/dec/07/london-riots-twitter

Schmidt, J. (2007). Blogging practices: An analytical framework. *Journal of Computer
Mediated Communication, 12*(4), 1409–1427.

Shirky, C. (2009). *Here comes everybody: The power of organizing without organizations*.
New York, NY: Penguin.

Shoemaker, P. J., & Vos, T. (2009). *Gatekeeping theory*. New York, NY: Routledge.

Spiro, E. S., Fitzhugh, S., Sutton, J., Pierski, N., Greczek, M., & Butts, C. T. (2012). Rumoring during extreme events: A case study of Deepwater Horizon 2010. In *WebSci
'12 Proceedings of the 4th Annual ACM Web Science Conference* (pp. 275–283). New
York, NY: Association for Computing Machinery.

Starbird, K., Maddock, J., Orand, M., Achterman, P., & Mason, R. M. (2014). Rumors,
false flags, and digital vigilantes: Misinformation on Twitter after the 2013 Boston
Marathon bombing. In M. Kindling, & E. Greifeneder (Eds.), *iConference 2014 Proceedings* (pp. 654–662). iSchools.

Sunstein, C. (2001). *Republic.com*. Princeton, NJ: Princeton University Press.

Thorson, K., & Wells, C. (2015). Understanding media effects in an era of curated flows.
In T. Vos & F. Heinderyckx (Eds.), *Gatekeeping in transition* (pp. 25–44). New York,
NY: Routledge.

Vos, T. (2015). Revisiting gatekeeping theory during a time of transition. In T. Vos &
F. Heinderyckx (Eds.), *Gatekeeping in transition* (pp. 3–25). New York, NY: Routledge.

Wallsten, K. (2010). Yes we can: How online viewership, blog discussion, campaign
statements, and mainstream media coverage produced a viral video phenomenon.
Journal of Information Technology & Politics, 7(2), 163–181.

Walther, J. B., Carr, C. T., Choi, S. S., DeAndrea, D. C., Kim, J., Tong, S. T., & Van Der
Heide, B. (2011). Interaction of interpersonal, peer, and media influence sources
online. In Z. Papacharissi (Ed.), *A networked self: Identity, community, and culture on
social network sites* (pp. 17–38). New York, NY: Routledge.

Watts, D. J. (2004). *Six degrees: The science of a connected age*. New York, NY: W. W.
Norton.

White, D. M. (1950). The "gate keeper": A case study in the selection of news. *Journalism Quarterly, 27*(4), 383–390.

Woodly, D. (2008). New competencies in democratic communication? Blogs, agenda
setting, and political participation. *Public Choice, 134*(1), 109–123.

SIXTEEN

Encouraging Information Search to Counteract Misinformation

Providing "Balanced" Information about Vaccines

SAMANTHA KAPLAN

I n this chapter I review the more common and overt ethical dilemmas of misinformation in physical and digital information environments and possible search modifications that may both mitigate some of the negative repercussions misinformation can cause and cultivate greater fluency in information seekers. I do this within the frame of the ongoing debates and controversy about vaccines in the United States. Because I consider the use of search to counteract misinformation within the framework of vaccination, it is beneficial to introduce or clarify several important concepts related to the issue and the context of vaccination in the United States. At the time of this writing, there is consensus in the scientific community about the safety of vaccines and the benefit of compulsory immunization to public health. Still, when evaluating misinformation, researchers ought to remember that information is "located socially and historically, and . . . this context inevitably influences" what is considered right or wrong, accurate or inaccurate, authoritative or nonauthoritative (Nielsen, 1990, p. 9). Because accuracy is context-dependent, researchers ought to prioritize educating information seekers about the context of information they might find rather than trying simply to refute, correct, or remove claims that run counter to official public health messages.

Immunization, Vaccination, and Herd Immunity

The World Health Organization (WHO) defines immunization as "the process whereby a person is made immune or resistant to an infectious disease, typically by the administration of a vaccine" (WHO, 2016). The United States' relations with immunization began in the late 1700s, with the smallpox vaccine (Stern & Markel, 2005). Since that time immunization via compulsory vaccination has expanded to include many other diseases, such as mumps, measles, rubella, tetanus, diphtheria, and chicken pox—a disease many perceive as non-life-threatening.

The United States has effected high adherence to the immunization schedules by instituting their absence as a barrier to entry to the public school system, a policy that has been adopted by most higher education entities as well. Exemptions from immunizations vary greatly and are determined at the state level (Bossaller, 2014). But for the most part, the childhood series of vaccinations has become a relatively accepted part of life, with fewer than 2% of parents of kindergarten students requesting exemptions of any kind (Steenhuysen, 2015) from the 30-plus shots for 14 diseases the U.S. Centers for Disease Control and Prevention (CDC) recommend (CDC, 2016a) that children receive before they turn 18. Without current immunization records, children may not attend school—and this applies not just to primary school. Provision of immunization records persists even in graduate school for some higher education entities. Not receiving one's immunizations can serve as a barrier to participation in everyday life; summer camps, day care centers, and even some places of employment require participants to be in compliance with the CDC's recommendations.

There are several predominant reasons children's parents—of whom there is not a consistent profile (Bossaller, 2014)—decline immunizations. The reasons go by various names according to states, but they are usually categorized as some form of exemption for medical reasons (for example, individuals with suppressed immune systems are not good candidates for vaccines) and nonmedical exemptions. Nonmedical exemptions may be religious or nonreligious, though the procedures to obtain them are usually the same. As long as exemptions remain below a certain threshold (for some diseases this threshold is less than 1%; for others it is higher), the immunity of others is not threatened.

Herd immunity, or *community immunity*, has multiple meanings but in this chapter refers to the reduction of risk reached when a "particular threshold proportion of immune individuals" has been immunized (Fine, Eames, & Heymann, 2011, p. 911). In plainer language, it is the number of people in a community that need to be immunized against a disease so that those who have not been immunized are not at risk for the disease. If this threshold is not met, there is no indirect immunity for nonimmunized individuals and the community is at risk. The herd immunity threshold varies greatly by disease, population, and other factors and is usually estimated by complex epidemiological models, so "the sensible public health practice is to aim for 100% coverage" (Fine et al., 2011, p. 914).

Herd immunity has been undermined in many communities as larger numbers of parents in the United States have begun to question the safety and necessity of vaccines. Fine and colleagues (2011, p. 914) note as much, commenting, "It is not surprising that a sustained low incidence of infection, caused in large part by successful vaccination programs, makes the maintenance of high vaccination levels difficult, especially in the face of questioning or negative media attention."

This is not a hypothetical or speculative situation. It used to be the case that the number of exemptions granted was small enough not to jeopardize herd immunity, but that is no longer a safe assumption. The controversy over vaccines has been charged with causing preventable outbreaks; 2014 saw the largest number of measles cases since 2000, and most of the infected were unvaccinated (CDC, 2016b). This has led to legislation that makes it harder to obtain exemptions in California (Bernstein, 2015). Canada is considering requiring parents seeking exemptions to take a course on the subject (Csanady, 2016). Concerns about compromised herd immunity should be given additional credence as recent outbreaks of Zika and Ebola have shown how quickly disease can spread in a globalized society. Ultimately, herd immunity "is about protecting society itself" (Fine, Eames, & Heymann, 2011, p. 915).

Recent Controversy in Regard to Vaccination

Some of the rise in the rejection of vaccines has been attributed to a now infamous and retracted paper written by Andrew Wakefield and colleagues and published in 1998 by the *Lancet*. The paper purported a causal link between the MMR (mumps, measles, rubella) vaccine and autism spectrum disorder (ASD). In the ten years between publication and retraction and the years since, the issue has become even more contentious and divided. Though Wakefield's findings have been rejected by further science (Chen, Landau, Sham, & Fombonne, 2004; Clayton, Rusch, Ford, & Stratton, 2012; Farrington, Miller, & Taylor, 2001) and in courts of law (Decoteau & Underman, 2015; Kirkland, 2012), it is possible these efforts have had a reverse effect and have been misconstrued as evidence that the government and the scientific community collude, an opinion observed by Bossaller (2014) in a content analysis of comments on news articles about vaccination.

We must also acknowledge that the vaccine delivery system in the United States has been improved over time. At least some antivaccine advocate arguments are based on outdated references to past practices, yet it will be useful to acknowledge that historical context. In the case of thimerosal, a preservative used in vaccines, the American Academy of Pediatrics and the U.S. Public Health Service recommended discontinuing it in the late 1990s. Holden (2003) has noted that increasing immunization will require acknowledgement and assessment of the historical seeds of antivaccine advocate complaints and assurance that current vaccine delivery systems actually include all necessary monitoring and controls to ensure that the complaints are not pointing to legitimate concerns.

Official inability to counter vaccine controversies successfully is distressing from a strategy perspective, as highly rigorous methodologies have been utilized to examine safety concerns. A national cohort study of children born in Denmark between 1991 and 1998 found no evidence to support arguments against vaccination (Madsen et al., 2002). Taylor, Swerdfeger, and Eslick's (2014) meta-analysis of five case-control and five cohort studies also found no evidence for a relationship between vaccination and ASD.

Repercussions from the Wakefield case of scientific misconduct have not been diminished by the extent of inaccurate information readily available and used by parents. Studies have shown that parents cite anecdotal evidence from friends and family as reasons to question or decline vaccines (Bossaller, 2014; Freed, Clark, Butchart, Singer, & Davis, 2010; Rochman, 2013). Parents may be inundated with this misinformation about the safety and necessity of vaccines from entertainment and social media; or, if they seek information from these platforms, they are not likely to find good information. One study of Facebook analyzed the 10 most popular vaccination groups, pages, and places (for a total of 30) and found that 43% could be considered antivaccination; those sites were significantly more active than provaccination sites; and "a substantial portion of the information . . . is not concordant with information provided by CDC and FDA" (Buchanan & Beckett, 2014, p. 230).

In a content analysis of online news comment sections (more than 1,500 comments from 7 sites), Bossaller found "personal experience was often cited as the ultimate authority" (2014, p. 236). Bossaller identifies overlapping ideas of authority and authoritativeness about vaccination "because the same entities that fund research often pursue compliance, especially regarding public health . . . [which] build[s] a tangled web of mistrust for wary information seekers" (2014, p. 232). The commenters made "numerous statements that doctors and scientists' recommendations were tainted by their affiliations with insurance and pharmaceutical companies" (Bossaller, 2014, p. 237). Bossaller found that "most often they asked for unbiased information," though "there was disagreement about what might constitute unbiased information" (2014, p. 238). The commenters' request identifies an opportunity for improvement; rather than providing unbiased information, perhaps educators can develop their faculties for detecting bias. All of this creates a challenging gauntlet for information seekers looking for authoritative, accurate, credible information on this topic.

Vaccination Information in Information Environments

Information providers have not yet resolved which information to include or exclude, what criteria to use, or how to educate individuals searching for information on vaccination. Providing vaccination information in different environments encounters different quagmires, starting with the physical (libraries) and finishing with digital (Internet-based). While mass media and other forms of communication are important information providers, receiving information from them is a somewhat passive experience, whereas a library or search engine is something seekers engage for a more active experience. In these settings, one can imagine that individuals already have some idea of what they are looking for; even if it is not fully conceived, it is an information need that they can articulate to a librarian or a search engine in order to be directed to more information.

Physical Information Environments

The controversy has started to seep into information and library science as public librarians are called to answer health information–related queries and provide resources about vaccination. As they do so, it is worthwhile to consider what belongs on library shelves as well as who decides that and how. Is it the will of the people, or should librarians arbitrate their collections? In this instance the viewpoints are so polarized that no matter which choice the librarian makes, it will be accorded a stance and potentially not fulfill its mission. What to do?

Libraries and librarians face "an inherent tension between collecting popular literature that may provide dangerous misinformation with regard to health and access to high quality, authoritative resources" (Flaherty, Tayag, Lanier, & Minor, 2014, p. 1). This tension was articulated by library workers themselves when interviewed regarding their personal beliefs about vaccines; in providing vaccination information, they "attempted to adhere to two not easily compatible positions: dedication to neutrality . . . and dedication to information quality" (Keselman, Arnott Smith, & Hundal, 2014, p. 208). The American Library Association's Library Bill of Rights (1996) appears to privilege neutrality, as it states that "materials should not be excluded because of the origin, background, or views of those contributing to their creation," and its second provision asserts that "libraries should provide materials and information presenting all points of view on current and historical issues." It is also important to remember the third law of library science, according to Ranganathan (1931): "Every book its reader"—every book or item has a reader. Further, one cannot, nor should one, presume to know how readers will use the information they find. Rather, to adhere to these principles without jeopardizing the welfare of their patrons, libraries and librarians must begin to consider "the best ways to provide the public not only with access to information but also with guidance and mechanisms for evaluating what they find" (Flaherty, 2013, p. 164). These concerns are amplified in an online information environment. Accordingly, Noruzi (2004) expands the laws of the library to the Internet in declaring that just as every book has its reader, every web resource has its user.

Digital Information Environments

If one considers the Internet as a library, one must recognize a global user base exceeded only by collection size, limited metadata and indexing, and a very murky concept of who the librarians are. Known avenues to removing something from the collection vary by country but include invoking the Digital Millennium Copyright Act (DMCA) in the United States and

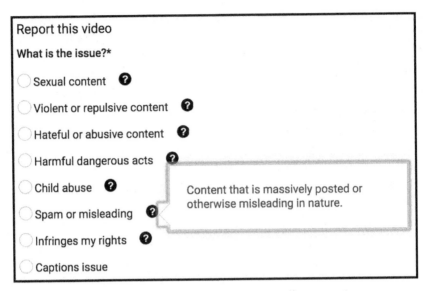

Figure 16.1. YouTube reporting criteria, retrieved from http://www.youtube.com

analogous laws in other countries. Such laws implement two 1996 World Intellectual Property Organization (WIPO) treaties and are concerned with copyright issues in digital environments (National Research Council, 2000). Through the laws, content can sometimes be removed if it fits definitions of certain forms of pornography and other activities for which there is a legal basis of removal.

Movements like the Right to Be Forgotten advocate to recognize individuals' right to have greater control over personal information on the Internet, including the right to have content about stigmatizing past events removed. They have gained some traction in the United States since the mid-2000s and have had practical success in Europe (Mantelero, 2013). No right is generally recognized to remove inaccurate information. The criteria used by large information entities like YouTube or Yahoo to arbitrate flagged content are largely unknown. If an individual chose to flag a video for YouTube moderators in 2016, for example, they were asked to select one of the eight options listed in Figure 16.1. Only one reflects misinformation—the "misleading" category. If libraries provide a transparent, limited collection, digital information providers are the opposite, supplying an opaque, limitless collection.

If the Internet is a constantly growing library staffed by technical services librarians who work only to ensure that the library's capacity is increasing, one must acknowledge that it is unrealistic to think weeding is the solution. In a library, weeding is necessary because of spatial and financial constraints, and criteria such as whether a newer edition of a book is available or whether a book has ever been checked out guide decisions to remove material from collections. Online, the shelf space appears inexhaustible. Digital deselection is also unrealistic, as it is questionable whether something can ever be removed from the Internet. Attempts to remove things have also backfired spectacularly. "The Streisand effect" was coined as a term when singer and actor Barbra Streisand attempted to limit the ability of Internet users to look at pictures of her house, which had the unintended consequences of heightening awareness of the availability of this information and popularizing interest in looking at pictures of her house (Jansen & Martin, 2015).

Online search environments may be at greater risk for accidentally promoting misinformation. While it is easy to laud algorithms, there is no bill of rights for Internet users, and search engine algorithms are proprietary, their flaws only revealed by trial and error—sometimes at the expense of hapless individuals. In 2009 a Syracuse undergraduate in good standing could not understand why his resume failed to attract interest; upon searching himself on Google, he realized he shared his name with a convicted felon and had no recourse for differentiating himself (Klara, 2014).

While libraries typically reflect a bit of the microcosms that fund them, such as having a local authors shelf and local transportation maps available, search engines are just beginning to adapt search results to searchers. For the most part, online searchers use the same Google or Bing. If two people in the United States both search a keyword combination they have never used before, each will likely receive top-ten results that are largely identical. What is inaccurate for one user is probably inaccurate for other users. While what is deemed accurate and correct changes over time, this suggests fewer inaccuracies to fix in online environments and highlights the potential for wide-ranging negative effects when search engines are not "right."

Online search environments offer the opportunity to teach broad audiences of interested information seekers with differing physical information environments through mechanisms that can be implemented concurrently from the source identification and presentation side, despite small differences in search results that are introduced with search personalization services. Therefore, it is important for Google, as the most-used search engine, to be accurate. Despite the potential to disseminate accurate information on critical though sometimes controversial topics such as health through Internet search services, in practice, this potential has not been realized. Nevertheless, because of the heterogeneity of librarians and library policies, compared to search engines, dissemination of erroneous information is much more likely to occur between librarians and patrons than between search engines and users. In a 2014 study, Flaherty and Grier found that only 67% of interactions between librarians and patrons resulted in provision of "authoritative, high-quality health information that directly addressed the query posed" (Flaherty & Grier, 2014, p. 299). Standardizing human interactions is a more complicated problem than standardizing search engine output. If a search engine is providing inaccurate search results, those results are likely inaccurate for everyone who searches using that query, whereas human error may be different in each instance.

Nascent search engines were primitive in power, limited in scope, and inaccessible to many, but later generations have grown to resemble titans—immensely powerful, infinite in scope, and permeating almost every digital device. Despite gains, they reflect the values and biases of the humans who create them as well as the queries they receive and the users they serve. Sweeney (2013) detected racial bias in search engine advertisements when queries contained a racially identifying name; searching more than 2,000 real names, the word "arrest" was much likelier to appear in ads returned to black-identifying names. Noble also has found racial bias when searching with racial or ethnic identity keywords, such as "black girls," for which pornographic sites dominated the results; search engine results may represent "the most explicit, racist, or sexist formulations" (Noble, 2012, p. 41), forcing the questions of whether, how, and in what ways Internet search service providers are ethically responsible for the nature of search results or recommendations.

When providing vaccination information, search engines reflect competing narratives that are dependent on keyword search terms entered by users. Wolfe and Sharpe conducted a content analysis of search results from four search engines and found that "as soon as words with the Latin root *vacca* are used, the percentage of anti-vaccination sites increases dramatically" (2005, p. 540). Concordantly, Hindman, Tsioutsiouliklis, and Johnson find that in this instance "the Internet funnels viewers . . . to a few Web sites" (2003, p. 29). Unknowingly, information seekers using words like "vaccine" and "vaccination" are potentially signaling to a search engine that they espouse antivaccination views.

Eli Pariser (2011) coined the term "filter bubble" to encapsulate how personalized search services could insulate users from opposing viewpoints and invisibly isolate users from different and new ideas. Filter bubbles become more dangerous when connected to providing health information. A searcher is provided with the links that the algorithm calculates the seeker wants to see, not what is authoritative or accurate according to scientific and medical professionals. While personalization has generated a whole subset of recommender systems, there does not appear to be any system devoted to recommending information outside of what a user wants to see that might in effect help pop her or his filter bubbles.

Balance

Perhaps at this point the battle may appear pointless because the amount of misinformation is insurmountable, and countering it appears an ineffective strategy; multiple modifications would have to be made, removal of content is not realistic, and the list would only continue. However, I have introduced this evidence and these examples for another reason—to suggest that the other side of the issue presents a greater opportunity for meaningful amelioration.

Scientific theory attempts to isolate variables and establish relationships. In the situation of the provision of vaccination information, scientific literature presents evidence of relationships between variables. Scientific theory should also prioritize whatever evidence is most useful to explain or predict a phenomenon. I introduce these concepts to underline my main point, that it is not useful to focus on fixing a collection even if that appears to be the primary source of the problem. Instead, it is more useful to focus on fixing how seekers interact with the search environment. What if teaching seekers about the flaws of the collection rather than trying to make a perfect collection could ameliorate this issue? In reviewing Dixon, McKeever, Holton, Clarke, and Eosco's (2015) study about the importance of presentation techniques, Southwell and Thorson (2015, p. 591) assert, "Results suggest that . . . contextualization can encourage nuanced thinking regarding vaccines."

Based on Wolfe and Sharpe's (2005) findings, the search term "vaccination" is compromised; while the skew associated with the term is not objective, it is necessary to introduce search mechanisms that inform seekers that searching this term alone will not show them the most authoritative perspectives on the issue. Rather than completely abandoning efforts to cultivate authoritative, credible collections, society must acknowledge that in this information age, sometimes it is more dangerous to exclude material than to include it with a warning. Contextualized presentation of material may be a more effective and pragmatic approach to countering promotion and dissemination of misinformation than suppression.

I also advocate for this choice because there are notable instances of search modifications making a meaningful difference in real-world outcomes. For example, pro-suicide information is readily available on the Internet (Recupero, Harms, & Noble, 2008). In the case of links that inform individuals about suicide methods, the inclusion of the phone number for a suicide hotline is helpful to those who are suicidal without censoring the information from those who might need it (researchers, mental health professionals, etc.). A Google blog notes that the inclusion of the National Suicide Prevention Lifeline phone number in search results accounted for a 9% rise in call volume (Zeiger, 2010). While some might still argue for censorship, I argue against that. Removing such information does not remove suicidal tendencies. Instead, it would drive that information behavior underground or, more realistically, into an information environment where it is harder to guarantee an intervention such as the hotline number.

Libraries are in a somewhat different position than digital information providers. Their collections are smaller, though they select from a vast pool of resources. However, I hope to have emphasized that avoidance of the information-quality problem has the potential to limit public librarians' ability to promote and support public health. Keselman and colleagues (2014) raise the larger questions of viewing librarians simply as conduits to sources containing answers to questions or more broadly as socially responsible agents in transactions.

It may be time for librarians to consider rating nonfiction materials. Every book in a collection has a barcode, so why not a small box explaining which of the library's selection criteria it meets or whether the librarians have found that it is considered authoritative, accurate, and credible and according to what criteria. Librarians embrace transparency of procedure and have experience organizing as a collective to produce records that can be used by one another, as the Online Computer Library Center (OCLC) cooperative demonstrates.

If information providers are not comfortable or realistically able to arbitrate what is good information, they can at least flag topics about which readers should be wary and might be wise to consult experts for advice. If individuals are given notice that information concerning some topics is contested, providers have the opportunity to let them know that there are multiple perspectives without endorsing one above the other, in effect achieving some neutrality and objectivity.

Conclusion

Theory is evaluated upon usefulness in a specific and limited context rather than as a universal truth that applies across time and space. What about information? For whom is information useful? Who is treating it as truth? Hypothesizing how information will be used and then applying hypotheses to justify censorship sets a dangerous precedent. However, if not directly through information providers, there exists an opportunity for society to protect itself from materials that could hurt it. In the age of mass media, the Internet, and social media, it is as if information seekers require herd immunity from misinformation.

Health care providers make every effort to eradicate disease by cultivating immunity through vaccination, though they are realistic that complete elimination is rarely achievable. However, with the use of vaccines they are able to lower the risk significantly of epidemics and death. Contextual information interventions that users encounter during the information-seeking process could help inoculate society against dangerous misinformation without jeopardizing commitments to providing information from all viewpoints. Bossaller says society cannot forget "that when doubt or skepticism is delegitimized or deemphasized as a proper part of knowledge creation or acquisition, participants in the debate will be unable to truly converse with each other" (2014, p. 238).

References

American Library Association. (1996). Library Bill of Rights. Retrieved from http://www.ala.org/advocacy/intfreedom/librarybill

Bernstein, S. (2015, June 30). California bill limits school vaccine exemptions. Reuters. Retrieved from http://www.reuters.com/article/us-usa-vaccines-california-idUSKCN0PA2CB20150630

Bond L., Nolan T., Pattison P., & Carlin J. (1998). Vaccine preventable diseases and immunisations: A qualitative study of mothers' perceptions of severity, susceptibility, benefits, and barriers. *Australian and New Zealand Journal of Public Health*, 22(4), 440–446.

Bossaller, J. S. (2014). Evidence, not authority: Reconsidering presentation of science for difficult decisions. *Reference & User Services Quarterly*, 53(3), 232–241.

Buchanan, R., & Beckett, R.D. (2014). Assessment of vaccination-related information for consumers available on Facebook. *Health Information and Libraries Journal, 31*, 227–234.

CDC. *See* U.S. Centers for Disease Control and Prevention (CDC).

Chen, W., Landau, S., Sham, P., & Fombonne, E. (2004). No evidence for links between autism, MMR and measles virus. *Psychological medicine, 34*(3), 543–553.

Clayton, E. W., Rusch, E., Ford, A., & Stratton, K. (Eds.). (2012). *Adverse effects of vaccines: Evidence and causality*. Washington, DC: National Academies Press.

Csanady, A. (2016, May 12). Ontario parents who object to vaccines could be forced to take a class in science of immunization. *National Post*. Retrieved from http://news.nationalpost.com/news/canada/canadian-politics/ontario-parents-who-object-to-vaccines-could-be-forced-to-take-a-class-in-science-of-immunization

Decoteau, C. L., & Underman, K. (2015). Adjudicating non-knowledge in the Omnibus Autism Proceedings. *Social Studies of Science, 45*(4), 471–500.

Dixon, G., McKeever, B., Holton, A., Clarke, C., & Eosco, G. (2015). The power of a picture: Overcoming scientific misinformation by communicating weight-of-evidence information with visual exemplars. *Journal of Communication, 65*(4), 639–659.

Farrington, C. P., Miller, E., & Taylor, B. (2001). MMR and autism: Further evidence against a causal association. *Vaccine, 19*(27), 3632–3635.

Fine, P., Eames, K., & Heymann, D. L. (2011). "Herd immunity": A rough guide. *Clinical Infectious Diseases, 52*(7), 911–916.

Flaherty, M. G. (2013). Consumer health information provision in rural public libraries: A comparison of two library systems. *The Library, 83*(2), 155–165.

Flaherty, M. G., & Grier, P. L. Jr. (2014). Statewide initiative to embed consumer health librarians in public libraries: A case study. *Public Library Quarterly, 33*(4), 296–303.

Flaherty, M. G., Tayag, E. K., Lanier, M., & Minor, J. (2014). The Jenny McCarthy conundrum: Public libraries, popular culture, and health misinformation. *Proceedings of the American Society for Information Science and Technology, 51*(1), 1–1.

Freed, G. L., Clark, S. J., Butchart, A. T., Singer, D. C., & Davis, M. M. (2010). Parental vaccine safety concerns in 2009. *Pediatrics, 125*(4), 654–659.

Hindman, M., Tsioutsiouliklis, K., & Johnson, J. A. (2003, April). Googlearchy: How a few heavily-linked sites dominate politics on the Web. In *Annual Meeting of the Midwest Political Science Association, 4*, pp. 1–33.

Holden, E. W. (2003). Pediatric psychology and public health: Opportunities for further integration in the 21st century. In M. C. Roberts (Ed.), *Handbook of pediatric psychology* (3rd ed.) (pp. 710–718). New York, NY: Guilford.

Jansen, S. C., & Martin, B. (2015). The Streisand effect and censorship backfire. *International Journal of Communication, 9*, 656–671.

Keselman, A., Arnott Smith, C., & Hundal, S. (2014). Library workers' personal beliefs about childhood vaccination and vaccination information provision. *Journal of the Medical Library Association, 102*(3), 205–210.

Kirkland, A. (2012). Credibility battles in the autism litigation. *Social Studies of Science, 42*(2), 237–261.

Klara, R. (2014, March 3). Are you a felon? According to Google you just might be.

Adweek. Retrieved from http://www.adweek.com/news/technology/are-you-felon-according-google-you-just-might-be-156027

Madsen, K. M., Hviid, A., Vestergaard, M., Schendel, D., Wohlfahrt, J., Thorsen, P., . . . Melbye, M. (2002). A population-based study of measles, mumps, and rubella vaccination and autism. *New England Journal of Medicine, 347*(19), 1477–1482.

Mantelero, A. (2013). The EU proposal for a general data protection regulation and the roots of the "right to be forgotten." *Computer Law & Security Review, 29*(3), 229–235.

National Research Council. (2000). *The digital dilemma: intellectual property in the information age*. Washington, DC: The National Academies Press.

Nielsen, J. M. (1990). *Feminist research methods: exemplary readings in the social sciences*. Boulder, CO: Westview.

Noble, S. U. (2012, Spring). Missed connections: What search engines say about women. *Bitch, 54*, 36–41.

Noruzi, A. (2004). Application of Ranganathan's laws to the web. *Webology, 1*(2), article 8. Retrieved from http://www.webology.ir/2004/v1n2/a8.html

Pariser, E. (2011). *The filter bubble: What the Internet is hiding from you*. London, England: Penguin.

Ranganathan, S. R. (1931). *The five laws of library science*. Madras, India: Madras Library Association.

Recupero, P. R., Harms, S. E., & Noble, J. M. (2008). Googling suicide: Surfing for suicide information on the Internet. *Journal of Clinical Psychiatry, 69*(6), 878–888.

Rochman, B. (2013, April 15). How social networks influence parents' decision to vaccinate. *Time Health and Family*. Retrieved from http://healthland.time.com/2013/04/15/how-social-networks-influence-a-parents-decision-to-vaccinate

Southwell, B. G., & Thorson, E. A. (2015). The prevalence, consequence, and remedy of misinformation in mass media systems. *Journal of Communication, 65*(4), 589–595.

Steenhuysen, J. (2015, August 27). U.S. vaccination rates high, but pockets of unvaccinated pose risk. Reuters. Retrieved from http://www.reuters.com/article/us-usa-vaccine-exemptions-idUSKCN0QW2JY20150827

Stern, A. M., & Markel, H. (2005). The history of vaccines and immunization: Familiar patterns, new challenges. *Health Affairs, 24*(3), 611–621.

Sweeney, L. (2013). Discrimination in online ad delivery. *Queue, 11*(3), 10.

Taylor, L. E., Swerdfeger, A. L., & Eslick, G. D. (2014). Vaccines are not associated with autism: An evidence-based meta-analysis of case-control and cohort studies. *Vaccine, 32*(29), 3623–3629.

U.S. Centers for Disease Control and Prevention (CDC). (2016a, February 1). Child and adolescent schedule. Retrieved from http://www.cdc.gov/vaccines/schedules/hcp/imz/child-adolescent.html

U.S. Centers for Disease Control and Prevention (CDC). (2016b, June 1). Measles cases and outbreaks. Retrieved from http://www.cdc.gov/measles/cases-outbreaks.html

Wakefield, A. J., Murch, S. H., Anthony, A., Linnell, J., Casson, D. M., Malik, M., . . . Walker-Smith, J. A. (1998). RETRACTED: Ileal-lymphoid-nodular hyperplasia, non-specific colitis, and pervasive developmental disorder in children. *Lancet, 351*(9103), 637–641.

Wolfe, R. M., & Sharp, L. K. (2005). Vaccination or immunization? The impact of search terms on the Internet. *Journal of Health Communication, 10*(6), 537–551.

World Health Organization (WHO). (2016, April 5). *Health topics: Immunization.* Geneva: WHO. Retrieved from http://www.who.int/topics/immunization/en

Zeiger, R. (2010, November 11). Helping you find emergency information when you need it [Web log post]. Google. Retrieved from https://googleblog.blogspot.com /2010/11/helping-you-find-emergency-information.html

CONCLUSION

An Agenda for
Misinformation Research

EMILY A. THORSON, LAURA SHEBLE,
AND BRIAN G. SOUTHWELL

As mass media systems evolve and change, misinformation will continue to play important roles both as noise complicating public understanding and as a source for belief and attitude formation and change related to a range of topics, including politics and health. In this conclusion, we point to several potential future areas of research that would expand the study of misinformation and misperceptions presented in this volume: opportunities to study misperceptions driven by cognitive biases, to examine the indirect effects of repeated exposure to misinformation and corrections, and to design interventions to stop misinformation before it spreads. Additionally, we discuss several important and emerging lines of research that are not fully considered in this volume but which could contribute to our understanding of misinformation at the center and periphery of mass communication systems.

Drawing a clear distinction between *misinformation* (false information) and *misperceptions* (false beliefs) opens up several promising avenues of research. Although "misinformation" is often used as a catchall for both concepts, using the same term for them masks two important points. First, not all misinformation causes misperceptions. Indeed, understanding when misinformation is not believed can shed light on how best to correct it. Second, not all misperceptions are caused by misinformation. Daniel Kahneman notes that humans are "pattern seekers, believers in a coherent world" (2011, 115), and this drive to understand can lead to incorrect inferences that then become integrated into larger belief systems. Maki, Carrico, and Vandenbergh in this volume point to misperceptions about how households can most effectively conserve water. These misperceptions arise not necessarily because someone or something is spreading misinformation but because of normal human biases in information processing and causal inference.

Widening the study of misperceptions to include false beliefs that are not directly attributable to misinformation may also help us identify misperceptions that are more correctable. Misperceptions that emerge largely from explicit misinformation have often been politicized, spread, and reified to such an extent that they are difficult to completely correct, such as misperceptions about President Obama's birthplace or about climate change. For these beliefs, motivated reasoning contributes to the creation and maintenance of misperceptions. In contrast, misperceptions that emerge from cognitive biases may be easier to correct because they are not subject to repeated reification by trusted elites.

A second avenue of research involves studying the indirect effects of misinformation. In their chapter, Poulsen and Young chart an enormous growth in political fact-checking organizations over the past few decades. Whether or not there is objectively more misinformation in the world than there was 10, 20, or even 100 years ago is difficult to answer. However, it is also plausible that this growing focus on misinformation and misperceptions itself has changed the public's perception of misinformation's prevalence. This perception may have the downstream effect of decreasing trust in politicians, health care providers, scientific experts, or news media. Decreased trust could then create a vicious cycle in which people resist corrections issued from those same institutions. Public understanding of misinformation and the possible adverse externalities of well-meaning efforts to track misinformation are notable avenues for future theorizing and research.

Another indirect effect of misinformation and misperceptions is on political attitudes more generally. Political compromise and negotiation require both sides coming to the table with the same set of facts. But as Weeks points out in this volume, if one side or both are misinformed, effective deliberation is difficult. Although this type of downstream effect is theoretically plausible, we have little empirical evidence to demonstrate how misperceptions shape willingness among political actors to compromise or shape attitudes toward the other side. We need more evidence in this vein.

To date, much of the research aimed at minimizing adverse effects of misinformation has focused on the point of *reception*—in other words, how and why people accept or reject false claims. As Boudewyns and colleagues describe in this volume, understanding how and when people recognize deception in health-related advertising is critical for building interventions that could increase audience awareness and skepticism about misinformation. Media literacy training might be beneficial in preventing some audience uptake of misinformation in the first place. The development of visual media literacy discussed by Hemsley and Snyder and the Smart Consumer education program proposed by Bullock would minimize misperceptions not by offering explicit corrections to specific misinformation but by training citizens to recognize misinformation as such right away.

However, it is also worthwhile to consider how to stop misinformation at the point of *presentation or dissemination*—before it enters the mass media. Thus, a third avenue of research involves understanding how and why misinformation emerges in media systems and how interventions can potentially stop it before it reaches the mass public. Bullock outlines several sites of intervention in the realm of consumer product labels, but other areas may require different approaches. Experimental research has shown that alerting legislators to the presence of fact-checking organizations in their area leads them to make fewer misleading claims (Nyhan & Reifler, 2014). Could similar interventions work for other sources of misinformation, such as advertising agencies, political campaigns, and pharmaceutical companies? Although research programs aimed at reducing incentives for organizations and institutions to spread misinformation pose logistical challenges, such efforts may pay substantial dividends. Nonetheless, we must acknowledge the regulatory structures in the United States and elsewhere—which are not geared toward absolute preemption, per se—and legitimate concerns some commentators have regarding the potential for undue censorship of free speech.

At the intersection of discussions by Cappella and colleagues on computational approaches to measuring misinformation and by Kaplan on the limitations associated with search and retrieval tools to help people distinguish information from misinformation lies the suggestion of developing tools to identify potentially harmful misinformation. Current work in this area has focused on topics such as characterizing and detecting disinformation on the web, including Wikipedia hoaxes (Kumar, West, & Leskovec, 2016), and detecting, tracking, and containing the spread of misinformation in online social networks (Del Vicario et al., 2016; Nguyen, Yan, Thai, & Eidenbenz, 2012).

Finally, topics addressed indirectly or only peripherally, albeit with potentially increasing importance for mass communication systems, include archival inquiry on misinformation in the historical record; work to understand misinformation in the context of national security, intelligence, and violent conflict (Lewandowsky, Stritzke, Freund, Oberauer, & Krueger, 2013); and research on the potential roles of misinformation as private information enters, or has the potential to enter, more public spheres. The first two of these topics have more established and developing literatures and are covered elsewhere. The potential role for misinformation in the context of privacy has been less discussed in a general context; for example, misinformation might be used to protect sensitive private information vulnerable to exposure in more public information spaces. There is some precedence for the use of "noise" to obfuscate activities and behaviors subject to online surveillance and tracking, such as Internet searches (Howe, Nissenbaum, & Toubiana, n.d.), and to preserve the privacy of individuals included in data sets (Mivule, 2013). Such initiatives suggest that the purposeful introduction of misinformation may play an increasingly important role in protecting private information, and so we would be remiss in not mentioning this potential function of misinformation.

What is clear from the work assembled in this book is that misinformation is a phenomenon that occurs regularly in mass media systems. Its emergence has many causes, and not every presentation of misinformation is the product of malicious intent. Nonetheless, the cynical application of misinformation likely will continue to pose a significant challenge for media systems that allow contributions from a variety of actors. This collection of work offers a theoretical and conceptual foundation for future intellectual engagement with misinformation as a feature of media systems. Future remedies will require not only continued theoretical consideration, however, but also the development and maintenance of consistent monitoring tools and a willingness among neighbors and fellow members of society to agree that some claims that find prominence on shared airwaves and in widely available media content are insufficiently based in scientific consensus and social reality and should be countered. Misinformation arises as a function of systems structure, human fallibility, and human information needs. Insofar as we want to overcome the worst effects of the phenomenon, we will need coordinated efforts over time rather than any singular, one-time panacea we could hope to offer.

References

Del Vicario, M., Bessi, A., Zollo, F., Petroni, F., Scala, A., Caldarelli, G., . . . Quattrociocchi, W. (2016). The spreading of misinformation online. *Proceedings of the National Academy of Sciences, 113*(3), 554–559.

Howe, D. C., Nissenbaum, H., & Toubiana, V. (n.d.). TrackMeNot. Retrieved July 1, 2016, from https://cs.nyu.edu/trackmenot/

Kahneman, D. (2011). *Thinking, fast and slow.* New York, NY: Farrar, Straus, and Giroux.

Kumar, S., West, R., & Leskovec, J. (2016, April). Disinformation on the Web: Impact, characteristics, and detection of Wikipedia hoaxes. In *WWW '16 Proceedings of the 25th International Conference on World Wide Web* (pp. 591–602). Geneva, Switzerland: International World Wide Web Conferences Steering Committee.

Lewandowsky, S., Stritzke, W. G. K., Freund, A. M., Oberauer, K., & Krueger, J. I. (2013). Misinformation, disinformation, and violent conflict: From Iraq and the 'War on Terror' to future threats to peace. *American Psychologist, 68*(7), 487–501.

Mivule, K. (2013). Utilizing noise addition for data privacy, an overview [arXiv preprint]. arXiv:1309.3958 [cs.CR]. Retrieved July 1, 2016, from http://arxiv.org/abs/1309.3958

Nguyen, N. P., Yan, G., Thai, M. T., & Eidenbenz, S. (2012, June). Containment of misinformation spread in online social networks. In *WebSci '12 Proceedings of the 4th Annual ACM Web Science Conference* (pp. 213–222). New York, NY: Association for Computing Machinery.

Nyhan, B., & Reifler, J. (2015). The effect of fact-checking on elites: A field experiment on U.S. state legislators. *American Journal of Political Science, 59*(3), 628–640.

Contributors

Douglas J. Ahler is an assistant professor of political science at Florida State University. He received his PhD from the University of California, Berkeley, in 2016. His work has appeared in the *Journal of Politics*, *Legislative Studies Quarterly*, and *Political Behavior*.

Kevin R. Betts is a social science analyst at the Food and Drug Administration's Center for Drug Evaluation and Research, Office of Prescription Drug Promotion, where he provides research and consulting services pertaining to promotional prescription drug communication. His areas of expertise include individual and group perception, judgment, and decision making.

Vanessa Boudewyns is a research scientist in the Science in the Public Sphere program in the Center for Communication Science at RTI International. Her work takes an interdisciplinary approach to the study of message effects, cognition, and behavior change, incorporating research from psychology, mass communication, and social marketing.

Graham Bullock is an assistant professor of political science and environmental studies at Davidson College. He received his PhD from the University of California, Berkeley, and MPP from the Harvard Kennedy School; he is the author of *Green Grades: Can Information Save the Earth?*, a book on information-based governance, published by MIT Press in 2017.

Joseph N. Cappella is the Gerald R. Miller Professor of Communication at the Annenberg School for Communication at the University of Pennsylvania. He is a fellow and past president of the International Communication Association (ICA), recipient of the ICA's Fisher Mentorship Award, and Distinguished Scholar of the National Communication Association.

Amanda R. Carrico is an assistant professor of environmental studies at the University of Colorado, Boulder. She holds a PhD in social psychology from Vanderbilt University. Her work examines processes of household and community adaptation to environmental stress and factors associated with the adoption of pro-environmental behavior.

John K. Donahue is an instructor at Columbus College of Art and Design. His research focus has been media psychology; he is the author of articles and book chapters on storytelling, journalism, and graphic design. His work has been presented at conferences in psychology and mass communication.

Ullrich Ecker is an associate professor at the University of Western Australia's School of Psychological Science, where he leads the Cognitive Science Laboratories. He is a former Australian Research Council postdoctoral fellow and a fellow of the Psychonomic Society.

Melanie C. Green is an associate professor in communication at the University at Buffalo. Her work has focused on the power of narrative to change beliefs. She has edited two books on this topic (*Narrative Impact* and *Persuasion: Psychological Insights and Perspectives, Second Edition*).

Catherine Slota Gupta is a health communication research scientist in the Patient and Family Engagement Research program in the Center for Communication Science at RTI International. Her research focuses on patient-provider communication, informed decision making, and medication adherence.

Jeff Hemsley is an assistant professor in the School of Information Studies at Syracuse University. His book *Going Viral* was published by Polity Press in 2013.

Samantha Kaplan is a doctoral student in the School of Information and Library Science at the University of North Carolina at Chapel Hill.

Alexander Maki is a postdoctoral fellow with the Vanderbilt Institute for Energy and Environment and the Vanderbilt Climate Change Research Network. His research explores how behavior change interventions lead individuals to engage in a range of related behaviors ("behavior spillover") and to try to spread their behaviors to other people.

Elizabeth J. Marsh is a professor of psychology and neuroscience at Duke University. Her research focuses on how students acquire, maintain, update, and apply their knowledge. Her work is supported by the U.S. Department of Education, the National Science Foundation, the James S. McDonnell Foundation, and the Spencer Foundation.

Amie C. O'Donoghue is a social science analyst in the Office of Prescription Drug Promotion, Center for Drug Evaluation and Research, U.S. Food and Drug Administration.

Yotam Ophir is a PhD candidate at Annenberg School for Communication at the University of Pennsylvania. He has received master's degrees in communication from the University of Pennsylvania and the University of Haifa, Israel.

Ryan S. Paquin is a research scientist in the Patient and Family Engagement Research program in the Center for Communication Science at RTI International. He applies attitude and behavioral theory to conduct research on judgment, informed decision making, and strategic communication planning and evaluation.

Shannon Poulsen is a graduate student at Ohio State University.

Laura Sheble is an assistant professor in the School of Information Sciences at Wayne State University and a research associate at the Duke Network Analysis Center at Duke University. Her work brings together information science and social network research.

Jaime Snyder is an assistant professor in the Information School and adjunct assistant professor in human-centered design and engineering at the University of Washington.

Gaurav Sood is the founder and chief scientist at a stealth-mode startup. Gaurav has a PhD from Stanford, a bachelor's degree in computer science from Rutgers University, and postdocs from Princeton, Stanford, and Georgetown. He also works on exploring the antecedents and consequences of group-based affect.

Brian G. Southwell directs the Science in the Public Sphere program at the Center for Communication Science at RTI International. He also is a faculty member at Duke University and the University of North Carolina at Chapel Hill and hosts a public radio show, WNCU's *The Measure of Everyday Life*.

Jazmyne Sutton is a doctoral student at Annenberg School for Communication at the University of Pennsylvania. She received her master of arts in communication from San Diego State University.

Briony Swire is a PhD candidate with the Cognitive Science Laboratories at the University of Western Australia. She was awarded a postgraduate Fulbright scholarship and collaborated with Massachusetts Institute of Technology's political science department on the processing of political misinformation.

Emily A. Thorson is an assistant professor of political science at Syracuse University.

Michael P. Vandenbergh is the David Daniels Allen Distinguished Chair of Law, co-director of the Energy, Environment, and Land Use program, and director of the Climate Change Research Network at Vanderbilt University law school. His research has been discussed in *National Geographic*, the *Washington Post*, and National Public Radio's *All Things Considered*.

Natasha Vazquez is a public health analyst in the Social Innovation and Communication Strategy program at the Center for Communication Science at RTI International.

Brian E. Weeks is an assistant professor in the Department of Communication Studies and faculty associate in the Center for Political Studies at the University of Michigan.

Brenda W. Yang is a PhD student in psychology and neuroscience at Duke University. She received her undergraduate degrees at the University of Southern California.

Dannagal G. Young is an associate professor of communication at the University of Delaware and research fellow affiliated with the University of Delaware's Center for Political Communication, Annenberg Public Policy Center, and National Institute for Civil Discourse.

Index

A-B-C model of behavior, 179
Adair, B., 243, 245
advertising: claim contextualization, 43; claim refutation/qualification, 43–44; counteradvertising, 214–216, 219–221, 223; deceptive claims, 35–46; and detection of deception, 37–40; direct-to-consumer (DTC), 5, 35, 39, 45, 158; direct-to-physician (DTP), 35, 158; false claims, 35–36, 39–40, 43; health-related, 35–46; misleading claims, 35–36, 38, 40–42, 44–45; moderators of deception awareness, 40–45; and skepticism, 38–42, 46; visual deception, 44–45
affect. *See* emotions
Affordable Care Act (ACA), 62, 268
Ahler, D. J., 7, 83
Aikin, K. J., 215
Ajzen, I., 63, 64
algorithms, 136, 144, 281, 283
All the President's Men, 119
Amazon's Mechanical Turk (MTurk), 79–80, 253
American Marketing Association, 225
American Society of Newspaper Editors (ASNE), 234–235
Anderson, S. J., 18
Ansolabehere, S., 78
Antman, E. M., 169–170
Antonio, L., 203
Appel, M., 118
Arai, K., 39
Aronson, J., 205
Asp, E. W., 38, 42

autism, 162, 164, 196, 276
automobile emissions, 212–213, 224

Barkeley, D., 131–132, 136
Barthel, M., 75
Barzilai-Nahon, K., 269
base rate fallacy, 79, 85–86
Bazerman, C., 166
Beam, M. A., 128
Beckstead, J. W., 205
belief perseverance, 115–116
Bennett, W. L., 144–145
Bergson, H., 125
Bernstein, C., 119
Bertin, J., 94
Better Business Bureau (BBB), 221–222, 224–225
Betts, K. R., 7
biased information processing, 147–149
Bigman, C. A., 55
Bisgin, H., 62
Blair, J., 113
blogging, 92, 100, 265–270
"Bluff the Listener" (NPR game), 15, 17, 28
Blumler, J. G., 237, 240
Bolls, P. D., 56
Bornstein, R. F., 20
Bossaller, J. S., 277–278, 285
Boudewyns, V., 7, 291
Boush, D. M., 39
Brexit, 87, 206
Brisbane, A., 252–253
Brock, T. C., 23–24, 111–112
Brossard, D., 251

Brown, C., 169
Bullock, G., 9, 215, 291
Bullock, J. G., 77
Burbano, V. C., 213
Bush, G. H. W., 240–241
Bush, G. W., 110, 217, 223, 250

Callaghan, K. C., 204
Cappella, J. N., 7, 291
Carrico, A. R., 8, 290
Carter, J., 236
Castells, M., 91, 264
causal illusions, 206
Chisholm, R. M., 39
citation bias, 168
Clarke, C., 283
climate change, 15, 54, 157, 290; and
    behavior, 177–178, 180–181, 183–184,
    187; belief in global warming, 183–
    184; global warming, 142, 150, 169,
    183–184; and misinformation, 162,
    169–170, 177–178, 187, 202–204; and
    source credibility, 202
Clinton, H. R., 110, 249
Clinton, W. J., 217, 236
co-activation of misinformation, 197,
    201–202
cognitive science, 7, 15–29; and assump-
    tion of truth, 16–18; and credible
    sources, 18–20; and ease of process-
    ing (fluency heuristic), 20–21; and
    emotions, 25–26; and motivation,
    24–25; and narrative information,
    22–24; and scientific window dress-
    ing, 21–22; and stored knowledge,
    26–28. See also heuristics
Cohen, G. L., 205
Colbert, S., 21, 24, 127–128
Colbert Report, The, 127–128
Colletta, L., 124–125, 130–131
Comedy Central, 8, 128, 134
commodity theory, 111–112
confirmation bias, 24
consensus, 3–4, 143, 146, 161–162, 183,
    274, 292
consumer information, 212–225

consumer opinion, 218–219
Consumer Product Safety Commission
    (CPSC), 222–223
Consumers Union, 214, 219–220, 225
Cooke, J., 117
Cooper, H. M., 166
correction, 1–2, 5, 7–9, 76, 195–197; and
    advertising, 44, 53–54, 64–65, 215;
    and belief change, 29, 38, 54, 147–
    148, 197, 201, 206; and credibility,
    202–203; and environmental misper-
    ceptions, 185–186; and fact-checking,
    242–244, 250–260; and factual alter-
    natives, 198; and gatekeepers, 264,
    271; and memory errors, 149–151; and
    mental models, 197–198; and moti-
    vated reasoning, 147–148; motivation
    to correct, 116–118, 202; and narra-
    tive information, 116; and political
    misinformation, 149–151, 242–244,
    250–260; public information cam-
    paigns, 164; refutation, 3, 43–44, 46,
    201–204, 274; retraction, 25, 28, 113,
    163–165, 197–206, 268, 276; and skep-
    ticism, 38, 147–148, 205–206; and
    trust, 18–20, 290; and unintentional
    misinformation, 110; and worldview,
    203–205. See also misinformation
Corsi, J., 133
Council of Better Business Bureaus
    (CBBB), 221–222, 224–225
credibility: and advertising, 38, 117, 220;
    and correcting misinformation, 202–
    204; and fact-checking, 252, 260; fac-
    tors of, 103; and libraries, 284; and
    media gatekeepers, 264–265, 268;
    and news, 119, 142; retraction source,
    202–203; and social media, 144, 145;
    and truth, 18–21; and visual artifacts,
    93–95, 100–103
Crichton, M., 116
curated flows framework, 263
curation logics, 263–265, 267–271

Daily Currant, 131–132, 136
Daily Show, The, 128, 134

Johnson, N., 236
Johnson, P. E., 41
journalism: American Society of News-
    paper Editors (ASNE), 234–235; citi-
    zen journalism, 92, 240; commercial
    pressures, 236–238; deregulation,
    236–238; early American newspapers,
    233–235; and fact-checking, 232–245,
    249–260; horse-race coverage, 237;
    muckraking, 235; and narrative infor-
    mation, 115; norms and mispercep-
    tions, 144–146; pressures affecting
    pursuit of facts and truth, 235–240;
    and professionalization of politics,
    238–239; and technology, 237, 239–
    240, 242–243; video news release
    (VNR), 238; watchdog journalism,
    235, 236; yellow journalism, 233–
    234

Kahneman, D., 289–290
Kaplan, S., 9, 291
Kassin, S. M., 118
Kata, A., 146
Kavanagh, D., 237, 240
Keeter, S., 232
Kerry, J., 112
Keselman, A., 284
Kim, M., 203
Kirby, J., 102
Kiviniemi, M., 63
knowledge: aggregation of, 219; codi-
    fied, 165–166; and cognitive science,
    17–20, 26–29; and environmental be-
    havior and policy, 177, 179–187; net-
    works, 159–160; persuasion knowl-
    edge model, 41; revision of, 114–116,
    201; specialized, 52, 216, 219–220;
    stored, 26–28; tacit, 165–166
knowledge assessment, 51–65; argu-
    ment repertoire, 59–60; close-ended
    questions, 54–57; computational
    approaches to text analysis, 60–62;
    found data, 60–62; open-ended ques-
    tions, 57–58; person-centric, 63–64;
    reaction times, 58–59

Kostelnick, C., 94
Krueger, J. I., 3

Ladle, R., 169
LaMarre, H. L., 128
Landau, J. D., 19
Landreville, K. D., 128
Lang, A., 56
Lariviere, V., 165
latent Dirichlet allocation (LDA) tech-
    nique, 61–62
Lawrence, R. G., 145
Lazarsfeld, P. F., 9
Leiserowitz, A., 142
Levine Einstein, L., 150
Lewandowsky, S., 3, 115–116, 119, 151,
    200, 205
libraries, 278–284
Lilienfeld, S., 205
Littell, J. H., 169
Liu, Z., 62, 105

machine learning, 61
Maibach, E. W., 142
Maki, A., 8, 290
Malečkar, B., 118
Malik, T., 110
Mancini, P., 238
market editors, 217–218
market facilitators, 216–217
Marsden, P., 102
Marsh, E. J., 7, 19
Mathison, S., 93, 103
Mattson, M. E., 17
McKeever, B., 283
McLeod, D. M., 251
media dependency theory, 40–41
media literacy, 5, 291; visual media liter-
    ary, 93, 103, 291
memory errors, 149
memory processes, 199–200
mental models, 62, 98, 115, 197–199,
    201
Meredith, M., 78
Messaris, P., 44
Miller, J., 110

and motivated reasoning, 147; motivated skepticism, 25; pluralistic ignorance, 179
Skurnik, I., 42, 200
sleeper effect, 19
Smart Consumer education program, 226, 291
Snopes, 23. *See also* fact-checking
Snowberg, E., 78
Snyder, J., 7, 291
Snyder, T. E., 201
social contagion, 26
social identity theory, 73–74, 148–149
social media, 64, 74, 110, 124, 134–51; accessibility of, 6; and Boston Marathon bombing, 196; and bots, 144; and credibility, 20, 203; Facebook, 91–92, 124, 134–136, 143–144, 203, 224, 277; and fact-checking, 147, 243–244; and fake news, 135–136, 144; and found data, 60–62; and gatekeepers, 264–265, 270; Instagram, 269–270; and journalism, 144–146; and Malaysian Airlines flight MH370 disappearance, 198; and news selection bias, 141; proliferation of, 8; and satire, 135–136; and social identity, 148; Twitter, 20, 62, 91–92, 99–100, 135–136, 143, 196, 203, 244, 265–266, 269–270; and vaccination misinformation, 277, 285; and visual misinformation, 91–103; and worldview, 204
social networks: and data art, 98–99; and middle-layer gatekeepers, 9, 263–271; network reinforcement, 5; and political misinformation, 141, 143–144; and scientific information, 158–160; and social media, 92, 94, 143–144; 3-D, 98–99; and visualizations, 92–93. *See also* network studies
Sommers, S. R., 118
Sood, G., 7
Southwell, B. G., 7, 283
Spanish-American War, 234
Spinoza, B., 4, 38
Spivak, C., 243
Stahl, B., 130

Stahl, B. C., 3
Stahl, C., 18
Stapel, D., 163
Stasko, J. T., 105
Steele, C. M., 205
stereotypes, 71–72, 74–75, 77–82, 85–87, 148–149
Stewart, J., 128
"sticky" information, 23, 26
story-telling, 22–24, 55, 109, 115–117, 119–120, 244
Streisand effect, 281
Stritzke, W. G. K., 3
Stupak, N., 205
Sullivan, M., 253
Surowiecki, J., 19, 219
Sutton, J., 7
Sweeney, L., 282
Swerdfeger, A. L., 277
Swift, J., 128–129, 131
Swire, B., 8, 200

Taber, C. S., 25
Tal, A., 22
Tan, A. S. L., 55
Tarbell, I., 235
Taylor, L. E., 277
Test, G. A., 124
Thomas, C. D., 169
Thompson, D., 134
Thorson, E. A., 8, 149–150, 267, 283
tobacco products, 71; litigation settlements, 214; measurement of knowledge of tobacco product advertising, 51–65; Public Health Cigarette Smoking Act, 214; and science, 157, 162; warning labels, 55, 59, 61, 215
Tong, W., 62
Toth, J. P., 21
Trump, D., 87, 112, 129, 245, 249
trustworthiness, 18, 93, 118–119, 202–203, 264
truth: assumption of, 16–18; and cognitive science, 15–29; and credible sources, 18–20; ease of processing as heuristics for, 20; and emotions, 25–26; journalistic pursuit of, 233–